Thomas Oswald Cockayne

Spoon and Sparrow, and Fvndere and Passer

English Roots in the Greek, Latin and Hebrew

Thomas Oswald Cockayne

Spoon and Sparrow, and Fvndere and Passer
English Roots in the Greek, Latin and Hebrew

ISBN/EAN: 9783337415631

Printed in Europe, USA, Canada, Australia, Japan

Cover: Foto ©Thomas Meinert / pixelio.de

More available books at **www.hansebooks.com**

SPOON AND SPARROW,

ΣΠΕΝΔΕΙΝ AND ΨAP,

FVNDERE AND PASSER;

OR,

ENGLISH ROOTS IN THE GREEK, LATIN, AND HEBREW:

BEING

A CONSIDERATION OF THE AFFINITIES OF THE OLD ENGLISH, ANGLO-SAXON, OR TEUTONIC PORTION OF OUR TONGUE TO THE LATIN AND GREEK; WITH A FEW PAGES ON THE RELATION OF THE HEBREW TO THE EUROPEAN LANGUAGES.

BY THE

REV. OSWALD COCKAYNE, M.A.,
FORMERLY OF ST. JOHN'S COLLEGE, CAMBRIDGE.

LONDON:
PARKER, SON, AND BOURN, 445 STRAND.
1861.

PRINTED BY TAYLOR AND FRANCIS,
RED LION COURT, FLEET STREET.

TO THE READER.

No task, on completing a toil, is more pleasing than that of acknowledging the assistance of friends. The Ven. Archdeacon Browne, Professor of Classical Literature, the Rev. Dr. McCaul, Professor of Hebrew, and the Rev. J. S. Perowne, Lecturer in Kings College, London, when I hoped to find some aid at Cambridge towards printing this work, gave me every kind assistance, after reading parts of the MS., by furnishing me with recommendatory letters. Inquiries on the spot convinced me, however, that no funds were available for the purpose; and consequently no application for assistance was made. The proved and well known scholar to whom I am indebted for some marginal remarks will find them entered on the record, as from Eudoxos; and gladly I see that he has negatived so few statements. Three or four comparisons with the Sanskrit I owe to the notes of a friend, from whom I borrowed the second edition of Bopps Glossary; they were, he tells me, all from German sources, not his own.

I wish to apologize for the use of the phrase " Anglosaxon," now too deeply established to be easily changed. The language of the Seaxan by its true name was English (Englisc); it is the tongue still spoken about our hedgerows and farmyards by the unbookish homebred sons and daughters of England. The uncouth Latinism " Anglosaxon " has separated too far the oldest English writings from ourselves; and every day, thanks to the learned, the gap, it seems, is growing wider. Unwillingly I concede to custom and convenience a phrase which our old folklore and the truth condemn.

CONTENTS.

	Page
Introduction	1
Cautions	17
Vowel Change	19
Gutturals interchanged with Gutturals	62
Anlaut	67
Inlaut and Auslaut	89
Labials interchanged with Labials	94
Anlaut	102
Inlaut and Auslaut	115
Dentals interchanged with Dentals	117
Anlaut	117
Inlaut or Auslaut	125
Gutturals interchanged with Labials	127
Anlaut	130
Inlaut or Auslaut	134
Labials interchanged with Dentals	137
Anlaut	138
Inlaut or Auslaut	139
Gutturals interchanged with Dentals	141
Anlaut	146
Inlaut or Auslaut	147
Dentals interchanged with L	149
Anlaut	150
Inlaut or Auslaut	151
S interchanged with R	153
Sibilation	156
Anlaut	163
Inlaut or Auslaut	175
Final N	189
Labials changed to R	190
V to L	191
Gutturals changed to M	192
Assimilation	192
Letters lost	194
Gutturals lost in Anlaut	196
Dentals lost in Anlaut	197
Labials lost in Anlaut	201
M lost in Anlaut	206
N „ „	206
R „ „	207
Gutturals lost in Inlaut	209
Dentals lost in Inlaut	217
Liquids lost or gained in Inlaut	219
Letters lost in Auslaut	235
Semitic roots	261
Families of Words	287

INTRODUCTION.

1. If there be any largeness of truth in the now common and much bruited tale, that the languages of Europe and India, the teutonic, greek, latin, persian and sanskrit are closely allied to one another, then it must be possible to compare the several members of the group, as for instance the english, greek and latin. In the english is found a true teutonic element, brought by the Angles from the mainland, when they won and sat down in the country of the Britons, and wholly like to the old and new forms of the german, and the scandinavian. If the anglosaxon, german and norse be fairly set side by side, read and traced out, it will be quite clear that they were but one tongue a few hundreds of years ago, say some five and twenty centuries, and might even now be called dialects, not much more differing from each other than the laconic from the attic. This ancient element then in the english being ascertained in a measure by an examination of the old writings and a comparison with corresponding speech in the other and older teutonic tongues, may be compared with the vocabulary of the greek and latin.

2. Studies of this kind are the natural result of reading in various languages: no one can fail as he follows the sense line after line, to be struck with the likeness of this or that word to what he had known before and elsewhere. Amused and instructed by what he thus observes, he becomes gradually more familiar with the changes, which are ever taking place, in the spelling and speaking of words, more entirely and

thoroughly convinced of the kinship of related languages, and more ready to give his belief in fresh examples.

3. At first sight, an english word having the form and expressing the sense of a greek or latin word seems to be borrowed, or only like accidentally. That the teutonic was borrowed from the languages, whose old books we have and read, was the opinion of the learned men in all countries to the close of the last century, and later. Not only professed etymologers, but the interpreters of ancient records helped themselves in their difficulties by deducing everything from hebrew, greek, latin. It is true that the oldest teutonic writings which have come down to us, have occasionally some words actually learned from the more civilized races with which they came in contact. Of this an example may be seen in the word Place. From Πλατυς 'broad,' was formed a feminine used as a substantive, Πλατεια, which crept into constant use in latin to signify broad street, the usual greek word for street, αγυια, never having obtained a footing in the latin language: this Platea descended to the french, and is in constant use still with the latin sense in such expressions as "La grande place" of continental towns. So also many streets in London are thus described, for example, Whitehall Place. The Germans, unwilling as mostly they are to adopt foreign terms, have nationalized the word as Platz. It was not wholly unknown to the Anglosaxon under the form Plæce, and appears in the mœsogothic as Plapya. In all these cases the word is, to all appearance, foreign, from a hellenic source, and the true teutonic words, for the sense we now give it, are stow, stead.

4. Of the anglosaxon especially, among the older teutonic dialects, it is true, that many words have been taken into it from abroad. An instance is found in the word Offer=agls. Offrian: this is mere latin, Offerre, and, what is rarely the case, it found its way at the same time into the german as Opfer. In the norse I do not recollect it, nor in the mœsogothic. The word is scarcely ecclesiastical, but it had its origin in an altered religious sense: for the mœsogothic Blotan, which expresses λατρευειν, σεβεσθαι is too nearly connected with Bloþ=Blood, to answer well to the unbloody sacrifices or

gifts of a more kindly system: hence probably a new word was admitted into the language of the Germans and the English (Anglo-Saxons).

5. The genuine teutonic character of any word cannot be assumed from its form or thorough incorporation with our speech. Some put on a deceptive appearance: the following are mere latin, Catch, Chase, Search, Measles, Pay, Shrive, Source, Cousin, Sure, Nurse, Benison, Tile, Chafe, Poison, Season, Pity, Ransom, Ferret, Chimney, Cannon, Shoal, Spice, Hotel, Pursue, Fashion, Parcel: these are greek, Place, Dish, Desk, Trout, Treacle, Tomb, Treasure, Liquorice, Quinsy, Dropsy, Palsy, Shark, Minster, Surgeon, Gillyflower, Bombazine, Apricot, Gulf, Date as a fruit, Alms, Dram. Carol is greek, as may be seen in Lye under Kyrriole, whose account is fully sufficient.

6. The anglosaxon affords no sufficient sole test of the true origin of any word, on account of its having learnt much of christianity and something of latin civilization. To assist us further we have a large part of a translation of the New Testament, quite independent of all saxon literature, and using a different alphabet, formed and read by the Goths as they lay in Mœsia upon the banks of the Danube, awaiting the plunder of imperial Rome. Here the language has far less admixture of the latin, though in a translation of the holy writings of a new faith some borrowed words were necessarily useful. The glossary of this volume being limited, many kinds of words, whole tribes, are of course wanting.

7. To check results still more, there lies an appeal to Scandinavia. The men of those climes spoke a dialect which belongs to the teutonic, frankish, english and gothic, and we have from them some early poems thoroughly heathen, quite untouched by christianity, the hero tales of which refer to events which took place while yet the scandinavian population had its home on the south of the Baltic, and was mixed with our saxon race. Yet even these tales of Oðin are not entirely beyond the influence of the latin, spoken by a race of superior skill and knowledge. Very little, however, appears which did not come to the people from their forefathers.

8. Among those who amuse themselves with words and languages there is generally a great heat about the sanskrit. In spite of all professions of a more rational and sober kind, the students and professors of this ancient tongue make almost an idol and an oracle of it, and no gainsaying is to be permitted. Let me ask, therefore, whether this is to be held unlike all other languages and to be supposed unworn, unsmoothed, unaltered; whether it has kept all its old asperities, all its concurrent consonants, all its throat rasping gutturals. The professors of sanskrit, who are at the same time among the most accomplished philologers, have themselves replied; they say that they cannot call this the primitive language; they announce that "the sanskrit has in many points experienced alterations, where one or other of the european sister idioms has more truly transmitted to us the original form." "Several languages, which are still spoken, retain here and there the forms of the primitive world of languages, which several of their older sisters have lost thousands of years ago." These admissions, however, go for very little; it is not a familiar idea with the learned, that the same causes, which have worn away the true radical letters in other tongues, have wrought also in the sanskrit: yet it cannot be denied but that the gutturals spoken over half our eurasian continent, have been in the sanskrit turned into sibilants and semi-sibilants; and for myself I am convinced and do assert that it has also dropped letters from the beginning of words, has rejected them from the middle, and sometimes thrown them away at the end.

9. Nobody, it may be presumed, is bound to pin his faith upon all that everybody has said about derivations from the sanskrit. The evidence is no greater in this case than in others. Latin and greek words must be like the sanskrit both in shape and sense, and variations must be in some way explained or paralleled, or else the comparison is unconvincing. To the derivational system, as given from the native authorities, the german professors do not unreservedly give their assent: they often pronounce the origin of a word uncertain, and often use phrases "volunt esse," etc., of hesitation.

10. In etymology a good many of the most familiar facts are not denied. Then some are probable, entertained by the student with content; some look dubious, some are mere speculations. Were we to admit all that can be made reasonably likely about the changes which words and letters freely suffer, still the case would not be mended. As a man sees with clear vision near and bright objects, distinguishes even some far off if they are well placed for light and contrast, but knows scarce anything of those which are away on the dark horizon, so if two words be letter for letter the same in Germany and England, if they have the same sense, they may be acknowledged to be of one origin ; if a change of letter occurs, provided it be frequent, a willingness to draw even for that upon credulity will be granted, but if we want two roots in the english greek and latin with some changes of letter to be identified, then doubt appears, and when many alterations have occurred, assent is hardly given at all. With practised minds there is some difference of detail, but the principles of faith and doubt remain the same. So that this branch of study has its limits, there are things that can never become credible ; there are mists upon the landscape. No amount of reading ought to remove such doubts; every several word ought to receive a different amount of confidence. Let some engaged in this pursuit continue of sound mind.

11. Undoubtedly from these maxims it follows that what is offered in these pages is open to refusal ; and that is true ; some words should be more alike ; some may now or sometime be set in a different light ; some we think of differently at different times. All that I believe of the whole scheme is this, that it is worthy the consideration of the reader. He will find some things that are new and true ; new only as now freshly dug up from their old burial ground.

12. The weak point in all the learned is their ignorance : the laity do not assume to know anything ; yet in an Englishmans mother tongue few clowns but would puzzle a doctor. We collect, in the rural districts, specimens of our tongue which are in no books, no glossaries, no dictionaries. The modern use of the word Buxom has surprised many before now ; it is

a compound from the agls. Bugan, Bow, and the adjectival -sum, and is therefore Bow-some, pliant, obedient: "Unbuxom to mother church" is a frequent expression in old books;

> [N]ild þai, wald þai, all gert he
> Bowsum til hys byddyng be.—*Wyntown*, vol. ii. p. 96.

The following lines are on the fourth (romanist) commandment.

> The ferd is worschip thi fader and thi moder
> Bo way of kynde thes too may noȝt be the to der
> To thaim oght * thou buxumnes and honor
> And also in thair [sickness?] help and socour.
> *The Myrrour of Lewed Men*, 99.

13. Shrewd is of these later days taken to mean 'keen,' and in the "Taming of the Shrew" we are supposed to hear a word of the same form but different sense, and of the weaker gender. When a horse-keeper calls a vicious brute a Screw, he uses the older form in the proper sense, and Shrewd is no more than Screwy. The following lines are of Satan: I have corrected an error of the hand or type in the word 'ueawe' for 'few,' which is printed 'neawe.'

> Therfore ther hys a mastryc schreawe,
> Wyth hym mo beth and thet nauȝt ueawe
> And neades mote;
> For he hys heaved of schrewednesse,
> Ase God hys cheaf of alle godnesse,
> And alle bote†.—*William of Shoreham*, p. 148.

> The good wyffe sayd, wer hast thou be?
> In schrewyd plas, as thynkys me.
> *The Frere and the Boy*, 283. Halliwell's ed.

> Be God, sayd the wyffe than,
> Her is a schrewed aray.
> *Id.* 290. (*English Miscellanies*, Warton Club.)

> Out fruit go and gather but not in the dew,
> With crab and the walnut for fear of a shrew ‡.
> *Tusser December*, p. 19.

Adelung gives eng. Screw, germ. Schraube, swed. Skruf,

---

* The MS. reads Oght'. This piece was printed by the Caxton Society with a wrong title, and 'oghten' read. Cf. norse Att for †agt.

† Bote is remedy, cure. Neades mote, needs must.

‡ Shrew, here thief.

dutch Schroeve, french Ecroue, ital. Scrofola, polish Szruba, finnish Scrunwi. The equivalent has never yet been found in any agls. writing. It comes to us of course in either shape from an english not a foreign source; it is quite english, for I do not learn that the Germans or Swedes would call a perverse horse a Screw. And it often happens that words which ought to be saxon cannot be shown to be so.

14. Inquiries are often made as to the relation of the phœnician group of tongues to ourselves, to what is called the aryan or indo-european. As we proceed I shall endeavour to show that concealed likenesses may be found, hitherto unremarked, between the phœnician tongues and the rest.

15. As to the relationship of the keltic there is among the wise in words no doubt. Zeuss, who attempted nothing on this head and has therefore no favourite theory to extol, says that they form part of our group; "lingua Celtica deprehenditur una linguarum Asiæ et Europæ affinium a primordio;" and any one who has looked at the tenses of an irish verb will be satisfied that this opinion is well grounded.

16. Some instinctive tests exist by which to discriminate between borrowed words and true parallels. Thus compounds can hardly be accepted: no one perhaps but the excellent scholar himself who committed the crude thought to paper, would suppose sorcerer to be Θεουργος. Afformative letters added to the visible root afford a strong ground of suspicion. Yet I would say 'instinctive tests' rather than rules, for it is not reasonable to suppose but that old roots had acquired some afformative letters while still some of the kindred nations were undivided from each other. Thus in the words Horn, Cornu, Κερας, קרן, with the horned Hart, Cervus, the presence of an N in the hebrew latin and english would not fairly be concluded to make one of these languages the lender and the other the borrower: for, first, the word may have been commonly applied to the thing B.C. 2000 or 2500 or sooner, secondly, the N may have been significant in all these languages. A similar method might be applied, reasonably to Screw.

17. It will often be found that my conclusions are at

variance with what better men than myself have taught. They are, I hope, carefully and thoughtfully at issue. Graff says somewhere that Pott, "scharfsinnig" as he is, took Signum to be = si — gnum = sanskr. sun — jnâ : here are two good names and two eminent men, but Signum is δεικ — end, Token. In another place Pott who had seen that there must be an affinity, as there is, between Αλειφειν and the mœsogothic Salbon, to Salve, accounted for the S by making it Sa, which Bopp accepts from him, reading Sa as sanskrit, while perhaps Pott did at least compound his word in elements of the same language and meant the mœsogothic article, either way producing a very curious something, quite exceptional in form. More things of this sort might be alledged, but as I write "nævos in corpore magno" rises to my memory and I am silenced. In regard therefore to illustrious names I shall say no more.

18. One or two principles may seem here sometimes to be tacitly assumed without proof; one is, that in the same syllables, or more exactly, in varied forms of equivalents, that which retains the greater number of letters is the more ancient. No careful statement of this proposition would perhaps exclude all exceptions, for language has continually its anomalies. But it ought to be admitted that Vestis which contains more letters than Εσθης is nearer to the ancient form, and though Virgil, for names sake, was later than Euripides, yet the syllables in Virgils mouth or from his stylus wore an older form than their equivalents in the poems of the other. Like Oðin, Woden, the two words were living at the same date B.C. or A.D. but the adhering letter shows a form less worn, less suffering from attrition. Hence if a somewhat lax use of the term old may be permitted, the modern english Work is older than the attic Εργον, and as old as the homeric Fεργον.

19. English readers are impatient of a perplexity of explanation: it is better to say at once that in such instances as May, Μεγαλα (pl.), Magnus, the shorter form May is older, having none of the afformative syllables of the others. In this instance a root which to Homer 800 B.C. had perished,

and was dead of age, still survives in the common talk of England. It is to instances of this sort that the learned professor alluded when he said that some words have retained a more primitive shape in this latter day in which we live, than they possess in writings two or three thousand years old. As an exception to this may be cited Daffodil which is Ασφοδελον, and has capped itself with a letter which eight hundred years ago did not belong to it.

20. Another principle that seems generally valid is that gutturals are older than labials and equivalent sibilants: some arguments will be offered on the question at 519, 637. If true, then latin words not directly adapted from hellenic art or science, are generally more archaic than their greek equivalents: Quinque is older than Πεντε, Equus than Ἱππος. This rule also is open to some remarkable exceptions: languages are found like the scotch, a dialect, observe, of the english, which bring back a long lost guttural, as Quhare, Quhite, Quhit, for Where, White, Wheat under their older truer spelling Hwær, Hwit, Hwæt. Here it may be urged that the Scotch do but add somewhat of force to the aspiration; a stranger example is seen in the irish, which has turned Πασχα, the passover or Easter into Cáisg, Cásga, and Πεντηκοστη Whitsuntide into Cincis. Yet generally, on the larger average by much, experience and consent affirm the rule.

21. If so, then our word Quick is very ancient in its spelling; meaning probably 'living,' as in "Quick and dead, Quick with child, Quicksilver, Quicksand, Cut to the quick," it descends into vic-tum with one guttural, Viv-ere with none, βιος with none. Should any contemner of english wish to argue that the hardening process has produced the word we utter, it will be seen by and by that the hebrew of the Pentateuch stands beside the english.

22. The rough old forms of words might well be preserved among the skythian wilds. All understand well enough that the germanic nations came from Skythia. There they lived while Moses gave laws to Israel, while Homeros sang of Troy, while Roman and Sabine fought. That in the camps

of these wanderers and warriors such a word as Quick might be spoken without much change, or such a verb as May, Magan might live, while altered or lost in towns and sunny fields, is not surprising.

23. As we have never seen presented to us all the words of our own people in any dictionary, not so much, I mean, the pedantic latinisms of the writers, as the genuine home-talk of the husbandmen, so it may be presumed we have not on paper the whole anglosaxon (English) tongue. Prose authors, poets, schoolboys, every craft, every county have something of their own, and as the historians, the essayists, and the poets have possession of print, they have got their words into the dictionaries, the others are pretty nearly shut out. In saxon then as the literature is mostly ecclesiastical, homilies, sacred songs, with addition of glossaries, it is not to be supposed we can have everything. In the old english, teutonic words often occur, which are in the dutch or german dictionaries not in the saxon. These were in most cases real saxon words, but not of the printed portion. Thus Qued 'bad,' is frequent in old english, and it must have been saxon though not found recorded.

The deficiencies of the vocabulary of anglosaxon books are supplied by glossaries. How many must have been the words that Ælfric never heard, how many that he refused to admit when he did hear them, how many that did not present themselves while compiling a glossary. A small examination of unpublished manuscripts will soon convince any one who can read the language, that the admirable industry of Lye and Manning had not completed the whole task: nor has any one equal to the undertaking yet appeared. Thus I find of the Nile that it is caldor fallicra ea, 'prince of noble rivers,' where occurs the latin Pulcer = norse Fallegr, a word not in the agls. dictionaries. Modern lexicon makers are not to be named in the same page as the old heroes of this battle.

24. All very similar words require a close examination lest by chance they be borrowed terms. The Skythians said that from heaven were borne, a plough, a yoke, a sagaris or sword, and a cup. These then were either heavenly blessings, or

were foreign improvements; if foreign, they were first known in Skythia about a thousand years before the invasion of Darius, or near the time of Moses. We may safely conclude then that words of this stage of civilization were not borrowed from the merchants, priests, or books of Greece and Rome. But a large list of words exists which it would be mere credulity to suppose original to the gothic races.

25. To guarantee a proper measure of circumspection I have selected from a list prepared by the late Sharon Turner, far the larger number of his parallels, and beforehand aver that I see no parallelism, but merely romanized phrases in them. The unlike likeness of saxon words with the latin is much more persuasive than an exact correspondence; the latter may be latinisms in saxon characters, the former are most likely due to a sisterhood of dialect. An advance in the arts useful to men is eagerly caught at by every nation. Glossarists and word theorizers are often over greedy: they swell their catalogues " si possunt reete, si non, quocumque modo." This error will gradually diminish before the increase of judgment in the science. Now Mr. Sharon Turner is reputed to have known something of anglosaxon, and his conclusions come with recommendation : I am willing therefore to claim a slower belief, a more suspensive caution than he exercised, by refusing or sometimes hesitating to admit to comparison with the latin the following : æbs, abies; ængel, angelus; ær, æs, æris; æren, æreus; æx, axis; alewa, aloe; amber, amphora; ancer, anchora; anakumbyan? accumbere (that word is mœsogothic and not native; the page of S. T. is vol. ii. p. 148); aplantan, plantare; arca, area though in Ulphilas; asal, assa, asinus, asellus (with germ. esel); box, buxus; calic, calicem; calo, calvus; cancere, cancer; candel, candela; cal(?) (colewort), caulis (id.); ccalc (=chalk), calcem (lime); ccale, calculus; ccaster, castra (on this word Dr. Guest says, " No word answering to ccaster is found in the celtic dialects, nor is it known to any german language except our own. The avenue by which it found its way into the anglosaxon may furnish a subject for consideration hereafter. No philologist will subscribe to the opinion that it came directly

from the latin Castrum." That is, it is a latin word, but not derived from contact with the Romans); cimbal, cymbalum; circol, circulus; ciste, cista; cisten-beam, castanea; coc(?), coquus; corn treow, cornus; cræsta, crista; croh, crocus; cryft, crypta; cycene(?), coquina; cylene, culina; cype-leac, cippus; cyrs-treow, cerasus; deofl, diabolus; eced, acetum; egor, æquor (here we have not one sense); elehtre, electrum; elm, ulmus; elpen-ban, from elephanta (acc.) (olfend, a camel, by distortion of meaning from elephanta); ened(?), anatem (acc.); fæcele, faculam; færs, versus; fic, ficus; finn, pinna; finnol, fœniculum; fiþele, fidicula; flum, flumen; fore, furca; fricca, præco; gamol(?), camelus; gigant, gigantem; gem, gemma; grad, gradus; grennian, grunnire (but ?); imne, hymnus; leon, leonem; linen, lineus; mæger, macer; mealwe, malva; meter, metrum; midd (bushel), modius; mil, mille passus; minte, mintha; mul, mulus also mullus; mant, montem; muscle, musculus; must, mustum; mynet, moneta; næpe, napum (acc.); offrian, offerre; Orc, Orca (the latin borrowed this word from Scandinavia; the Orkneys, lat. Orcades, are the walrus islands from Örkn in islandic)—

"The ugly orks that for their lord the ocean woo."
"That all the armed orks of Neptune's grisly band
With music of my verse amaz'd may list'ning stand."

pal, palum (acc.); papig, papaver; pawo, pavo; pic, picem (acc.); pil, pila; pill, pulvinar; pise, pisum; pitt, puteus; plante, planta; plaster, emplastrum; pund, pondo; port, portus; pur, purus; pyngan, pungere; pirige, pirus; regol, regula; rude, rute, ruta; salh, salicem (acc.); sape, sapo; segnian, signare; sagne, sagena; segn, signum; sutere, sutor; turtle, turtur; ynce, uncia (inch); yndsa, uncia (ounce). To suppose all these words to be independent specimens of cognate dialects is to put history, comparative philology, and experience out of consideration.

26. Other words exist where a likeness is strong, but a critical watchfulness prevents our conceding a full confidence that the forms were indigenous. Dr. Guest has argued that some words having reference to a better condition of life were

carried through a Keltic medium and learnt by the Saxons before their arrival in England, while still out of the reach of roman contact, and in their inveterate heathenism. Thus our Tile = agls. Tigle = dutch Tegel = germ. Ziegel was taken from the latin Tegula; for Tacitus expressly says "Ne cæmentorum aut tegularum usus." The word would probably be adopted not long after the roman power was firmly established in Gaul.

27. Dr. Guest takes also our Wall = agls. Weall = germ. Wall = dutch Wal, and observes that they signify properly a wall of defence. "The wider meaning assigned to the english word may perhaps admit of the following explanation. In the north of England wall was pronounced wa', as all was pronounced a', and thus it seems to have been confounded with wa, answering to the agls. Wah 'a partition'." In these sentences there seems to me a great deal of reserve. Dr. Guest does not say that Wall is latin, he only places it among a list of latin words: and he seems to turn aside from the older equivalents, lest his argument should be obscured. Now the mœsogothic for τεῖχος, a city wall, is ᛒᚪᚾᚴᚱᛋ-ᚹᚪᛞᛞᚷᚾᛋ, a borough waddyus; for partition wall, μεσοτοιχον, is ᛗᛁᚦᚱᚪᚴᚪᚼᚹᚪᛞᛞᚷᚾᛋ, mid-house-waddyus; for foundation, θεμελιον, is ᚱᚴᚾᚾᚪᚾᚹᚪᛞᛞᚷᚾᛋ ground-waddyus. Here is no distinction between the wall of a house, and the murus of a city as far as regards the word Waddyus. Now of this gothic word the agls. Wah, genit. Wages, is the equivalent, just as Twegen is the saxon form of mœsog. Twai, genit. Twaddye, or as the sanskrit Duh for Dug answers to mœsog. Daddyan. The saxon remains in Wainscot, which is Wagen-scid, -schedula; dutch Wagenschot; and the islandic has Veggr. We find this form in old english—

An aundiren he kept in his honden tho
**With that aundiren he thret Sir Gy
**Into the wongh it fleye to fot and more.
Sir Gy of Warwike, p. 250.

In further illustration it may be added, that considering the form naturally taken by primitive life, this mœsog. Waddyus must be held as akin to Wattle, for both the external fence of an encampment and the internal partition, which separated a silvan hut into chambers, would naturally be wattled. Against this the reader may object that according to what appears above, it is the mœsogothic which puts dd for g; and now I am tracing back to a dental; I do not assent to any limited theory of letter-change. What is true of the mœsogoths must be true of others; and in anticipation of art. 1027 I shall express a speculative opinion that Wattle, Withy, Vitis, Viere, Bind, are of the same origin with Twine, Twist, Twig, and have for their oldest root some shape of Two, perhaps Twegen. Now it is clear, if these premises be admitted, admitted I mean, to probationary consideration, that Vallum is but another form of Wattle, Waddyus; and if agls. Weall be a latinism, this latinism traced further back is teutonic.

28. The next word which Dr. Guest mentions is Street, agls. Strǣte, which we at once recognize as no derivative from Strew, but a roman idea and a roman word. Out of system and wise policy that vigorous people carried their paved roads to Bagdat eastward and Carlisle northward.

Quam bene vivebant Saturno rege priusquam
Tellus in longas est patefacta vias.

29. The word Mill I cannot attribute to a latin origin. Unless the teutonic races sprang out of the ground, one hardly sees how they could escape the knowledge of a word and a process which was known to and named by Homer. A large trade with the shores of the Black Sea was carried on by the merchants of Hellas, and a favourite theme with late writers were the adventurous journeys of the Skyths, Anacharsis and Toxaris to Athens. $Μυλη$ in Homer is a hand-mill. All the while, however, there was an indigenous word Quern for the same thing; but to set against that, the mœsogothic has not only Malan, Luke xvii. 35, of the hand-mill, but the very similar word Malwyan $συντριβειν$, the german Zermalmen; and this cannot fail to remind us of Malleus, and the norse Miöllnir, Thor's hammer. Two terms may have concurrently existed, one from Whirling, Vertere, and another from crushing to pieces.

30. It may be necessary to say a few words upon the relationship of the Keltic languages to the english: and these remarks will be taken only at a low value, unless they seem to be intrinsically worth something. One or two surprising coincidences may be observed; compare irish, gaelic, welsh Brú, the womb, with $E\mu\beta\rho\upsilon o\nu$; welsh Bu 'was' with sanskr. Bhu, greek $\phi\upsilon$-$\epsilon\iota\nu$, lat. Fu-i: welsh Byw 'to live' with the homeric $\beta\epsilon\omega$ probably $\beta\epsilon\digamma\omega$, see art. 1024: irish Ceóac 'dark' with Cæcus, especially as used by the poets: irish Cluas = welsh Clust, the ear, with $\kappa\lambda\upsilon\epsilon\iota\nu$; irish Col, $K\omega\lambda\upsilon\mu a$; Colaim, $\kappa\omega\lambda\upsilon\omega$ (i. e. $\kappa\omega\lambda\upsilon o\mu\iota$); welsh Cudd (pronounced Cuð), hide, $K\epsilon\upsilon\theta\epsilon\iota\nu$; welsh Dagr, $\Delta a\kappa\rho\upsilon$; irish Dearg 'an eye,' Dearcaim 'I see,' Dreach 'aspect;' welsh Edrych 'to look,' $\Delta\epsilon\rho\kappa\epsilon\sigma\theta a\iota$; welsh Enw, irish Henw, gaelic Ainm, $O\nu o\mu a$; Ffer, $\Sigma\phi\upsilon\rho o\nu$; welsh Gân 'a birth,' irish Geinim 'beget,' $\Gamma\epsilon\nu o\varsigma$, $\Gamma\epsilon\nu\nu a\epsilon\iota\nu$ ($\gamma\epsilon\iota\nu o\mu\iota$); welsh Iach 'sound, whole,' $I a\sigma\theta a\iota$; irish Leagaim 'lick,' $\Lambda\epsilon\iota\chi\epsilon\iota\nu$ ($\lambda\epsilon\iota\chi o\mu\iota$); welsh Mir 'the visage,' cornish Mirer 'to look,' spanish Mirar 'to look,' cf. Mirari; welsh Pryn 'purchase,' cornish Perna, $\Pi\iota\pi\rho a\sigma\kappa\epsilon\iota\nu$, $\Pi\rho\iota a\sigma\theta a\iota$; irish Seile, 'spittle,' $\Sigma\iota a\lambda o\varsigma$, Saliva. These words can scarcely be borrowed from the latin, and historical evidence is wanting to induce a belief that they could be from the greek. Rather, joined to some pronominal forms and the mode of inflecting the verb, we conclude that the Keltic nations are not alien from the common stock.

31. Suspicion attaches to a large number of words which are like the latin, since the Kelts, we know, were all for a long space of time, within the influence of latin arts and a latinized priesthood. Many welsh words not found in irish may be fairly assumed to be taken from the latin, many more from the saxon, many of recent date from the english. Archdeacon Williams appears to take a true and unprejudiced view of the facts, when he says that once "it was foolishly imagined that the welsh was a language per se, without parentage or cognation, and only to be explained on its own principles and to be illustrated from its own resources. This system, supported by the great industry and illguided ingenuity of Dr. Owen Pughe, has exerted a most baneful effect upon the more modern

race of welsh scholars." A good many lists of words common to the welsh and latin, or common to the welsh and teutonic, have been made out. In looking through these it must always be kept in mind that novelties take their names from the people from whom they came, that highly civilized nations have many more new things than such as are less advanced, and that always a nation superior in war, in trade and in arts exercises a vast influence over its inferiors. Hence we shall rather draw the conclusion that the Kelts borrowed from the Romans, than the Romans from them : or from the Saxons, rather than the reverse. Even in the most recent lists, by the most able scholars, are quite untenable propositions. Thus Ystaen with the sense of extension, ductility, is no original for Stannum, for Ystaen is but the latin word Extendere transplanted into the welsh. Button is from no keltic botwm, but a french word, and from a Bud, as is clear from Boutonner, which is both 'to bud,' and 'to button.'

> He dradde nat that no glotons,
> Should steale his roses or bothoms.
> CHAUCER, *R. R.* 4307.

The history of Funnel I take to be this : Fundibulum gave Funnel in its ordinary sense, χοανον, then came Funnel-shaped chimneys, reversed funnels, used in glass-works, &c., and they were soon called also Funnels, then applied to the furnaces of steamboats they became to the unmechanical eye only iron chimneys. It would be very odd if we had borrowed Funnel from Wales from Ffyn, of the same family as Πνεειν. What Cæsar says of the barbarism of the Welshmen, when he first set foot in Britain, ought to induce much hesitation in setting down for keltic any terms which have a savour of the easier life about them, or which relate to objects as well known and probably better discriminated in Rome than Britain. There are no doubt keltic words which came into latin and into english, but it must be a very short list, Cabin, Mutton, Flannel, &c. Those seem to be employed on a more hopeful subject, who compare the irish with the sanskrit, as Pictet has done, for of the words common to the keltic and greek most are known in the sanskrit also.

A few cautions are desirable.

32. The latin in its old words preserves ruder and more archaic forms than the attic greek, which is best known to us. It approached very near to the æolic, of which we know little.

33. No one language is to be derived from any other, except in words and things which have been borrowed. In the home talk words are common to two languages, and have been probably in both cases drawn from some earlier spring. A remarkable instance is Agni 'fire' in the sanskrit, Ignis in the latin, certainly not borrowed either way.

34. S is the nominative masculine singular termination in the sanskrit, greek, latin and mœsogothic, the radix therefore is seen by removing this S, with its vowel, if it have one. The sanskrit has partly changed this S into H, the islandic always into R. Hence in islandic R is to be separated from the radix.

35. The islandic largely uses assimilation, as Baggi 'baggage,' from mœsog. Balgs, 'bag'; none of the teutonic languages employ this sort of change so much as the islandic. Sometimes the nominatival R disappears by the force of it, as Spónn for Spón-r.

36. The islandic, called in its oldest form, norse, drops the digamma, vau, or W, much as the hellenic did between the days of Homer and Thukydides; the mœsogothic and anglo-saxon very regularly, though neither of them always, preserve it. The latin also mostly retained it. Thus Worm in the norse is Orm, in latin Vermis, in mœsog. Waurms, in agls. Wyrm.

37. For the ancient K, the mœsogothic in the middle of words almost always substitutes the softer sound of H; the agls., though less often, writes H for G or K, and sometimes the english brings back the G. The German has two sorts of H, one of which represents an ancient guttural as in Herz, καρδια; the other is merely an indication of a long vowel as the second H in Hahn=mœsog. Hana 'cock,' our Hen.

38. The J of the sanskrit has the sound of the english J as in Jack. Short A in sanskrit is a mere help sound; pronounce as in America.

c

39. The J of the german is the english Y; in transferring some languages, as for instance the mœsogothic to the common type, many who treat of etymology use german books and adopt the german J. J was no part of the saxon alphabet, they had neither the character nor the sound.

40. The J of latin books is a mere imitation of the german method of printing; Cujus, Ejus, Jupiter are not latin at all, they should be Cuius, Eius, Iupiter. The romans had neither the letter nor the sound.

41. The latin had four conjugations, perhaps five; one simple, as Regere: one in A contracted, †amao=Amo; †amais =Amas; †amaimus=Amamus, and so on: one in E contracted, as Moneo, †moncis=Mones; †moncimus=Monemus, and so on: one in I contracted, as Audio; †audiis=Audis; †audiimus=Audimus, and sometimes Audiebam=Audibam, Audibo. The fifth was in V (u), which we with correctness probably regard as a consonant sometimes, sometimes a vowel, thus SOLVO, SOLVTVS, Solvo, Solutus, VOLVO, VOLVMEN, Volvo, Volumen, the roman character being the same either way.

42. Latin verbs are very often of two or three conjugations: they are written, simply, as Regere, with A, as Amas, with E, as Mones, and with V, as Solutus. Parens 'a parent' is a participial substantive from †parere=Ferre; the frequentative of this †parere is Portare: in the sense 'bear children' the infinitive mood remains Parere, but in Pario, Pariunt, the verb adopts the conjugation in I. Capere, Rapere, Facere are like Regere; but Capio, Rapio, Facio, Capiunt, Rapiunt, Faciunt, Capiens, Rapiens, Faciens are like Audio, Audiunt, Audiens. Capere of the simple, Capio of the I conjugation are accompanied by Occupat of the A conjugation, and by Aucupatur, Aucupari. So also Facere, Faciebam, stand by the side of Significare, Magnificare, yet Magnificentem. Densare appears in Virgilius and Horatius as Densere, Addensere. Compare Legere, Elegans; Liquare, Liquere; Vomere, Ἐμεῖν; Sanare, Insanire; Sternere, Consternatio; Κλινειν, Clinare; Λειβειν, Libare; Θορυβεῖν, ταρασσειν, Turbare; Ερροντι=Erranti (ἡ μ' οιῳ ερροντι συνηντετο νοσφιν ἑταιρων.

δ. 367). Lavit, Lavat; Luere, Lavare, Λουειν; Affligere, Confligere, Profligare. Dicere was originally identical with Δεικνυναι, and meant 'to shew.' Festus informs us that in the older latin it was capable of the A conjugation; which we see in Dedicare, Indicare.

43. The verbs in -eo should make -evi, -etus, as Neo, nevi, netus, Impleo, implevi, impletus, and the more common conjugation Moneo, monui, monitus consists of Moneo with E, Monui with U, and Monitus on the simple model; it is therefore made up of three conjugations.

44. The termination μι in the first person singular whether found in τιθημι, ἱστημι, διδωμι, φημι, ειμι, or in δαμνημι, αϜειδημι archaic words, or in κοπτοιμι in the barytone conjugation, with all those terminations of the other persons most in analogy with it, is more ancient than the ending in -ω.

45. Languages do not limit themselves to one form of a root, but the same original radix often appears in derivatives which are not very like, as ALL, WHOLE, HEAL, WELL, Salvation.

46. Marks over vowels are intended to distinguish those which are read long. The printers, it seems, rarely possess types to mark the difference in the manner of latin prosodies, and this awkward contrivance is a substitute. The matter has not been much, perhaps not enough, attended to in these pages.

47. The first and easiest step in changing the aspect of words is a change in the vowels. As was wittily but fairly said, in etymology the vowels are of no account and the consonants of little. Many examples occur in which the change can be accounted for fully, for example we know why Κυνα has a different vowel from Canem, and we know that the υ does not represent the a at all. When such examples occur they encourage us to the conclusion that a change of vowel ought not to prevent our comparing words. Within the precincts of any separate language the changes of inflexions will change vowels; words will also be deduced from a common root, and in their descent receive vowels of different values. Nor do the written characters represent commonly the actual

sound. Many different sounds are represented by one character in english, as in What, Can, Call, State, Dictionary. The long a of the anglosaxon is often written o in English, as Stan, Stone; Ban, Bone; Ham, Home; Rap, Rope; Gast, Ghost; Sar, Sore; Wrat, Wrote. The short vowels in corresponding greek and latin words are often different, they are different in the different dialects of all languages, different at different ages. The change of a vowel is then often no sufficient reason for denying the relationship of words, and sometimes it is a hardly sufficient reason. A strong vowel change will be a reason for doubt, but not enough to close the argument. J. Grimm in his 'Deutsche Mythologie,' p. 10, gives an opinion that God is not of the same stock as Good; the mœsogothic Guþ is not to be compared with Gods, neuter Goþ, because of the change of vowel. Rather than compare these two vowels, he explains God as persian Khoda, a contraction of zend Quadâta = sansk. Swadâta, 'a se datus.' Grimm has here put himself to unnecessary trouble: the mœsogothic Guþ no longer retains its vowel in the norse, but becomes Goð, and has been so printed in the Edda since the edition of Professor Munch. The difference also between a long and short vowel, if short, is not insuperable. It by no means, however, follows from this that the ancient gods were good. The germans tend too much to scruple in comparing vowels: the principles of 'Vocalismus' have as yet received less light than the laws of consonant changes, and, as the vowel element is more volatile, afford greater difficulties. Thus Sol, Ἥλιος; Dies, Biduum have vowels hard to reconcile. Add to this, that a very important branch of the subject, the change of consonants, and of consonants coupled with vowels into other vowels, have never yet been properly examined. Thus Σημα seems related to Signum. The german philologs get over difficulties of vocalization by a halfword about exception or anomaly or the like: we may lay down more broadly that much yet remains unexplained in vowel change: at the outset we have only to maintain that changes, and occasionally unexpected changes, are found. Compare Ἀρνευτηρες with Urinatores.

48. The great extent of change, often of systematic change, in words, may be illustrated by comparing one or two word families. Thus engl. to Drink=agls. Drincan=mœsog. Driggkan [sound ng]=germ. Trinken=isl. Drecka : engl. a Drink=agls. Drinc=mœsog. Draggk=eng. a Draught=isl. Drecka=agls. Drenc=eng. a Drench : engl. he Drank=he Drunk=agls. he Dranc pl. hig Druncon=mœsog. pl. weis Drugkun (1 Kor. x. 4. etc.) : engl. to Drench=agls. Drencan =mœsog. Draggkyan=germ. Tränken ; to Drown=agls. ? =isl. Dreckia=dansk. Druknc=germ. er-tränken, the intrans. er-trinken. Here we have all the vowels and some of the diphthongs.

> The see him gon adrynke
> That Rymenil may of thinke.—*Kyng Horn*, 978.
>
> Tho fond hue hire sonde
> Adrouque by the strond.—*Id.* 987.

49. Thus again agls. Bugan=engl. to Bow=agls. Beogan, Bigan, Bygan=mœsog. Biugan=germ. Beugen ; engl. Bowed =agls. ic Beag, pl. we Bugon ; part. Bugen, Bogen. Derivatives a Bay, stand at Bay, Bay window, Bow, Bow window, Bight, Bough, Buckle, Bosom, Buxom, Beigh, french Bague. The anglosaxon Beag was not a ring only, or an armlet ; it was also a coronet or diadem. Stephanus is Grecisc nama, þæt is on Leden, Coronatus, þæt we cweðað on Englisc, Gewuldor beagod ; for ðan ðe he hæfð þone ecan wuldor beah. (Homilies I. 50) The Bays then of our poets, and the Bay tree were in reality the Coronet and the Coronet tree. Lye rightly set Beah 'corona' first. Wuldorbeh was in constant use for a crown of Glory, and Beh stands by itself for the same, as in the Martyrdom of St. Margaret, fol. 73. The latinized form Boiæ, Bays, cited by Lye, seems to shew that the french term for a stag at bay, abbois, is of teutonic origin.

50. With the mœsogothic Maþyan 'φαγειν' are connected Maggot=isl. Maþkr=mœsog. Maþa, 'a worm,' Moth, Mite, Meat. Several pairs of words may serve also as examples, Syrop=Shrub; Deal=Dole; Dent=Dint; Gargle=Gurgle; Spire, Spear, Spirt=Sprout ; Snake with Sneak ; Nighest= Next; Brat, Brood; Float, Fleet ; Sip, Sop, Soup, Sup ;

Writhe, Wreathe. So in latin, Capio, Cepi, Recipio, Recupero (Recover), Reciprocus?

51. To relieve the heaviness of the subject let me recall the lines of Spenser on the compound word Thames, Tamesis, F. Q. IV. xi. 24.

> So he went playing on the watery plaine;
> Soone after whom the lovely bridegroome came;
> The noble Thames, with all his goodly traine.
> But him before there went, as best became,
> His auncient parents, namely th' auncient Thame;
> But much more aged was his wife then he,
> The Ouze, whom men doe Isis rightly name;
> Full weak and crooked creature seemed shee,
> And almost blind through eld, that scarce her way could see.

52. Short A changes place with E, as bank, bench; arma, inermis; pars, expers; gradior, ingredior; farcio, confertus; βαλλω, βελος; ετραφην, τρεφω; εσπαρην, σπερμα; Σαραπις =Σεραπις; βαραθρον ion. βερεθρον; αρσην ion. ερσην; φαλαρα, phaleræ; παθος, πενθος; dor. ποκα, att. ποτε; dor. γα, att. γε; dor. αλλοκα, att. αλλοτε; dor. Αρταμις, att. Αρτεμις; ion. μεγαθος, att. μεγεθος; ion. ταμνειν, att. τεμνειν; καλυπτω 'cover,' κελυφος 'husk, pod'; ψαλια=ψελλια.

53. With I, as ϝεικατι=Viginti; ζαγκλη, sickle; facio, conficio, artificem; manus, cominus; amicus, inimicus; capio, anticipo. Samson, in german Simson; sanskr. agni, lat. ignis; sansk. panchan, lat. quinque; sanskr. ashwah, ἱππος; sanskr. saptan, mœsog. sibun, engl. seven; sanskr. chatur, mœsog. fidwor.

54. With O, as papaver, poppy; partem, portionem; scabo, scobem; κρατα, κροταφοι; παρδαλις=πορδαλις; δαμαρ=δομορτις; καρηναι, κορμος; σπαρηναι, σποριμος; ἁμα, ὁμος; τραφηναι, τροφη; ϝεικατι, εικοσιν; att. στρατος, æol. στροτος; att. ανω, æol. ονω; att. ανιαις, æol. ονιαις; βαλλω, βολη.

With U, παϊς=puer; αφλαστα=aplustra; κραιπαλη=crapula; καλαμος, calamus, culmus; Ἑκαβη=Hecuba; Ἡρακλης=Hercules; χαμαι=humi; Θριαμβος=triumphus; αγκιστρον, uncus; ἁμα=ξυν; capio, aucupor; salsus, insulsus; calco, conculco; taberna, contubernium.

55. Short A is also exchanged with long vowels and di-

VOWEL CHANGE. 23

phthongs, and some of these changes are by rule and method, as λαθειν, λησω; λαθεσθαι, ληθη; μακρος, μηκος and μηκων 'poppy' from its length; παρα, παραι; τεσσαρακοντα, ion. τεσσαρηκοντα; καλος with short a in attic, καλος with long, homeric; Χαριτες, Gratiae; doric κρασσων with κρατος, κρατιστος, att. κρεισσων; πλατυς probably latus; capio with κωπη? dbtfl.; At, αταρ, αυταρ, autem; ὑδατος, ὑδωρ; ἑταρος, ἑταιρος; in oscan Aut=At; Malli now Mooltan.

56. It is suppressed, as βαλλω, βεβληmαι; θανατος, τεθνηκα; δαμνημι, δεδμηκα.

57. As an application, the yew tree, Taxus, with its excellent bows, Τοξον, and its poisonous leaves, Toxicum, may be an example.

58. Long a is found exchanged with η in many examples from the greek dialects, as dor. ματηρ, att. μητηρ; att. πρασσω, ion. πρησσω; att. ἑδρα, ion. ἑδρη; halare, anhelare; with ω, as dor. πρατιστος, att. πρωτιστος; accipiter as if ωκυπτερος; with αι, as Θηβαγενης, Θηβαιγενης; ἰθαγενης, ἰθαιγενης; αετος, αιετος; that Haurio is Αρυω seems well confirmed by αρυταινα 'a ladle' οινηρυσις. Compare Naves, ναυς, νεας, νηας.

59. It is suppressed, as balare, βληχασθαι.

60. Short e is exchanged with a, as above. With i, as teneo, contineo; specio, conspicio (this change does not hold before R, as tero, obtero: Grotefend); θεος, lacon. σιος; κερασαι, κιρναν; ισθι, εστω; †πετω, πιτνω; πελαζειν, πιλνασθαι; μελεταν, meditari 'practise'; ανεμος, animus, anima; σκεδαννυμι, σκιδναμαι; πεπερι, piper, pepper; τεκειν, τικτειν; πλεκω, plico; indicem, index; Σικελια, Sicilia; ἑστια, ion. ἱστιη; λεγω, lingua. With short o, as tego, toga; pendo, pondus; terra, extorris; βαλος, βολη; φερειν, φορτιον; Ερχομενος in native inscriptions=Ορχομενος; γενος, γονεις; τρεφω, τροφος, τροφη; φρενες, φρονειν; æol. εδοντες, οδοντες; æol. εδυνη, att. οδυνη; λεγω, loquor, ετυμολογω etc. With u, as tego, tugurium; contemno, contumelia (if so, and not from tumeo: Grotefend); peiero, iuro; γενναν, γυνη; σφενδονη, funda; ἑλκος, ulcus; αμελγω, mulgeo; νεφελη, nebula; τεος, tuus; the latin -mus of the first person plural, with the doric μες.

61. It is also suppressed, as μενος, mens, μεμνημαι; γενος, γιγνομαι; βελος, βεβλημαι; τεμνω, τετμηκα; γερανος, grus; †πετω, †πιπετω, πιπτω. Short E exchanges also with long vowels and diphthongs; as σπερμα, σπειρω; γενος, εγειναμην; στελλω, εστειλα, and thus frequently; κεας, εκηα; φρενες, φρην; ἑνα, unum; νεφος, nubes; στρεφω, στρωφαν; πετεσθαι, πωτασθαι; νεμειν, νωμαν.

62. Long E is exchanged with A, as above; with short E, as sedes, sedeo, ἑδρα; legem, lego; regem, rego; regula, rego; tegula, tego; legi, lego; with O, as pedere, podex? agls. reaf, in the Heliand, girobi, spanish, italian roba, engl. robe; deal, dole: with u, as celo, occulo; steed, stud; feel, frequentative danish famle, english fumble.

63. To give more bone and substance to this making of lists, let us examine the forms taken by the verb to Ken. In old english often Can, and the common Cau, posse=norse Knaga; in the causative, mœsogothic Kannyan; in lowland scotch Ken 'know,' in german Kennen, in islandic Kenna, in some agls. forms cennan; in mœsogothic and agls. Cunnan, whence Cunning, in isl. Kenning; with Y, in the islandic causative Kynna; then with the vowel suppressed, Know, Knowledge, then with a diphthong Quaint, as in Acquaintance=germ. Bekantschaft.

> And preyed hire per charite and for profites love
> To kenne hem sum coyntice ȝif sche any couþe*.
> *William and the Werwolf*, fol. 24. B.

> After him spak Dalmadas
> A riche almatour he was,
> A faire mon, quoynte, and vertuous,
> Feol† and hardy and coragous.
> *Kyng Alisaunder*, 3041.

> A shipman was ther, woned fer by west;
> For aught I wote, he was of Dertemouth.
> He rode upon a rouncie as he couthe.—*Chaucer, C. T.*, 390.

---

* Here couþe is knew, could, the l being a mere modern intrusion. Chaucer has couthe, coud, coude: it is formed by rejecting N in Kend.
† Feol, fell.

Aftur kyng Annisag, of wam we habbe ytold
Marius, ys sone, was kyng, queynte mon and bold,
And ys sone was aftur hym, kyng Coel was ys name,
A noble man and queynte and of good fame.
Robert of Gloster, p. 72.

A wise wif if that she can hire good
Shall beren hem on hond the cow is wood.
Chaucer, C. T., 5813.

This sely carpenter goth forth his way,
Full oft he said alas and walawa,
And to his wif he told his privitee,
And she was ware, and knew it bet than he
What all this queinte cast was for to sey.
Chaucer, C. T., 3601.

64. I here submit an explanation of CUDDLE differing from what is found in the authorities. From Ken with its passive participle Cup, 'known,' comes Uncouth, 'unknown.'

To dyne I have no lust
Tyll I have some bolde baron
Or some unketh gest,
That may paye for the best.
Robin Hood, 22.

I wyll forsake both lande and lede
And become an hermyte in uncouth stede.
Squyr of low degre, 136.

Hence in the sense of an adjective equivalent to 'familiar.'

And ȝif another treutheth sethe
Wyth word, of that hys nouthe:
The ferste dede halte beth
Ne be hy nase couthe
As none;
Bote ȝef ther folȝede that treuthynge
A ferst flesch ymone.
William of Shoreham, p. 60.

He is speaking of ceremonial betrothal, and teaches that if after a first betrothal a second follow in word, of that no account is made; the first deed binds both, be they never so familiar, as none ever were; except if the betrothal be followed by consummation, flesh in common. The glossaries state this sense to be still used in the provinces. From this was formed a verb.

þan ciþer hent oþer hastely in armes,
And wiþ kene kosses kuþþed hem togidere.
William and the Werwolf, fol. 15.

Whence would come a frequentative verb Cuddle. The dutch has Kudde 'a flock,' Kudden 'to go in shoals.' 1 Peter, v. 2: Weydet de kudde Godts die onder u is. In the North, Cutter 'to fondle' (Brockett). A ewe cutters to her lamb. (MS. notes on Norfolk words.) Kudden, 'coire, convenire, congregari, aggregari' (in Kilian).

Coddle on the other hand is the frequentative of Cade, 'to pet.'

65. Short I is exchanged with A, E, as above. With U, as facilis, facultas; consul, consilium; exul, exilium; famulus, familia; compare locus, illico; in the numerals which have -ginta, and -κοντα; imber, ομβρος; ficus, συκη; gibbus, κυφος; and the cases in which a consonantal or semiconsonantal I answers to a consonantal or semiconsonantal U, as δια, δυο, δοιοι; καιω, καυσω; κλαιω, κλαυσαι; διχα, δυο; διπλοος, duplex; so ζεϝα, ζειδωρος; and other examples with digamma, see Art. 383. This change is recognized in the semitic languages, and deserves more attention in the greek and latin.

66. Short I is exchanged with long in liquorem, liquare; liquidus has the first syllable either way; suspicor, suspicionem, (†suspictionem); video, vidi; with long O, as cognitus, notus. In english the short I is often diminutival, as drop, drip, dribble; top, tip; tramp, trip; sup, sip.

67. Short O is found for A, E, I as above. For short U, as ομου = ξυν = συν = con : γονη, γυνη; ονομα, æol. ονυμα, with ανωνυμος, επωνυμος. In common with other short vowels it is dropped, γονη, γνησιος. It is also exchanged with long vowels and diphthongs, as πνοαι, πνοιαι; κορη, κουρη; æol. ορα, for ωρα (Gregor. Korinth); æol. οτειλη, for ωτειλη (id.); φευξομαι, φευξουμαι.

68. Short υ is exchanged as above. It is dropped, as in πυρ, πυρος, πιμπρημι, πρηστηρ; it gives place to diphthongs, ερυθρος, ερευθος; δυο, δευτερος; κυνες, κουνες (Etym. M. 632. 53); to long ω, in χωλος, Κυλλοποδιων (Homer), κυλλος (Aves, 1379).

69. There seems no doubt of the identity of Σφυρα, 'a hammer,' Σφυρον = welsh. Ffer 'the ankle, malleolus pedis,' Σφαιρα 'a ball': compare Ferire, ferrum.

70. The long vowels and diphthongs undergo changes which would not, from their fullness of sound, have been expected; as κειρειν, κουρευς; σπευδω, σπουδη; εκ τῶ θαλαμω for εκ τοῦ θαλαμου; and many like this; μουσας, μωσας; accusatives in -ους become in doric -ως -ος; ποιεω, ποεω, poeta; διδου, διδοι; Θουκυδιδης, Θευκυδιδης; ελθειν, æol. ελθην; κυμα, κουμα (Etym. M. 632. 53); ιθυς, ευθυς?

71. Here again it must be said that a further, and a better account may be given of several of these interchanges. Some may be traced up without breach of analogies to a common source; some may have intermediate forms. But the object here is to prove that a great change in "Vocalismus" is no sufficient reason for denying affinity. Not always, seldom rather, can the various steps of alteration be traced out: remote links of a chain may be thought to hold together without our seeing all that intervenes; and when a group of languages extends from the Himâlayas across Asia to England and thence to America, some considerable changes may be looked for.

72. As an appendage to these remarks on vowel change, and vowel omission, let me here add instances in which the initial vowel of one form has disappeared in another, and that without determining whether the vowel have been added or subtracted, a question which belongs to each word separately. Δυρομαι, Οδυρομαι; Post, Οπισθεν, oscan Pusst, Pust, sanskr. Pashchât; Agrigentum, Girgenti; Scutiger, Esquire; Ipsum? Ψε æol. for Σφε (Apollonios Dysk. p. 128, πως ψε και γιγνωσκομεν); Αλειφειν, Λιπαρος; Apem, Bee; Episcopum, Bishop; Aper, Boar; Αριθμος, Ρυθμος; Adamanta, Diamond; Apulia, la Poule; Ariminum, Rimini; Amaracus, Marjoram; Ερυθρος, Red; Οροφη, Roof; Αστερα, Star; Αριθμος, Rime, agls. Rim 'number,' or the equivalent Ρυθμος; Εθελοντης, Volunteer; for θελειν, †βολειν are probably one; Ελευθερος, Liber; Αποινα, Ποινη; Αμελγω, Mulgeo; Ερετμος, Remus; Ελαφρος, Levis; Pert is usually Impertinent, but sometimes Apertus,

"pert brother" (William and the Werwolf. fol. 73. 'true,' Sir F. M.).

73. Some languages which do not readily approve some or other two initial consonants, will prefix a euphonic vowel. As this is more common in french and welsh I shall be short on the topic.

> Quhare with grete slauchter bludy Diomede
> Distroyit all and to his tent can lede
> The milk quhite hors, fers, swift and gude,
> Or cuir they taistit ony Troiane fude
> Or drunken had of the flude Exhantus.
> *Gawine Douglas*, En. lib. I.

74. Since $\Sigma\tau\epsilon\phi\epsilon\iota\nu=\Sigma\tau\epsilon\gamma\epsilon\iota\nu$, so also $\Sigma\tau\rho\epsilon\phi\epsilon\iota\nu$ may have been †$\sigma\tau\rho\epsilon\gamma\epsilon\iota\nu$, and $A\sigma\tau\rho\alpha\gamma\alpha\lambda\sigma\varsigma$, which in Homer means vertebra, may be made out of it. A confirmation of this supposition is found in $\Sigma\tau\rho\sigma\gamma\gamma\nu\lambda\sigma\varsigma$ 'round,' apparently a derivative of †$\sigma\tau\rho\epsilon\gamma\epsilon\iota\nu$.

74*. We now proceed to consider examples. Since it shall be a condition upon our english words that they may be found in the ancient teutonic, it must naturally be presumed that the teutonic dialects themselves afford a much larger range of instances: by way of curious illustration the rare agls. Eorp 'wolf'=isl. Erpr=sabine Hirpus; Frefele=Frivolus. The mœsogothic Aistan=lat. Æstimare, and since the suffix in M is probably participial, will be earlier. $M\alpha\chi\epsilon\sigma\theta\alpha\iota$ and Mactare (and $\mu\alpha\gamma\epsilon\iota\rho\sigma\varsigma$?) may belong to agls. Mece=mœsog. Meki, a $\mu\alpha\chi\alpha\iota\rho\alpha$, 'large knife': etc. etc.

75. AN, A. See ONE.

76. ACHE=$A\chi\sigma\varsigma$=agls. Ece, with verb Acan = sanskr. Ak-an, 'pain, affliction.' $A\chi\epsilon\rho\omega\nu$ cannot be $\alpha\chi\epsilon\alpha$ $\rho\epsilon\omega\nu$, since derivatives take the form $\chi\epsilon\iota\mu\alpha\rho\rho\sigma\nu\varsigma$, nor can it be α, $\chi\alpha\iota\rho\omega\nu$, for such a compound could not have the participial formation -$\sigma\nu\tau\sigma\varsigma$.

77. AIL=agls. Eglan, may be $A\lambda\gamma\epsilon\iota\nu$, involving a somewhat dubious transposition. The mœsog. Aglo, '$\theta\lambda\iota\psi\iota\varsigma$, $\mu\sigma\chi\theta\sigma\varsigma$, $\sigma\delta\nu\nu\eta$,' is allied to Agls, '$\alpha\iota\sigma\chi\rho\sigma\varsigma$,' UGLY.

78. $A\nu\tau\iota$ had its equivalent in agls. And as prefix=mœsog. And=norse prefix And. It remains to us in ANSWER.

VOWEL CHANGE. 29

79. ANEAL contains agls. Ælan 'to burn,' whence Eld 'fire,' Ele 'oil,' etc. It is close in form and signification to Ελαιον, Adolescere ' blaze,' Oleum.

80. ARM = agls. Earm = mœsog. Arms = norse Armr. This word must have been latin, since we have Armilla, ' bracelet :' Armus is applied to the shoulder of animals.

81. ARROW. Grimm on Elene 239 observes that as spiculum is related to spica, so is Arrow to Arista; also that Arcus 'a bow' may belong to the family. Correspondence of letters gives more force to the last observation, since agls. is Arewe, mœsog. Arhwazna: and the four first letters of the mœsogothic are the representatives of the four first of Arcus, the u being radical, as in Arcubus.

82. Ass = agls. Assa, Asal = mœsog. Asilus = germ. Esel = lat. Asinus, Asellus. This correspondence goes for little; the animal is probably a native of the hotter climates. Hebrew is Aþôn.

83. AXE = Αξινη = lat. Ascia = agls. Eax = mœsog. Akwizi (Luke iii. 9.) = isl. ˮOx, ˮOxi. In anglosaxon the word seems not common Ll. Inæ. 43. sco eax bið melda nakes þeof. ' the axe is a tell tale not a thief.' Of these forms the mœsogothic with its quertra, kw, may be judged most ancient. Οξυς, Acuo, Hack, Hew are doubtless of its kindred.

84. AYE, YEA = germ. Ja, may be traced in mœsog. †aikan found only as yet in the compound afaikan translating αρ-νεισθαι. The latin equivalent is Aio, which had an affirmative sense as may be seen in Forcellini. " Diogenes ait, Antipater negat." Cic. " Quasi ego id curem, quid ille aiat aut neget." Cic. And in reply to questions " Hodie uxorem ducis ? Aiunt."

85. CALL = norse Kalla = lat. Calare = Καλειν with numerous derivatives : cf. Κολωος ' a cry,' Κολοιος ' a jay,' erse Callan ' prating,' Caol ' calling ;' cf. also Clamare like Κληδων, Κλησις. Kalendæ is a participial derivative. Varro L. L. V. Primi dies mensium nominati Kalendæ, ab eo quod his diebus calentur eius mensis Nonæ a pontificibus, quintanæne an septimanæ sint futuræ, in Capitolio in curia Kalabra [dicta, sic, quinquies] Te kalo Iuno Novella, vel septies, Te

kalo, Iuno Novella. The same at greater length in Macrobius I. xv. Hebraists compare Kôl ' a voice ' with call.

86. CACK = Κακκαν = Caccare = isl. Kúka = welsh gaelic erse Cachu, with subst. Cach = agls. Cac.

87. CAM ' crooked,' " S. This is clean cam. B. Merely awry" (Coriolanus III. i.), cf. Καμπτειν, lat. Camurus, as "et camuris hirtæ sub cornibus aures" Virgil, also Campso, "Leucaten campsant" Ennius frag. 380. Χαμον, καμπυλον, Hesychios. The gaelic and welsh employ the word largely. I do not find the word in the anglosaxon; Kilian has only Kamus, Kamuys, Simus, and his editor quotes Vondel (died 1679) Terwyl de kamutze geitjes de struicken afscheeren. Dum tenerae attondent simae virgulta capellæ. It was of frequent use and is still retained provincially: "The deck of a ship is said to lie CAMBERING when it does not lie level, but higher in the middle than at either end." (Kersey.) Cammerel is a crooked piece of wood with three or four notches at each end on which butchers hang the carcases of slaughtered animals. (Craven gloss.) So Gambrel (Moor). Gambrils, Cambrils are the hocks of a horse. Cammed is crooked, also cross, ill-natured; Cammock is a crooked tree or beam, timber prepared for the knee of a ship (Halliwell): camber-nosed is cited by Junius (Etym.). Chaucer C. T. 3931.

> A Shefeld thwitel bare he in his hose,
> Round was his face and camuse was his nose.

Id. 3972.

> This wenche thike and wel ygrowen was
> With camise nose and eyen gray as glas.

Skelton in his description of Elynour Rummyng,

> Her nose som dele hoked
> And camously croked.

Again in Poems against Garnesche,

> Your wynde shakyn shankkes, your long lothy legges,
> Croked as a camoke and as a kowe calfles.

Also in Why come ye not to courte (against Wolsey),

> Be it blacke or whight,
> All that he doth is ryght,
> As ryght as a cammocke croked.

VOWEL CHANGE.   31

88. CARE = lat. Cura = mœsog. Kara = agls. Caru. The mœsog. Kaurs 'heavy' seems akin.

89. CARVE = Κειρειν = agls. Ceorfan. The agls. and english are used of all sorts of cutting. Thus, Thæt timber acorfen wæs (Orosius IV. vi. = 396. 15), of the building of the first roman fleet. Cf. erse Cearb, 'a cutting,' Corran 'a sickle,' Cear 'kill.' Lat. Curtus is the passive participle. Κειρειν is 'cut,' as ἡπαρ εκειρον. Κρεας is 'meat for eating,' and may belong to this verb, though its latin equivalent Caro, Carnes do not clearly support that conjecture. For the sibilate forms of this root, as ξυρος, see SIBILATION.

> And ten brode arrowes held he there
> ─── sharpe for to kerven well.
> CHAUCER, *Romaunt of the Rose*, 930.

90. CHAP. cf. Καπηλος, a CHAPMAN. Chap = agls. Ceapian = mœsog. Kaupon = norse Kaufa = germ. Kaufen = CHEAPEN. Cf. CHEAPSIDE, Chippenham, Chipping Norton, Chipping Sodbury, Copenhagen = Kjöbenhavn, and numerous names in Sweden, Norway and Denmark, Ringkjöbing, Nyköping, Norköping, Linköping, etc.: in all of which the word signifies market, place of trade. *Cape, Chaffer, Chapman.*

> All throw a luke that I haif coft full deir.
> DUNBAR, *Goldin Terge*, xv.

> Is chaffer fit for fools their precious souls to sell.
> PHINEAS FLETCHER.

> Master, what will you copen or by?
> Fyne felt hattes or spectacles to reede?
> LYDGATE'S *Minor Poems*, p. 105.

91. CHOP, diminutive CHIP, occurs in the salique laws under the frequentative form, Capulare *e.g.* "Si quis in sylva alterius materiamen furatus fuerit aut incenderit vel concapulaverit aut ligna alterius furaverit, DC. den. culpabilis indicetur." (Eccard, p. 27.) Cf. Κοπτειν, Caponem (acc.). Kappe 'cut,' of trees, in friesic.

92. CHURL, the agls. Ceorl = germ. Kerl = norse Karl, fem. Carline = norse Kerling are commonly applied to old peasants. If Κουρος, Κορη are related, a change of sense has come in. See GIRL, 282.

93. CLAW = χηλη = agls. Claw = dutch Klauw = germ. Klaue = swed. Klo.

94. CLIMB = agls. Climban = germ. dutch Klimmen. Cf. Κλιμαξ 'ladder.' This evidence is scant, but see art. 192.

95. COMBE = agls. Comb, Cumb = welsh Cwm is to be compared with Campus : for the vocalization see 1026. Field, Vallis show a converse change of application, supposing them kindred words.

> No small delight the shepherds took to see
> A coombe so dight in Flora's livery.
> W. BROWNE, *B. P.* II. ii.

96. COP 'head, top' = lat. Caput = agls. Copp = germ. Kopf. Cf. COPING stone. Halliwell quotes " In the tenthe monethe, in the firste dai of the monethe, the coppis of hillis apeeriden."

> "For Cop they use to call The tops of many hills."
> DRAYTON, Polyolbion, xxx.

HOB nails have large heads.

97. CRAB = agls. Crabba = germ. Krabbe = dutch Krab. Cf. Καραβος. It appears by Aristot. Hist. Anim. IV. ii. that καρκινος is crab, καραβος lobster, καρις shrimp, αστακος crayfish. But the letters K, R are common to these and to their distinctive CRustaceous covering : cf. welsh Crag ' a hard crust or covering.' Sanskr. is Karkat.

98. CROP 'summit' = agls. Cropp = Κορυφη. This is not convincing. Κορυφη must be connected with Καρα: we have the word in use of the "cropping out" of mineral strata. As we have no large induction here, Crop may be another form of Cop.

99. CROAK, CROW = Κραζειν, Κοραξ, cf. Κεκραξομαι = agls. Crawan, Craw = germ. Krähen, Krähe = lat. Crocire, Corvus, Cornix. In the Isle of Wight crows may be heard called Cracks, and thus the various words are probably imitative of the bird's cry. Thus with a variation sanksr. Kâkas ' a crow' is formed on Caw, and kardas 'crow' on the first element of Crouk. With Κραυγη Pott compares sanskr. Krush, ' to call, cry, weep.'

100. CUCKOO = lat. Cuculus = Κοκκυξ : from the sound. Sanskr. kôkilah, 'indian cuckoo.'

101. DARE, DROWSY = lat. Dormire = Δαρθανειν = with a

slight change lat. Torpere. The islandic at Dura 'sleep by fits,' Dur 'a nap.' Sanskr. Drai 'to sleep.' The dutch Bedaaren 'appease, allay, quiet,' seems to display the metaphorical use. Cf. DREAM. In dutch Dat Weer bedaart, ' the storm is stilled ;' He bedaart wedder, 'he is quiet again.' Een bedaart Man, 'a sleepy fellow.' In lower saxony Drömken ' to lie in a light doze.' The sense here given to Dare is not that of the glossaries. In the Promptorium Parvulorum, under Daryn, or drowpin, or prively to be hydde, latito, lateo, Mr. Way cites Palsgrave (A.D. 1530) ' to Dare, to prye, look about, je advise alentour,' and Cotgrave 'squat.' It seems to have escaped his notice that these citations do not illustrate the word in the glossary, as latitare is simply the very common adjective Dern=agls. Dearn, Dyrn ' secret,' in a verbal form. I think the sense given above is confirmed by the passage:

> Nece, quod he, it ought ynough suffice
> Five houres for to slepe upon a night,
> But it were for an olde appalled wight
> As ben thise wedded men, that lie and dare.
> CHAUCER, *C. T.* 13034.

> Ich mai iseo so wel on hare
> Theȝ ich bi daie sitte au dare.
> *Owl and Nightingale*, 383. (Ou=an.)

> For hire love y carke ant care,
> For hire love y droupne ant dare,
> For hire love my blisse is bare,
> Ant al ich waxe won.
> *Percy Soc.* vol. iv. p. 64.

(Languish, which the editor's glossary gives, is near enough to the sense of the sentence, but has no support in the kindred tongues.)

> Y droupe, y dare night and day,
> My will, my wytt is all away.
> *Erle of Tolous.* 553.

The word TRANCE, which has come to us from the french, seems to have the same origin; for to be in a reverie, is not remote in sense.

> He dared as doted man for þe bestes dedes
> And was so styf in a studie þat none him stint miȝt.
> *William and the Werwolf,* fol. 60.

102. DEEM, DOOM=agls. Deman=norse Dœma=mœsog. Domyan=lat. Damnare:

> And ye schul bothe demed be,
> And heye hong on galwe tre.
> *Gy of Warwike,* p. 160.

103. DEW, cf. Δευε δε γαιαν, Ψ. 220. Agls. Deaw=norse Dögg=germ. Thau. Cf. Τεγγειν art. 479.

104. DOUGHTY is a derivative of the agls. subst. Duguð, from the verb Dugan 'to be excellent'=mœsog. Dugan, συμφερειν, χρησιμον ειναι,=norse Duga=germ. Taugen with Tuchtig. This teutonic root produces in latin the participial adj. Dignus.

105. EAR=lat. Arare=Αρουν=agls. Erian=mœsog. Aryan =isl. Eria. Ploughing is in irish and gaelic Ar. Genesis, xlv. 6: Neither earing nor harvest; where the LXX. have αροτριασις and the hebrew Kharish, which is of the same sense, and, as we shall see, of the same root.

> I have, God wot, a large field to ere;
> And weke ben the oxen in my plow.
> CHAUCER, *C. T.*, 887.

> I have an half acre to erie
> By the heighe weye;
> Hadde I eryed thei half acre,
> And sowen it after,
> I wolde wende with yow,
> And the wey teche.
> *Piers Ploughman,* 3800.

> Heo howsede and bulde faste and erede and sewe
> So þat in litel while gode cornes hem grew.
> *Robert of Gloucester,* p. 21. ed. Hearne.

(Heo, they; hem, them: agls.)

> The erthe it is, which evermo
> With mannes labour is bego,
> As well in winter as in Maie.
> The mannes honde doth what he may
> To helpe it forth and make it riche
> And forthy men it delve and diche
> And eren it with strength of plough.
> *Gower,* lib. i. p. 152.

VOWEL CHANGE. 35

But Ysis, as saith the cronique
Fro Grece into Egypte cam,
And she than upon honde nom
To teche hem for to sowe and ere
Which no man knew tofore there.
Gower, lib. v. p. 154.

106. Ear=lat. Aurem (acc.)=agls. Eare=mœsog. Auso =norse Eyra=germ. Ohr. Further see Hear.

107. Earn 'an eagle'=agls. Earn=norse Ari. Grimm compares Ορνις 'bird.'

108. Eat=lat. Edere=Εδειν, homeric, superseded in later authors, in the present by Εσθιειν (for εδθιειν, a combination of dentals intolerable to the greek)=agls. Etan=mœsog. Itan =norse Eta=sanskr. Ad.

109. El in Elbow=agls. El boga, that is the el-bending, represents Ωλενη, welsh Elin, 'elbow,' Hrabanus Maurus Helina, 'cubitus:' so that an N seems to have dropped off; it is retained in Elne, an ell.

110. Else=agls. Elles, which is used adverbially : El— and Ellor— are frequent in compounds. The mœsog. adj. is Alis, adverb Alya=Αλλα. These are branches of the same stock as Αλλος, Alius. Observe LI in latin is ΛΛ in greek, like φυλλον = folium : the neuter Αλλο is for †αλλοδ = Aliud.

111. Eme (frater matris) =agls. Eam=germ. Oheim, Ohm. Hence the latin feminine Amita (soror patris) =Aunt. Eme is still in use in Lancashire, and is frequent in old english. In a poetical genealogy printed by Hearne, it is said of King Stephen

A good man he was bedene
I trewe King Harry was his eme.
Appendix to Rob. Glouc. p. 587. (bedene, very.)

The child aparceiued wel this,
And held hit in his herte, I wis.
His emes work he gan aspie
Till he couthe al his maistrie.
Seuyn Sages, 1022.

112. Ever=agls. Æfre=Αιϝει, a form of Αιει, found in a Krissæan inscription. Thus Αιϝων=lat. Ævum, which in

D 2

passing through the french becomes Age. Derivatives are Ætas, Æternus. Varro in Pseudolnea, "Per æviternam hominum domum tellurem propero gradum." ΑιϜων is life in Iliad T. 27. The mœsogothic Aiws translates αιων, and in negative clauses the adverbial Aiw answers to ποτε 'ever,' as Mark ii. 25. All these forms are to be referred to Quick.

113. Errand=agls. Ærend=norse Erendi. The origin is from norse Arr=mœsog. Airus, 'αγγελος' producing Airinôn, 'πρεσβευειν,' which is to be compared with Ϝιρις, the goddess messenger, and with Ϝιρος in the Odyssey, the suitors' errand-man:

Ἀρναῖος δ᾽ ὄνομ᾽ ἔσκε· τὸ γὰρ θέτο πότνια μήτηρ
ἐκ γενετῆς· Ϝιρον δὲ νέϜοι κίκλησκον ἅπαντες
οὕνεκ᾽ ἀπαγγέλλεσκε κιών, ὅτε πού τις ἀνώγοι.
Od. Σ. 5.

The evidence for the digamma in Ϝιρος is derived from the homeric versification only, but it is strong. An A sometimes took the place of digamma even in the mœsogothic, which preserves the vau generally: the word Aiws as compared with Vivere, gives one example. In Alan belonging to Valere, Alere, and in Aurtya for †Waurtya for †Ϝριζα, †wradicem, †wroot, the Vau has been lost. Of the earlier source of these words see the word family Swee, Swer.

114. Elm=agls. Ælm=norse Almr =Ulmus.

115. Ewe=lat. Ovis=OϜις, Οἶς, Οἶς=agls. Eowu=a mœ-sogothic root †awi, existing in Awebi, 'flock,' Awistr 'fold' =isl. A'=erse Oi, Ai, Aoi=sanskr. Avis.

116. Fare, Ford, Ferry, Freight, Fraught, welfare, farewell. Cf. lat. Ferre, Ferri, Φερειν, Φερεσθαι, with agls. Ferian 'to bear, carry,' Faran, Feran 'to go,' germ. Führen '.to convey,' Fahren ' to go,' mœsogothic Faryan (act.), Faran (neut.), islandic Færa, 'to carry,' Fara 'to go,' För, Firð, 'a journey.' For the rest see Bear, and Fare in art. 400, 429.

116 a. Fast, Fasten, agls. Fæst, germ. Fest, mœsog. Fastan, norse Fastr are as probably related to Fangen, to be compared with Manifestus.

117. Fear=lat. Formido. The exact word Fear seems not to be saxon; Thorpe has Fear, 'craft, peril' (Analecta).

Fright represents the agls. adj. Forht 'timidus, pavidus,' with derivatives. The mœsogothic Swers 'εντιμος,' Sweran 'τιμαν' answers to lat. Vereri, and neither seems exactly to suit this signification: we have the true mœsog. equivalent in Faurhts, 'δειλος, cowardly.'

118. Flog. Cf. Flagellum. Sure that these words are a collateral form of Slay with agls. Slagan=germ. Schlagen, I am obliged to confess that the precise form does not show itself to me in a teutonic tongue, see 415. Fillip from germ. Fillen 'to scourge'=Filian 'flagellare' in the Heliand appears to be a diminutive. About Bremen the Flail is usually called Flogger (Brem. Wörterb.).

119. Flow=lat. Fluere=agls. Flowan=germ. Fliessen: cf. agls. Flod = mœsog. Flodus = germ. Fluth = Flood. The sanskr. flow is Plu.

120. Froth =Αφρος=norse Freyða=welsh Broch=erse Bruchd.

121. Fuller=lat. Fullonem (acc.) =agls. Fullere=mœsog. Wullareis. The mœsogothic word seems to come direct from Wulla 'wool,' so that a fuller may be a wooller. But in agls. we have Fullian 'to baptize,' Fulluht 'baptism,' Fulluhtere 'the baptist.' Ulfilas translated βαπτιζειν by Daupyan, to Dip, as the rubric of the baptismal service of our church does; the missionaries of Gregory chose another term, which may have been related to the cleansing of the fuller, or on the contrary to Πλυνειν 'wash clothes,' with a long list of words, which denote water; fluo, fulica, palus, pluit, pluviæ, lavare (for plavare?), πελαγος, πλεῖν, λουειν (for πλουειν?) float, fleet, erse and gaelic Fual ' water.' Walker is fuller.

122. Grass =agls. Gærs, Græs=mœsog. Gras = norse Gras =Γραστις=lat. Gramen. Γραστις is genuine greek, see art. 275: the latin as a passive participle is commonly, and it seems truly, derived from a lost verb graere, rare in greek Γραειν. The sanskrit has Gras 'to devour, swallow,' which Bopp, in the second edition of his glossary, compares with the words above.

123. Hand is found in lat. Prehendere, and, Prof. Key adds, in Ansa. Agls. Hand=mœsog. Handus=norse Hönd.

124. HERON=lat. Ardea=Ερωδιος.=agls. Hragra=germ. Reiger=danish Heire. Whether Heron be french or nay, its relationship to γερανος another long-legged grallator shows the antiquity of its form. The root in †gar 'leg.'

125. HOLE='Ολος. The spelling Whole is a corruption: HEAL, HEALTH are of the same family. Root semitic.

126. IN=lat. In=Εν=agls. In=mœsog. In=norse I. This is not all quite clear. Εν was †ενς=Εις and of the same form as εξ: the sanskrit has Inter, Under, in the form Antar, also Antaran=Εντερον: it remains therefore to conclude that the ancient †ενς was a substitution for †εντ, like προς for †προτ, προτι, since a dental termination was always altered by the Achivi: and †εντ is fully established by the old latin Endo.

127. INTER in Interloper=bremish Enterloper 'zwischenläufer,' in dutch Enterloopen, applied to a coasting vessel, is the german Unter 'among, between,' a sense lost in our Under: and=lat. Inter. On loper see art. 810.

128. KEEP=lat. Capere?=agls. Cepan. Lye shows that the agls. is captare, capessere, tenere: root hebrew Caf, the hollow of the hand?

129. KEN=Κοννειν, Æsch. Suppl. 175. see KNOW.

130. KENT=lat.? or british? british doubtless, Cantium= agls. Cent. Canterbury=agls. Cant-wara-burh, 'borough of men of Kent.' Cant is corner, as in Κανθος 'corner of the eye,' Γωνια being not altogether dissimilar. QUOIN, and with s SQUINT: a Cant rail is a triangular rail, to Cant a vessel, is to set it on edge (Forby). So a Canton in heraldry is in the corner of the shield.

> For nature hath not taken his beginning
> Of no partie ne cantel of a thing.
> CHAUCER, *C. T.* 3010.

> See how this river comes me cranking in
> And cuts me from the best of all my land
> A huge half moon a monstrous cantle out.
> SHAKSPEARE, *Henry IV.*

As a gloss of Hesychios connects Κανθος, ὁ του οφθαλμουκυκλος, rather with another sense and another radix, I quote the proofs that it is corner. Κοινον της βλεφαριδος μερος της ανω και κατω κανθοι δυο, Aristot. H. A. I. ix. Τα εκατερωθεν των βλεφαρων ακρα, Pollux, ii. 71, etc., Steph. Lex., Paris ed.

131. Kiss = Κυσαι = agls. Cyssan = norse Kyssa = germ. Küssen. The supposed present κυνεῖν?

132. Knuckle = norse Knui = Κονδυλος.

133. Lane = friesic Lona, Lana is not altogether remote from Limes, which is properly a ridge of grass down ploughed land serving to separate the allotments and for a footway.

134. Lap = Λαπτειν = agls. Lappian = isl. Lepja.

135. Leak. In Lye Leccian [Leccan] is 'rigare, irrigare,' and the participle Leht is 'madefactus.' The teutonic usage is wider: dutch Leken 'Liquere, stillare, manare, perfluere, liquorem transmittere' (Kilian), Bremish Lekken 'to run, drop, dribble,' also 'let through, leak.' Not only do they say 'the vessel leaks, the ship leaks,' but 'the water leaks,' Lekkende Ogen are streaming eyes. Norse Leka is 'drop' and Logr is 'moisture,' usually 'lake.' Hence Lake = lat. Lacus is allied. Liquidus belongs to Liquet, ''tis clear;' and if Liquor is related, then Liquet is of the kindred of all these. Lavare had probably a common original, and it appears by Laȝamon, i. 320, that Lather is not remote. An example of the copious flow of water implied in the teutonic usage of the root occurs in the Ormulum, where he speaks of Pharaohs host overwhelmed in the sea þa lec þe waterr oferr hemm. ii. 161.

136. Left hand = lat. Læva = Λαιη, Λαια. The word Left is believed by german philologs to be connected with the old teutonic Laf, 'flaccidus, languidulus, segnis, imbecillis' (Kilian). The gaelic has Clè 'left hand,' Clith 'left.'

137. Less = Ελασσων = agls. Læs. Least = Ελαχιστος = agls. Læst. From ελαχιστος and the rule for such comparatives as ελασσων developed by Grimm, whence it must be for ελαχ-ζων, it seems such a root as Lack is contained in the word. When we come to compare dentals with gutturals we shall try to make ολιγος the positive and = little: in the mean time agls. Lecan 'privare' is given by Lye.

138. Ley is, says Grimm (G. D. S. p. 60), Lucus, because

pasture is woodland. Ley is usually so spelt for pasture, and Lay for fallow: the history of the words is wanting.

139. Lick=Λειχειν=agls. Liccian=mœsog. Laigon in the compound bilaigon, Luke xvi. 21=isl. Sleikja, with sibilant=lat. Lingere, with liquid=sanskr. Lih=hebrew לקק or biliterally לק=erse Leagaim ('I lick').

139 a. Long. Cf. Λογγαζω 'linger' cited by Pollux from the Κηρυκες of Æschylus, and mentioned by Photius, Phrynichos, Hesychios, Aristoph. frag. 641, Languere. Passow, who is not brilliant in etymology, declares the connexion with the german cannot be mistaken. Agls. Lang=mœsog. Laggs.

140. Lay, Lie. The saxon forms thus differed: Lecgan 'lay' actively, Licgan, 'lic' intransitively, and the latter is frequent as Liggen in old english. Lie=also mœsog. Ligan =norse Liggja=germ. Liegen=homeric Λεγεσθαι. Lay= mœsog. Lagyan = norse Leggja=germ. Legen = homeric Λεγειν. In lat. Lectus, Lectica, the same root remains.

> The chorle they founde hem aforne
> Liggin under an hawthorne
> Under his head no pillow was,
> But in the stede a trusse of gras.
> CHAUCER, *R. R.* 4001.

> Ho that passeth the bregge
> Hys armes he mot legge
> And to the genunt alowte*.
> *Lybeaus Disconus*, 1252.

> She was a primerole, a piggesnie,
> For any lord to liggen in his bedde,
> Or yet for any good yeman to wedde.
> CHAUCER, *C. T.* 3270.

141. Lock (allure)=germ. Locken=lat. Lacere, Lactare. Not accepting Festus's explanation, I believe the root to be Lac, γαλακτ; for I find the agls. Spanan 'allure' similarly allied to Span 'mamma.' Lac belongs as much to the teutonic Milk as to γαλακτ. "I am no hyrde to be locked ne take by chaf:" Reynard the Foxe, p. 155.

142. Lute=lat. Latere=Λαθειν=agls. Lutian. Cf. Lytig

* Aloute, 'bow down.'

and the norse Laun: the fullest form is in Clam, Celare; Latere for †clatere.

> For love is of him selfe so derne,
> It luteth in a mannes herte.
> GOWER, lib. i. p. 107, ed. 1857.

> Aventures for to layt in land.
> Ywaine and Gawin, 237.

143. MARCHES: the agls. Meare 'a boundary'=mœsog. Marka 'ὅριον, μεθόριον'=isl. Merk is near to latin Margo. Cf. to MARK=agls. Meorcian=isl. at Merki.

144. MARGARET, a pearl: a compound mere grit, a sea stone=agls. Meregrot=Μαργαρίτης=lat. Margarita, which Pliny, ix. 35, says is vox barbara, a word of foreign origin. Μαργαρίτης is found as early as Theophrastus, B.C. 322 (ap. Athenæum, iii. p. 93). Þat gode meregrot 'the goodly pearl,' Matth. xiii. 45. Ulphilas treats the word as foreign. A stone in the bladder is in germ. Gries. The norse Griót is lapis, saxum, and produces a compound Griótbiörg, Gritbergs. The erse has Greit 'a precious stone.'

145. MEADOW=agls. Mædewe. Cf. Madere 'to be moist.' Kilian has Maede 'cænum, lutum,' Mad is 'terra palustris' (Ihre cit.), Máde in friesic is a low swampy piece of ground which though now it be used as pasturage was formerly marshy (Outzen). Meadow is now in a proper sense a piece of flat ground next a stream, or a slope supplied with artificial irrigation. The word has little connexion in sense with Metere. So MUD, MOIST.

146. MEAL=agls. Melu=lat. Mola the sacred meal. Also MILL=agls. Mylen, Miln=lat. Mola=Μύλη. These words have been discussed in the introductory remarks. The sanskrit Peshanan, 'a hand-mill, any apparatus for grinding or pounding,' is from pish related to Pinsere.

147. MELT=agls. Meltan. The norse has Melta 'to digest;' but the word signifies also 'to subject to the action of heat,' and Björn Haldorsen translates Melta bygg til ölgerða 'torrere hordeum,' 'to heat barley for ale making,' that is to MALT. The homeric Μέλδειν is the same thing, Φ. 363:—

'Ως δὲ λέβης ζεῖ ἔνδον ἐπειγόμενος πυρὶ πολλῷ
κνίσσῃ μελδόμενος ἁπαλοτρεφέος σιάλοιο.

with var. lect. κνίσσην(?).

148. Mere=lat. Mare=agls. Merc=norse Marr=mœsog. Marci. Neither in agls. compounds nor in german (Meer) is the word confined as in english and agls. simple use, to inland sheets of water. We have not the means to determine whether these forms be akin to the semitic term, æthiopic Mâi 'water,' also Marr, Amarus, 'bitter,' and to Μυρεσθαι and Myrrh so called from its dropping. Marsh comes nearer to the usual vowel, Moor and Mire are scarce distinguishable in the older style of english.

149. Mesh=agls. Max, Masc=germ. Maschen=welsh Maschen=lat. Macula. These evidences do not at all prove that the word is not a latinism; but the absence of the final L in all cases goes some way to prove it. We shall come by and by to instances in which M arises out of B; and I believe Mesh, Basket, Fiscus to be so far one as that they have all arisen by dropping the L in Πλεκειν, Flasket, Flask, see 398.

150. Monger in Fishmonger, Costermonger, Fellmonger =agls. Mangere=isl. Mángari, with the verb at Manga 'mercaturam facere,' and the subst. Máng, 'mercatura,' are the northern equivalents of lat. Mangonem (acc.) which is applied to dealers in slaves, horses, jewels, unguents.

151. Mid 'with, among'=germ. Mit=agls. Mid=mœsog. Miþ=norse Með=Μετα. Cf. sanskr. Madhyas=Medius= Mid with Middle, Midst, Moiety, Μεταξυ, Μεσος. Since Μετα implies change, we have allied words in lat. Mutare, mœsog. Maidyan, especially in the compounds Inmaidyan translating μεταμορφουν, μετασχηματιζειν, αλλαττειν, and in Inmaideins, ανταλλαγμα 'compensation.' The german often has in compounds, like the greek, the sense of participation, as in Mitschuld, μετα-scelus; but I do not know that this is the case in the mœsogothic and norse. From the sense of change comes Mutare, from participation Mutuus. As an example of old english Mid, take:—

With that he sholde the Saterday
Seven yer thereafter
Drynke but myd the doke
And dyne but ones.
Piers Ploughman, 2621.

152. Milk = lat. Mulgere = Ἀμέλγειν = agls. Meolcian with subst. Meolc = mœsog. Miluks = isl. Miólk, with verb at Miólka = germ. Melken, with subst. Milch. From the sweetness of both, it seems probable that milk is connected with Mel 'honey,' Μελι, Mulcere, Mulsum, Mulcedo. The keltic languages have B for M as erse Bleacht. It is impossible but that γαλακ- and Milk must be different forms of the same word.

153. Min is a teutonic root found in the latin Reminisci, Meminisse, Mentem, Monere, Monstrum, Monstrare, &c., and in the greek Μεμνησθαι, Μιμνησκειν. It occurs in the agls. Mingian ' monere,' Mænan ' memorare,' in the mœsog. Munan, δοκειν, ἡγεισθαι, λογιζεσθαι, νομιζειν, οιεσθαι, Muns, βουλη, προθεσις, προθυμια, προνοια &c. : in the norse Minna ' remind,' Muna. ' remember.' In Mean, Mind it bears a form and is capable of senses which show it to be no latinism. " Never mind." " Mind your business."

> O dinna ye mind, Lord Gregory.
>> *Minstrelsy of the Border*, ii. 62, in Jamieson.
>
> To ground he fell, so alto rent
> Was thar no man that him ment.
>> *Ywaine and Gawain*, 2619.
>
> Be that rech that y er of mene*.
>> *Lybeaus Disconus*, 1038.
>
> Sothe sawys y wylle you minge†.
>> *Octavian*, 6.
>
> And fore thi frynd and fore thi foo
> And fore thi good doeres also
> Alse mone as thou mai myn‡.
>> John Audelay, p. 72.

---

* By the brach that I ere made mention of.
† True tales I will to you tell.
‡ As many as you can recollect.

> Dame, he seyde ur daughter hath ment
> To the soudan for to weende.*
>
> *Kyng of Tars,* 257.
>
> Of the greyhound we wylle mene
> That we before of tolde.
>
> *Sir Tryamoure,* 473.
>
> They wyste not what to mene.
>
> *Id.* 348.
>
> The kyng in herte was full woo
> When he herd mynge tho
> Of her that was his quene.
>
> *Emare,* 924.

154. MIN = mœsog. Mins = germ. Minder = norse Minni = lat. Minor. The root is found in agls. Minsian, used by Cædmon, and in the homeric Μινυνθα, Μινυνθαδιος. It is however rare in agls. and english; cf. Jamieson. In friesic as a positive, "Min, wenig; so min, so wenig" (Outzen).

> The levedy and whosoever syttes withinne
> Alle browers schynne have bothe more and mynne†.
>
> Boke of Curtasye, 665.

Compare MINNOW a very small fish; the greek usage of the root is that of a positive.

> They rose up more and myn.
>
> Emare, 915.

155. MOCK is of good antiquity, since the gaelic has Mag 'to mock.' We seem to get it from the french Moquer. It occurs in Aristot. H. A. i. 9, and Athenæus, who imitates the Iliad, II. 324.

> τοῖς δ' ὁ κόλαξ πάμπρωτος ὑφαίνειν ἤρχετο μῶκον. (V. 187.)

The hebrew uses מוק in the Hiphil. In Richardson the first example is from a Bible of 1551; Piers Ploughman employs in its place Lakken (6574). It must have come to the french from a frankish source. Mocken 'buccam ducere,' that is to pull the MUG (a word which appears in the san-

---

* The context requires, 'has made up her mind.'

† Browers I conjecture to mean 'hot water;' cf. dutch Broeijen 'to grow hot, to scald,' also Brew, Brewis. Levedy = Lady; Schynne = agls. Sind ? = lat. Sunt, and Schynne here means 'are to have'? an agls. construction, Rask, 257. In this poem To is constantly omitted after Schynne, and some doubt remains. More the greater, Mynne the less.

skrit) Moffelen ' buccas movere' (Kilian). His jeering mocks and Mows : the merry Puck (Halliwell).

156. Moon = Μηνη = agls. Mona = mœsog. Mena = norse Máni = germ. Mond; all the teutonic dialects have it masculine, except the english. Month = lat. Mensis = Μην = agls. Monað = mœsog. Menoþs = norse Manaðr. Observe that the greek makes Month take a radical aspect. The sanskrit enthusiasts are anxious to believe Mas, Mâ 'to measure,' the ultimate source.

157. Moss = lat. Muscus = agls. Meos = isl. Mosi.

158. Mother = lat. Mater = dor. Ματηρ, att. Μητηρ = agls. Modor = norse Moðir = erse Mathair = sanskr. Mâtri. The sanskrit has Matran in the sense 'elementa,' very like Materies, Matter. The mœsogothic for mother has Aiþei and generally for father Atta.

159. Mourn = agls. Murenan, Murnan = lat. Mœrere. This is not sufficiently proved old teutonic.

160. Mouse = lat. Mus, acc. Murem = agls. isl. Mús = sanskr. Mûsh, where the Germans readily accept the native derivation from Mush, Mûsh, 'to steal.'

161. Mow = agls. Mawan, seems by Hay-Mow, Barley-Mow compared with agls. Muga, 'a heap,' to mean 'gather' as well as 'fell by scythe;' if so, it corresponds both ways to Αμαειν. B. H. translates isl. Mugr, 'a swathe of newly cut grass.' Bede i. 1. = 474. 32. And þær nænig mann for wintres cyle on sumera heg ne mawcð : better 'gathereth' than 'cutteth.' This involves the loss of a G in αμαειν, of which see 828.

162. Murder = agls. Morþor, with norse at Myrða. These words are applied to secret homicide, and have not a sense directly deducible from Mortem. Since the root is copiously employed in sanskrit, and is used in the Edda, it may be no latinism in english.

163. Name = agls. Nama = mœsog. Namo = sanskr. Nâman. The difficulty of reconciling these forms with the latin Nomen, once †gnomen, as in Cognomen, Agnomen, may be removed by supposing them to have all lost the initial, which for the teutonic would be K, and for the sanskrit its

softened substitute J. But this is asking a great deal; for
these languages are not in the habit of dropping the K in
any word derived from Ken, nor is the sanskrit. The difficulty is increased by the greek form Ονομα, which to correspond with the latin ought to be †γνωμα: still more, the
older spelling was Ονυμα, as in Επωνυμος, Ευωνυμος; and
the importance of not neglecting this spelling is visible in its
welsh equivalent, Enw (erse Ainim, gaelic Ainni, cf. breton
Anat 'known'). While these considerations seem to convey
a doubt, the agls. verb Nemnan, retaining, as it does, the
participial men, mn, with the norse Nefn which changes only
the labial liquid for the labial mute, bring back certainty.
The hebrew and syriac have a trace of the word, כנה 'cogno-
minavit.'

164. NE is the old negative particle of the saxon language,
as of the modern french,=mœsog. Ne. It has suffered contraction in NOT=Ne a whit, 'not a whit'=agls. Ne an
hwæt. Ne with short vowel was also the old latin negative:
it appears in Nefas, Neque, Nequeo. Non is some contraction, perhaps Ne unum. Nought, Naught are merely varied
spellings of Not; and the agls. Wiht, Wuht should be Hwit,
Hwæt=Quid=agls. Ceat. Wiht is either fem. or neuter.

165. NEW=lat. Novus=Νεος, say Νεϝος=ags. Niwe=
mœsog. Niuyis=sanskr. Navas.

166. NOSE = lat. Nasus = agls. Næse = germ. Nase =
sanskr. Nâsâ, &c. The norse Nef is not much like; but
Nes, a Ness, a projecting tongue of land=agls. Næs with
pl. Nasas, comes very close. Cf. Cape=arabic Ras=a Head-
land, Start Point, from agls. Steort 'a tail.' Κολπος, 'a
gulf, a bosom.'

167. Now=lat. Nunc=Νυν=agls., mœsog., isl., swed., dan.
Nu. It seems that an adverbial termination of time, as in
donec, ἡνικα, τηνικα, tunc, forms that latter part of the greek
and latin words: the comparison of the sanskrit form Nûnan
does not remove the impression. Nuper, as compared with
Semper, draws us back to New.

168. OAK=agls. Ac, a form which remains in ACORN, germ.
Eichel: the greek for which is Ακυλος. Do Quercus, Ilicem,

contain Ac? Is Accr 'a maple' related? Acorn is adjectival, not a compound of Corn.

169. Oar=agls. isl. Ar. The nearest approach is in Νηϝος εϝεικοσοροιο μελαινης Od. 4. 322: 'a twenty-oared vessel.' πεντηκοντορος, a fifty-oared galley. Then it must be compared with Ερεσσειν, Ερετμος, which last is very like the agls. Reðra, Reðer with its compounds.

170. Oil=agls. Æl, Ele=mœsog. Alew=lat. Oleum= Ελαιον. From the use of oil in lamps it appears connected with agls. Ælan 'accendere,' a root which we retain in Aneal; norse Eldr, 'fire,' = danish Ild. The same root is found in Adolescere, "Adolescunt ignibus aræ." This Adolescere must be distinguished altogether from Adolescens, Adultus, where the root is Valere.

171. Onde 'life, breath, rage' is from the same mœsogothic root Anan, found also in the sanskrit An 'to blow,' as produces Ανεμος 'wind,' Animus 'spirit, rage,' Anima 'breath, life.' Onde=agls. Onda, Anda=norse Ond.

> So sone so they to him come
> Into bote they him nome;
> Quyk they ladde him to londe,
> In his body tho was litel onde.
> Kyng Alisaunder, 3498.

(Nome, took.) The D in Onde is merely a dental adhering to the dental liquid.

> He no may sitt no stonde
> No unnethe* drawen his onde.
> Sir Gy of Warwicke, p. 7.

172. One=agls. An, Æn=mœsog. Ains=norse Einn= 'Eva (acc.)=lat. Vnum (acc.)=old latin Oinom.

173. Open=agls. Open=norse Opinn=dan. Aaben=germ. Offen. These are adjectives: cf. lat. Aperire=welsh. Agori= Οιγειν.

174. Ord, 'point, first point, beginning,'=agls. Ord.=norse Oddr, by assimilation: cf. Ordiri. In Beowulf, 6212: Hilderinc sum on handa bær æled leoman, se þe on orde geong. 'The warrior who walked in the first place (=at their head)

---

* unnethe=uneasy, scarcely.

bore in hand a kindled light.' I am surprised at the translation 'who went in order.'

> With fuyr brenuyng and with sweord
> With ax and mace and speris ord.
>   Kyng Alisaundre, 1900.

> Heort and armes through scheldis bord
> He clevyd with speris ord.
>   Kyng Alisaundre, 3609.

Some intimate connexion probably exists between this root and germ. Ur, lat. Oriri.

175. Pillow = Pulvinar may belong to Pluma as Voss gives it, with a vowel interposing like Πλευμων Pulmo. But it may also be another form of the mœsog. Balgs, Bag, Bulga, Vulva. As commencing with P, it cannot be in its present shape an old teutonic word, and it may be a mere alteration of Pulvinar.

176. Pool = agls. Pol, Pul = isl. Pollr 'standing water, swamp' = lat. Paludem (acc.). See art. 121 on Fuller. Some try to explain the -ud syllable of the latin as Vdus; but then they take Pal- as Πηλος.

177. Prate, Prattle. Ihre, under Prata ' loqui,' compares these with Interpretari. Let our eyes turn towards Φραδ-, where we find Φραδης, Φραδη, Φραδμων convey the sense of prudence, understanding: this sense must lie at the root both of Φραζεσθαι, and also of Φραζειν, and may without difficulty be applied to Interpretari. The mœsogothic has Fraþyan, which is the version of φρονειν, συνιεναι, γιγνωσκειν, νοειν, αισθανεσθαι and Froþs, φρονιμος. That this is the equivalent of φραζεσθαι has been remarked by Gabelentz and Löbe. The norse is Frœða.

178. Rag, 'Ρακος. I do not know the history of Rag, and dare not compare these words.

179. Rain, as compared with Ραινειν ' sprinkle,' involves the question whether a guttural in inlaut can be omitted in greek, as has been in this english word. See art. 811.

179 a. Ready = agls. Ræd. = mœsog. Raþs (ευκοπος). The agls. Hræd and the norse Hraðr retain an aspirate older than the mœsog. In the agls. piece De Mirabilibus Indiæ

(fol. 99, b. 12) we have Ne mæʒ nan man raypelice on þæt land gefaran. 'No man may easily in that land fare' (cf. 'Ραδιος)

180. RIND = agls. Rind = germ. Rinde. These are used of trees and fruit. 'Ρινος is the skin of an animal, and not remote in sense, not more than Pellis and Peel. The D adheres easily to N, being both dentals.

> And mochell mast to the husbande did yield
> And with his nuts larded many swine,
> But now the gray moss marred his ryne.
>   Spenser: Shepherds Calendar February.

> His hose and doublet thistle downe
> Togeather weau'd full fine :
> His stockins of an apple greene
> Made of the outward rine.
>   Tom Thumbe, 43.

> And to berye hym was hys purpos
> And scraped on him bothe ryne and mosse.
>   Sir Tryamoure, 392.

181. ROOT with its norse swed. dan. equivalents; only Rotfæst Sax. Chron. 1127. in agls., cf. lat. Radicem : it is probably ancient teutonic, as it is found several times in the Sæmundar Edda.

182. SACK = Σακκος = lat. Sacculus = agls. Sacc, Sæc = mœsog. Sakkus 'sackcloth' (Matth. xi. 21, Luke x. 13) = erse Sac. The hebrew also has it. Another form Σακτας, θυλακους, Herodian. Philet. p. 100.

183. SAD is of the same origin as Sedere.

> I shall seye thee, my sone,
> Sæide the frere thanne,
> How seven sithes the sadde* man
> On a day synneth.
>   Piers Ploughman, 4952.

> Hy comen to the on werldes ende ;
> And there hy founden thing of mynde ;
> Of pure golde two grete images
> In the cee stonden on brasen stages ;
> After Ercules hy weren ymad
> And after his fader of golde sad †.
>   Kyng Alisaundre, 5582.

---

* *i. e.* sedate.   † Solid.

The mœsogothic employs the root copiously, Sɪᴛ=Sitan; Sᴇᴛᴛʟᴇ=Sitls; Sᴇᴛ=Satyan; Satur=Saþs. The sanskrit also connects these ideas in Shad.

184. Sᴀʟᴛ=lat. Sal='Αλες=agls. mœsog. norse Salt=erse Salan=gaelic Salann=welsh Halen. In latin Sal 'the sea' ='Αλς=erse Sáill 'sea or salt.' Cf. sanskr. Salan=Salilan, 'water,' lat. Saliva, Σαλευειν.

This may be the same root as was looked for in the article on Fuller, 121.

185. Sᴀᴍᴇ=mœsog. Sama, appears in the latin compounds, Simul=Same While, Similis=Same Like. Its earlier form is Con. See art. 662.

185 a. Sᴀᴜɴᴛᴇʀ. "After the christian world had run à la santa terra or in English a sauntering about 100 years." (Defoe, History of the Devil.) This is wit, not fact. Saunter =mœsog. Sainyan βραδυνειν, with agls. Sæne, 'slow,' and Sᴀᴡɴʏ, to be compared with lat. Segnis.

186. Sᴄᴀᴛʜᴇ=agls. Sceaðian, Sceðan=mœsog. Skaþyan with derivatives=germ. Schaden=isl. Skeðia. The compound Ασκηθης, αβλαβης, unscathed, is frequent in Homer, nor can any rational origin for it within the greek itself be found.

187. Sᴄᴀᴛᴛᴇʀ=Σκεδασαι. The agls. Scateran with the R, is not found except in a late passage of the Saxon Chronicle, anno 1137. But the monosyllabic root is in agls. Sccidan 'to divide'=mœsog. Skaidan 'διχαζειν'=germ. Scheiden.

188. Sᴄᴏғғ=Σκωπτειν. Unfortunately for the closeness of the parallel, the english word cannot be sustained by the cognate dialects; germ. Spotten is near, but the agls. is wanting. Schimpen, Schimpfen, Schoppen, Schobben in dutch and german will not do. What Kilian has under Schofflieren seems a different class of ideas. Whether the word be traceable to the mordacity of the poets I do not know. A saxon poet was called a Scóp, 'a maker' from Scapan, 'to Shape, to make;' as a greek bard was a ποιητης. Compare the following passages, in the former of which Skof is poet.

> Alisaundre wexeth child of mayn,
> Maistres he hadde a dosayn.
> . . . . .

The serethen* maister taught his pars,
And the wit of the seoven ars;
Aristotel was on thereof.
This nis nought ramaunce of skof.
King Alisaundre, 668.

The sonne ariseth, the day springeth;
Dewes falleth, the foules singeth.
The oost arist on erne morrow †
That hath had a nighth of sorowe.
Nor it is ypassed by ne don thereof;
Bot gamenen togedres and ek scoll.
Ibid. 5456.

188 a. SENESHALL is a compound from the mœsogothic, from Sins 'old' and Skalks a servant; like Marshal, from Mare, in agls. Mearh (masc.) = norse Marr (masc.) a horse, and Skalks. The mœsogothic Sins has a derivative Sineigs which is lat. Senex.

189. SHALL = agls. Ik Sccal (for the infinitive had become obsolete) = norse Eg Skal = mœsog. Skulan (inf.) 'Ὀφείλειν.' This original sense 'to owe' had become very rare even in old high german. Graff vi. 161 quotes Tatian 99. er scolta zehen thusunta talentono 'he owed ten thousand talents.' To this early sense is due lat. Scelus, and the germ. agls. isl. have the same sense in the substantive. "Guilt" is similarly from the notion of payment, gold.

189 a. SHAPE = agls. Scapan = mœsog. Skapyan = norse Skapa = germ. Schaffen, and used in a very wide sense may be compared with Σκευος, Σκευαζειν. Our termination -ship as in Lordship, the german -schaft, as Gesellschaft, arises from this verb.

190. SHARD = agls. Scearn 'dung' = isl. Skarn = Σκωρ, the nominative. From this root the beetle which deposits its eggs in dung takes it name Scarabæus, a compound, in which we should regard Beetle or Bug as the second element. It is said, that the Egyptians observing this creature rolling about spheres of dung, in which its eggs were deposited, regarded it as an emblem of the great world shaper.

* Read seveneth.
† Erne morrow = early morning.

> The shard born beetle with his drowsy hums.
> Macbeth.
>
> Such souls as shards produce, such beetle things.
> Dryden, Hind and Panther.

We may, I think, observe the approximation of the termination Bug = swed. Bagge = danish Basse (see on sibilation) as in Skarnbasse, to Beetle, in the Kentish term for the creature Sharnebude. Other names, as germ. Mistkäfer, that is, dung chafer, and agls. Tordwifel, confirm the derivation given.

> Lyke to the sharnebudes kynde
> Of whose nature this I fynde
> That in the hotest of the day
> Whan comen is the mery May
> He spret his wynge and up he fleeth.
> Gower, lib. i. p. 173.

Scarabæus does not appear to be greek, although it springs from a greek word; but it also is not english, though it springs from an english root. A derivation from καραβος seems favoured, but what καραβος I do not see; is it Lobster? or a coleopterous insect of that name (Aristot.)?

191. SHIP = agls. Scip = mœsog. norse Skip = germ. Schiffe = SKIFF = Σκαφη, Σκαφος 'a boat, a vessel of a meaner sort,' πλοιαριον. Cf. SKIPPER.

192. SH— = agl. Scitan = isl. Skita = germ. Scheissen. The genitive Σκατος corresponds. Lye gives no reference for the verb, but only for the substantive Scitta.

> And shame it is, if that a preest take kepe
> To see a shitten shepherd and clene shepe.
> Chaucer, C. T., 505.

193. SHOOT = agls. Scēotan = norse Skióta. Cf. Sagitta = erse Sciot.

194. SIX = agls. Six = norse Sex = mœsog. Saihs = lat. Sex = Fεξ, εξ. = sanskr. Shash = שש.

195. SKIN. It seems probable that some connexion exists between this word and Σκηνη 'tent,' since tents were of skins (Pott). So Leather, which has nothing keltic, belongs to mœsog. Hleiþra, 'σκηνη,' 'tabernacle.' The SK has a sense of shading as in SHAW, SKY = in norse Sky 'cloud,' at Skyggja

'overshadow,' Shade, Σκια. Eudoxus observes that the skin is the tabernacle of the flesh : that would reverse the order above, and make the greek the older.

196. Smoke = agls. Smic, Smeoc = germ. Schmauch. Σμυχειν in Homer is 'burn with dull combustion.' Hesych. Σμυξαι, φλεξαι, εμπρησαι, μαραναι. Cf. erse Micch = welsh Mwg 'smoke.'

197. Sow = lat. Sus = Συς (Homer) = agls. Sugu = germ. Sau. Cf. Swine = agls. Swín = mœsog. Swein.

198. Sow = agls. Sawan = mœsog. Saian = norse at Sá = lat. Sa-tum, Sev-i.

199. Some was originally 'one,' and it is probably identical with the roots of Semper, Singuli and Semel 'one while;' perhaps also with 'Ενα. The sense 'one' I do not find developed in the glossaries : " All and some " is frequent in o. e. and is " All and each one." The usual sense of the singular agls. Sum = mœsog. Sums is the indefinite quis, τις, but examples occur in which it is necessary to the sense that it be reckoned as a numeral. Lye cites passages where Sum in one clause, against Sum in another, mean 'the one, the other.' In Beowulf 6210 : Eode cahta sum, 'he went one of eight,' not as has been translated by a scholar whose name has weight, 'accompanied by eight,' for in the previous lines he chose seven, seofone being legible. In 4797 Gewat þa XIIa sum, ' went then one of twelve,' for the thirteenth man mentioned 4808 was not of the hero band, but " against his will, bound, sad of mind, went to guide them."

200. Sound = lat. Sanus = agls. Sund. The mœsogothic equivalent I take to be Swinþs, ισχυρος, for the latin may drop the W as it has done in Canis, and the saxon may vocalize it, as has occurred in Hund, Hound.

201. Speed = agls. Spedan ' to prosper' = Σπευδειν to be diligent about. Cf. Σπουδη. The agls. is used of diligence, purpose, and the like. Cædmon, 36 : Swa wit him butu an sped spreacað; 'so we both to him one purpose speak.' 66 : se þarh snytro sped smið cræftega wæs ; ' who through wise diligence a smitheraftsman was.' The T in Σπευδειν corresponds with another agls. form Speowan.

202. Spit=agls. Speowian=mœsog. Speiwan=isl. Spyta
=lat. Spuere. Spittle=agls. Spatl=lat. Sputum. Spew
=agls. Spiwan=isl. Spya seems near akin to lat. Spuma.

203. Stand = agls. Standan = mœsog. Standan = norse
Standa=lat. Stare='Εστηκεναι: the greek radical form is
active. Stand=sansk. Sthâ=etc. The special form of stand
may be explained by supposing it a new verb formed on a participle like κυλινδειν art. 915. The radical letters are in Set
='Ισταναι=Sistere: and the other derivatives are numerous,
see art. 183: also Stack, Staff, Stab, Stay, Stead, Steady,
Staid, Stake, Stick, Stalk, Stall, Stallion (kept separate in a
stall to itself), Stanch, Stiff, Stilts, (probably Sting, Stick and
Stitch like Stab and Stoccado,) Stock, Stow, Stoke, Stout,
Stub, Stubble, Stabilis, Stagnum, Stamen, Statim (on the
stead), Statuere, Stimulus, Stipes, Stipula, Stirps, Stupere,
Stolidus, Stultus, $\Sigma\tau\alpha\theta\mu o\varsigma$, $\Sigma\tau\alpha\sigma\iota\varsigma$, $\Sigma\tau\alpha\tau\eta\rho$, $\Sigma\tau\alpha\upsilon\rho o\varsigma$, $\Sigma\tau\epsilon\lambda\epsilon$-
$\chi o\varsigma$, $\Sigma\tau\eta\mu o\nu\alpha$ (acc.), $\Sigma\tau\iota\beta\alpha\rho o\varsigma$, $\Sigma\tau\iota\zeta\epsilon\iota\nu$, $\Sigma\tau\iota\chi\alpha$ (acc.), $\Sigma\tau\iota\chi o\varsigma$,
$\Sigma\tau o\iota\chi o\varsigma$, $\Sigma\tau\epsilon\lambda\lambda\epsilon\iota\nu$?, $\Sigma\tau\upsilon\pi o\varsigma$, $\Sigma\tau\upsilon\epsilon\sigma\theta\alpha\iota$, $\Sigma\tau\eta\lambda\eta$, $\Sigma\tau\epsilon\iota\chi\epsilon\iota\nu$.

204. Star=agls. Steorra=mœsog. Stairno=norse Stiarna
=Αστερα (acc.)=lat. Stella. The comparison of Αστραπη
'lightning' with its verb αστραπτειν, shows the existence of a
root capable of explaining all these terms at once. Χαλκου τε
στεροπης 'flashing light.' Od. p. 437. In sanskrit, Vastar,
'mane, in the morning,' is supposed to come from an obsolete
root Vas, 'to shine.'

205. Sting=germ. Stecken, Stechen=$\Sigma\tau\iota\zeta\epsilon\iota\nu$ (with $\Sigma\tau\iota\gamma\mu\eta$)
=lat. †stinguere in Distinguere, if that account of the word
be correct. The mœsog. Staks translates $\Sigma\tau\iota\gamma\mu\eta$, Galat. vi.
17.

206. Strew=lat. Sternere (with Stravi) = $\Sigma\tau\rho\omega\nu\nu\upsilon\nu\alpha\iota$,
$\Sigma\tau o\rho\nu\upsilon\nu\alpha\iota$, $\Sigma\tau o\rho\epsilon\sigma\alpha\iota$=agls. Streowian = mœsog. Strauyan
Mark xi. 8, xiv. 15=norse Strá=germ. Streuen. Cf. Straw
=agls. Streow=norse Strá=germ. Stroh=lat. Stramen. To
this root seems to belong Stercus, which is properly manure
for the fields.

207. Sull 'plough'=agls. Syl, Sulh (for sulg). Hence
lat. Sulcus 'a furrow' (Grimm, Gr. iii. 415). Sul is plough
in Cornwall, Devon, Wilts.

208. Sweet=lat. Suavis=agls. Swæte, Swæs=germ. Süss =sanskr. Swâtu.

209. Teat=Τιτθη, Τιτθος, Τιτθιον=agls. Tit, Titt=germ. Zitz=welsh Diden=דד=דש.

   Hyre tyttes areu an under bis*
   As apples tuo of parays †
   Ou self ȝe mowen seo.
     Percy Soc. vol. iv. p. 35.

210. Tingle=lat. Tinnire, Tintinare. Tintinant aures, επιβρομεισι δ' ακουαι. Tingle is the frequentative of Ting, Ting, the voice of a bell : but it is not in the saxon lexicons.

211. Tire. The agls. Tirian 'to vex, annoy,' Teorian 'to faint, to fail,' norse Trega 'to trouble,' danish Tære 'to consume, waste,' Tærge 'to exasperate, irritate,' Træt 'tired,' swedish Trötta 'to tire,' Trött 'tired' are similar to lat. Terere, Trivi, Τειρειν, Τριβειν. So ὥσπερ ὄνοι μεγάλοις ἄχθεσι τειρόμενοι. Tyrtæos.

212. Token=agls. Tacn=mœsog. Taikns=Τεκμωρ, Τεκμαρ, Τεκμηριον.

213. Tolls=Τελη, 'taxes, payments,' see Deal, art. 472. The italian form of the gothic root Tagliare, gives us Tailor, Entail, on an indented parchment, Retail, Tallagium, etc. Thus though the word be not saxon it appears to be gothic. Some gothic words remain both in Italy and Spain. Tolls were in early times part of the load. Spelman compares Excise, and an irish tax, Cutting.

214. Tor=lat. Turris=Τυρσις=agls. Tor, Turr=isl. Turn. The devonian Tors are like castles on hill tops, they are formed by the disintegration of the granite at the sides, leaving heavy masses to be acted on by future winters. In some cases the tor has been quite eaten away and the hill of fragments only remains.

214 a. Umb, 'around'=agls. Ymb, Emb=norse Um= germ. Um=lat. Amb- =Αμφι.

   As he was syttand at þe mete
   Wyth myis he was swa wmbesete.
     Wyntown, i. 206, 106 †.

---

 * Bis is a fine silk. † Parays=paradise.
 † See also Halliwell or Jamieson.

215. Un prefix = lat. In = Αν = agls. mœsog. Un = norse O. The supposition that Αν may have been ava rests, among critics, upon two very suspicious words αναεδνος Il. ix. 146, 288, and αναελπτα παθοντες, Hesiod. Theog. 660. The hiatus in these words might be admissible, on Alexandrine principles would be admitted readily, but now rather on the supposition that Fεδνα, Fελπις had the initial Vau. If so, the passages will read ανFεδνος, ανFελπτα, or aveFεδνος, aveFελπτα, which would bring them into conformity with the suggestions of the comparison of languages. Αμβροτος is correctly formed from Αν and μβροτος by rejection of the first consonant as the rules of euphony require; had the original primitive been ava the compound would have been αναμβροτος.

216. Under = agls. Under = mœsog. Undar = norse Undir = lat. Inter = sansk. Antar. These are not always alike in signification, but are undoubtedly the same word. The german has occasionally the sense conveyed by the preposition in Interire, Interimere, Internecio, as also has the sanskrit. Prepositions are so capricious that their meanings are hardly traceable. See Interloper, art. 127.

217. Wade = agls. Wadan 'to go' = lat. Vadere. The norse Vaða is often accompanied with the idea of force, like invadere.

218. Wag = lat. Vacillare = agls. Wagian = mœsog. Wigan, Wagyan. To this word Wave = agls. Wæg, appears akin, from the swaying vibrating motion; then the mœsog. is used to express σαλευειν, κλυδωνιζειν, and Wegs is σεισμος, κλυδων, κυμα.

219. Wall = lat. Vallum : see introduction, art. 27.

220. Wallow = agls. Wealwian = mœsog. †walwian in compounds, also Walwison, κυλιεσθαι, Mark, xx. 20. The active form is Fελειν, Fελισσειν = Volvere. Cf. Wheel = agls. Hweol = norse Hvel. Of the existence of an earlier form †hvolv, kvolv, there is no doubt, from κυλιειν. Observe that while the simple Vau leaves no aspirate, as in οικος, οινος, these Kw initials leave an aspirate, which belongs not to the W but to the K.

221. Wamble 'nauscare' = isl. at Væma cf. Voma 'nausea' = dan. Vammel. Cf. lat. Vomere, with Ἐμεῖν presumed †Fεμειν. "If anything overchargeth it, undigested, it wambleth = escam fastidit et ingestam [indigestam?] respuit." Ianua Ling. 292. "Wil hardly escape wambling of stomach = nauseam vix effugiet." Id. 467.

222. Ward = agls. Weardian = norse Varða, seems not to turn the eyes but the mind to the wardens charge : it is probably akin to lat. Vertere.

223. Wards = agls. -weard, -weards = mœsog. -wairþis, -wairþs, is the latin Versus, -orsus.

224. Wart = lat. Verruca = agls. Weart = isl. Varta = germ. Warze. The agls. Wear ' callus, nodus,' comes still nearer in form to the latin. This may be connected with Wear = agls. Werian, as it appears where the hands are worn with toil.

225. Wasp = lat. Vespa = agls. Wæps, Wesp = germ. Wespe. Are these latinisms?

226. Weave = agls. Wefan = norse Wefa = sanskr. Vap, is represented in greek by Ὑφαίνειν, a derivative of Ὑφη, a form of Wef with the W vocalized. The epithet αργυφος applied in Homer to sheep, seems to indicate that ὑφ- might be wool; it is also applied to a ladys dress. As the lexica do not recognize the second member of the compound, the places shall be cited. Od. E. 230, K. 543 : αὐτὴ δ' ἀργύφεον φᾶρος μέγα Fέννυτο νυμφή. K. 85 : ἄργυφα μῆλα νομεύων. Hymn. Merc. 250: ἄργυφα Fείματα νύμφης. Il. Ω. 621 : ὄφιν ἄργυφον ὠκὺς Ἀχιλλεὺς σφάξ'. One passage Σ. 50, τῶν δὲ καὶ ἀργύφεον πλῆτο σπέος, would be much better as ἀργυφέων. In the mœsogothic, as far as we have it, no word of corresponding sense exists: Waibyan belongs to Weipan. The passage " woven from the top throughout," John, xix. 22, is not extant.

227. Wed, originally 'pledge,' = agls. Wed = mœsog. Wadi = norse Veþ. Compare with what hesitation soever, lat. Vadem 'a surety, bail,' Ἐδνα believed Fεδνα ' wedding gifts.' Hence Wedding, Wedlock.

> I wedde myne cris.
> Piers Ploughman, 2374.

And leieth his lif to wedde.
P. P., 12135.

His maners* he ded to wede sett.
Sir Cleges, 62.

228. Were 'man, husband' = agls. Wer = mœsog. Wair = norse. Verr = lat. Vir = sanskr. Varah = erse gaelic Fear. The compound Weregild is familiar to our ears.

For hit itit ofte and ilome
That wif and were beoþ unisome †.
Owl and Nightingale, 1519.

229. While, Whilom = agls. Hwile, in the dat. pl. Hwilum = mœsog. Hweila, dat. pl. Hweilom = lat. Olim. The root While is also found in Semel, somewhile, Simul, 'same while.' Duration is not implied in the ancient word more than it is in Olim: mœsog. Hweila translates ὥρα, χρονος, καιρος. Some other adverbs in -im may turn out to be old datives or ablatives, call them accusatives who may: thus, Passim, Sensim, Statim 'on the stead.' The O in Olim arises from vocalization of the W. I am sensible that closely examined, these words are better singular than plural, as Statim 'on the stead' not 'on the steads.' I am not content to reply that in agls. and in swedish the termination -um is often adverbial; for there is great reason to suppose, against the grammar, that substantives as well as adjectives and pronouns, made originally the agls. dative singular in -um: so that Lustum is 'with pleasure,' Miclum Spedum is 'with much speed.' This had occurred to my own study of the language before I read Mr. Goodwins remarks to the same effect in his notes to Guðlac p. 106. The argument would be much strengthened by a collection of examples where the singular would be much more appropriate than the plural. Perhaps therefore -im in Olim is dative singular. Seldom still remains to us, an adverbial dative.

230. Whoop = agls. Wopan (incorrectly sometimes even in saxon written with h, as Hwcop in Cædmon, 159. 18) = mœsog. Wopyan, which means, as in John xii. 17, 'call.'

* Manors.
† Betides; frequently; not at one.

To this the homeric Ϝοπα=lat. Vocem (acc.) belongs. The word must have the Vau, as in Od. E. 61, αϜειδουσα Ϝοπι καλῃ.

231. Wick=agls. Wic, 'a place of residence'=mœsog. Weiks 'κωμη, αγρος'=Ϝοικος=lat. Vicus. The digamma in Ϝοικος is ascertained by inscriptions, having been, since Bentley, presumed from homeric versification. Οικος was not the proper old word for 'house' or building, that was Δομος; but it signified 'a dwelling,' and this sense remains in οικειν 'dwell,' αποικια 'away from home, colony,' οικαδε 'homewards,' οικοι 'at home,' μετοικος. Boeckh had mentioned that perhaps the O represents the digamma; if so, the true homeric word was Ϝικος, Wick. (Boeckh Staatshaushaltung, p. 393, not in the translation.) The lokrian inscription (Philolog. Soc. vol. v.) gives however both the O and the Vau, μεταϜοικεοι. There are, nevertheless, reasons enough for accepting Boeckhs suggestion, art. 383. In a fragment of Korinna Ϝυκια. I entertain no doubt but that all these words are forms of Quick : see art. 1024.

232. Widower, Widow=lat. Viduus, Vidua=agls. Wuduwa, Wuduwe=mœsog. Widuwo or, Luke, vii. 10, Widowo (fem.)=sanskr. fem. Vidhavâ, which according to the native authorities signifies 'without husband.'

233. Will=agls. Willan=mœsog. Wilyan=norse Wilja =germ. Wollen=lat. Velle (Volo)=βουλεσθαι, βολεσθαι (Buttm. Lex. p. 28), εβολλομαν Theokr. xxviii. 15.

234. Win=lat. Vincere?. There is good scope of analogy to induce a supposition that the radical syllable in Vinco is Vic, and that N has been inserted to strengthen the imperfect tenses. Against this foregone conclusion I can in this instance contend but weakly. There is however a possibility that N has been ejected : see "All these are passing good knights and are hard to winne in fight." Mort d'Arthure, vol. ii. chap. xxi. "And there Sir Sauseise had wonne Sir Meliagaunt, had not reseewes come there" id. ii. cxxvi. So also in the norse at Vinna; Guðrunarkviða ii. 30 : Unz þik aldr viðr; 'usque dum te senectus vicerit.' So in Saxon Chron. anno 1138 : On þis gær com Dauid King of Scotland

mid ormete færd to þis land, wolde winnan þis land. Winnan occurs for 'war' (Orosius III. ix.=p. 362. 28), and Gewinn is a constant expression for warfare. So also as to me appears in Owl and Nightingale, 1098:

> For þen the kniȝt forles his wunne
> An ȝaf for me an hundred punde.

the knight lost his victory and had to pay for killing the bird a hundred pounds.

> The sowdanne hymselfe was therinne
> That Cristendome was commene to wynne.
> Sir Isumbras, 225.

> Sewes him to sum cite and aseye him þere
> Til ȝe wiþ fin fors þe freke have wonne.
> William and Werwolf, fol. 16 B.

235. WIND = lat. Ventus = agls. Wind (masc.) = mœsog. Winds (masc.) = norse Vindr (masc.).

236. WINE = lat. Vinum = Ϝοινος (Ϝινος?), Οινος = agls. Wín = mœsog. Wein = armenian Gini = hebrew Yayin construct. Yeyn = arabic æthiopic Wayyn. The northern nations, it must be supposed, borrowed this word from more genial climes; the pleasant drinks of Skythia were mead and ale. Loðbrokar Qviða. 25. Dreckom bior at bragði or biug-viðom hausa. Soon we will drink beer from the capacious skull.

237. WINNOW = agls. Windian. Cf. agls. Winnung, 'winnowing:' the lat. Vannus is the machine used in threshing floors for producing an artificial wind. Columella, II. 21: At si compluribus diebus undique silebit aura, vannis expurgentur (frumenta). This cannot have been a cradle.

238. WITE = lat. Vituperare = agls. Witian = mœsog. Hwotyam, 'επιτιμαν.'

> The kynges sone, kene and proud
> Gaf kyng Richard swylke a ner clout,
> That the fyr of hys heyen sprong;
> Richard thawt he deed hym wrong;
> "I swer by Seynt Elyne,
> To morwe it is tyme to pay myne."
> The kyngys sone on him lowgh,
> And bad, he schulde have his will now,

Bothe of drinke and of mete,
Of the beste that he wolde ete ;
That him ne thorst yt not wyte,
For febyl his dynt to smyte*.
                Richard Coer de Lion, 676.

239. Withy = agls. Wiþic, Wiþige = lat. Viticem (acc.) = Fιτεα. The digamma is fairly supposed in this word, from Homers versification and what is found in Hesychios, γιτεα, ιτεα. [In Φ. 350. πτελεαι τε, edd.]

Καίοντο πτελέαι καὶ Fιτέαι, ἠδὲ μυρῖκαι.
                Il. φ. 350.

Μακραί τ' αἴγειροι καὶ Fιτέαι ὠλεσίκαρποι.
                Od. κ. 510.

240. Woe = agls. Wa = mœsog. Wai = lat. Væ = Φευ.

241. Wool = agls. Wull = mœsog. Wulla. Cf. lat. Villus. Vdisque aries in gurgite villis mersatur. Virg. Georg. iii. 446. Compare the article on Fleece.

242. Work = agls. Weorc (neut.) = mœsog. Waurstw (neut.) (the verb is Waurkyan) = norse Verk (neut.) = Fεργον, εργον : where the digamma is established by the Eleian inscription. Zeuss on the keltic Guerg 'efficax' (Oxford Glossary) considers it the root of Virgilius.

243. Worth = agls. Weorð, Wurð 'honour, dignity, price.' The mœsog. has Wairþs 'ἱκανος, αξιος,' as subst. τιμη 'price,' Wairþon, τιμαν : germ. Würde, 'dignity.' Compare lat. Vereri, reverentia, which have no nearer parallel in the sibilate form mœsog. Sweran. The agls. Wurþian means Vereri (as Exod. xx. 5) ; and we express the same sense by Worship, a compound. Fear, art. 117, is a ruder kind of respect, compare also Ware, Beware, Wary, Guard, which approach in sense.

244. Worm = agls. Wyrm = mœsog. Waurms = norse Ormr = lat. Vermis. The mœsogothic translates οφις and the norse is snake, the original form of the word being some such root as †kwer, 'creep.' See the sanskrit index.

---

* Richard is in prison in Austria ; the dukes son and he exchange fisticuffs ; such an ear clout. That he might not dare to charge it on him (that he had starved him) to make the return blow feeble.

245. Wroth=agls. Reþe=norse Reiðr. This may serve as a probationary root for lat. Irritare. The W is doubtful; danish swedish Vred.

245 a. Wult. Whether in the citation this word be a mere appropriation from the latin I know not: lat. Vultus clearly =agls. Wlit=mœsog. Wlits (with verb Wlaiton περιβλέ-πεσθαι)=norse Litr dropping as usual W (with verb Lîta).

Pert of wult and eloquent*.
Wyntown Croniel. p. 116. 881.

246. Young=lat. Iuvenis=agls. Geong=mœsog. Yuggs =norse Ungr=sanskr. Yuvan.

The following parallels have been rejected. Foul, Φαυλος; make, μηχανασθαι; Earth, Ερα; Thane, Θητα; Creak, Κρεκειν; Hulk, Ὀλκας; Rib, Ῥαβδος; Dock, Δεχεσθαι; Stork, Στεργειν; Balteus, Belt.

In speaking of the commutations of consonants let me remark that some are so familiar from the grammars that they pass for nothing; while a due reflexion would ask whether such changes go no further; some are so difficult that they are not at this present day admitted, and obscure even the sense of Shakspeare (art. on Top). Every faulty sound has its instruction, every national peculiarity. Eudoxos observes with truth that the pronunciation of children, of drunken people, of sufferers with catarrh and great snuff takers often illustrates changes of consonants.

247. Let the incredulous student, who regards his own language with distrust, be led on to an easy proposition, that the gutturals, κ, γ, χ, C, K, G, Q, H, are among themselves interchangeable. The ancient Greek alphabet had its H, but the character was usurped by long E, and the later scribes employed half an H, Ⱶ, to represent the sound; the current hand made this ʻ a comma. Q stands for KW; it is the Kôf of the hebrew, the kâf of the arabic, and the Ⰴ of the mœsogothic; it is found on some greek coins as ϙ, koppa, always they say before an O. It has apparently, then, some claim to be called a double letter, but this claim has never been admitted, it makes no position in prosody, and was represented

* Pert, open.

in the old alphabets by a single character. It soon passed out of the greek language, very little trace of it remaining to us, giving up its words to kappa : the latin exchanged it with C, and even the hebrew, which gives it full employment, will exchange it with Caph, and Kheth. These letters may be sufficiently for our purposes termed gutturals, though some of them be more strictly palatals, and a refined sense designates some of these as uvals.

248. To this class of letters belongs the hebrew Ain. Some english writers express, following the spanish Jews, this letter by ng, gn; a practice which better orientalists, with abundant reason, condemn as utterly false. As is shown from the Septuagint, the Ain when hardest is nearly a G, as in Gomorrha, and when softest almost without sound, as Eli, Amalek.

249. Among the gutturals the hebrew and arabic grammarians class the Aleph, Alif. Without asserting any such paradoxical doctrine as that the absence of aspiration has a guttural sound, we shall be able to admit that to K, G, Q, X, H is allied that sound which arises by diminishing the aspiration to the lowest point. As we proceed we shall have examples in which κ, γ, χ often entirely disappear at the commencement of a word, whether before consonant or vowel; and though the steps of the process be lost, it may be easily supposed that a K or G might become a hard strong H, then a softer, and then be lost. Thus between $K\alpha\pi\rho o\varsigma$, Aper, may have intervened †hhaper, haper.

250. These remarks may be illustrated and confirmed by a few words of Ewald on the arabic gutturals. [Gr. p. 27.] "Omnium lenissimus spiritus est Alif, talis scilicet qui vocalem ab initio syllabæ positam necessario præcedat, 'post vocalem quoque vocis intensione audiri queat, ut 'awara, yas-'alu, ra'sun. Fortior est Hâ latino et nostro H, Græcorum spiritui aspero respondens; intentior etiam Hâ (hebr. Kheth) Græcorum χ et nostro Ch paullo mollius pronunciato respondens. A quibus 'Ain ita differt ut spiritum palato non extrudat, sed extrinsecus haustum intrudat magis palatum pungens, qui sonus nobis ægre imitando attingitur."

251. When vocalized the gutturals tend to a Y and I sound :

thus agls. Geong=engl. Young, and the english spelling is nearer to Iuvenis and to Yuvan: agls. Geoc=Yoke, and the english is again nearer the latin and sanskrit: the anglosaxon system of writing did not use at all, it is true, the letter Y as a consonant, but if Geoc were pronounced Yoke, and Geong, Young, which I should not wish to dispute, still the G must have been esteemed akin to the sound of our Y. In Alfreds Orosius the consonantal I of proper names is turned into saxon by a G. The mœsogothic alphabet had separate letters for G and Y, the latter of which ???, would pass into the vowel ï, as ???ΑΛΙVISKS, ???ΝΑΛΙΝS and in one instance at least ???ΑΙΝS, εκεινος, answers to the guttural K. The anglosaxons knew nothing of the convenient alphabet of Ulphilas, and in rejecting the Runes, accepted the inadequate A B C of the latin. The ancient element which in mœsogothic is Ga, ΓΛ, and german Ge, was reduced in saxon times to a simple Y; as yblent, yclept: the mœsogothic Gards, becomes both Garden, and Yard, in english; Gairnyan becomes Yearn; the germ. Gestern is our Yesterday; the german Gerte is our Yard (staff); our pay is pacare. Changes of this sort would be expressed in semitic, greek, and latin words by I, and thus Μεγ·ζων makes Μειζων.

252. Where KW was superseded by a K sound there often remained some trace of the original W in a U: thus mœsog. Kwairrus=lat. Cicur, a reduplicated form; mœsog. Kwens=γυνη; Quoius=Cuius, Quatere=Concutere; an old †kwan=κυν-α. But this not always, for †kwan=Can-em; καπνος=Vap-or.

253. Among the liquids N adheres to gutturals rather than M, and its place is rather before the guttural than after it. On this see the sanskrit.

254. K, χ are interchanged, as in the formation of tenses in greek; thus τεταρακται, εταραχθην; τεταρακται, ταραχη; διδασκειν, διδαχη; δεχεσθαι, πανδοκος, προσδοκαν; χνους, κνους; ρεγχειν, ρεγκειν; εχειν, εκεχειρια; δεχεσθαι, ionic δεκεσθαι: χιτων, ionic κιθων; Μαχαιρα=mœsog. Meki=agls. Mece.

255. The sound χ is unknown to the english, anglosaxon,

mœsogothic, norse, and pure latinity. Cicero tells us he was compelled by a corrupt fashion to adopt the aspirate in some words (Orator, 48) : Quin ego ipse, cum scirem ita maiores locutos esse, ut nusquam, nisi in vocali, aspiratione uterentur, loquebar sic, ut pulcros, Cetegos, triumpos, Kartaginem dicerem; aliquando idque sero, convicio aurium cum extorta mihi veritas esset, usum loquendi populo concessi, scientiam mihi reservavi. Orcivios tamen, et Matones, Otones, Cæpiones, sepulcra, coronas, lacrimas dicimus, quia per aurium iudicium semper licet.

256. Κ, χ are exchanged with γ, as in the forms of verbs, τεταραγμαι, τεταρακται, λελεγμενον, λελεκται; λεγομαι 'lie,' λεχος; γναπτω, κναπτω; hebrew Khilbnâh, χαλβανη, Galbanum; κυφος, κυπτειν, gibbus; χαρις, gratia; Χαριτες, Gratiæ; κολπος, ital. golfo, engl. gulf: this word as Niebuhr teaches (Lectures on Ethnology, ii. 140) passed into the italian from the greek towns in the south of Italy, where the hellenic language was not extinguished till the third or even the eighth century after Christ; καμπτειν, 'bend,' γαμψος 'bent;' δεικνυναι, digitus; the tens in -κοντα answer to the tens in -ginta, as τριακοντα, triginta: κομμι, gum; aquila, eagle; κολλα, glue; κυβερναν, gubernare; γογγρος = conger; κιθαρα = guitar; hebrew gâmâl = καμηλος; ονυχα = unguem (acc.); ελαχυς = ολιγος; Cuckoo = Gowk; secare, segmentum; ilicem (acc.), ilignus; salicem (acc.), salignus; κυκνος, cygnus; Κνωσσος, Gnossus; Κνιδος, Gnidus; Προκνη, Progne; Ακραγας, Agrigentum; κραβατος, grabatus; globus, glomus belong to κυλιειν; the ulcer γαγγραινα is also καρκινος, and it is apparently the feminine form of cancer; Ceres was Geres "quod gerit fruges,' Varro IV.: is it not rather Ger, of the saxon rune song (12), annona, anni proventus? Cic. de Nat. D. ii. 26. By the norse Smiúga 'to sneak' it appears that Sneak and Smuggle are very close in sense and form : to Sneak Snake belongs.

257. The κ, γ, χ letters became H. Compare κυφος, κυπτειν, gibbus with ὑβος; χαμαι, humi; κοιρανος, germ. Herr (Buttm. Lexil. i. 35); keep gives hapse, hasp; a cooper makes hoops; Call, Halloo; Camisia 'chemise' = germ. Hemd;

χειμων 'winter' seems rightly compared with sanskr. Himan 'frost, snow' whence the mountains Himâlaya, Hæmus, Emodes; Emathia (Macedonia), Hiems, Hibernus, χιμετλον: χειρ = Hir, 'the hollow of the hand,' in Cicero, Varro, etc.

258. The κ, γ, χ, H, also disappear altogether, χαρασσειν is nearly ορυσσειν; carpere is nearly ερεπτειν; γλημαν, γλημη are λημη, lippire; χλιαρος = λιαρος; κυλινδεισθαι = ἀλινδεισθαι, whence αλινδηθρα; γαια = αια; γδουπος as in εριγδουπος with δουπος; κελευθος with ακολουθος, show the origin of †ελευθειν, ηλυθον; αἰμυλος = æmulus; ἑνα = unum; haurire = αρυειν; γνωναι may give νοος; gnatus = natus; καπρος = aper; gagates = agate; taking its name from Gages a river in Lykia. (Plinius, xxxvi. 19.) χλαινα = læna; colaphus = alapa; glubere = λεπειν; with liber, 'bark;' calcem gives λαξ; gallus should be compared with αλεκτρυων, the common notion from λεκτρον being irreconcileable with the sense of *a* privative, he appears in welsh as Ceilliog applied to the cock pheasant, heath cock, cock thrush, drake, and grasshopper, erse Cailcac, and perhaps takes his name from Call, and agls. Galan 'sing;' χηνα becomes anatem (acc.) and then νησσαν; γλαυσσειν, λευσσειν; γλυκυριζα, liquorice; the first syllable in Erinaceus, Urchin, is apparently χηρ akin to χοιρος; one of the names of the hedgehog is χοιρογρυλλις; tunica is for †etunica, χιτων, from the hebrew, with a root 'to cover;' gif is an old form of if, as was fully illustrated by Horne Tooke; though it does not necessarily follow it was the imperative Give, for even the norse has Ef; Gippeswic is the saxon name for Ipswich, it has a stream, the Gipping, which flows into the Orwell; †cubi as in alicubi was the old form of ubi; an old †euter became uter; in Quicumque, the cumque represents quumquum, for the latin doubles its indefinites like quisquis, ut ut, unde unde, quoquo, 'ever' therefore was quumquum and is now unquam; quod became ut 'that;' †eunde in alicunde became unde. In the anglosaxon and mœsogothic the change of gutturals to H is constant. In almost all instances, say not in all, the harder guttural seems earlier than the gentler.

259. With the KW the case is the same; thus mœsog.

Kwainon 'πενθειν'=agls. Cwainian, Wanian=germ. Weinen (but not whine). The lat. Quies=mœsog. Wis which translates γαληνη; Zeuss in the old keltic glossary (1079) has Poues = Quies; does then παυειν belong to this group? hither perhaps Κεομαι, Κειμαι and the sanskrit Shî 'sleep, repose.' Tranquillus has a correspondent mœsog. in Anakwal, το ἡσυχαζειν and norse Hvîla 'to rest' Hvilld 'repose.' Are γαληνη, κελλειν, οκελλειν connected with it? With Vacuus compare welsh Coeg. With Vanus compare Κενος, with Venter Κενεων 'belly,' and sanskr. Shûnyas 'empty;' with Vapor, Καπνος.

260. The object in these lists is to set before the mind such examples as may persuade it to accept the now received doctrine that gutturals change: not to exhaust all that can be said, or to produce all that has been said. Hence a list of other supposed parallels approved by men whose names have great weight in Germany shall not be given here, since they are somewhat doubtful. Not all probably by many, of the examples given, have been printed before.

ANLAUT.

261. Lat. Con=erse Coimh, Comh=mœsog. Ga=agls. Ge=germ. Ge=engl. prefix Y='Aμα, 'Ομου. That the mœsogothic Ga in one of its senses signified together is evident from gawairþi translating ειρηνη but meaning 'amity' since the elements are con=συν and γενεσθαι; from gabauryoþus translating ἡδονη, and gabauryaba ἡδεως, but made up of the elements συμφερει; from gabinda, συνδεσμος; gabundi, συνδεσμος; from gahlaiba translating συμμαθητης, συστρατιωτης and made up of con and hlaifs 'loaf;' probably from galigri, Rom. ix. 10; from gamains which is in sense and form communis; from gaman κοινωνος, from gamarko συστοιχουσα; from gayuko, συζυγος; from gatiman, συμφωνειν; from gawaurdi, ὁμιλια, made up of con and word=verbum; from gawaurstwa, συνεργος; from gawidan, συζευγνυναι; from gawizneigs wisan, συνηδεσθαι; from gakwumþim conventibus (John, xvi. 1). Surely the comparison need be no further pursued: I have been so full here because Grimm,

though he sets ga by con, has not been understood to assert the identity of the two, nor has he recounted them in his list of mœsogothic words with latin equivalents in the preface to Schulze. The other senses and the weakness of sense found in the latin Con in composition are largely paralleled in the mœsog., in agls., and in german. Thus Gamaitano is the Concision of St. Paul, Philipp. iii. 2. It is proper to add that the original form of Ga was Gan as is evident by comparing Cuncti with germ. Ganz 'all' $\pi\hat{a}\nu$. The agls. has also Ge as Con, in gebedda, gebedde, 'a bedfellow,' gebeorscipe, 'a compotation,' gefera, 'a companion,' gegada 'comes,' gehada, qui eiusdem status vel ordinis est, the root being Had 'a state'= mœsog. Haidus, translating $\tau\rho o\pi o\varsigma$=engl. Hood as in boyhood. Ge is Con again in gehleoþ 'consonus,' as gehleoþre stæfne sungan, Bed. i. 25, 'consona voce cecinerunt' (Lye) (to make the english 'agreeable' is very wide of the mark); in gehlyt 'consors' (con-lot) Ps. xliv. 9; in gelaþung 'a congregation;' in geligen, 'a lying with;' in gelodan 'fratres,' Lye, that is, gelcodan, germ. leute; in gemæn, 'common' as in mœsog. and german; in gemana 'consortium;' in gemot 'an assembly,' as in Witenagemot, with several collateral forms; in gerefa 'comes,' also germ. Graf 'count;' in gereonung 'coniuratio' and geruna, symmystes, from the same root; in geþwær 'concors;' in getoge 'a tugging together,' a spasm. There are many anglosaxon words which are wholly unintelligible without this key to their signification. Abraham wæs Godes gespreca (Homilies, i. 90). Lye was very far from the truth in explaining Gefol; which is applied to a camel (Genesis, xxxii. 15) attended by her foal; similarly of a cow with her calf Gecelf (v. 13). Gemedrydran means having a common mother (Genesis, xliii. 29). "Without doubt," says Niebuhr (Hist. Rome, i. 512) "the name Consules means nothing more than colleagues," it is therefore the german Gesell. Perhaps oportet, it comports, $\sigma\upsilon\mu\phi\epsilon\rho\epsilon\iota$ is from con; thence opportunus, for to draw it from portus is not appropriate. That $\kappa o\iota\nu o\varsigma$, $\xi\upsilon\nu o\varsigma$, $\alpha\mu\alpha$, $\dot{o}\mu o\upsilon$ belong to this family has never been questioned. I shall show that the german Ganz 'all'=$\pi\alpha\nu$

GUTTURALS INTERCHANGED.

=cunctus and that παν in composition=Con. To this word with loss of aspiration must be carried a copulative, in αδελφος, αλοχος, ακοιτις, ασπαζεσθαι, ακολουθος, απτερος (Agam. 276). For αδελφος we have Aristot. II. A. III. i. 10, δελφυς όθεν και αδελφους προσαγορευουσι: similarly Hesychios. Observe that this a is nearer to mœsog. Ga than to any greek type. 'Απαντα (acc.) a double Con, retains the softened guttural. For further remarks see arts. 520, 662. An example of the sense con in english is worth giving.

> Hit is unrijt and gret sothede*
> To misdon one gode manne
> And his ibedde† from him spanne‡.
> Owl and Nightingale, 1486.

262. GAIN in Gainsay, or AGAIN or AGAINST=agls. Ongean, Ongegen, is related to Gan as Contra to Con. With, which has now in our language the place of Con, to the exclusion of the old Mid, was originally possessed of the sense Contra, which still remains in Withstand, quarrel with, differ with, etc. The similarity of sense is but shadowy, yet it has been active in all these prepositions. I may be permitted here to offer some account of AJEE, OGEE. In the old english, final letters among the rest were frequently dropped. Man was Me, Done became ydo, Been, ibeo. The agls. Agen thus became Age. Examples are of constant occurrence, I take the first that comes to hand.

> And dude here beste aje the prince; ac ever eft he was wo.
> Thomas Beket, p. 3.

> Tho heo were aje thulke house, ther this Gilbert was.
> Id. p. 5.

Thus Agee, Ogee meant Contra, and contained the same ancient radical element. In architecture an Ogee arch is one, the head of which is completed by two circles drawn contrary, that is, with centres on the outside of the span. Ajee may be used provincially as awry; but this seems to be the history of the word.

* Sothood, sottishness.   † Bedfellow.   ‡ Allure.

263. Ape = Κηπος, κηβος = hebrew Kôf קוֹף = germ. Affe = agls. Apa = sansk. Kapi-as with vowels short. The κηπος is one of the long-tailed apes; modern naturalists have misapplied the term to the Sapajous of America, which could not have been intended by the hebrew and the sanskrit. In their 'Wörterbuch' the Grimms consider this word of importance to the history of language.

264. Carve = Κειρειν art. 89, in another form Gird? Gird means cut, whatever its origin. Since agls. Gyrd, a Yard, can hardly be considered a cutting instrument, perhaps Ceorfan may be admitted.

> Thurgh girt with many a grevous blody wound.
> Chaucer, C. T. 1012.

> And girdeth of Gyles head
> And lat hym go no ferther.
> Piers Ploughman, 1284.

The editor illustrates by the Towneley Mystery of the Shepherds

> "If I trespas eft, gyrd of my heede."

265. Chill, Cool, Cold = agls. Col adj.; Celan, Cilian, Colian verbs = norse Kala. Cf. Gelu, Gelidus.

266. Chin = agls. Cyn = germ. Kinn; cf. mœsog. Kinnus 'cheek' = isl. Kinn. Cf. lat. Gena 'cheek,' Γενειον, 'chin' = Γενυς. Cf. Γναθος, 'jaw.' Gnaw.

267. Chirp. Cf. lat. Garrire; Queri also, "Dulce queruntur aves," "Queruntur in silvis aves." Greet, Cry = agls. Gretan = mœsog. Gretan = norse Gráta. Many forms of Chirp are found. Agls. Girran (past pl. Gurron, Andreas 748), garrire, Ælfric. Cirman 'make a noise, cry out,' Cyrm 'cry, scream' (Thorpe), Ceorian 'murmurare,' Hreman, Hræman 'clamare, vociferari.'

> And kisseth hire swete and chirketh as a sparrow.
> Chaucer, C. T. 7387.

> All full of chirking* was that sory place.
> Id. 2006.

---

* Noise.

GUTTURALS INTERCHANGED. 71

With chirm of earliest birds.
Milton, Par. L. iv. 642.

Vorþi ich am lop smale fo;le
That flop bi grunde an bi þuuele *
Hi me hichermet and bigredeþ
And hore flockes to me ledeþ.
Owl and Nightingale, 277.

268. CHOOSE = agls. Ccosan is allied to Gustare, Γενεσθαι. For in mœsog. Kiusan expresses δοκιμαζειν, and Kausyan γενεσθαι. This leads to the identification of γενεσθαι with agls. Ccowan = CHEW. Cf. also CHEEK = agls. Ceaca.

269. CLUE = lat. Glomus = agls. Clowe, Cliwe which seems to be connected with Κλωθειν, Κυλιειν, ניל, גלה.

270. COME = agls. Cuman = mœsog. Kwiman = norse Koma (making past pl. Kvámum) = Venire. The dutch also in Qvam retains the old V. The original spelling is retained in the old english word Queme which is a corruption of the mœsogothic gakwiman, convenire. It is of very frequent occurrence and well known.

Horn me wel quemeth,
Knyght him wel bysemeth.
King Horn, 490.

An initial V in latin had, often, a letter preceding it; that this was a K is clear, in Vivus, Vis, Vires, Venire, Vastare, Venus, Venari, Vermis, Valere, Vigere, Vegere, Vigilare, Vas (vasa), Verres, Vertere, Vita, Viscera, Velox, Vapor, Vanus, Venter, Veru. A dental has been lost in Viginti. The antiquity of the initial V is more or less supported by the sanskrit in Vocem, Vitulus, Vomere, Vir, Verres, Vicus, Vestis, Virus, Vehere, Ve (or), Ventus, Ve (prefix), Videre, Vidua, Vertere, Vacillare. As the sanskrit loses initial letters, even according to its worshippers, Verres, Vertere may rightly stand as ancient and at the same time not original.

271. CORN = agls. Corn (neut.) = mœsog. Kaurn (neut.) = isl. Korn (neut.) = lat. Granum. Cf. Kernel = agls. Cirnel; they say in east Anglia "a kernel of wheat," "a kernel of salt" (Forby). GRavel, GRit, from the GRating sound, seem to

* þuuele = agls. þufe, 'germen, frons.' Hore = agls. Heora = their.

point to the first letters as imitative. Hebr. Gârôl, rough, and arabic Jarila 'lapidosus fuit,' have been compared.

272. COURT, GARDEN, GARTH, YARD, ORCHARD, WEAR. Cf. lat. Hortus, co-Hors, Urbs, Orbis, Χορτος (αυλης εν χορτῳ· Λ. 773). The mœsogothic has Gards, οικος, Aurtigards, κηπος, Midyungards, οικουμενη, Weinagards, αμπελων, vineyard, where the english word according to all reason should have begun with a W; Garda, αυλη. In the semitic languages is a copious supply (see 1046) of similar examples. All these are forms of Cir-ca, Cir-cum, Gird, Girdle; and the various senses may be in a good measure illustrated by the uses in the Edda of the word Garðr, which means 1. a hedge, ringwall, or plankfence; 2. the space so enclosed, either as 3. court, or as 4. field, garden; or as 5. dwelling. From Tigranocerta, Novgorod, and the tatar Yourts to Carthage this word is spread. A Garth is 'a yard,' 'a little close;' and a Fishgarth is a dam in a river for the catching of fish (Kersey). Garth an inclosure is also welsh. A Wear in a river=Were, 'defensio, munimentum, agger' (Kilian) is of this group. Ware, Ward (see 222), Guard may be. For other members of the group see art. 280 and 1026.

273. CRANE=agls. Cran=lat. Grus=Γερανος. Cf. Ερωδιος, Ardea, HERON a similar bird. The root I suppose lies in the length of the leg; cf. Crura 'legs,' Grallæ 'stilts,' Gradus 'a stride,' erse gaelic Cara 'a leg,' Corr 'any bird of the crane kind.' Science names them nowadays Grallatores, 'stilters.'

274. CREEP=lat. Repere=agls. Creopan. Other forms are Krim, with the labial liquid M for the labial P, and Serp, with the guttural become sibilant. Cf. CRAWL, CRIPPLE.

275. CRESS=GRASS=mœsog. Gras, Mark iv. 28, Frumist gras, πρωτον χορτον; 32. allaize grase maist, 'greatest of all herbs.' Rom. xiv. 2, gras matyiþ 'eateth herb,' λαχανα εσθιει := isl. Gras 'herb,' especially Iceland moss=agls. Græs, Gærs, Cressa, Cerse = l'ραστις, Κραστις (Aristot. H. A. VIII. x. 1; Mœris, Hesych. εστι δε ὁ χλωρος χορτος). Art. 122.

276. EAR=lat. Auris (see art. 106) is a difficult word; Ακουειν, with Ανηκουστειν, Auscultare, and the mœsog. Auso,

GUTTURALS INTERCHANGED. 73

Ουας, welsh in an old glossary Scouarn 'an ear,' go some way towards indicating an original form †Kous, or †Akous.

277. Gall=Χολη=agls. Gcalla=isl. Gall. Χολος, 'anger,' Χαλεπος 'indigestible,' are of this root, also Cholera, Choleric, &c. Further back in its life it was related to Yellow=agls. Geolo, to Gold=norse Gull, to Χλωρος.

278. Gander=Χην=lat. Anser=germ. Gans=agls. Gandra=sanskr. Hunsah हंः, which is goose, gander, swan. It appears then that in Κυκνος 'swan' exist the same elements KN in a reduplicate form, and the latin word for duck Anatem (acc.) is with loss of guttural similar; it seems to bring in Νησσα, which, however, might be †νηχσα. As a full discussion here would be premature, see in Word families art. 1048.

278 a. Gape=agls. Geápan=norse Gâpa, the germ. Gaffen 'to stare,' i. e. with open mouth. With sibilation Gasp. Both related to Καπτειν as well as Χασκειν (351). Odyss. ε. 467 :

μή μ' ἄμυδις στίβῃ τε κακὴ καὶ θῆλυς ἐέρση
ἐξ ὀλιγηπελίης δαμάσῃ κεκαφηότα θυμόν.

Yet perhaps this κεκαφηως is from καμνω, as if κεκαμηως.

279. Gar, now a scotch word, frequent in old english; the norse is Görva=Görfa=Gerva=Göra=Gera 'to make, prepare.' This is referred by Pott with reason to sanskr. Kri, 'make,' with which Χειρ is connected and Creare, and Crescere, and Carmen, and Iccur. The old english has Graith, 'prepare,' is it not the norse past Görða? Carmen then is of the same sense as ποιημα.

280. Geotan is almost extinct in english: it represents Χειν, and Gutta : if Gutter be french, Gout, a homely word for a sewer, and for a gush as of blood, is probably from the saxon direct. Mœsog. Giutan=germ. Giessen. See art. 852.

> Ther was ycome with the messangers
> A queynte mon, a metal geoter ;
> That couthe caste in alle thyng.
> He avysed* than the kyng ;
> And tho he com hom, sykirliche,
> He cast a forme the kyng yliche

---

* Avised, stood vis à vis.

In face, in eyghnen, in nose, in mouth,
In leynthe, in membres, that is selcouth*.

Kyng Alisaundre, 6734.

281. Gird, Girth, Girdle = agls. Gyrdel: Curl: in these appears the root Cir-cum, Cir-ca, Cir-culus, Γυρος, Gyrus, Gyrare. No doubt the original form was †kwer, as in Quern; the υ in γυρος, κυκλος cf. circulus, was a vocalization of the W, and in Vertere, the guttural has been removed. See art. 272 and 1046.

282. Girl was of either sex "Gerles that were Cherles" (Piers Ploughman, 528 of 'Ammon and Moab'). "Grammer for Girles" (id. 5961). "Knave gerlys" (id. glossary). It answers to Κουρος, Κουρη, Κορη and seems to arise out of the verb Car, Kri, Grow. Churls, Earls, Girls seem to be all of one stock.

283. Glad = Lætus = agls. Glæd = mœsog. Hlas, ἱλαρος = norse Glaðr = sanskr. Illâd.

284. Gnat = agls. Gnæt = Κωνωπα (acc.). A derivative of the greek is Canopy, properly Conopeum, a musquito net. קֵן 'a gnat.'

285. Gore = agls. Gor = lat. Cruor.

286. Gourd = lat. Cucurbita = agls. Cyrfæt = germ. Kurbs. See art. 1026 and cf. Cucumis. Hagars bottle of water is not very different, חֶמַת. Gurkens are little cucumbers; germ. Kurbs is nearly Kürke 'cucumber.' The agls. Cyrfæt treats the gourd as a Vat; we have only the compound.

287. Grab = Rapere = Ἁρπαζειν with transposition of R. To Grab are allied Grip, Gripe, Grapple, Grope, Grasp (sibilated) = agls. Grapian, Griopan, Gripan, Gripe, Grap = mœsog. Greipan, with Gagrefts, δογμα = norse Gripa = sanskr. Grabh, the earlier form of Grah. Here the english has retained an earlier form than the greek, than the latin, than the ordinary sanskrit.

288. Gris 'a pig' = isl. Gris = Χοιρος = sanskr. Kirah or Kiri. The root may lie in the habit of the animal to make furrows in grass land, Κειρειν, arare: the sanskr. verb Krî to which the word is referred, signifies with Ap to make furrows.

* Selcouth, strange.

289. Guest = agls. Gæst = mœsog. Gasts = norse Gistr = lat. Hospitem, Hostem (acc.) [Grimm].

> The kyng of Alemaigne gederede ys host
> Makede him a castel of a mulne post;
> Wende* with is prude ant is muchele host,
> Brohte from Alemaigne mony sori gost†,
> To store Wyndes ore.
> Richard of Almaigne, 20.

290. Hair. Od. χ. 188: τὼ δ' ἄρ' ἐπαίξανθ' ἑλέτην ἔρυσάν τέ μιν εἴσω Κουρίξ. Il. 1. 178: ἐν καρὸς αἴσῃ (?). Cf. Hircus even if Fircus, Hirtus, Hirsutus.

291. Hal 'a hiding place.' The radical letters KL occur in a great number of words signifying covering and concealment: lat. Celare, Occulere, Clam, "Calim antiqui dicebant pro clam" (Festus), and I take Calim for a dative, 'in hiding;' καλυβη 'a hut,' καλυξ 'the covering of the blossom in a plant,' κελυφος 'the covering of the seeds, pod;' gaelic Ceil, 'conceal;' welsh Cêl, 'concealment, shelter,' Cil 'a retreat,' erse Ceilim 'I conceal;' Culmen 'the covering of a house, the roof, the thatch, sometimes the reed, culmus:' mœsog. Hulyan, translating περικαλυπτειν; agls. Helan 'to cover;' old english Hele, whence Hillier 'a roofer;' agls. Hlid = Lid 'the covering of a vessel.'

> Ich was in one sumere dale,
> In one suþe diȝcle‡ hale,
> I herde ich holde grete tale
> An hule and one niȝtingale.
> Owl and Nightingale, 1.

The last glossary on this passage follows Grimms idea and gives Hale = Hollow; but Lye has Hal, latibulum, from the word-for-word version of the Psalms, xvi. 13. The latin Cella, usually the dark recess where the idol deity was placed, is derived by Festus and Servius from Celo, "quod ea celentur, quæ velimus esse occulta." In this sense Hal, agls., occurs in St. Guðlac (p. 82, line 22), þa gemette he hine hleonian on þam hale his cyrcan wið þam weofode, 'leaning in the cella of his church against the altar.' Gluma the chaff or

---

* Weened. † Gost is here foreigner.
‡ Suþe diȝelo, very secret.

husk of the grains of corn can scarcely be separated from κελυφος; and Glubere 'to peel, flay, strip off the covering,' as we say "to bark a tree, to peel an orange," must go with it. If so, Liber, λεπειν, λεπας, λεπτος, Limpet have all lost a K.

> No longer hele y nille*
> Al that sothe tellen y wille.
> Sir Gy of Warwike, p. 9.

> Als the bark hillest† the tre
> Right so sal my ring do the.
> Ywaine and Gawin, 741.

> Thyn balle agrayde‡ and hele the walles
> With clodes and wyth ryche palles.
> Launfal, 904.

> And alle the houses ben hiled,
> Halles and chambres
> With no leed but with love
> And lowe speche as bretheren.
> Piers Ploughman, 3680.

292. Halm = Καλαμος = lat. Calamus, Culmus, agls. Healm (masc.) = isl. Halmr. With this compare Quill, the hollow of feathers, lat. Caulis 'stalk,' Columen, Columna, welsh Calaf 'a stalk, a reed,' Called 'the stalk of thistles,' gaelic Cuile 'a reed, bulrush, cane,' the erse Cuile, Ciolceach, Golcog, Giole, Giolcach 'a reed,' Coll 'a post or pillar, the stalk of a plant,' the æthiopic ሐእት 'calamus,' the greek Αυλος 'a pipe.' These lead us to Hollow. Since the word Colbhta, Colpa, erse, the calf of the leg, can hardly fail to be akin to Colb 'pillar,' cf. welsh Celff 'a stock, a pillar,' we must conclude that Calf = lat. Columen.

> In champion countrie a pleasure they take
> To mow up their hawme for to brew and to bake;
> And also it stands them instead of their thacke
> Which being well inned they cannot wel lacke.
> The hawme is the straw of the wheat or the rie,
> Which once being reaped they mow by and by.
> Tusser, August 14.

---

* Nille = ne wille, will not.

† Conceals, as appears by what follows: "For of the sal thai have no syght."

‡ Agrayde, prepare.

GUTTURALS INTERCHANGED. 77

293. Hals = lat. Collum = mœsog., norse, agls. Hals. Gallows seems to be another form = agls. Galga, 'patibulum.'

> Al this route of ratons
> To this reson thei assented.
> Ac tho the belle was ybrought
> And on the beighe* hanged,
> Ther ne was raton in al the route
> For al the reaume of France
> That dorste have bounden the belle
> About the cattes nekke
> Ne hangen it about the cattes hals,
> Al Englond to wynne.
> Piers Ploughman, 346.

> The crueltee of thee, queen Medea,
> Thy litel children hanging by the hals,
> For thy Jason, that was of love so fals.
> Chaucer, C. T. 4493.

And hence the verb to Halse.

> Halsethe and kissethe and wol him not withseyne†.
> Lydgates Minor Poems, p. 32.

294. Halt = agls. Healt = mœsog. Halts = norse, Haltr = lat. Claudus = χωλος = welsh Cloff.

295. Hand = Κονδ-υλος? = agls. Hand = mœsog. Handus = norse Hönd. Cf. 123.

296. Harns = germ. Gehirn = norse Hiarnr = isl. Hiarni = dan. Hierne = swed. Hjerna, can scarce be but mœsog. Hwairnei 'skull;' cf. Κρανιον, Cerebrum, Καρα.

> He cleft the helme and the hern-pan.
> Ywaine and Gawin, 660.

297. Head is a contraction of agls. Heafod (neut.) = mœsog. Haubiþ (neut.) = norse Hofuð = lat. Caput = Κεφαλη. The german has two forms, Haupt and Kopf. The sanskr. Kapâl masc. or neut., but it means 'a skull.' From the final L of the greek, T of the latin, it is evident that the first syllable contains the root: this exists in agls. Cop, Copp 'top.' See art. 96. Another form, Κυβη, existed in greek, whence the homeric Κυβισταν 'to go head first,' 'tumble over;' and

---

* Beighe, something bent, here collar.
† With-say = contradict.

hither refer one way or other, Κυβερναν 'steer' = Gubernare, which gives us Govern: the second syllable may be Oar. Apex belongs to this group, for Servius quotes with a half sneer the derivation from apere, saying 'unde apicem dictum volunt (In Æneid. x. 270).

298. HEAP is of the same origin as Copia. In the singular the senses are not remote; and, for the plural Copiæ, the agls. Heap frequently means 'troops, bands;' thus Engla heapas 'troops of angels' (Ælfric. Homil. i. p. 340, 342). Þes hearda heap (Beowulf, 858. K.), 'this hardy band.' The swedish form is Hop, which is used in the same sense, as, Mark x. 46, en mägtig stor hop folk. Haufe in germ. is both 'heap' and 'band, crowd.'

   Fast lepeth your English heap*.
       Richard Coer de Lion, 1789.

   And he that lov'd me or but moan'd my case
   Had heapes of fire brands banded at his face.
       Browne Brit. Past. I. iv.

   Unarmed were the most hep.
       Gy of Warwike, p. 189.

   The most hepe wepen for blis.
       Ibid. p. 142.

   The wisdom of an hepe of lered men.
       Chaucer, C. T. Prologue, 578.

   Ye shal catche myse by grete heepis.
       Reynard the Fox, p. 25.

   A grete heep of houndes.
       Id. p. 159.

299. HEART = lat. Cor, Cordis = Κηρ, Καρδια = mœsog. Hairto = agls. Hcorte = norse Hiarta = germ. Herz = sanscr. Hrid; cf. CORE.

300. HEEL = agls. Hel (Ælfric) = norse Hæll = lat. Calcem. This exists in the greek adverb λαξ for †κλαξ, and in the derivative λακτιζειν for †κλακτιζειν: see art. 1028. The mœsog. is Fairzna, translating and of the same source as πτερνα, compare lat. Perna, 'a shank of bacon' not 'a gammon.' The corresponding saxon Fiersna = germ. Ferse, occurs only

      * Band.

in Cædmon 56. 19, where Mr. Thorpes translation cannot be accepted by any who recollect the mœsogothic and the text Genes. iii. 15, " It shall bruise thy head and thou shalt bruise his heel." Professor Dietrich acknowledges ' heel,' proposing to print thus : þu scealt fiersna sætan tohtan niwre : ' du sollst den Fersen (des Weibes) nachstellen mit neuem Kampf.'

301. HEMP = Κανναβις = lat. Cannabis = isl. Hanpr = agls. Hænep, Henep = sanskr. Shan-an, with sibilation. Herodotus iv. 74 describes it as a novelty to his countrymen and as skythian. See Nettle.

302. HIDE = Κευθειν = agls. Hydan = cornish Kyth, Kytha (Lluyd) = welsh Cuddio.

303. HIDE = Cutis = agls. Hyd = isl. Hud = germ. Haut.

304. HIVE. In mœsog. Heivafrauya is οικοδεσποτης, where Heiv is evidently = agls. Híw ' a family,' by us applied to bees only. With the mœsog., Grimm (Gram. i. 540) compares lat. Civis. That it is also οικια, and Quick, seems probable.

305. HOBBY, COB may be the same word as Caballus, which is as early as Lucilius; cf. welsh Ceffyl = irish Capall; the gaelic has Capall ' a mare.'

> Long after Phœbus took his lab'ring team
> To his pale sister and resigned his place
> To wash his couples in the ocean stream.
>   Drayton.

The danish Hobbe, J. Grimm says, comes from the hobbling gait. We should perhaps be ashamed to say that it may be Ἱππος. The Bœotians (Boeckh, Corp. Inscr. 2554) seem by the names Ὑππαγρα, Ὑππασια to have made ἱππος into ὑππος.

306. HOE seems related to mœsog. Hoha, ' αροτρον,' and lat. Occare 'to harrow' according to Grimm (Gr. iii. 415). Also (?) to HEW, HACK, HOGG = norse Hoggva ' cædere.' A Hog is a cut boar, a Hog sheep is one whose wool has been clipped the first year, a Hog mane is cut near the neck.

307. HORN = lat. Cornu = Κερας (κερατος) = קֶרֶן Keren = mœsog. Haurn = norse Horn = welsh Corn = erse Corn ' a drinking horn.' On account of its great horns HART = lat.

Cervus. In isl. Horn signifies also Corner=welsh Cornel=
erse Coirneul, Corr, and so agls. Horn, o. c. Hirn.

> Or for to ripe that holkit* huge belly
> And the hid hirnis to serche and well espye.
>   Gawin Douglas, lib. ii. (Of the wooden horse.)

To this root some refer Aries, Κριος; but see art. 757.

308. Hornet=germ. Hornisse, Hornus (Wachter)=agls. Hyrnet=erse Cearnabhan=lat. Crabronem (acc.). The antennæ of this wasp are not remarkably large. I am told that it may take its name from its whirring sound, as the hebrew Zirrah (if with dagesh occultum). Cf. the erse Cronan, 'the buzzing of a fly or insect.' The hornet is of a pale yellow, and another root might be suggested, the sanskrit Gaur yellow, which produces probably Crocus, Cera, and by removal of the guttural, Aurum. Yet the Gloss. Arg. has Horn-beron, Crabronis.

309. Hollow=agls. Hol=Κοιλος (?). The mœsog. has Ushulon, λατομειν, 'to hollow out (?),' Hulundi 'σπηλαιον.' More probably between o and ι in κοιλος a consonant has fallen out.

310. Hound=agls. Hund=mœsog. Hunds=norse Hundr =Κυνα (acc.)=lat. Canem=sanskr. Shwan (of which the nominative is Shwâ). The original root beyond doubt †Kwan. Kennel retains the K.

311. Hunt=Venari=agls. Huntian. These are altered forms of the above undoubted root †Kwan, Hound. The vocalization by E long, as compared with Canem, is remarkable. There is no connexion with mœsog. Hinthan, which is the o. c. Hent.

312. Hurry=old germ. Hurschen (to which Rasch 'quick' with our Rash, 'temerarius,' is perhaps allied) may be unhesitatingly compared with Currere. I shall attempt to show that χαιρειν=σκιρταν, and means leap, jump; Currere I take to be of the same root, with KW, and W vocalized.

313. Javelin=agls. Gafeloc. Cf. Οβελος 'a spit.'

314. Ken, Know=agls. Cunnan=mœsog. Kunnan=norse

---

* Holkit is interpreted 'sunk,' by Sir F. M. in Sir Gawain.

GUTTURALS IN ANLAUT CHANGED. 81

Kenna = germ. Kennen = lat. Gnoscere, Noscere, with incep-
tive sense and inceptive-sco = Γιγνωσκειν, Γνωναι, Κοννειν
(Æsch.) = sanskr. Jnâ. Gnoscere is asserted by Cæcilius ap.
Diomed. I. 378 ; it occurs in dignoscere, cognoscere, ignoscere.
The sanskrit according to its custom puts a sibilant J for the
guttural: the german and north country english have much
more ancient forms. Like the latin we drop in pronunciation
the K of Know.

> If I sholde deye bi this day
> Me list nought to loke :
> I kan noght parfitly my paternoster
> As the preest it syngeth :
> But I kan rymes of Robyn Hood
> And Randolf erl of Chestre ;
> Ac neither of oure Lord ne of oure Lady
> The leeste that evere was maked.
> Piers Ploughman, 3273.

Like Eγνωκεναι, γνωμη, Know sometimes means resolve.

> Then was the soudan glad and blithe
> Mahoun be thonked foole* sithe
> That heo was so biknowe.
> Kyng of Tars, 460.

315. KEN = lat. Gignere (for †gigenere, Genuisse) = Γενναν,
Γεινεσθαι = erse Geinim (I beget) = agls. Cennan = sanskr.
Jan. So KIN = lat. Genus = Γενος = agls. Cyn = mœsog. Kuni
= norse Kyn = erse Cine. The list of words belonging to the
root is too long to give. Some forms show by the vocalization
that an earlier root †Kwen existed, as Γυνη, QUEAN, mœsog.
Kuni, and -kunds used as a termination = -γενης, agls. -cund
as termination, with the latin isl. agls. engl. for det kvindelige
Skamlem. The dutch Kinderen is so much like Children,
having the plural termination twice, that the words are probably one: Rask (68) says of the agls. Cild 'child,' that it,
"according to Lye, forms cildru, but the usual plural is like
the singular cild ; yet in Legg. Ælfredi þa steopcilde occurs
twice ; though the c final is probably mute in this instance."
If then the agreement of the plural forms be accidental, still
Cild compared with germ. Kind, appears the same, like Tent,

* Feole = many.

G

Tilt. In the goddess Venus the K of the older root has fallen away, and among the various ideas the root contains, the tendencies of ruder life point to a worship like that which travellers tell of the Druses of the Syrian Oberland. It is impossible to shake off the impression that the Chemosh of the Moabites כְּמוֹשׁ is the same deity, and bears a name not accidentally but by affinity similar. For a time I felt this conclusion overthrown by a note of Ludolfi on ከሞሽ, but I now see that to the root †kwen belongs not only Venus, but also Venter, Κενεων and Κενος. Hence the significations vary, and the semitic languages have two forms, both of them originally one, in hebrew כמוש, חֹמֶשׁ, æthiopic ከሞሽ, ኈሞሽ. This conclusion is borne out by חֵמָת 'a water skin'=lat. Vter for Venter. See further art. 1026. As examples of some english forms now forgotten, take

> He bicom sone þerafter pur gydi and wod:
> For he was in ys moder wombe, as he understod.
> He þo3te he wolde wyte and se how faire þe chambre were
> Warinne he was ykenned, ar ys moder hym bore.
> Robert of Gloucester, p. 63.

> He come of Woden þe olde lowerd, as in teþe kne*.
> Id. p. 228.

> Hi3t mo3t be do ine kende watert
> And non other licour.
> William of Shoreham, p. 8, de baptismo.

> That he wald go to get his pray,
> His kind it wald‡, the soth to say.
> Ywaine and Gawin, 2020.

316. KID=isl. Kid (neut.) Kida (fem.)=Hœdus. Near this lies GOAT=agls. Gat, Gæt=hebrew Gedî, גְדִי.

317. KISS=agls. Coss=germ. Kuss=lat. Osculum for †cosculum. Cf. Κυσαι. Not however to deny that Os and Osculum are connected, for it seems probable that Os also had lost a guttural; cf. Ostrea, χαος, χασκειν, χαινειν, Gustare, etc. etc. Ostrea is surely 'yawner.'

318. KNEE=mœsog. Kniu (neut.)=norse Knê (neut.), also

---
* Tenth generation. † It must be done in natural water.
‡ His nature would, willed it.

GUTTURALS IN ANLAUT CHANGED. 83

later isl. Huie=agls. Cucow (neut.) =lat. Genu=Γονυ. The pronunciation now in use with us omits the K, and is an example of dropping a guttural.

319. Knot=agls. Cnott=isl. Knuttr, Hnuttr=lat. Nodus. Cf. 605.

319 a. Know: cf. Νους. The norfolk people use the word thus: "He lost his know some days before he died, but he got it back just at the last and called to me."

320. Knit=agls. Cnytan = isl. Knyta = lat. Nectere. עָנד alligavit?.

320 a. Ladder=agls. Hladder, comes I think from †κελευθειν=†ελευθειν=mœsog. Leiþan. Lead appears to be causative of the same verb. In modern german Geleise 'a path' assigns no force to the preposition, but Geleit and Geleiten 'accompany' preserve its old sense 'con.' In agls. ʒelǽt occurs as 'the meeting of roads' in the singular (Genesis xxxviii. 21). Near Keswick is a path on the shores of the lake called Lord Derwentwaters ladder. Ladder we may conclude is κελευθος. Ελευθερος and Liber are participial derivatives of †ελευθειν, ελθειν.

321. Lift=mœsog. Hlifan=old lat. Clepere=Κλεπτειν. This is a border word; we retain Shoplifter. The root is Kal 'conceal;' and Latro is for †klatro, λαθειν for †κλαθειν.

322. Leme, Light, Lustre, Lightning, Lowe; agls. Liget, Leoma, Lig; mœsog. Liuhaþ, φως, Liuhtyan, λαμπειν, Lauhatyan, αστραπτειν, Lauhmuni, αστραπη, φλοξ; latin Lucem, Lucere, Lumen, Illustris, Lucerna,(Luna?); Λαμπειν, Λευκος, Αιγνυς (Aristophanes), Λυκιος (Απολλων), αμφιλυκη (νυξ), Λυχνος, Λευσσειν, Λυγδος (Lydius lapis); erse Leos 'light,' Lasaim 'I burn, light, kindle,' are all words which have lost their initial letter: for the present compare these with Gleam, Glow, Glare, Glance, Glitter, Glister, Gloss, Glass, Glede, Glim, Glimmer, Glimpse (these forms with 1 are diminutives), Gloze, Clean; agls. Gleam, Gleuge, Glære 'amber,' Glæs 'glass,' Glawan, Glitenan, Glisnian, Glistenung 'a flash of lightning,' Gled; mœsog. Glitmunyan, στιλβειν; norse Glóa, Gler; isl. Glama 'whiteness,' Glampi 'splendour,' at Glana 'to dawn,' Glans 'bright-

G 2

ness, lightning,' Glansi 'ray,' Glitnir 'bright,' at Glora 'to
glare,' Glossi 'a shining, a flame,' at Glossa 'to blaze,' at Glyssa
'to sparkle,' at Glytta, 'to glitter,' Glædur 'gledes,' Glæsir
'splendour;' in the Edda, Eygló 'ever glowing' is the suu;
erse Glium 'light, the sky, clean, plain,' Glor 'clear, clean;'
lat. Clarus; γληνη (?) and the old radical word Γελειν, λαμπειν,
αιθειν in Hesychios, of which Σελας is a sibilate form. Γελαν,
αυγην ἡλιου; Γλαινοι, τα λαμπρυσματα των περικεφαλαιων,
οἷον αστερες; Γλαυκος, λευκος; Γλαυσον, λαμπρον; Γλαυσσει,
λαμπει; Γλεφαρα, οφθαλμοι, l'ηνος, φαος (Hesych.); Γλαυ-
κιοων 'having flashing eyes,' Γληνη 'the pupil of the eye'
(Homer). Sanskr. Glau 'the moon;' welsh Golc 'splendour,'
with thirty similar welsh words. The fire lowes is quoted by
Hickes as a Yorkshire phrase.

> As rede as any gleede.
> Piers Ploughman, 903.
>
> Nis na moore to the mercy of God
> Than in the see a gleede.
> Id. 3056.
>
> O thou of Troy the lemand lamp of licht.
> G. Douglas, p. 48, 21.
>
> Be than the wallis lemand bricht and schire
> Of the unhappy Didois funerall fyre*.
> Id. 127. 21.
>
> And all maketh love, well I wote,
> Of which min herte is ever hote,
> So that I brenne as dothe a glede,
> For wrathe, that I may nought spede.
> Gower, lib. iii. p. 280.
>
> But I fare like the man that for to swele his flyes
> He stert into the bern and after stre he hies
> And goith about the wallis with a brenning wase
> Tyll it was at last that the leem and blaze
> Entrid into the chynys where the wheate was,
> And kissid so the evese that brent was all the plase†.
> History of Beryn, 1611.

* Mœnia respiciens quæ iam infelicis Elissæ Collucent flammis.
† Swele=burn, stre=straw, wase=wisp, chynys=chinks, evese=
eaves.

GUTTURALS IN ANLAUT CHANGED.   85

> Ther wende of him a lem that toward the north drou
> Evene as it were a launce, red and cler inou*.
>> Rob. Glouc. p. 548.

> Therinne lay that lady gent
> That after syr Launfal hedde yseut
> That lefsome lemede bryght.
>> Sir Launfal, 288.

> That brennand fire withouten ende so gretlye hit glowes
> That al the water in the warld may not sloke his lowes.
>> Myrour of Lewed Men, 1127.

323. LEAN = agls. Hlinian = Κλινειν = lat. clinare in compounds.

323 *a*. LICK, art. 139, is shown to have been originally †glick by the greek for 'tongue,' Γλωσσα = לשׁין with לחך 'licked,' the sibilants are of letter change.

324. LISTEN = agls. Hlystan = norse Hliðan = Κλυειν. The Heliand has Hlust 'the ear' = erse and gaelic Clúas = welsh Clust with Clyw 'hearing as a sense.' Cf. the second syllable in Auscultare. Scotch and english Lug 'an ear.'

325. LOAF = agls. Hlaf = norse Hleifr = mœsog. Hlaifs, Hlaibs seems connected with Κλιβανος, a portable oven, in which cakes were often baked upon the hearth (Acharn. 1123, Herodot. ii. 92). So Bread from agls. Brædan 'to roast, etc.'

326. LOOF 'palm of hand' = mœsog. Lofa = norse Lófi, which is apparently related to Λαβειν, may be akin to GLOVE = agls. Glof = isl. Glofi. Λαβειν seems akin to a Claw, Χηλη, Clasp, and they may be collateral forms of Grab, Grasp.

327. NAME, if really a form of Nomen, has lost a G, †gnomen, as in Agnomen, and, what is surprising, the sanskrit has lost its corresponding J. Nomen has its full form in Cognomentum. In the islandic we find our Ken = norse Kenna, used for 'name.' Hundingr het rikr konongr, við hann er Hundland kent. 'There was a powerful king called Hunding, after him is Hundland kenned, named.' See the semitic usage of בנה. B. H. in Kendr.

328. NAP = agls. Hnoppa (Somner, unde?). Cf. Γναφευς, Κναπτειν.

* Of a comet after the battle of Lewes.

329. NEIGH=agls. Hnægan=danish Gnegge=lat. Hinnire. Cf. NAG.

330. NETTLE=agls. Netle=Κνιδη. Hemp is a plant of the nettle tribe, and the forms Κνιδη, Κανναβις appear to arise from some common element. This remark will have some value in determining the affinities of skythic and hellenic.

331. NEVE (fist)=isl. Knefi may be related to Κονδυλος 'fist.' To Knefi refer KNEAD. By change of labial to corresponding liquid I suspect an affinity with agls. Niman 'take,' which however is Niman, not hniman, in the mœsogothic. Shakspeare uses Neve, " give me thy neafe, Monsieur Mustard Seed." Mids. N. Dr. iv. 1. " Sweet knight, I kiss thy neif." Henry IV. Pt. II. ii. 4.

332. NITS=agls. Hnite=swed. Gnete=Κονιδες.

333. NUT=lat. Nucem (acc.) = agls. Hnut = isl. Hnot, where the H points to an older K, found in the welsh Cneuen 'nut'=gaelic Cno.

334. QUEAN, QUEEN=agls. Cwen=Γυνη=mœsog. Kwens, Kwino=norse Kona, Kvaen, Kvân. See Ken, 315.

335. QUICK=mœsog. Kwius=lat. Vivus=agls. Cwic= norse Kvikr. In the oblique cases the norse retains the two original koppas, as acc. Kvikvan. The second guttural survives in lat. Vixi, Victum; the first in the mœsogothic. The affinities of this word are too numerous for this place; see art. 1024.

335a. QUENCH=agls. Cwencan is to cause to vanish, and is therefore an active answering to Vanescere; cf. Vanus, Κενος for †kwen-os. Sibilation might give Swoon=agls. Aswunan : cf. s'évanouir.

336. QUERN=agls. Cweorn, Cwyrn=mœsog. Kwairnus in the compound Asilu-kwairnus = norse Kvern. Cf. welsh Chwyrn, a WHIRL. These words are of the same origin as lat. Vertere, γυρος, etc. So Veru perhaps, 'a spit' as turning.

337. RAVEN=agls. Hrafen=norse Hrafn=lat. Corvus: cf. Cornix.

338. RIDDLE = agls. Hriddel = erse Creodhar = lat. Cri-

GUTTURALS IN ANLAUT CHANGED.   87

brum. Κρινειν 'judge' is also 'sift.' Cernere used poetically for 'see' is properly to 'distinguish' objects. Cernuus
is one who stoops with eyes straining to distinguish. The
sanskrit Krî 'cast, throw' is scarce near enough in sense.
The english word is half forgotten. To riddle with bullets is
to make as many holes as there are in a sieve. Riddle,
γριφος, is from Read, 'explain' = mœsog. Raidyan, 'ορθοτο
μειν,' Garaidyan 'διαταττειν.' For the relation of the N of
Κρινειν, to the D of Riddle, see art. 877.

339. RING = agls. Hring = norse Hringr = Κιρκος. Cf. Circulus. Compare the islandic forms in Kring. An iron ring
bevelled to receive a rope on board ship is a Kringle; and
hence the naval tale Tom Cringles log. Root †kwer, see art.
1026.

340. WALLOW = Κυλιειν = agls. Wealwian = mœsog. Walwian = Volvere. Cf. WELTER.

341. WASTE = agls. Westan = lat. Vastare. The mœsog.
Kwistyan, απολλυναι, seems the original form.

342. WHAT = agls. Hwæt = lat. Quod, Quid interrogative
and indefinite = erse Ciod Ciodh = welsh Peth = sanskr. Kat
obsolete (Wilson, Gram. p. 84). The anglosaxon does not
use this pronoun as a relative: nor Hwa = Who; What here
given is found in Somewhat. WHIT (not only feminine but
neuter) seems closely akin: NOT is compounded of na-whit;
and AUGHT of a-whit; so NOUGHT: the spelling with a G is
mere custom.

> The kerver schalle kerve the lordes mete,
> Of what kyn pece that he wylle etc.
>   The Book of Curtasye, 795.

343. WHEN = agls. Hwænne = mœsog. Hwan = erse Cuin
= welsh Pan = lat. Quando, Quum, Cum = sanskr. Kadâ.
The mœsog. and agls. words are sometimes indefinite, and so
in old english.

> But whan* she dotyth and wyl be nyse.
>   Lydgate, Minor Poems, p. 202.

344. WHETHER = agls. Hwæþer = mœsog. Hwaþar = lat.

* Sometimes.

Vter for †cuter, †quuter = Ποτερος, Ὁποτερος with labials = sanskr. Kater-as.

315. WHENCE = agls. Hwanon = mœsog. Hwadro = lat. Vnde for †cunde, †quunde as in Alicunde. The greek rejects N, Ποθεν: sanskr. is Kutas.

346. WHILE. Does this contain the same root as Tranquillus? The norse Hvîla is 'rest,' and the subst. is 'bed;' mœsog. Hweilan translates παυεσθαι, and Gaweilains ανεσις. (See art. 258.) There is nothing inconsistent in ώρα, αναπαυσις, and both norse and mœsogothic make the connexion etymologically close.

347. WHO = agls. Hwa, both as indefinite and interrogative = mœsog. Hwas, indef. or interrog. = Quis = sanskr. Kas = erse Ci = Τις where a guttural becomes a dental, and a labial is possible. As an example of the old indefinite, take—

> In Maie at the furthest twifallow* thy land.
> Much drout may else after cause plough for to stand:
> This tilth being done ye have passed the worst
> Then after who ploweth, plow thou with the furst.
>
> Tusser, May 23.

348. WHOM = agls. Hwæne = mœsog. Hwana = lat. Quem = sanskr. Kam.

349. As a corollary to these articles Qualis = WHAT-LIKE, Talis = THAT-LIKE, as Similis = Same-like, Puerilis is Boy-like, and the rest of the terminations in -lis, except where the former element is a verb, as agilis, habilis, facilis.

350. WORSE = agls. Wyrs = mœsog. Wairs = norse Verri. By analogy this should be Χερειων, Χειρων, could we assume the first letter to have been koppa, KW.

351. YAWN = agls. Ginnan = norse Gîna = Χανειν, Χασκειν = lat. Hiare, Hiscere. Compare Χαος, GAP, GAPE, Χασμα.

352. YESTERDAY = agls. Gæstran dæg = lat. Hesternus dies; cf. Heri = Χθες = sanskr. Hyas. The mœsogothic Gistradagis is a difficulty, for it is used for 'tomorrow' (Matt. vi. 30). Instead of meddling with the mœsogothic text, I should say that whether we look at the sanskrit or the latin Heri for keri,

---

* Twifallow is twice plough a fallow.

and Cras, there is a great similarity of form and perhaps the words are one.

353. Yet=agls. Git=Ετι. That Ετι was †κετι appears probable from the form Μηκετι, for to suppose the K inserted to match ουκετι is not admissible in the face of a better explanation.

354. Yard=agls. Gerd 'a yard, a twig.' Cf. Verberare, and art. 541.

355. Yon=agls. Geond=mœsog. Yains=isl. Inn=germ. Jener=Κεινος, Εκεινος. Hence Εκει seems to be for Εκειν. Cf. welsh Acw 'yonder.'

INLAUT AND AUSLAUT.

356. Acre = agls. Æcer = mœsog. Akrs = norse Akr = germ. Acker=lat. Ager=Αγρος. In all these languages, modern english excepted, the word is masc. and means field. The hebrew Ikkâr 'a digger, husbandman' hardly comes here, for Αγρος is not specially ploughed land, but rather includes unreclaimed ground, even so that αγριος is 'savage.'

357. Angle from agls. Angel 'a hook' = lat. Vncus, though a fish hook be Hamus. The form Αγκιστρον 'a hook,' since τρον signifies that wherewith an action is performed, supposes a verb †αγχιζειν 'to angle.'

358. Awn=mœsog. Ahana=islandic Ögn=Αχυρον=lat. Acus (aceris). The agls. is Egla. Forby gives in East Anglia "Haw, the ear of oats ; Havel the beard of barley ; Avel, the awn or head of barley." Avenæ 'oats' akin? Radix Ac, 'sharp.' In Oxfordshire they say Hoyl, as I myself learnt, in Dorset also as may be seen in Halliwell who prints Hoils ; but if the root be Ac 'sharp,' the true spelling is Hoyl. A saxon name for a hedgehog with its prickles is Igil.

358 a. Bays, berries (see Halliwell). Since the agls. had Beigbeam for Moses burning bush, Luke xx. 37, and Begbeam 'morus, mulberry tree' it must have had Beg, Beig 'a berry'=lat. Bacca. Berry in 627, 756.

359. Bray=breton Brengi=welsh Brefu. Cf. βρυχασθαι. "Επι ονων βρωμασθαι, λεγουσι δε αλλα σπανιον." Zenodotos ap. Valck. Ammon. p. 228. Βρωμασθαι seems to be

the frequentative of Fremere, of which the preceding are variations: cf. Rumorem, art. 931, Roar. That there is imitation no doubt, but the sounds also are of kin.

360. Day=agls. Dæg=mœsog. Dags=lat. Dies. Cf. Daw, Dawn. The sanskrit gives Div 'to shine,' as a subst. 1. 'heaven,' 2. 'sky' Divas, Divan, a day. From the sense 'heaven,' Deus; from 'sky,' sub dio. I assume the iota to be a vocalization of the teutonic G.

361. Egg=agls. Æg=isl. Egg neut.=erse Ugh=Ωον. For Ovum see 513.

362. Edge=agls. Ecg=norse Egg=lat. Acies. Egg (on) =agls. Eggian=norse Eggja, seems better referred to Quick. (1024.)

363. Eye=agls. Eage, Æg, in the Heliand Oga=norse Auga=mœsog. Augo=lat. Oculus=Οκος, Οκκος, the Bœotian hard form of †οψ, Οφθαλμος. Can we not to this root refer Ox=mœsog. Auhsa, the large eyed animal, a characteristic which is remarked in the homeric βοϜωπις. Another disguised form is in agls. Ætywian=mœsog. Ataugian 'to set before the eyes.' Ey in Anglesey, Bardsey, Chelsey (= agls. Ceolsig, from keels, barges), Sheppey, Molesey, Chertsey, Orkneys, and in the Aits or Eyets of the Thames, signifies 'island' and seems to be so called from a pictorial resemblance to an eye. Cf. norse Ey=agls. Æg, Ig 'island.' Compare danish Öje 'eye,' Öe 'island;' swedish Öga 'eye,' Ö 'island,' erse Iag 'island.'

> Blessed is the eye
> That's between Severn and Wye.—(Ray.)

" Hence the use of the word eye to designate any separate object in the midst of a mass of heterogeneous materials, as a small spot surrounded by an expanse of a contrasted colour.

> A. The ground is indeed tawney.
> S. With an eye of green in it.

Red with an eye of blue makes a purple. Boyle (Nares). So (?) we speak of the eyes of a potato, and in swiss the round cavities in a gruyere cheese, the drops of grease swimming on broth, the knots in wood are also called eyes.

Stalder." (Wedgewood.) A spring of water is called by the same name as eye in hebrew. The modern english Island is a mispelling of agls. Iglond, properly englished as pronounced, Eyland; on the other hand Isle=ital. Isola=lat. Insula. Some saxon scribes thought it, and some saxon scholars think it Ealand, 'water land' which appears to describe badly. Insula I should compare rather with the keltic Inis 'an island,' than with ' in salo.'

364. EKE = agls. Ecan = mœsog. Aukan = norse Auka = lat. Augere=Αὐξειν, Αὐξανειν, sibilate. Hawker, Huckster are reputed to come from this verb, and the learned editor of the Ormulum endorses the opinion.

365. FAGOT = Φακελος = lat. Fascis, sibilate. I do not know how this word came to us; the french probably had it from the same source as ourselves. The welsh have Ffagod but not the gaels.

366. I=o. e. Ik=agls. Ic=norse Ek=mœsog. Ik=Ego =Εγω=old greek Εγων=sansk. Aham.

> So the* ik, quod he, ful wel coude I him quite
> With blering of a proude milleres eye,
> If that me list† to speke of ribaudrie
> But ik am olde; me list not play for age;
> Gras time is don, my foddre is now forage.
> Chaucer, C. T. 3864.

The agls. Ic under the sibilate form Ich produced Icham, Ichill in the old language, and was cut down also to Cham, Chill.

> Bot thou haue merci on me
> For sorwe Ichil meself sle.
> Sir Gy of Warwike, p. 9.

> To hir Ichil tellen al mi thought
> Whi that Icham in sorwe brought.
> Id. p. 7.

> Chill tell thee what, good vellowe,
> Before the vriers went hence,
> A bushel of the best wheate
> Was zold vor vourteen pence.
> Plain Truth. Percy Reliques, vol. ii.

---

* The=agls. þeon=mœsog. þeihan προκοπτειν, prosper.
† Me list, impersonally, mihi placet.

Cham zure they were not voolishe
That made the masse, Che trowe.
Ibid.

"Chill not let go, zir, without vurther 'casion." "Chill pick your teeth, zir." King Lear.

367. Lay, Lie = Λεγειν, Λεγεσθαι, art. 140. Besides what was there cited we have forms with other gutturals, λεχος, αλοχος, λοχος, λεχω, λεκτρον. It would be heresy to turn ones eyes towards Lucina, the attendant of the Λεχω.

368. Mickle = agls. Micel = mœsog. Mikil (the neuter) = norse Mikill (masc.) = Μεγαλα (neut. pl.) = Magnus = sanskr. Mahat-as. The greek λ exhibits an adjectival, and the latin N a participial derivative from the verbal root, extinct in both those languages, but existing in the english: for May = agls. Magan = mœsog. Magan, δυνασθαι, ισχνειν = sanskr. Mah 'amplificare.' Hence Main, Might, Much.

The Fader hys God, for he may alle.
William of Shoreham, p. 142.

For the sense 'to be full grown' see art. 834. The verb also might mean 'to be well:' in Friesland at a wedding, Dass (=dat is) Breed en Bredigams Sünheit, dat's (=dat se) lang lave en wél mäge. 'Here's bride and bridegrooms soundhood (health), that they long live and well May.' (Outzen.)

369. Night = agls. Niht = mœsog. Naht (acc.) = Νυκτα (acc.) = lat. Noctem (acc.) = erse Nochd = welsh Nos (sibilate). The old sanskrit form Nak in the Veda (Max Müller) is found in Nactam ' noctu, by night,' while the usual word is of the sibilate form Nishâ.

370. Reach = agls. Ræcan = mœsog. in the compound ufrakyan, 'εκτεινειν' = germ. Reichen = dan. Række = swed. Räcka = Ορεγειν = lat. Regere in Porrigere and generally, for Regere means to keep in a straight line; Regula is 'a ruler,' Regio 'a reach of land,' also 'a border, a limit.' In regione viarum is 'in the reach of streets,' e regione 'in a direct line.'

371. Reech (Retch) = agls. Roccetan, Roceytan = lat.

Eructare = $Ερευγεσθαι$. Cf. germ. Rülpsen. Hence Rumen, Ruminare.

372. RICH. The agls. has Rice 'rich,' also 'a ruler,' also 'kingdom, rule;' Riesian, Rixian 'to rule:' the mœsogothic has Reiks '$αρχων$' (as subst.), $εντιμος$ (adj.), Reiki '$αρχη$;' the norse has Riki 'power,' Rikr 'powerful:' the german orientalists agree in the identity of Regem and Rajah, rejecting native notions, and the Vedas have Ranj 'to rule,' the usual sanskrit has Râj: the latin has Regere, Regem, Regnum, Regula, &c. The names Alaric, Theodoric = þiudareiks, retain the gothic root.

> Bring us to thin riche ther* is joie most.
> > Percy Soc. vol. iv. p. 94.

> Nammore maystrye nys hi3t† to hym
>   To be ine bredes lyche,
> Thane hym was ine the liche‡ of man
>   To kethen§ ous hiis ryche.
> > William of Shoreham, p. 20.

> And i sal tel yow swilk‖ tithandes
> That ye herd never none slike
> Rehereed in no kynges ryke.
> > Ywaine and Gawin, 140.

> Nis non his yliche
> In none kinges ryche.
> > King Horn, 19.

372 a. STY = agls. Stigan = mœsog. Steigan = norse Stîga = germ. Steigen = $Στειχειν$. Sty is in agls. and english generally 'mount,' but this is not exclusively its sense. STEP is but a labial form of the root, and STEEP. So Stairs from Stigan are also called Steps. STAGGER is a frequentative. The rungs of a ladder are stails, not stales.

373. TAKE = agls. Takan = norse Taka = $Τεταγειν$. Buttmann, Lexil. i. 162, long ago thus explained Iliad, A. 591: '$Ρῖψε ποδὸς τεταγὼν ἀπὸ βηλοῦ θεσπεσίοιο$; and O. 23: $ὂν δὲ λάβοιμι$ '$Ρίπτασκον τεταγὼν ἀπὸ βηλοῦ$.

---

* Ther = where. † Hi3t = It, a false spelling.
‡ Liche, body. § Kethen, make known.
‖ Swilk and Slike are alterations of the mœsog. Swaleiks, and Such is the modern form.

374. W<small>AG</small>=agls. Wagian=mœsog. Wagyan=lat. Vacillare, פוק?

375. W<small>AY</small>=agls. Wey=mœsog. Wigs=norsc Vegr=lat. Via. "Rustici etiam nunc quoque viam vcham appellant." Varro R. R. ap. Forcell.

376. W<small>AGON</small> is probably akin to Vehere, Vehiculum, which once had C, as in Vectum, Vectigal. Some bring in οχος, οχημα, in which is no appearance of the Vau: and the old idea, εχειν is sufficiently explanatory. The norse Aka with its aorist ôk, seems connected with Ok, Yoke; and as that root produces in greek ζυγον, ζευγος, it is more difficult to imagine a second form οχος: though words are Protean in their changes.

377. W<small>AKE</small>=agls. Wæcan=mœsog. Wakan=norsc Vaka =Vigilare. The root is in all likelyhood Quick, 'alive;' to be awake is to be alive: on this root the latin formed an adjective by the adjectival L, Vigil, which produced the latin verb. W<small>ATCH</small>, W<small>AITS</small> are other forms of Wake.

<blockquote>
The corses, which with torch light
They waked had there all that night*.
Chaucers Dream, 1906.
</blockquote>

378. Y<small>OKE</small>=lat. Iugum=Ζυγον=agls. Geoc, Ioc=isl. Ok =mœsog. Yukuzi=sansk. Yug-an, Yuj. Ζευγος=mœsog. Yuk. Cf. Iungere=welsh Ieuo. The radix is Two, and probably the saxon form of it, Twegen: this I say, with the sanskrit Yu, iungere, before my eyes.

LABIALS INTERCHANGED.

379. The labials, P letters, or π, β, φ, V and W are interchanged among themselves.

380. It is to be observed that P is scarcely a teutonic letter, though frequent in old high german. The words which commence with P in the mœsogothic are almost all adaptations or proper names: no character had been appropriated to it in the runic norse alphabet, but the letter when it occurs appears as a dotted B: in the elder Edda only three words begin with

* Hence Irish wakes.

it. Many P's in the inlaut or auslaut as in Sleep, Speak had older forms, as Swaf, Swee. The latin V was a consonantal U, and had the sound of W; one character represented the vowel in either case. The english V commonly marks latinisms, so that Waste and Devastation, Wine and Vintage come to us by different channels; but a few exceptions appear to exist, as Vineyard, Vails, Vat, Vinewed, Vie.

381. A few words upon the homeric digamma are required here. Of the nature of Alexandrian criticism some idea may be formed from the name given to this letter, based upon its shape Ϝ: yet the letter still lived in some of the old dialects, and Alexandria had one quarter of the city devoted to Jews, nor was it very distant from Sidon and Tyre, which lent their alphabets to Hellas. The time is past when one need put faith in Heyne, who, it is evident, had paid little attention to this subject; for he begins his big book by prefixing the Vau to the augment, as Ϝηνδανε, and it does not dawn in upon him, till well on in the Iliad, that if Ϝανδανειν begins with a consonant its augmented form must be εϜανδανεν. This blunder, subsequently corrected, still blots the pages of many an edition with the name of a scholar on the titlepage. Nor has he even applied the instruction derivable from the forms of the latin, so fully as he might. To accuse him of having learnt nothing from the mœsogothic or the norse would be unreasonable; yet it would be equally unreasonable to follow him. Nor is anything equal to the occasion, as far as I know, to be gained from the recent edition of the Iliad by Immanuel Bekker, who goes to work in the spirit of the last century, or, as he says himself, cautiously.

382. The evidence for the existence of the digamma in any old greek word is such that we must remain ever watchful. Not even in inscriptions let us put full confidence; thus in his work on pottery Mr. Birch (ii. 19) mentions that vases have ϜΕΡΑΚΛΕΣ and ϜΥΨΙΠΥΛΗ, and believes the first letter to be the digamma: no one, who has a tolerable portion of inquisitiveness, can doubt but that here is a form of the He, H, or aspirate. In a Lokrian inscription, ὅτι 'whatever' is stamped on the brass Ϝοτι; the inscription is among the most ancient

in dialect, whatever it be in date; but it is strange if the W have remained in this instance, while it had disappeared in Homer. Therefore, though ὅτι = quod-quid, it is probable the stamping was in error and that a He was intended. Then again it is by no means certain that usage was uniform in this letter: on the contrary there is sufficient proof of variety. Nor is it altogether fair to assume that, when a letter has been lost, that letter must be Vau. In Homer's time the disappearance of S initial, perhaps also of the inlaut, was growing and strengthening; in some words as Συς, Ὑς it was established. In the words which depend on the root †ϵικϵιν, be like, the evidence of other languages is in favour of the restoration of L, not W, †λϵικϵιν 'be like;' though this is not to be regarded as a very probable conjecture. The instruction derivable from grammarians is on the whole trustworthy, but it is of various degrees of applicability; thus the words in Hesychios, which have a superabundant gamma, do not stand on a good footing as evidence.

383. Let us remark in the first place that the digamma may be vocalized, and, while we expect a υ as in κυνα, γυρος, we find an ο as in οικος, οινος, οιδα. Thus, at art. 728, Withy, Ϝιτεα is compared with οισυη, a word which seems to have no digamma in the only line in which it occurs. Now if ο be a substitute for the Vau, so that Ϝι = οι, then Ϝοικος, Ϝοιδα, Ϝοινος are incorrectly written, and should be Ϝικος, Ϝιδα, Ϝινος: but see 231. Some examples of an α compensative of a digamma may be found. Thus engl. Wort = mœsog. Waurts appears in Or-chard = mœsog. Aurti-gards. Our Errand comes from mœsog. Airus, which is in the same stage of change as the goddess Ϝιρις, the celestial messenger; we retain the W in Word: Α in Airus is therefore a compensation for the Vau. The Α in Αιων, Αιει, from Ϝιϝ-end, is a greek example. There are I believe some examples in greek of an intrusive Θ, as εσθλος for εσλος, εδειν, εσθειν, εσθιειν; and Λισθεσθαι may be connected with the root Wit, by a somewhat circuitous process: Λ compensative, θ intrusive, σ to prevent concurrence of dentals. I suspect the root Ϝιϝ in εξαιφνης, αιφνιδιος, αιψα. If in οιδα omicron is for Vau, then is also epsilon in ειδεναι

LABIALS INTERCHANGED.   97

and the other moods: also in Εικοσι = Viginti, in Εικειν = germ. Weichen, Ερεικειν = Break, Wreck, Ερεσθαι as connected with germ. Fragen, Ερευγεσθαι with βρογχος, angls. Hraca, Hreak, Sereare, Ερυθρος with βροδον, and the long syllable in Ειπειν may be accounted for. Secondly, since at least a noninitial Vau might become a vowel υ, so conversely the υ becomes a consonant Vau. Hence while the sanskrit and latin invite us to read Νηϝος, yet the spelling of the nom. Νηυς, and of the dat. Νηυσιν must not be disturbed. Such words as εὕαδε are not to be altered to εϝαδε, *e. g.* P. 647 : ἐν δὲ φάει καὶ ὄλεσσον ἐπεί νύ τοι εὕαδεν οὕτως. On the contrary there can be no objection to καϝϝαξαις for καναξαις since the unassimilated form was κατ-ϝαξαις. Observe that the vowel in Sol 'the sun,' arises out of the digamma; ηϝελιος (in Hesychios Αβελιος, ήλιος, Κρητες) = mœsog. Sauil = by contraction Sol. Again, as in the semitic languages, and in some greek examples, κλαιειν, κλαυσαι, καιειν, καυσαι, the vowels υ and ι interchange, so, similarly, Vau becomes ι. Therefore lat. Novus and eng. New give us Νεϝος; but νειατος, νειαιρα must remain as they are. It is by no means clear that a word beginning with a digamma did not also drop it. In a criticism at art. 985, upon ἑκαστος, I have shown, to my own conviction at least, that having regard to its origin this word could be written either with or without digamma : we know that in the Bœotian inscriptions it has none. Other words may be similarly affected. To speak more generally, however, it is possible that in Homers age the language might be in transition and it might be indifferent in many cases whether the digamma were used or not. This is a distasteful supposition ; it seems the refuge of ignorance ; and some of the examples are not arguments in favour of it, but to be otherwise explained. It is a very different thing to show that the language itself, comparing century with century, was subject to movements and alteration, and to make the same visible during the lifetime of a poet. (For Homers existence need not yet be disbelieved.) Therefore, though in Sword, Answer, Woolwich, Greenwich, Warwick, Berwick, we drop the true and written W, these changes do not apply well to a single poem. If we admit that there was a time of uncertainty, yet one man probably spoke one manner of speech, and there are no such broad lines of distinction in the Iliad as to make us recognize different forms of one dialect. This however belongs to the history of the Vau, that the word ἱδρως, which every one now knows to have commenced in latin, english and sanskrit with Sw, has in the homeric poems no trace of an initial consonant (Δ. 27?). Another such word is Ϝιδιος, which certainly comes from Σϕε, sanskrit Swa, as †σϕιδιος, like μαψιδιος, μινυνθαδιος, and in the Lokrian brass and Heraklean Tables is found Ϝιδιος, with a possibility of reading it in Pindar, Olymp. xiii. 49: ἐγω δε Ϝιδιος. This has no consonant in Homer. I think I find an example of a similar process in Αἷρα 'a hammer,' a word used by Kallimachos. Antiquarian researches connect the notion of a flint pebble and a hammer, Σϕαῖρα and Σϕῦρα, and Αἷρα seems to be Σϕαῖρα without the initials. We have an example in our Errand, which is allied to Swear, Answer. Dionysios and Priscianus (p. 546 b.) both assure us that the name of Homers heroine was Ϝελενη, whereas the scansion of his lines makes her Ἑλενη. One word seems to be transitional in the homeric pages. In ὈϜις, Ewe, the iota is not compensative, but of the root, and the digamma must have disappeared before the two vowels could make one syllable in the contracted form of the word as οἰων, which is common in Homer. Another word offers itself, but the argument from it will have slender force. To derive οιωνος a bird, from οιος 'alone' is a whimsical example of the notions of lexicographers. Suppose it comes from Avis, as οιων from Ovium, then it also has lost the Vau, or lost it in most cases.

384. The authority of inscriptions gives us Ϝαξος, that is by compensation, Ὀαξος, a city in Krete standing on a precipice and connected it may be with Ϝαγνυμι: also Ϝελατη=Ελατεια; Ϝρατρα=ρητρα; Ϝαλειοι=Ηλειοι; ΕυϜαιοιοι=Ευαιοι; Ϝετεα=ετη; Ϝεπος=επος; Ϝαργον=εργον; Ϝετας=ετης; Ϝαδων, Ϝαναξιων proper names; Ϝαρνων=Αρνων, proper name; Ϝισοτελιαν confirming the presumed Ϝισος; Ϝεικατι=εικοσι; Ϝεξ=ἑξ; ΔιϜι=Διΐ; ΑιϜας=Αιας; Ϝιδιος=ιδιος; κωμαϜυδος = κωμῳδος; τραγαϜυδος = τραγῳδος; κιθαραϜυδος = κιθα-

ρῳδος; αυλαϝυδος = αυλῳδος, from all which αϝειδω, αϝηδων are clear; ϝασστος = αστος; ϝοικεειν = οικεειν; αιϝει=αιει; κλεϝος=κλεος.

385. The kindred languages combine their testimony with the older versification in ϝηδυς, ϝανδανειν, ϝαστυ, ϝεαρ (lat. Ver: O. 307, τ. 519); ϝειδον (Vidi); ϝειδος; ϝεισομαι, ϝοιδα; ϝεικοσι; ϝεικειν (norse Vikja, germ. Weichen, agls. Swician); ϝεκαστος or ἑκαστος, see art. 977; ϝεκυρος ϝεκυρη or Σϝεκυρος, Σϝεκυρη (sanskr.); ϝελισσειν with its cognates; ϝενετοι, Veneti; ϝεννυμι, ϝεσθης; ϝου, ϝοι, ϝε=†σφου, †σφοι, σφε, sui, sibi, se, with its adjective ϝεος=†σφεος, suus; ϝεπος, ϝειπον; ϝεργον; ϝειρω, ϝερεω; ϝεσπερος; ϝεστια; ϝις; ϝινες (= Venæ?); ϝιον; ϝιτεα; ϝιφι; ϝοικος; ϝοινος; ϝοπα = Vocem; οϝις; ὑλϝη; ωϝον.

386. Conclusions drawn from homeric versification alone are not very secure, since other initial letters, S, D, T, L, G, K are omitted as words change their forms; and all along lies the possibility of hiatus, congenial to the ionic dialect, and certainly existing in the text as we have it.

387. From the presence of a υ in Πηλευς, Ατρευς, we may conjecture Πηλεϝιδης, Ατρεϝιδης, which were long ago observed to be quadrisyllabic, Πηληϝα, Ατρεϝος (one passage only is in the way), and so of all substantives in -ευς. From the υ in θευσομαι, θοϝος.

388. Grammatical tradition testifies to ϝειραναν, δαϝιον, Δημοφαϝων, Λαϝοκαϝων, ϝανηρ, in the first and last unexpectedly. Of ϝειρηνη see 1016.

389. The labials often become vowels; thus τεθηπα, of which the imperfect tenses have the form θαμβειν, makes the passive participial θαυμα; eng. Swamp=germ. Sumpf; Reversus = Rursus; aves capit make aucupem; ab fert make aufert; favere, fautor; soluo in solutus, solvo; volvere, volumen; κυνα, Hunt from †kwan; γυρος from †kwer: Baptismus=span. Bautismo; debitor=span. deudor; capital=span. Caudal. Chaucer has Sote for Sweet, Sustren for Swestern= Sisters.

390. Among the liquids the labial M belongs to and precedes the labials, and when concurrent, if either changes, the

other changes with it. Thus in turning Lamed into greek, a β was required to facilitate the pronunciation, Lambda; in Longobardus, Lombard, †lonbard was impossible. Στρεφειν= †στρεγειν, but †στρεγειν required Στρογγυλος with NG, while Στρεφειν required Στρομβος. In turning Samech into greek a transposition was the resource, Sigma. Τυπτειν is related to timbrel, thump, τυμπανον, as Step to Stamp, Trip to Tramp. Quinque has N according to rule before the guttural, so has πεντε, but πεμπαζειν changes both at once. When εν, παν, συν, in which the N is radical, or παλιν precede π, β, φ, the N becomes M. When cannabis loses a vowel it becomes hemp.

391. M exchanges with the labials as Hiemem, χειμερινος, hibernus; μυρμηκες, formicae; μολυνειν, polluere; μορφη, forma; ματαιος, fatuus; promulgare = provulgare (Festus); dirimere, diribitor, diribēre; tremere, trepidus; σεβειν, σεμνος; ερεβος, ερεμνος; germ. Himmel=engl. Heaven; murmur cf. purr; μολιβδος, plumbum; λημη, lippire; μεμβρας = βεμβρας (Athenaeos, P. 287); camera from cavus; μετα = πεδα; Servius says forcipes a forbicapes nam forbum est calidum (Æn. viii. 351, Voss.), so that it=formum; πολλοι= multi?; πολυ=μαλα?; pap=mamma?; marble from marmor: creep, worm: palma, palpare: germ. Reif=Rime (frost), Tervagant=Termagant, Malmsey=Malvoisie, Cormorant=Corvorant.

392. The affinity of M with the labials may be understood by trial, since we find it is pronounced with the lips. In the grammatical systems of the sanskrit and arabic it accompanies the labial mutes, and in the keltic languages is constantly changing places with them. Thus welsh Anfesurol = immeasurable; Anfoesol = immoral (moes = mores); Enfil, Anifel = animal; Arfal is a toll on grinding Meal; Difynio = to mince; Dof=domare, Ufel=humilis; Melfed=velvet. In irish M is the eclipsing letter to B, so that the nominative singular may begin with B and the genitive plural with M, as Bád, 'a boat,' gen. pl. na mbád. Thus again in the breton at Vannes 'bellows' is Bégin (cf. moesog. Balgs, bag), but elsewhere in Brittany it is Mégin. Vindemia became french Vendange

and passed into breton as Bendem, Mendem; Mint=breton Ment or Bent (Legonidec). So our Sumersault, or Sumerset = spanish Sobresalto. In old english (agls.) MSS. may be occasionally observed some false readings, as mæstm for wæstm, which show that the letters are more nearly allied than they seem to us; yet we say Molly or Polly, Meg and Peggy. The arabic nicely distinguishes M as a nasal labial.

393. Examples of the interchange of labials among themselves are κρυπτειν, κρυβδην; επτα, εβδομος, observing here how two tenues become two medials at once; Φρυγες, Βρυγες; Βερενικη, Φερενικη; fascinare, βασκαινειν; θριαμβος, triumphus; rufus, rubere; parere, ferre; portare, ferre; canopus, κανωβος; palpebra, βλεφαρον; pascere, βοσκειν; Alpes, albus, αλφος; nubere, nuptiæ; populus, publicus; scribere, scripsit; vis, βια; balæna, φαλαινα; ambo, αμφω; gibbus, κυφος; glaber, γλαφυρος; nebula, νεφελη; nubes, νεφος; orbus, ορφανος; scribere, γραφειν; suber, συφαρ; figere, πηγνυναι; umbilicus, ομφαλος; ab, απο; Absyrtus, Αψυρτος; Arabs, Αραψ; Byrrhia, Burrus from πυρ; buxus, πυξος; carbasus, καρπασος; sub, υπο; procurator, broker (?).

> He waketh all the night and all the day
> He kembeth his lockes brode and made him gay,
> He woeth hire by menes and brocage
> And swore he wolde ben hire owen page.
> Chaucer, C. T. 3376.

Præpositus, provost; episcopus, bishop; duellum by dropping D, †uellum and bellum; blench, flinch.

> And therewithal he blent and cried, A!
> As though he stongen were unto the herte.
> Chaucer, C. T. 1082.

Bent = pent 'sloping,' as in penthouse;

> And downward from an hill under a bent,
> Ther stood the temple of Mars armipotent.
> Chaucer, C. T. 1981.

Plat = flat (Chaucer, C. T. 792, 1847); Hispalis, Seville; βρογχος, φαρυγξ; ervum, οροβος; averruncare, απερυκειν; ovis, opilio; bubalus, buffalo; buffoon, ital. buffa, beffa, rebuff,

ital. sbuffare, puff; basin, vas; William, Billy; episcopus,
évêque; wake, bivouac; botch, patch; purse, bursar; prove,
probare; devil, diabolus; καλυπτειν, καλυβη; κρυπτειν,
κρυφα, κρυβδην; Tibur, Tivoli; βρεμει, fremit; rapere, ravish:

> O had I Virgil's verse or Tully's tongue,
> Or raping numbers like the Thracian's song!
> W. Browne.

ANLAUT.

394. BAG = mœsog. Balgs, ασκος (on the omission of L see
895), found also in the compound matibalgs 'meat bag,' πηρα
= lat. Pellis 'skin of an animal' (used as a bag, a water or
wine skin) = FELL. A large number of forms are akin to this:
BELLY, BELLOWS, BUDGET, BILGE, BILLOW, BULGE, BOLSTER;
probably also POKE (a pig in a poke), POUCH, POCKET, POACHER
(with a bag), PAUNCH; lat. Follis, Bulga, Vulva. The affinity
of the several senses may be illustrated by the various meanings
of the norse Belgr: 1. pellis inflata animalis cuiuspiam; 2.
follis; 3. bulga, a leathern sack; 4. venter. It has lately been
argued that the english word Bag is the islandic Baggi rather
than a teutonic word; yet it was the older form balg which
produced the islandic bagg according to the rule prevailing in
that language for the assimilation of concurrent consonants.
The antiquity of the L is visible in welsh Bol, gaelic and irish
Bolg 'belly.'

395. BALL, BULLET, BALLOON, BILLIARDS, BOLL "and the
flax was bolled," το δε λινον σπερματιζον, LXX., und der Flachs
Knoten gewonnen: the hebrew is uncertain. Cf. germ. Bolen
'to revolve,' swed. Bol 'a ball,' dutch Bol 'head,' lat. Pila
'ball,' Pilula, 'pill,' Bulla 'a hollow globe of gold worn by
patrician boys,' also 'a bubble,' Bullire, Bulbus, and agls.
Beallucas 'testiculi.' Wachter compares πολος, sky as re-
volving, whence Polus, pole; πολευειν 'revolve,' πολειν drive
round. The saxon for Boll is perhaps hidden in the gloss Bul,
bulla; cf. welsh Bul, a seed vessel.

396. BANE = agls. Bana = mœsog. Banya ἑλκος = norse Bani
'a violent death,' Ben 'a deadly wound' are to be compared with φονος (J. Grimm). If φονος be from †φενειν,

επεφνον, and this mean strike like lat. †fendere in defendere, offendere, secondly 'kill,' the parallel is close.

397. BARGAIN 'battle,' apparently from norse at Berja= lat. Ferire. "They foyne at uthir and eggis to bergane," Gawin Douglas, p. 142. 8. Immiscentque manus manibus pugnamque lacessunt. "Of wikkit bargane tharein the furius rage, Id. book i. p. 22. 9.

398. BASKET=lat. Bascauda, a gallic word, seems to be Fiscus, Fiscella.

399. BE = agls. Beon = germ. Ich bin = sanskr. Bhu = lat. Fui 'was'=Εφυ 'was,' Φυναι 'to be'=erse Bim 'I am.' The welsh Byw 'to live,' seems to connect it with Vivere.

400. BEAR = agls. Beran, occasionally Feran = mœsog. Bairan = norse Bera = macedonian Βερειν = Φερειν = Ferre. BURDEN, BURTHEN, BAIRN, BIRTH, Φορτιον, Φορειν, Portare, Parere, Partus, Parens are all of the same original.

401. BEAVER=agls. Beofer=isl. Bifr=lat. Fiber. The similarity to Faber 'a carpenter' is note worthy.

402. BEECH=angls. Boc=lat. Fagus=φηγος. Some have doubted whether fagus be really beech : the glossary of Ælfric has Fagus, boc, and the spanish Haya, representing according to the spanish rules of letter change Fagus, is beech. Book= angls. Boc has been supposed to be so called from the beechen material: another conjecture might be based upon its similarity to Pagina which was originally 'pannel, tablet.' Yet since the mœsogothic Boka means γραμμα a letter, and since the Heliand has Bôcan, 'signum, portentum,' it is certain that both these notions are errors. It seems the word belongs to Beck, Beckon, Beacon.

403. BECK=agls. Bece=isl. Bekkr=according to J.Grimm, Πηγη 'spring'(?).

404. BEE=agls. Beo=isl. Bí=lat. Apis. We know episcopus, bishop; aper boar ; but letters are lost off old skythian roots, not from latin words only. Observe that Honey=agls. Hunig is very remote. We have not the greek word for bee, since μελισσα is an adjectival formation on μελι and means the honey-fly. The gaelic Beach is no safe guide, since -ach is a suffix in gaelic : the welsh is Cacynen.

405. BEND=agls. Bendan. Cf. lat. Pandus, BANDY. The games Bandy, Hockey are played with Bent, Hooked sticks.

406. BERE, BARley = agls. Bere = mœsog. †baris, the assumed root of Barizeins, κριθινος (cf. also Fraiw 'seed'=isl. Frá, Frio 'seed'), cf. lat. Hordeum for fordeum, 'barley,' Far 'a kind of bread corn,' Πυρος 'a sort of wheat.' בַּר 'corn' mostly as separated from the chaff, yet in Ps. lxv. 14 still in field. Βορα 'food?'. Since BEER is made from barley the connexion seems close.

407. BID=agls. Biddan 'bid or pray'=mœsog. Bidyan=norse Biðja=lat. In-vitare. Is Invitus, Unbidding? The mœsogothic seems to have once contained a parallel form, †weitan of the same sense as Bidyan occurring in Inweitan, John xii. 20, and producing Witoþs 'the law;' a trace of this root remains in isl. Veiting, Veitsla 'convivium.'

408. BILL = agls. Bill = german Beil = erse Biail, welsh Bwyell. Cf. Πελεκυς?

409. BIND = agls. Bindan = mœsog. Bindan = norse Binda =lat. Vincire=sanskr. Bandh.

409 a. BIRCH=agls. Beorc seems related to Virga, Verberare. Beorkes abiden in Laȝamon ii. 438, may be Virga.

410. BLEACH, BLAZE, BLAST, BLANK, BLANCH, FLUSH, BLUSH, BLOWZY; with the anglosaxon Blac 'pallidus,' Blæcan 'bleach,' Blæse 'fax,' Blætesung 'coruscatio' (germ. Blitzen), Blican 'fulgere,' belong to the latin Flamma, Fulgere, Fulmen, and the greek Φλεγειν, Φλοξ, περι-φλευειν 'to singe' (Nubes 396, Herodot. V. 77). It is remarkable that BLACK is of this group, for it represents the latin Fuligo, soot, the deposit of flame: the agls. is Blac and norse Blakkr. In the same manner Αιθαλος, Αιθαλη, Λιγνυς, greek words for soot, are derivatives of Λιθειν, Φλεγειν 'to burn, blaze.' None of these words are found in the limited collection of mœsogothic roots which have come down to us; but Blika 'to shine' occurs in the elder Edda. A more peculiarly saxon word occurs in Swart, from which Soot may be formed by vocalization and assimilation. The devon Blunk 'snow flake' may belong to the group.

411. Blister=Φλυκταινα : this engl. form has sibilation; Bladder is the same thing without : see Blow.

412. Blossom = agls. Blosma = lat. Flos. It believed by the german etymologs that Florem is an alteration of Floscm: see SR, 624. The mœsog. Bluma stands (Matth. vi. 28) for κρινον, lily: it seems closly akin to Bloom=isl. Blomi=germ. Blume. The verb Blow=agls. Blowan=germ. Blühen=lat. Florere=sanskr. Full. Cf. cornish Blodyn 'a flower.'

413. Blow=agls. Blawan=lat. Flare. The mœsog. †blesan found in the compound Ufblesan=norse Blàsa=agls. Blæsan (Lyc)=germ. Blasen, produces to us Blast, Blazon.

414. Blow. The mœsogothic Bliggwan, κατακοπτειν, μαστιγουν, δερειν, φραγελλουν, ῥαβδιζειν, shows the affinity of Flog, Flagellum, Affligere, Confligere, Πληγη, Πλησσειν. Flail is rather the flogger than the flyer. Blow, Flog are not as yet found in agls. Junius says old dutch Blouw is 'colaphus.' Blouwe alapa, Blouwen alapas impingere (Kilian) : see 118.

415. Boar=agls. Bar, Eofor=germ. Eber=lat. Aper= Καπρος. Cf. Porcus, porca, verres=sansk. Varâhas.

416. Bore = agls. Boran = germ. Bohren = isl. Bora = lat. Forare: cf. Foramen. Connected with Per.

> A sunne beme ful bright
> Schone opon the quene
> At a bore
> On her face so schene.
> Sir Tristrem, p. 156.

417. Borough=agls. Burh=Πυργος? The original sense is that of defence, as in Beorgan 'to protect,' whence Borh, Borrow 'security, pledge,' Borgian 'borrow, lend,' i.e. on security.

> With that ye me from deth borwe,
> And forgeve me youre covel will.
> Kyng Alisaundre, 4523.

> To this forward* he borows fand
> The best lordes of al that land.
> Ywaine and Gawin, 1953.

---

* Forward, 'promise.'

> Tary we no longer here;
> We shall hym borowe by gods grace,
> Though we bye it full dere.
>
>   Adam Bel, 200.

> Yet goe to the court, my lord, she sayes,
> And I myself will ryde wi' thee:
> At court then for my dearest lord
> His faithful borrowe I will bee.
>
>   The Rising in the North, 25.

> And therfore hath she laid her faith to borow.
>
>   Chaucer, Troilus and Creseide, 963.

I am tempted to add here that the old saxon root Beorgan 'protect' may be recognized in a warm BERTH, a snug Berth, properly †beorgþ, which is not to be found in the books.

> Yong broome or good pasture, thy ewes doe require,
> Warm barth and in safety their lambs do desire.
>
>   Tusser, January.

where the annotator has "A Barth is commonly a place near a farm house well sheltered." "Tis a poor barthless and motherless child, her said" (Devonshire Dialogue, p. 19). Hence we see also that BARTON is Barth-tun.

418. BOTH. The agls. is Ba, gen. Begra, dat. Bam, acc. Ba: the mœsog. is Bai and also Baioþs = norse Baðir = sanskr. Ubhau = lat. Ambo = $A\mu\phi\omega$. See art. 788.

419. BOTTOM = agls. Botm = $\Pi\upsilon\theta\mu\eta\nu$. The agls. is applied to vessels, as tunnan botm, a tuns bottom (Ælfric, Gl.). Small vallies are called Bottoms: cf. $Bo\theta\rho o\varsigma$ 'ditch,' $Ba\theta\upsilon\varsigma$ 'deep.'

420. BOX = lat. Buxus = $\Pi\upsilon\xi o\varsigma$. Borrowed?

421. BRAN in the first two letters seems connected with lat. Furfures.

422. BREECHES = lat. Braccae, a gallic word, derived by the keltic lexicographers from welsh, gaelic, irish Breac 'particoloured.' Cf. lat. Varius, and Brindled. The Edda has Brôk, plural Brœkr, the upper part of hose from the hip to the knee.

423. BROOK = agls. Brucan 'eat' (rather say 'swallow') = $B\rho\upsilon\kappa\epsilon\iota\nu$ (as Trachin. 987), cf. $B\rho o\gamma\chi o\varsigma$, $\alpha\nu\alpha\beta\rho o\xi\epsilon\iota\epsilon$, $\beta\iota\beta\rho\omega\sigma\kappa\epsilon\iota\nu$ = lat. Vorare, devorare. In a secondary sense, agls.

Brucan = germ. Brauchen 'use' = lat. Frui 'enjoy;' but the original sense remains in Frumen the larynx, Frustum 'a morsel' = scotch Brok = germ. Bruch, and Frumentum. Cf. Ασφαραγον, Φαρυγγα, Βρογχον. "Surely there can be nothyng so bitter but wysedome would brooke it for so gret a profyte" (Sir Thomas More, Works, p. 72, in Richardson).

> Sore sicke in bed, her colour all forgone
> Bereft of stomake, savor and of taste,
> Ne could she brooke no meat but brothes alone.
> Sackville, Induction, etc.

To brook an affront = to swallow it. In this sense take

> Senne hys swete and lyketh
> Wanne a man hi deth,
> And al so soure hy bryketh
> Wane ho venjaunce yseth.
> William of Shoreham, p. 102.

(Lyketh = placet; the construction is, it swallows sour, as if, it eats bitter, it tastes nice : Syn, sin, is usually fem. in agls. and hi, hy = agls. hig, feminine). According to the usual transmutations another form would be agls. Frettan = germ. Fressen, whence our Fret. BROWSE I take to be a sibilation of Brook, which is used for bite as well as eat, swallow. The agls. Byrgian 'taste' is closely akin to Brucan.

424. BROTHER = Frater. See change of dentals.

425. BROW = mœsog. Braw = agls. Bræw = norse Brún = erse and gaelic Brá, Brai = Οφρυς = sanskr. Bhrû.

The norse has also Bra 'eyelash, eyelid,' and from the connexion with οπ- the greek form seems the oldest.

426. BROWN = agls. Brun, from Brennan and πυρ. Similarly Πυρρος 'red,' Πυρραμος = Πριαμος, proper names like our Rufus.

427. BURN = anglos. Bærnan = mœsog. Brinnan = norse Brenna. Cf. BRIGHT = agls. Beorht = mœsog. Bairhts = norse Biartr. Cf. Πυρ and perhaps lat. Vrere, and perhaps burere in Comburere (so Wachter).

428. BUTT = lat. Petere ? Cf. petulcus, petulans ?. The word is not found in the agls. dict.

429. Fare has been already compared with Φερειν, Φερεσθαι; it has been also set beside πορος, περαν, πορευειν, πορευεσθαι.
430. * * * = agls. Peorð (Feorð?) = norse Frata = germ. Furzen = Παρδειν. The sanskrit in one form sibilates the initial letter as if a guttural had preceded the forms recited, Sharddh-as, root Shridh. The latin rejects R.

> Ac for I kan neither taboure ne trompe
> Ne telle no gestes,
> Farten ne fithelen
> At festes, ne harpen,
> Jape ne jogele,
> Ne gentilliche pipe,
> Ne neither saille ne saute
> Ne synge with the gyterne
> I have no goode giftes
> Of thise grete lordes.
> Piers Ploughman, 8486.

The word will not be found in agls. dictionaries, but it exists in the Runclay (14) under the form Peorð, baffling Wilhelm Grimm. There can be little doubt but that for the sake of the alphabet a word which usually began with F was assigned to P.

> Peorð byð symble plega and hleahtor
> Wlancum [on middum] þær wigan sittað
> On beorsele bliðe æt somne.

'A —— is always play and laughter amid men where warriors sit in the beerhall blithe together.'

431. Father = Πατηρ = Pater. See dentals.
432. Fee = agls. Feoh 'money, etc.' = mœsog. Faihu, χρηματα, κτηματα, αργυριον = norse Fê = germ. Vieh = lat. Pecus 'cattle,' joined with pecunia 'money.' In the agls. the old sense of 'cattle' was so fixed that king Alfred in his Orosius (e. g. III. vii. III. ix.) distinguishes inanimate wealth, as "liegend feoh," 'lying fee,' not walking fee. Pott truly observes that Pecus must not be connected with πεικειν, πεκτειν, ποκος, since cattle not wool bearing are included in the term. Pascere may do as well. So sanskr. Pashu 'pecus,' Push 'pascere.' Vails = lat. Peculium both derivative forms. This last parallel I owe to Dr. Latham and Professor Key.

> Robin sat on the gude grene hill
> Keipand a flock of fie.
> > Robin and Makyne, Percys Reliques, vol. ii.

> To a hart he let renne ;
> xii fosters* dyscryed hym then,
> That were kepars of that fee.
> > Sir Tryamore, 1054.

> Solinus sayis in Brettany
> Sum steddys† growys sa habowndanly
> Of gyrs, þat sum tym, [but] þair fe
> Fra fwlth of mete refrenyt be,
> Dair fwde sall turne þame to peryle,
> To rot or bryst or dey sum quhyle.
> > Wyntown Cron. I. p. 14.

433. FEEL = agls. ge-Felan = lat. Palpare ? = Ψηλαφαν ?

434. FELE = agls. Fela = germ. Viel = mœsog. Filu = norse in compounds Fiöl = Πολυς. Πολις and Populus seem to be variations of Πολλοι : it is acknowledged that Πληθος, Plebs are so.

> Hadde she loked that oother half
> And the leef torned
> She sholde have founden fele wordes
> Folwynge ther after.
> > Piers Ploughman, 2053.

> I not in what maner I sholde
> Of worldes good have sikernesse
> For every thefe upon richesse
> Awaiteth for to robbe and stele.
> Such good is cause of harmes fele.
> > Gower, lib. v. p. 134.

> Hir fair quhite breist, thare as scho did stand
> Fele times smat scho with hir awin hand.
> > G. Douglas, lib. iv. p. 120. 44.

435. FELL = agls. Fell = mœsog. †Fill, found in derivatives, = isl. Fell in compounds, Felldr 'pellis, exuviæ' (B. II.) = lat. Pellis. Cf. sanskr. Pâl 'to protect,' also FILM, PEEL, FLAY. There is an approximation in meaning amid mœsog. Filhan κρυπτειν, norse Fela 'tegere, occultare,' and Φυλασσειν. The notion of skin or cover may prevail in Πελτη, Pallium, Palla, Paludamentum, Pileus, Pilus.

* Foresters. † Places.

And sayd he and all his kinne atones
Were worthy to be brent, both fell and bones.
Chaucer, Troilus and Creseide, I.

Alle buen * false that bueth mad bothe of fleyshe ant felle.
Percy Soc. vol. iv. p. 94.

436. FEVER=agls. Fefer a reduplicate form of fire=lat. Febris a similar reduplication = Πυρετος = germ. Fieber. Formus, Fervere, Fornax contain the root Fire.

437. FEW=agls. Feawa=mœsog. Faws in the sing. translating ολιγος, in the plural Fawai ολιγοι = norse Far = lat. Paucus, Pauci, Pauxillus, Paullus, Pusillus = Παυρος, Παυροι. If the diphthong αυ do not represent aw, the comparison would belong to another class of changes, C and R. Puer seems to be Paucus.

438. FIGHT=agls. Feohtan=mœsog. Weigan=norse Vega =lat. Pugnare. FIST is a sibilate form. VIE is identical.

439. FILE defile = agls. Fulian = lat. Polluere = Μολυνειν. Foul=agls. Ful=mœsog. Fuls, οζων. The substantive FILTH is more familiar to us than the verb. From the mœsogothic sense, Frauya, yu fuls ist, Κυριε, ηδη οζει, the radical notion may be that of Putere=sanskr. Pûy.

The forty day cam Mary myld,
Onto the temple with her schyld
To schewyne here alone that never was fyld.
Songs and Carols, p. 99.

The haly ymage, grisly for to tell
Pullit and filit.
Gawaine Douglas, p. 44. 19.

þat næfre ma ne shall itt ben
O name wise filedd.
Ormulum, 15038.

439 a. FILL=agls. Fyllan=Plere. See 453.

439 b. FIN = agls. Finn = dansk. brem. Finne = dutch Vin = lat. Pinna, perhaps for †pitna, †petna. FENNEL = lat. Feniculum may be so called from its feathery appearance.

440. FIND=agls. Findan=mœsog. Finþan=norse (by assimilation) Finna. Gabelentz compares Πυνθανεσθαι. It is

---

* Buen=Bueth=Be, are.

commonly believed that here the radical syllab... this may not be true, as will be seen when we come to θ ... sider the elimination of N. The sense of the english is n... removed from that of the greek; but the mœsogothic is used as the version not of εὑρειν, but of γνωναι, and suits well to the parallelism. The texts may be compared: they are, Mark v. 43, xv. 45; Luke ix. 11; John xii. 9; Rom. x. 19. It is possible also that the old english FOND (try) = agls. Fandian, is of the same origin as Find.

> That soght aventures in that land
> My body to asay and fande.
> > Ywaine and Gawin, 314.

141. FIRE = agls. Fyr (neut.) = norse Furr (masc.) = germ. Feuer (neut.) = Πυρ. The gender of the norse word surprises the scandinavian scholars. Fire, like the german, becomes a disyllable in Shakspeare and many of our older poets:

> For who can hold a fire in his hand
> By thinking of the frosty Caucasus?

and so the greek: Simonides, frag. 29.

> Τοῦτο γὰρ μάλιστα φὴρ ἔστυγε πῦιρ.

141 a. FIRTH a scotch word = norse Fiörðr. Cf. lat. Fretum.

142. FLAT, FLITCH of bacon, in east Anglia FLICK 'a flitch of sawn plank' (Forby), FLAKE, FLAG stone, FLANGE, FLEACHES 'the portions into which timber is cut by the saw' (Forby), FLAG 'a broad leaved water plant,' with agls. Floc 'a flat fish,' Floh 'fragmen, frustum,' germ. Flach, Platt, dutch Vlak are all to be compared with Πλακα (acc.) 'a plain,' Πλακουντα (acc.) 'a flat cake, a bun usually served up hot,' Πλακινος 'of planks,' lat. Planus if for †placnus.

> The wary bird a prittie pibble takes
> And claps it twixt the two pearle hiding flakes
> Of the broad yawning oyster, and she then
> Securely pickes the fish out.
> > Brownes Brit. Past. II. iii.

142 a. FLAX = agls. Fleax = germ. Flachs. That this word belongs to Πλεκειν becomes clear enough by the agls. passage in the Hexameron of Basilius printed since Lye wrote

floxfc, 'web footed.' Ða fugelas soþlice ðe on flodum Wiað syndon flaxfote be Godes foresceawunge: Hexame-.on, viii. 'The fowls indeed that dwell on floods are flax footed by Gods foresight.' If flaxfote is web footed, then must flax contain a root like weave, which is Πλεκειν. The mœsog. had Flahta or Flahto πλεγμα, the isl. at Flietta 'nectere.' Pleach is a latinism. See Lock of hair, 810 a, and Fleece, 443, Flask, 819, Fold, 447.

443. Fleece = agls. Flys = germ. Vleis = lat. Vellus: cf. Villus. Also Flock of wool, Floss silk, Floo the woolly material which collects on the floor of bedrooms, also lat. Floccus, and possibly Wool with ουλος to which the idea woolly is not alien (Buttm. Lexil. i. 187). Fell, pellis may not be far off. Forby says Fleek is the down of hares or rabbits torn off by the dogs. "Dryden has Flix in the same sense."

444. Fly = agls. Fleogan = norse Fliúga = lat. Volare. The G appears as C in Volucris? Cf. Flutter, Flicker, agls. Fliccerian 'motare alas.'

445. Foal (masc.) = agls. Fola (m.) = mœsog. Fula (m.) = isl. Foli (m.) = Πωλος. Cf. Filly (fem.). The latin Pullus is applied to the young of any animal; it is also used as Pusillus, of which it seems to be a contraction: the teutonic languages have the root and may have the same contraction. See 437.

446. Foist, Fizz, Fizzle = lat. Visire. "Bull-fiest. The puff-ball, Lycoperdon, called in other counties puck-fiest, Fuzball, Mullypuff, Frogcheese, and probably by other names. Bullfiest, the german Bofist, and the Bovista of Dillenius are derivable from the idea which gave rise to the old name of Crepitus lupi, on which Lycoperdon is so far an improvement as being less intelligible" (Moors Suffolk Words). Foist must be first a substantive then a substantival verb. In Kerseys Dictionary, 1715, To Fizzle or Foist, to break wind backwards without noise. Swed. Fisa = isl. Fysa = germ. Fisten = dutch Vysten. Fizz as applied to the sound of frying grease is the same word.

    A little fusball pudding stands
    By, yett not blessed by his hands.—Herrick.

LABIALS INTERCHANGED IN ANLAUT.

Changing F to a guttural, it seems that GUST = agls. Yst, Gas, GHOST = agls. Gast, YEAST = agls. Gist, with germ. Gäschen = Gähren 'to ferment,' are connected with the word Fizz.

417. FOLD = agls. Fealden = mœsog. Falþan = norse Falda = germ. Falten = lat. Plicare = Πλεκειν. The latin and greek represent also entwining, plaiting, which are kinds of folding. Πλοκαμος, LOCK, probably in strictness braided hair which the ancient statues of women exhibit. The compounds, as Twofold Threefold and in mœsog. in -falþs, in agls. in -feald, in latin in -plex as Duplex, Triplex, in greek in -πλοος as Διπλοος, Τριπλοος.

418. FOLK = agls. Folc (n.) = norse Folk (n.) = lat. Vulgus. These seem derivations of πολ- see FELE. Gawin Douglas (Prologue to Book V.) thus translates "Quot homines, tot sententiæ:"

How many hedis als feil consatis bene.

419. FOOT = agls. Fot (m.) = mœsog. Fotus (m.) = norse Fotr (m.) = lat. Pedem (acc.) = Ποδα (acc.) = sanskr. Pâda, with the optional substitute Pad in all cases (Wilson, Gr. p. 56), accus. Padam, Pâdam. The root may have been formed on the Pitpat sound of a foot fall. Cf. PATH, agls. Peððian 'callem facere, conculcare,' Πατειν, βαδ-ιζειν, Vadere, Wade, Waddle.

450. †FOR, the inseparable preposition conveying a sense generally of mischief, bale = agls. For, inseparable also = mœsog. Fair, Fra, inseparable = germ. Ver, inseparable = Παρα in παρακουειν 'hear amiss, hear without regarding,' παραβαινειν 'transgress,' παραγειν 'lead astray,' παρορχεισθαι 'dance wrong,' παρορνις 'in contravention of bird omens,' παρῳδη 'a parody, a song distorted,' παροινειν 'err through wine,' παρατεκταινειν 'do carpenters work amiss' = lat. Per in perire 'go to ruin,' perdere 'fordo,' perimere 'do to death,' periuria 'forswearing,' periculum 'going wrong.' In modern english, examples are Forbid, Forbear, Forget, Forlorn, Forswear. Froward seems to be mœsog. Fra-waurhts = παραερδων 'doing amiss.'

And she was wonder wroth withal
And him, as she which was goddesse,

LABIALS INTERCHANGED IN ANLAUT

Forshope anone and the likenesse
She made him take of a herte.
Gower, i. p. 54, of Actæon.

The flessh is a fel wynd * * *
And forbiteth the blosmes
Right to the bare leves.
Piers Ploughman, 10864.

So harlotes and hores
Arn holpe with swiche goodes,
And Goddes folk for defaute therof
Forfaren and spillen.
Id. 9886.

He was not pale as a forpyned ghost.
Chaucer, C. T. 205.

The miller, that fordrouken was, all pale
So that unethes upon his horse he sat.
Id. C. T. 3123.

"Sir knight, said the two brethren, we are forfoughten and much blood have we lost through our wilfulnesse." Mort d'Arthur, vol. i. chap. 1. "Their shields and their hawberkes were all forhewen." Id. vol. i. chap. cxxix. "Because he had forjusted the noble knight Sir Palamedes." Id. vol. ii. chap. xxii.

451. FORE adj., FORE prefix, FORMER, FOREMOST, FIRST, FAR, FURTHER, FURTHEST, with the agls. se Forma (def. only), For, Fore (prefix), Fyrmest, Fyrst, Feor, Furður, and the mœsogothic Faur, Faura (prefix), Frums $αρχη$, Fruma, Frumists, Fairra, are to be compared with Pro, Prior, Primus, Porro, Porrigere, Procul, $Προ$, $Πριν$, $Προτερος$, $Πρωτος$, $Πορρω$. The norse also has the terms.

452. FROG. $Βατραχος$ had other forms found in Hesychios "$Βριαγχονην$, $βατραχον$, $Φωκεις$. $Βροαγχος$, $βατραχος$ $Βρουχετος$, $βατραχος$, $Κυπριοι$." The T therefore is intrusive and $βαραχος$ is the old form of $βατραχος$. These words are near enough to Frog=agls. Frogga=germ. Frosch (sibilate)=dutch Vorsch. The FR is distantly connected with fire as the gaelic Losgann 'frog or toad' with Loisg= welsh Llosgi 'to burn;' and so the frog is named from his burnt or brown colour. Thus also $Φρυνος$ is 'toad,' $Φρυνιον$

a plant was also called Βατραχιον; the famous Φρυνη was so called from her pale froggy complexion; cf. Φρυνιχος, Φρυνωνδας. "The old high german brün is in the glossaries Furvus and Fulvus" (Grimm). Fry = Frigere = Φρυγειν, is also from Fire. Parch whence?

453. Full=agls. Full=mœsog. Fulls=norse Fullr=germ. Voll=lat. Plenus=Πλεος, Πληρης. So Fill=lat. Plere. The hebr. מלא with the allied M is supposed akin.

454. Mold has the inorganic D, see art. 742, which it has not assumed in Mole an abbreviation of Mol-warp, otherwise Mouldiwarp: friesic and bremish Mul=dutch Ghe-mul 'dust' (Kilian)=agls. Myl, Mold. The teutonic lexicons cf. mœsog. Malwyan, art. 45, and Meal. I would here cf. Pulvis. The german has Mold in Maulwurf. Cf. agls. Molsnian, Formolsnian 'reduce to dust.' Meal as corn reduced to dust is akin, and Mallet.

455. Vat=agls. Fæt=lat. Vas, Vasis.

456. Warm=agls. Wearmian=mœsog. Warmyan θαλπειν = norse Varmr (adj.) = lat. Formus from Fire. Nearly so Brim in Brimstone; a sow in heat is said to be Brimming; isl. Brundr, 'ovium appetitus coeundi,' Bruni 'burning,' Brimi 'flame:' so Brand. Although for fire the sanskrit word is Agni=lat. Ignis, yet that tongue possessed the root, as in Bhrisht- 'fried,' Bhráj 'to shine,' Bhrej, 'to shine.'

457. Well=agls. Weallan 'to well, to boil, to be hot.' Cf. Ebulire : a Volvendo, from the rolling motion.

457 a. Whale = lat. Balæna = Φαλαινα = agls. Hwæl = norse Hvalr. The mœsog. of Matth. xii. is lost. To Balæna is Bellua akin?

INLAUT OR AUSLAUT.

458. Climb, Clamber belong to Clamp, probably Claw, and contain the notion of a fast hold. Clivus, acclivis may be referred to them rather than to Cleave, since the idea of a climbing steep applies better than that of a precipice, rupes, prærupta. The friesic also has Klieve=dan. Klyve 'to climb,' and en Klaft, Kliff, 'a stile to get over a wall,' quasi Κλι-μακα (acc.). Klammeren is 'hold fast with hands or claws.'

"Kaum sah er den Kater | Über den Käficht (small room) geklammert" (Zachar). Din minne ist gar ein range mir | Si klemmert mich, ich muos zuo dir (Otto von Bottenl.) (Adelung).

459. CLUB = lat. Clava = swed. Klubba. Akin to Clog, Log, germ. Kloben, Klopfen?

460. DEFTLY=agls. Dæftlice akin to Dæftan not inserted in the dictionaries. Homil. I. 362. Dæfe, Dæfte, Dafenlicnes, containing the idea, 'congruus, opportunus, idoneus,' and found in the early sense in Gedafenað 'decet,' and literally=lat. Decet, a relative of Dignus: see Doughty.

461. HAVE = agls. Habban, Hæbban = mœsog. Haban = norse Hafa = lat. Habere. The agls. and mœsog. like the latin signify hold as well as have. See art. 1026.

461 a. LAPPET, LAPPEL may be diminutives of LAP as in Dewlap, which is found in the agls. Earelæppe, Lifrelæppan, in the same sense as Λοβος. To the interchange of labials and gutturals would belong Lacinia. Was Lacerna a mere Lappet? The dutch Lapje in Kilian Lap is equivalent to our word.

462. LEAVE = agls. Læfan = norse Leifa = mœsog. hypothetical †leiban, with derivatives bilaibyan, περιλειπειν, Laiba καταλειμμα, aflifnan περιλειπεσθαι = λειπειν. For Linquere see Interchange of Labials and Gutturals. In Lap, properly a remnant, see the swedish and danish, and in the saxon form of Only a P is found: art. 957.

463. LIP=agls. germ. Lippe=erse Liobar=lat. Labium, Labrum. Cf. Lambere, with many others. Grimm (Gr. III. 400) thinks lip formed on the latin. That is because the mœsog. has Wairilo 'a lip' and the agls. Wæleras, pl. with liquids transposed like lat. Miraculum spanish Milagro, etc. The agls. seems near to χειλη, as if it had been †kwæleras, compared with Gula, germ. Kehl and the sanskrit. The modern welsh is Gwefus, but Lhuyd gives Guevl=cornish Guelv, 'lip.'

463 a. OF, OFF=Απο=lat. Ab, Λ=agls. Of=mœsog. Af= norse Af.

464. OVEN = agls. Ofen (m.) = mœsog. Auhns (m.) = isl.

Ofn (m.): with this Grimm compares ιπνος; add οπταν and hebrew אפה, 'coxit, proprie panem et similia farinacea.'

465. Rob = agls. Reafian = mœsog. †raubon found in biraubon συλαν = lat. Rapere. Hence Ruffian = agls. Reaffiend, also Sea Rovers, the danish being Röver, with Rov, 'rapine.'

466. Seven = agls. Scofon = mœsog. Sibun = norse Siau = germ. Sieben = lat. Septem = 'Επτα = sanskr. Saptan = שֶׁבַע.

DENTALS INTERCHANGED.

467. The dentals τ, δ, θ exchange with one another; as Ορθιος, arduus; θορυβειν, ταρασσειν, turbare; τριχες, θριξιν; ταχυς, θασσων; τρεχειν, θρεξομαι; τεινειν, tendere, germ. Dehnen, with according to Varro, pertinax, obstinatus; mentiri, mendax; σπαθη, spatula: dormire, torpere; επτα, εβδομος. Dade makes frequentative Toddle. A goose Daddles (Somerset).

> Which nourished and bred up at her most plenteous pap
> No sooner taught to dade but from their mother trip
> And in their speedy course strive others to outstrip.
> Drayton, Polyolb. I.

468. The dental liquid N attaches to dentals, and will often draw a dental after it, as tyrannus, tyrant; vermin, varmint; germ. donner, engl. thunder; lat. tonat, engl. it thunders; τεινειν, tendere; βαλανον, glandem; root †kwan, hound, hunt; kin, kind; min, mind; †τεκειν, yonder; country seems to me the saxon Cynrice.

> All Rome of were ner womyn had (Brennus)
> Ná had bene þat a gamyr made
> Sá hwge crakyng and sic cry.
> Wyntown, Cron. Sc. p. 73. 8.

N often loses a dental, as Span for Spend (Thomas Beket, 1387, 1472).

> As when the sun doth shine
> On straw and dirt mixt by the sweating hyne.
> Browne, Brit. Past. II. iv.

See also a remarkable example in Tines under Tooth, 925.

ANLAUT.

469. Dapper though for centuries used in our present sense, yet is thought by all to be old dutch Dapper, 'strenuus,

animosus, fortis, acer, gnavus, masculus, agilis' (Kilian): germ. Tapfer is 'brave.' Many compare Topper in Festus, "in antiquissimis scriptis 'celeriter ac mature.'"

470. Dare = agls. Dearran = mœsog. ga-daursan = norse þora = Θαρρειν, Θαρσειν. Cf. agls. þrist 'bold' = irish Tresa (Zeuss): sanskr. Dhrish 'be proud, overbearing.' The norse has also Drifa, with cognates. And agls. þræc 'robur.'

> For ich kan craft and ich kan liste
> On þareuore ich am þus þriste.
> Owl and N. 757.

> Thir wordes herd the knightes twa
> It made tham for to be more thra.
> Ywaine and Gawin, 3669.

> King Merkel was ful wo
> To fihten anon he was ful thro.
> Kyng of Tars, 1078.

So Octavian, 547, 834.

471. Daughter = agls. Dohter = mœsog. Dauhtar = norse Dôttir (by assimilation) = germ. Tochter = armenian Duystr = erse Dear = Θυγατηρ = sansk. Duhitri, from Duh 'to milk' as one, say the sanskrit professors, quæ mulgendi officium habuerit in vetusta familiæ institutione. This appears to me very doubtful: see sanskrit index.

472. Deal seems to be Τελειν. Σιτον τελειν, Xen. Hell. V. iii. 21, is 'to deal out corn.' Τελη taxes, may be deals, parts, of the goods taxed. Cf. agls. Dal 'a part' = germ. Theil, erse Dal division. Σ. 297. νῦν μὲν δόρπον ἕλεσθε κατὰ στρατὸν ἐν τελέεσσιν ('in deals, divisions'). Τελη in the sense of magistrates may be perhaps compared with the rude idea of a chieftain, the distributor of meat and armlets; the Deilir of the norse. Ευτελης 'cheap,' good to deal in? Cf. Dole.

473. Deer originally 'wild animal' = agls. Deor = mœsog. Dius = norse Dýr (even amphibious) = germ. Thier = Θηρ, Θηριον. On the latin see art. 558. The text (Mark i. 13) 'he was with the wild beasts,' ἦν μετὰ τῶν θηρίων, is in agls. "he mid wild-deorum wæs;" in the islandic Hann vaar þar ok með Villdudyrum; in danish Oc vaar iblant Diur; in swedish "War med wilddjuren;" in german, "War bei den Thieren;"

in dutch, " Was by de wilde gedierten." Rats and mice and such small deer, Shakspeare.

> Vor he ne recþ noȝt of clennesse
> Al his þoȝt is of golnesse,
> Vor none dor no leng nabideþ
> Ac curich upon oþer rideþ.
> Owl and N. 492.

474. Dim, Dun = agls. Dim = norse Dimmr, Dökkr? with germ. Dunkel. Here we seem to have the root of lat. Tenebræ, Δνεφας, Δνοφερος, Νεφος, Nubes, Nebula, etc. Cf. agls. Dumba 'dimness,' Dumbóttr ' of a dim colour;' germ. Dampf which is Nebula, our Damp having turned its sense a little; also æthiopic Daman ' obscurum seu nubilum fuit,' Damanâ 'nubes;' sansk. Tam-au ' darkness,' Tamas ' darkness.' The augurs made a Templum in the sky, usually at night, the temple had its dark cella for the idol, hence Templum may be referred to this root. Tempestas is also appropriate, and Contemplari.

475. Door = agls. Duru = mœsog. Daur = norse Dyrr (f. pl.) = Θυρα = sanskr. Dwâr ' gate.'

476. Drag, Draw = agls. mœsog. Dragan = norse Draga = lat. Trahere for †tragere with traxi for †tragsi, like maximus for magsimus, and tractum for tragtum, since softs require softs, medials require medials, like οκτω, ογδυος.

477. Dregs = isl. Dregg = Τρυγα (acc.).

478. Dry = agls. þyrr, þyr = mœsog. þaursus ξηρος, εξηραμμενος (verb þairsan) = norse þurr (verb, at þerra) = germ. Dörre, Trocken = danish Tör = swed. Torr, produces Tergere ' wipe,' Torrere ' scorch,' Τερσαινειν, Ετερρατο, εξηρανθη, Hesychios. Od. ζ. 98 : Ϝείματα δ' ἠϝελίοιο μένον τερσήμεναι αὐγῇ ' to get dry in the sunshine.' Compare Thirst = agls. þyrst = isl. þorsti with þyrstr ' thirsty.' Cf. mœsog. þaurseiþ mik ' it thirsts me,' sanskrit Trish ' thirst.' Add probably lat. Durus ' hard.'

479. Dye = agls. Deagan = lat. Tingere. So Dew as compared with Τεγγειν. Provincially Dag, to drizzle, Dag ' a drizzling rain,' a Daggy day (Brockett). In Norfolk a shower

of rain is a Dagg for the turnips (Wilbraham). Dag is a thin and gentle rain (Jamieson). Cf. Dew, art. 103.

479 a. DUMB. Cf. Θαμβειν the root of τεθηπα, θαυμα, θαυμαζειν.

480. TAKE, see art. 373. Cf. not only Τεταγειν, but Δεχεσθαι. So the subst. for the taking hand mœsog. Taihswo= Δεξια=Dextra. The Indian faces the east and calls the south the right hand, the Deccan : so the welsh Deheu; the erse and gaels, Deas. Cf. TOUCH, 497.

481. TAME = agls. Tamian = mœsog. ga-tamyan = norse Temja=Δαμναναι, Δαμαζειν=lat. Domare=sanskr. Dam.

482. TEACH=agls. Tæcan=lat. Docere=Διδασκειν.

483. TEAR = agls. Tear = norse Târ =mœsog. Tagr=Δακρυον, Δακρυ. On Lacryma see 613.

484. TEN=agls. Tigun=mœsog. Taihun=norse Tiu = lat. Decem = Δεκα = sanskr. Dashan. Here observe that the greek has lost the final consonant, and the sanskrit uses its customary sibilation.

485. THAT=agls. þæt=mœsog. þata=sanskr. Tad or Tat =To for τοδ. A dental does not end a greek word; To for That is like αλλο, aliud; ò, quod; τι, quid. THAT LIKE=agls. þyle=lat. Talis. Thus Similis=Same like. WHAT LIKE= agls. Hwyle=mœsog. Hwileiks=lat. Qualis. As an example of the neuter saxon article retained in english, take.

> And wanne he deithe, ne mey me* wite
>   Woder he cometh to wisse;
> Bote as a stocke ther lithe thet body,
>   Withe thoute alle manere blisse.
>   William of Shoreham, p. 1.
>
> The signe hiis that hys boute ydo
>   That thynge hys grace bynnet†.
>   Id. 40.

The agls. þæt is used for a neuter article as much as the το of attic greek. On Laʒamon, 1301, vol. iii. p. 450 : Sir F. Madden says "although I am aware some of our best scholars in A.-

---

* Me=man.

† The sign is that which is outwardly done, the thing is grace within. So six times on p. 55.

Saxon and Early English have sanctioned its use [as a demonstrative pronoun] in their versions, yet I am at loss for any examples which ought not properly to be translated by the definite article." Were this to the full extent true, our That would hardly be precisely an equivalent for the agls. þæt. But Lye and Manning give examples in some of which the demonstrative use seems undeniable: as Se Hælend soþlice þæt wiste, Matth. xii. 15. Cf. Bœth. p. 17. line 6.

486. THATCH = agls. þæc ' thatch, roof ' = norse þak ' roof ' = lat. Tectum = Τεγος. The verb to DECK ' cover ' = agls. þeccan = norse þekja = Tegere = Στεγειν. The Deck of a ship, to Deck with ornaments are of the same. Decus, Decorus, Decet with welsh Teg, pulcer, are of kin to agls. Gedafan, and their relationship to Tegere is doubtful. It seems more probable that they are related to Dugan and Dignus, art. 104. Gawin Douglas, II., thus translates Danaos ad tecta ruentes :

> The Grekis rusch and to the thak on hicht
> Sa thik they thrang about the portis all nycht.
>
> Then said the lords of the host
> And so conclude least and most
> That they would ever in houses of thacke
> Their lives lead and wear but blacke.
> Chaucers Dream, 1771.

487. THEN = agls. þonne = mœsog. þan = lat. Tunc. On τοτε see 914.

488. THIN = agls. þin, þyn = norse þunnr = germ. Dünn = lat. Tenuis.

489. THOLE = agls. þolian = mœsog. þulan = norse þola = germ. Dulden = lat. Tolerare, Tollere. Cf. Tetuli, Tuli, Tolleno, Τληναι, Τολμαν, Ταλας, Τλημων, THOLE PIN. The present tense, lost in the latin simple form of the simplest sense, is found in Opitulari. The sanskrit Tul means ' to weigh, to measure;' and Ταλαντον is a participle in this sense: the sanskr. Tulâ is a balance, the sign Libra, &c. Thole is found as late as 1770 in a letter of Watts the inventor of the steam-engine. "The vaguing about the country and bodily fatigue have given me health and spirits beyond what I commonly

enjoy at this dreary season, though they would still thole amends."

> There nys lyves mon noon so slygh,
> That he neo tholeth ofte mony annye.
> Kyng Alisaundre, Prologue, 10.

> Tho this lettre was rad and herd
> Mony on redid in the berd;
> And saide they wolde with him fyght
> Ar they wold thole such unryght.
> Ibid. 2046.

> Two theves also
> Tholed deeth that tyme
> Upon a croos besides Crist.
> Piers Ploughman, 12217.

490. THOU = agls. mœsog. norse þu = lat. Tu = doric Tυ = sanskr. Twam. There seems to be a connexion with Duo, as of εγων, aham with ekhad אֶחָד.

491. THREE = agls. þry (m.), þreo (f. n.) = mœsog. þreis = norse þrir (m.), þriar (f.), þriu (n.) = lat. Tres, Tria = Τρεις Τρια = sanskr. Tri.

492. THRASH = agls. perscan = mœsog. þriskan = isl. þreskja = lat. Triturare? THRESHOLD = agls. þyrscel = isl. þreskiölldr, compounded of Scel 'sill,' from Scylan 'divide, split,' being so called because it was the cottagers threshing floor, for we find a difficulty in making it door-sills. Wald, wood, cannot be admitted. So Oferskege from Over and slagan, strike.

493. THUNDER = lat. Tonitru = agls. þunor = germ. Donner = isl. Duna. The sanskrit has S additional, Stan, so that the third singl. Stanayati = Tonat. Cf. DIN, STUN = agls. Stunian. The homeric Στενειν was 'make a loud noise,' as ποντος εστενε: 'groan,' is a derivative sense.

> The weder wex than wonder blak
> And the thoner fast gan crak.
> Ywaine and Gawin, 360.

494. THUS = agls. þus = Τως homeric: ὡς 'thus,' seems to me another form of the same word. This is the adverb of the demonstrative pronoun THAT. It is probable that in some ancient shape all the cases of this pronoun might appear in

DENTALS INTERCHANGED IN ANLAUT.

the languages we are dealing with, visibly the same. It may be instructive to set out the easiest of recognition.

SANSKRIT.

nom. s.	Sah	Sâ	Tad or Tat	pl.	Te	Tâah	Tâni
acc. s.	Tam	Tâm	Tad or Tat	pl.	Tân	Taah	Tani

DORIC.

nom. s.	Ὁ	ἁ	το	pl.	Τοι	Ται	Τα
acc. s.	Τον	ταν	το	pl.	Τους	Τας	Τα

where Το is for †τοδ, and Τους for †τονς.

MŒSOGOTHIC.

nom. s.	Sa	So	þata	pl.	þai	þos	þo
acc. s.	þana	þo	þata	pl.	þans	þos	þo

NORSE.

nom. s.	Sâ	Sû	þat	pl.	þeir	þær	þau
acc. s.	þann	þa	þat	pl.	þâ	þær	þau

ENGLISH (agls.).

nom. s.	Se	Seo	þæt	pl.	þa in all genders
acc. s.	þone	þa	þæt	pl.	þa in all genders

Of the agls. some forms are found preserved in english.

> Gy oftoke sone that ferrede
> And seye than knight with them lede*.
>   Gy of Warwike, p. 168.

> þar com Eneas:
> & grette þen alde king.
>   Laȝamon, verse 132.

> & þene deaðƗ þolien.
>   Id. verse 284.

> For oyle smereth thane champion
> That me Ɨ ne schel on him evel festne.
>   William of Shoreham, p. 14.

> Aȝen him the develen come anon and nome thane wrecche faste.
>   St. Brandan, p. 24; and often so.

---

* Oftoke = overtook, Ferrede = company, Seye = saw, Than = τον.
†Deað is masculine.   Ɨ Me = man.

495. TIMBER. The agls. verb Timbrian 'build'=mœsog. Timryan = norse Timbra = Δεμειν. The B is merely a help sound to the M. Germ. Zimmern is 'work up timber for building.' Δενδρον is perhaps δεμ-τρον.

496. TOKEN = agls. Tacn = mœsog. Taikns = isl. Takn = Τεκμωρ, Τεκμηριον, connected with Δεικ-νυναι, in-dex, in-dicare, Digitus, Δεξια. Dicere ' say ' must have been originally δειξαι ' shew,' as Dicare in prædicare, dedicare, is ' say :' so Festus abridged " Dicassit, dixerit."

497. TOUCH comes to us from the french Toucher = ital. Toccare : it is one of the words left by the Ostrogoths ; for Tangere remains, like Frangere, from the latin. Lye on the word Wapentak has observed that the anglosaxon does not use this form in this sense. Touch therefore = mœsog. Tekan, Teikan, ἁπτεσθαι = lat. Tangere = Θιγειν : it is also probably connected with Δεξια.

498. TREE = agls. Treow = mœsog. Triu = norse Tre = Δρυς (oak), Δορυ (wood) = lat. Trabem (beam). Δορυ is ' wood ' in δουρειος ἱππος; Δουρα are ' pieces of wood,' Od. μ. 441, 443 ; in the sense of ' spear ' it was first ' the shaft.' The sanskrit is Tarah, Taru, Drumah, Druah. The anglosaxon has also the form Dur which remains in Appledore near Bideford, in the Isle of Wight and Sussex. The sanskrit is found in the favourite Deôdora pine, Deorum δορυ. In Trenails, Axle tree, Saddle tree the sense ' wood ' continues to the present day.

> Othir in this tre ar Grekis closit full rycht
> Or this ingyne is biggit to our skaith.
> Gawin Douglas, p. 40. l. 8.

> For James the gentile
> Jugged in hise bokes
> That feith withouten the feet
> Is right no thyng worthi
> And as ded as a dore-tree
> But if the deds folwe.
> Piers Ploughman, 8:33.

> A qwyte cuppe of tre therby shalle be,
> Therwith the water assay schalle he.
> The Book of Curtasye, 701.

So " and hanged on a tree ;" " the gallows tree." Τρεχνος in

Hesychios and Zonaras is a harder form of agls. Treow; it is interpreted στελεχος, κλαδος, φυτον, βλαστημα. In the first signification it = Truncus. Cf. Θρονος, Θρηνυς 'footstool,' Θρανος 'bench for rowers,' Θρανιτης: the Θρανογραφος of Hesychios is thus explained, meaning ευπρεπης τοιχογραφος, a wainscot painter. In these words I presume the N to be adjectival, as in Treen: see on participials.

499. Tug = agls. Teon (with præterite plural, we tugon) = mœsog. Tiuhan, with the sense of αγειν = isl. Toga = lat. Ducere.

500. Two = agls. Twegen (m.), Twa (f. n.) = mœsog. Twai (m.), Twos (f.), Twa (n.) = norse Tveir (m.), Tvær (f.), Tvau (n.) = lat. Duo = Δυο = sanskr. Dwi.

INLAUT OR AUSLAUT.

501. BROTHER = agls. Broþor = mœsog. Broþar = norse Broðir = lat. Frater = welsh Brawd = erse, gaelic Brathair = sanskrit Bhrâtri. Αδελφος was originally an adjective, ὁμομητριος; but Φρατρια 'a clan gathering' seems to retain the form: and Hesychios has an imperfect gloss, Βρα..., αδελφοι ὑπο Ηλειων. Harpokration the best authority for the orators, says, Φρατρια εστι το τριτον μερος της φυλης, but Hesychios and others add the notion of συγγενεια.

502. FATHER = agls. Fæder = mœsog. Fadar = norse Faðir = germ. Vater = lat. Pater = Πατηρ. In more frequent use the mœsogothic has Atta 'father.' The keltic languages often turn F into H or drop it, so that the gaelic and irish Athair is of the same origin. Some welsh words appear to be derivatives. Sansk. Pitri.

503. FEATHER = agls. Feþer = norse Fiöðr = Πτερον. This greek word is sometimes poetically or carelessly used for wing, but Πτερυξ is wing. Cf. Πετεσθαι 'fly,' Πετασαι 'spread abroad?' Patere? Pandere? Penna for †petna.

504. FERN is a contraction of agls. Feþern = Πτερις, so called from its feathery form. How is Filicem (acc.) to be explained? is it connected with Fliegen? and Pluma?

506. FOOT = Pedem = Ποδα (acc.). On the labial change see before, art. 449.

507. Glad=Lætus. On the omission of G see before, art. 283.

508. Good =agls. God=mœsog. Gods, with Goþ sometimes in the neuter=norse Goðr=Αγαθος.

509. Hide=lat. Cutis: on the C and H see before, 303.

510. Hide=Κευθειν: on the C and H see 302.

510 a. It = agls. Hit = mœsog. Ita = lat. Id. The whole pronoun in all cases and genders presents parallels between the latin and mœsogothic: the norse Itt seems to be for †Int and that for Yon-t, our Yon with the neuter termination T.

511. Mead, Meth, Metheglin=agls. Medu=norse Miöðr =welsh Medd=Μεθυ 'intoxicating liquor'=sanskr. Madyan; cf. sanskr. Madhu 'honey.' Hence sanskr. Mad 'to be drunk, insane,' Madah 'drunkenness,' Mad. From $\mu\epsilon\theta\upsilon$, $\mu\epsilon\theta\upsilon\sigma\alpha\iota$ (act.), $\mu\epsilon\theta\upsilon\sigma\theta\eta\nu\alpha\iota$ (mid.). These are all derivatives of the older form Mel; see art. 618, and on $\mu\alpha\iota\nu\epsilon\sigma\theta\alpha\iota$ art. 854.

> Hire mouth was swete as braket or the meth
> Or hord of apples laid in hay or heth.
> Chaucer, C. T. 3261.

> He sent hire pinnes, methe and spiced ale
> And wafres piping hot out of the glede.
> Ibid. 8379.

512. Mid=Μετα, art. 151.

513. Mother, art. 158.

513 a. Ready, Rather, both belong to one saxon word Hræð Rathe 'early, quick, sudden,' also agls. Ræd, 'ready, easy.' 'Ρᾳδιος. The saxon dictionaries give no example suited to ready. I quote from an MS. I hope to publish: for þara dracena micelnesse ne mæg nan man rayþelice on þæt land gefaran: for the greatness of the dragons (snakes) no man may readily on that land fare (travel). Cf. 179 a.

514. Sad, see art. 183. Cf. Satis, Satur which are only Settled.

> Lene he was and also lang
> And most gentil man tham omang,
> Ful perfiteli he couth* in partes
> And sadly† of al the sevyn artes.
> Sevyn Sages, 58.

---

* Couth, knew, præterite of kan, ken.   † Sadly, solidly.

In gon the speres sadly in the rest.
                              Chaucer, C. T. 2603.
                  For ȝeres
            Ne maketh so nauȝt thane* prest ald
            Ac sadnesse of maneres.
                              William of Shoreham, p. 52.

515. Sweat = lat. Sudare = agls. Swǽtan = norse (subs.) Sweiti = sanskr. (verb) Swid, (subs.) Swedah. The german sibilates the final syllable Schweiss, the greek drops the two first letters Ἰδιειν, Ἰδρωτα (acc.) : the latin vocalizes the W.

516. Udder = agls. Uder = Ουθαρ.

517. Wit from agls. Witan 'to know,' whence Witega 'a prophet,' and lat. Vates: norse Vita = mœsog. Witan = Φειδεναι = sansk. Vid. Since knowing comes from seeing, lat. Videre = Φιδειν is of the same root, and a Vates is also 'a seer.' For Wise see 705.

GUTTURALS WITH LABIALS.

518. The gutturals or κ, γ, χ letters exchange with the labials or π, β, φ sounds. In general the presumption is that the guttural rougher sound is older than the labial, but this is not always true. Thus Quattuor = πισυρες : a nearer form †πετορες is found in Petorritum 'a four wheel;' the word may be keltic, but the elements welsh Pedwar 'four' Rhod 'a wheel' are also found in the latin: Quinque = †πεμπε = Πεντε : the form †πεμπε is found in Πεμπτος, Πεμπαζειν 'to count' (Eumenid. 718), Πεμπασσεται (Od. δ. 412), Πεμπαστης (Persæ, 981) etc.; λυκος = lupus; γαλη = felis; equus = ἱππος, the latin itself having the labial in Epona, Iuvenal, viii. 157. Iurat solam Eponam et facies olida ad præsepia pictas : the sanskr. is Ashwas which had its origin in a guttural †Akw = welsh Echw = gaelic Each = runic Eh ; see the saxon runesong (19) and consider norse at Aka, Οχος, Bigæ, Quadrigæ. Coquere = †πεπειν, Πεπτειν, with Πεπων, Πεπαιτερος, Πεσσειν in att. with fut. Πεψειν. Στεφειν is only Στεγειν, compare Buttmann Lexil. p. 98, who quotes Archilochus, ἥδε δ' ὥστ' ὄνου ῥάχις "Εστηκεν ὕλης ἀγρίας ἐπιστεφής. I have argued also that Στρεφειν = a lost †στρεγειν. Lat.

* Thane = τον, the.

catinum 'a dish' with I long = patina with I short. Cf. Columba 'a dove,' Palumbes, Palumba 'a wood pigeon.' Sequi ='Επεσθαι; Βραχυς = Brevis; Frequens = Creber; Scintilla = Σπινθηρ. Cf. Uterque for †quuterque with the oscan Puturuspid; Quinctius with the oscan Pontius; Quidquid with Pitpit which the epitomator of Festus gives as Pirpit. Hallex 'the big toe' = Pollex 'the thumb.' Camillus and Famulus supposing the S in Casmillus, an old form, to be an insertion like Cosmittere (Festus in Dusmosus) for Committere. Glans = Βαλανος; Γληχων = Βληχων: dor. Γλεφαρον = Βλεφαρον. The dialectic Κως, Πως; Ὀκως, Ὀπως, Κη, Πη; Κοσος, Ποσος; Ὀκοσος, Ὀποσος; Κοιος, Ποιος; Ὀκοιος, Ὀποιος; Κοτε, Ποτε; Ὀκοτε, Ὀποτε; Κυαμος, Πυαμος. Σηκος 'an enclosure,' Sepes 'a fence;' Μαλαχη, Malva; Στρογγυλη, Stromboli, the liquid changing also; Stragulum, Stravi; some refer Ασπαλαξ, Σπαλαξ 'a mole' to Σκαπτειν, which seems dubious. There is a strong likeness between Gerere and Ferre, adding Vehere from 759 a: also between Guard, Ward, and agls. Beorgan. We pronounce as F the GH in Rough, Enough, Tough. Engl. Scoff = germ. Spotten. Cod is bag, as in peascod; it = agls. Codd, as Matth. x. 10, Marc. vi. 8, ne codd, ne hlaf, ne scoh on heora gyrdlum; 'not a bag, not a loaf, not (fee) money in their girdles.' For Cod, Pod is now more common; Forby says Pod in east Anglia is a large fat protuberant belly, and that Tusser has the word in the sense of a large leathern bag. The Scotch and Dutch say Keek for Peep, and Chaucer has Pike: Troilus and Creseide, iii. 56. Germ. Kriechen = engl. Creep: Soft = dan. Sagte; Sift = dan. Sigte; Mock = spanish Mofar; After = dutch Agter and the dutch frequently has gutturals for english labials. Cf. Garnish with Furnish, Squirt with Spirt; danish Spröite 'to syringe, squirt, spirt' as subst. 'a squirt, a fire engine,' germ. Spritze 'squirt, syringe, fire engine,' Spreitzen 'to fly about in the form of drops or sparks.' Cf. Strike, Streak with Stripes. The agls. Stigan 'to mount,' which gives us the Sty or hill path of the lake district, and Stirrup = agls. Stige-rap 'mount rope' and stairs = agls. Stæger, and Stails of a ladder, and Stickelpath

GUTTURALS EXCHANGED WITH LABIALS. 129

a devonshire name for a climbing track, is to be compared with Steep=agls. Steap, and with Step=agls. Step, Stæp.

> This was Ambition, rash desire to sty.
> Faery Queen, II. vii. 46.

Cf. Clog, Block. A Clump of trees is in the north called a Plump. Cf. Slap and Slay = germ. Schlagen = agls. Slagan, Slean, and especially the mœsog. version of John xviii. 22. Sums andbahtc standands gaf slah lofin Iesua, εἰς των ὑπηρετων παρεστηκως ἐδωκεν ῥαπισμα τῳ Ἰησου, "one of the 'ambacti' standing gave a slay (slap) of the loof to Jesus." The agls. Cocor has become Quiver.

> To a quequer Roben went
> A god bolt owthe he toke
> So ney on to the marke he wente
> He fayled not a fothe.
> Robyn Hode (and the Potter), 201.

Quake in Chaucer becomes Quappe, cf. Quaver.

> And lord so that his herte began to quappe*.
> Troilus and Creseide, iii. st. 2.

The bœotian Βαva 'woman,' is often considered as a form of Γυνη; perhaps it is so; the keltic languages have, welsh, Benyw 'a woman' = irish Ben = gaelic Ban, Bean. Bergk prints the fragment of Korinna thus:

> Μέμφομη δὲ κὴ λιγουρὰν Μουρτίδ' ἰώνγα
> ὅτι βανὰ φοῦσ' ἔ,3α Πινδάροιο ποτ' ἔριν.

(Here the η = αι, ου = υ, ἰωνγα = ἐγών γε = ἔγωγε). Is λεγειν, legere 'gather' akin to λαβειν? Is BEND = agls. Bendan, akin to Καμπτειν, Γαμψος? it is true that Bend may be a participial derivative of agls. Bugan, Bow = sanskr. Bhuj with Bhugn-ah, 'Bent.'

519. Let it not escape notice that to the exchange of gutturals and labials the interchange of F and H is to be referred: as Horrere = Φρισσειν, Hordeum = Fordeum, Hœdus = Fœdus (Quintil. I. iv.). See Hore, Hasten, Horse, Home, Hair. Thus it is not uncommon in old english to find Finger for Hunger.

* Riming to Lappe.

So longe hi wendo this holi men in the see aboute so
That hi were afingred sore, for here * mete was al ido.
St. Brandan, p. 19.

ANLAUT.

520. Con. It has been already remarked that lat. Con is the mœsog. Ga, the agls. and germ. Ge and the prefixed Y of our old authors. Con is also the root of Cuncti=germ. Ganz=Παντα (acc.). The affinity is evident. In compounds Con often has the meaning of All as Comburere, Comedere, Complanare, Complere, Concoquere, Conficere, Convalescere. These correspond to the hellenic compounds of Παν as Παντελης, Πανωλης, Πανοπλια, and the like. From this comes, with a diminished energy, that Con which, like the german Ge, seems to be slightly intensive, as Conturbare, Contueri, Conspicere, Contorquere, Consistere. Nowadays, since Buttmann looked shy upon it, the intensive Α of the homeric period is regarded with mistrust. It was however acknowledged by the old grammarians, and had a real footing in the language. In form, observe, it is nearer to its mœsogothic relative Ga, than Παν. Τὸ ā μόριον ποτὲ μὲν δηλοῖ στέρησιν ὡς τὸ ἄκλητος· ποτὲ δὲ ἄθροισιν ὡς τὸ ἅπας· ποτὲ δὲ τὸ πολύ, ὡς ἐν τῷ ἄχανες πέλαγος, τὸ μέγα πάνυ καὶ ἐπὶ πολὺ κεχηνός. (From an anonymous lexicon, p. lxxvii. in Tittmanns ed. of Zonaras.) A strong example in Λ. 155, ὡς δ' ὅτε πῦρ ἀΐδηλον ἐν ἀξύλῳ ἐμπέσῃ ὕλῃ. The explanation in Passow exhibits very loose ideas of the value of terminations.

521. Bunny=Coney=lat. Cuniculus (not saxon).

522. Cheeks, Chaps, in agls. by various forms Ceacas, Ceaflas, Ceaplas (?) with Ceowan, Chew, whence Jaw. "In either chap are sixteen teeth" (Phineas Fletcher). The mœsogothic has with sibilation Kausyan, in two senses, first in sense 'and form=lat. Gustare=Γενεσθαι, and secondly, δοκιμάζειν=our Choose=agls. Ceosan = norse Kiósa. Lat. Fauces seem to be, in form, the agls. Ceacas. In Ps. xxxi. 12, the words "In camo et frœno maxillas corum constringe," are translated by the literal but inexact saxon, according to the

* Here. · their.'

Cambridge MS. (Spelman), on hælftre and brydylse ceacan heora geteoh : hold fast their jaws in halter and bridle : and in other passages the saxon words incline rather to the sense of jaws. Fauces is no doubt used of the back of the mouth, the opening of the gullet, but Focale is a wrapper for the outside. Horat. Sat. II. iii. 254 : Ponas insignia morbi, fasciolas, cubital, focalia ; and cf. Martial, vi. 41 : Qui recitat lana fauces et colla revinctus, Hic se posse loqui, posse tacere negat. Suffocare seems to take its origin from external throttling; perhaps focare = CHOKE. Bucca also = Cheek, germ. Backen = welsh Boch, so that Fauces = Buccæ.

523. COLT = agls. Colt = lat. Pullus = Ηωλος = FOAL = mœsog. Fula = isl. Foli. Cf. dan. Kylling 'chicken' with lat. Pullus 'chicken' PULLET. See art. 415.

524. COUGH = dutch Kuch = Βηχα (acc.). Prov. c. HOST with o short = germ. Husten has weaker guttural and sibilation.

525. CREEP as related to Vermis, see before. The erse is Cruimh, which the welsh makes Pryv 'a worm.'

526. Cow may = Βουν (acc.) = lat. Bovem, for the germans are of opinion that the sanskr. Gô, 'cow' represents either.

527. GALL = Χολη = agls. Gealla = isl. Gall = lat. Fel, Bilis. The agls. Gealo = YELLOW is related to lat. Fulvus, Flavus, as Gall to Fel. YOLK = agls. Geolca. GOLD. A connexion exists between all these words.

528. GAMMON, HAM = lat. Femur, gen. Feminis (?). If art. 1026 has any solidity in it, Gammon, like Thigh, means 'thick, fat' and answers to Thumb; but that article is speculative.

529. GLOW, GLEAM, GLARE, GLANCE, GLITTER, GLISTER, GLOSS, GLASS, GLEDE, GLIM, GLIMMER, GLIMPSE, GLOZE, CLEAN, Γελειν, Clarus, with their teutonic relatives (art. 322), are to be compared with words of the same sense which have labials in place of gutturals : Φλεγειν, Φλογα (acc.), περι-Φλευειν (Νubes, 396 ; Herodot. v. 77), Flamma, Fulgere, Fulmen, Fuligo, Blanch, Blank, Blaze, Blast, Bleach, Black.

530. HAIR with Hircus, Hirsutus, Hirtus. The sabine

form of Hircus was Fircus (Varro, iv.); and Horrere seems akin to Φρισσειν, πεφρικεναι.

531. HASTEN=agls. Efstan=lat. Festinare. HASTE=agls. Ofest. Cf. FAST, Confestim.

532. HOME, HAM = agls. Ham = mœsog. Haims = norse Heimr, may be supposed to have had a more ancient form with K, so that Κωμη is possibly allied to Hamlet. Lat. Camillus = Famulus seems of this stock: Casmillus may have S intrusive.

533. HORE (now erroneously spelt Whore) is represented in mœsogothic by Hors, 'μοιχος, πορνος,' Horinon, 'μοιχενειν' Horinassus 'μοιχεια, πορνεια:' these are the greek Πορνος, Πορνη, Πορνευειν, and lat. Fornicari; for the tale about vaults is to be regarded as guess work. The norse also has Hôr, or rather Hôrr masc. 'adulterer.'

534. HORSE=agls. Hors=germ. Ross=norse Hross. This I conjecture to be the hebrew Pârâsh, 'a horse' פרש, and possibly the Persians, who were renowned for their cavalry, took their name hence: the hebrew is either horse, or horseman: Persia is פרס Pâras. This word seems to occur in Chaucer.

> At the chesse with me she gan to play
> With her false draughtes full divers,
> She stole on me and toke my fers,
> And when I saw my fers away,
> Alas! I couth no lenger play.
> The Booke of the Dutchesse, 652.

Tyrwhitt from Hyde says this term is Persian and represents the Vizir; hence our glossaries give it as the Queen: Richardson in his persian dictionary translates 'the knight at chess.' It at any rate signifies horseman. See art. 1040.

535. PLUM=agls. Plume. I take the notion of this word to lie in the two first letters denoting the colour of the fruit. The german Pflaume makes the P an F. The latin Pullus in the uncertainty of the application of names of colours was commonly applied to something near black. Πελλος, Πελιος, Πελιδνος were a deep blue as in the livid mark of a blow. Πέλαν τὴν πορφυρᾶν οἷν φασί· τὴν γοῦν μέλαιναν τοῦ σώματος

ἐπιφάνειαν, ἡνίκα ἂν δι' ὑποδρομὴν αἵματος μελαίνηται, πελίωμα καλοῦσι. Greg. Kor. p. 133. Πέλειας 'a dove' seems to take its name from this root, for a dove colour is a deep blue. Similarly can we not refer Dove=mœsog. Dubo, to keltic Dhu 'black'? Plumbum 'lead' is of the same hue : Πέλοψ must have been 'blue eye.' Plum is of the same deep purple, and Prunum is perhaps an alteration of the root Πελ to Pr. Damm with probability regards the Πλειαδες as doves. Πελαργος 'a stork' is a bird partly dark, πελ, partly white, αργος. Besides these forms we have Columba 'dove' =agls. Culfre=o. e. CULVER as in Culver Cliff of the isle of Wight, and the cannon called a Culverin, 'a little dove.' Κελαινος of blood, a wave, a storm, night, the ground, a skin covering a shield, scarcely answers so exactly as all the above derivations to PL : and some connect it with μελας, μελαινα. COAL that is charcoal, represents black, as in isl. Kolmyrkr, 'coal murky,' danish Kulsort 'coal swart.' "Bicollede is swere," blackened. Kyng Horn, 1072, so 1088. BLUE= agls. Blæ=germ. Blau=norse Blår compares exactly with welsh Glas 'blue,' whence Glastum 'woad' a plant cultivated fifty years ago, but now driven out of the market by indigo. Blat is also livid (Andreas, 2177). Blcomen (Lazamon, 25381) are 'black men,' negroes of Ethiopia. "Blacere þen ener eni blamon" (Seinte Marharete, fol. 15, l. 1). Lividus may be presumed to have lost a letter before L, so as to make it parallel to Blue, Black, 410.

> And bett hym tille his rybbis braste
> And made his flesche fulle blaa.
> Sir Isumbras, 310.

536. SCUM=swed. Skumm=germ. Schaum=dutch Schium =lat. Spuma.

537. SPADE=agls. Spad, Spadu (Ælfric gloss.)=isl. Spadi. Σπαθη is, 1. a sword; 2. a broad piece of wood for driving close the threads in weaving; 3. the shoulder blade; 4. a Spatula, etc. From 1 seems to come the italian Spada, and the spanish Espada 'sword:' of all the senses the earliest might be the third; in which Σπαθη=lat. Scapula, whence by likeness of form SHOVEL=agls. Scofl=germ. Schaufel.

Scapula Voss unavoidably connects with Σκαπτειν, which he says is 'cavare' to Scoor. Cf. art. 1015.

538. STAVE, the mœsog. Stabs which translates Στοιχειον and partakes of its form. Στοιχος 'a row' seems to be a row of STAKES, STICKS (dimin.) to support hunters nets, and STAVE is STAFF. The application as agls. Stæf=germ. Buchstab, 'a letter,' is to the characters standing in rows. Staves of a psalm are appropriate because there is a row of them.

539. SWEEP, SWAB=agls. Swapan=isl. Sopa. Cf. lat. Scobræ 'a besom.'

540. WRITE=Γραφειν=lat. Scribere : on the T, and other matters, see 578.

541. YARD=agls. Gyrd 'a stick'=lat. Virga.

> At this holi mannes tumbe, a nijht and a day
> Of ech monek of the hous, he let him discipline
> With a jurd.
> Thomas Beket, 2267.

INLAUT OR AUSLAUT.

542. CRAVE=agls. Crafian=norse Krefja, represents perhaps lat. Precari, Rogare.

543. EGG=agls. Æg=isl. Egg=erse Ugh (Luke xi. 12) = lat. Ovum=Ωον. Professor Max Müller says no one who has studied in the school of Bopp and Pott would think of comparing Egg and Eye. Egg is common to us and the keltic, Eye to us and the sanskrit. By the gaellic Ubh it would appear that APPLE, Ubhal is akin. Even cucumber is Earth apple (Numbers xi. 5).

> þat oþer ʒer a faucun bredde
> His nest noʒt wel he ne bihedde
> þarto þu stele in o day
> And leidest þaron þy fole eye.
> Owl and Nightingale, 101.

544. EYE=lat. Oculus (see 363)=Οφθαλμος, with Οψεσθαι, Οπωπα, γλαυκωπις, βοϝωπις. There is also a sibilate form Οσσε dual.

545. FEW=Pauci=Παυροι, see 437.

546. FLABBY=lat. Flaccus, Flaccidus. Flauw 'semianimis

etc. imbecillis, languidus' (Kilian).   Mœsog. þlakwus with changed initial, see 554.

547. Kiss (of which an account 317) is to be compared with lat. Basium, and Bess=welsh Pocyn. Cf. erse Pus 'a lip,' as os and osculum : see 1037.

548. Lakken 'to catch' = agls. Læccan = $\Lambda\alpha\beta\epsilon\iota\nu$. The latin seems by Laqueus 'a noose,' and Lappa 'a bur,' to have had this root. Lasso and Lace are sibilations of Laqueus.

> Leccherie him laughte.
> > Piers Ploughman, 518.

> And if ye lacche Lyere
> Lat hym noght ascapen.
> > Id. 1286.

> How Poliphemus whilom wrought
> When that he Galathe besought
> Of love, whiche he may nought lacche.
> > Gower, lib. ii. p. 163.

> Lacchis him in armes.
> > William and Werwolf, fol. 67.

> A grisly best, a ragged colt,
> They had hit laught in the holt.
> > Kyng Alisaundre, 685*.

> Now byleve thyn outrage,
> Or thou mygh lache dedly damage.
> > Id. 2968.

> On the Gregies quyk they dasschith
> And feole of heom theo deth lachith.
> > Id. 3735.

> And I shall yeve thee eke ywis
> Three other thinges that great sollace
> Doth to hem that be in my lace†.
> > Chaucer. Romaunt of the Rose, 2788.

> But certes, Love, I say not in such wise
> That for to scape out of your lace I ment.
> > The Complaint of Mars and Venus, 348.

---

* Of Bucephalus.   † Lace=Laqueus.

> Sche schalle me bothe hoder* and happe†
> And in her lovely armes me lappe‡.
>
> Bone Florence, 112.
>
> Out of that brom thai lepen anon
> And bilapped ous euerichon.
>
> Gy of Warwicke, p. 292.

Mr. Halliwell supposes Lappe to mean 'covering' in the following passage cited by him.

> And alle ladis me lowttede that lengede in erthe
> And now is left me no lappe my lygham to hele.
>
> Morte Arthure, MS.

In this, as far as visible in print, Lappe means leaving, remnant, λοιπον. This is the sense of the mœsog. Laiba, the danish Lap, swed. Lapp, germ. Lappen, and in our old saxon word Onlipig the radix occurs with a P. Or it means Flap, ora, fimbria, which is the sense of the agls. Læpe, and of germ. Lappen also. For an example of the sense 'cover,' see the Ormulum in Bilapped. The agls. Glappa = Lappa 'bur' (in Analecta), but that hinders not, see Loof, Glove.

549. LAW = agls. Lagu from Leegan, LAY, Λεγειν = norse Lag from at Leggja. The Romans say Legem (acc.) is from Legere 'read,' or is ab eligendo from Λεγειν, ξυλλεγειν 'pick.' Let us take into consideration the lost root legere 'lay,' the middle of which, Lie, is in Lectus, Lectica. This view is in some measure confirmed by the greek words, θεμις, θεμιτος, θεμισται, which are based on θεμα having the same sense. Participials are not unfrequently the foundation of new forms as in θεμελιον, σημαινειν, ασθμαινειν.

550. LEAVE = lat. Linquere, Liqui = Λειπειν: see art. 162.

551. LIGHT = agls. Leaht = germ. Leicht = lat. Levis = Ελαφρος = sanskr. Laghu: the norse is Lettr by assimilation for †legtr.

552. OPEN (see art. 173) = lat. Aperire = Οιγειν = welsh Agori.

553. SAP = anglosaxon Sæp = german Saft = Οπος = latin Succus.

---

* Hoder, cuddle.   † Happe, have, hold.
‡ Lappe seems to me a softer form of Lack, Lachch.

LABIALS WITH DENTALS.

554. The labials and the dentals are interchanged, as σπουδη, studium; σταδιον, spatium, which coincidence appears most strikingly in the application of both to the distance once round the race course. Gregorius, de æolica dialecto, 44: αντι δε του τ̄ το π̄· στολην, σπολην, σταλεις, σπαλεις. Latro 'robber' may be supposed to have some connexion with κλεπτης 'thief,' and Laverna, the goddess of thieves, "pulcra Laverna," gives a labial: since, also, latro belongs to latere, λαθειν, it seems likely that these are forms of κλεπτειν and stand for †clatere, like clam, †κλαθειν like κλεπτειν: so in the norse laun is 'secrecy' clam. Βραδυς 'slow,' was in the older form βαρδος plainly = tardus; Il. Ψ. 309: αλλα τοι ιπποι βαρδιστοι θειειν. Βηχα = tussim, sibilation having altered the guttural. Βριζειν, δαρθανειν, dormire, may be related: also fores, θυρα. Φλαται = θλαται; φηρες = θηρες; οβελος = οδελος (doric, Acharn. 796); formus = θερμος; lapis = λιθος; vulva = δελφυς. There seems to be some value in the suggestion that Valva 'door' = hebrew daleth 'door,' to which add δελτος 'tablet.' Λειπειν is akin to λοισθος; Vellere = τιλλειν; δαιτα = dapem: probably fumus = θυμος (Grimm); cf. θυμαλωψ 'hot coal' (Aristophanes); φρισσειν, φρικη seem to belong to τριχες, θριξιν; carpere seems origin of card (wool); with carduus, as teazle, a sort of thistle, was long cultivated for teazing wool; suet is sevum, sebum; spread = agls. stredan, stregdan, but, notwithstanding, belongs to spargere. Several examples occur in the mœsogothic, some not observed by Grimm, mœsog. þliuhan = agls. Fleogan = Flee: mœsog. þrafstyan = agls. Frofrian 'comfort;' mœsog. plakwus = lat. Flaccus; mœsog. Hrot = Roof; mœsog. plahsyan (act. εκφοβειν), answers to εκπλαγηναι passively: mœsog. þwastyan = Fasten: mœsog. Gaplaihan =, in the Heliand, Gitlehan. The agls. Fengel = þengel; the isl. Fön = þön 'lamina cornea;' isl. Fiol 'a file' = þiol; isl. Fiosnir = þiosnir; agls. pafian = lat. Favere. Toper, Tipple, I suppose, are traces of the existence among us of the german Topf, which is now Pot. Dote is, I think, the agls. Dofian. We find First for Thirst.

> The kniȝth had fouȝten as a bare
> Therefore him fersted ful sare;
> The mayde brouȝth him ful ȝare
> The spyces and the wyn.
>
> Sir Degrevant, 1696.
>
> The beggares bueth afurste.
>
> Kyng Horn, 1120.

Forby says, in east Anglia, Fapes 'unripe gooseberries' = Thapes: "we sometimes call a Thistle a Fistle." "Fill horse 'the horse in the shafts,' is probably 'Thill horse,' from þill, Thill, temo." Ihre points out that swed. Missfirma = misþyrma. Φυλλον, Folium=? sanskr. Dal-an=welsh Dalen, Dulen=irish Duillcog, Duille, Duillein; the irish has a secondary form Billcog.

555. Add the sibilate forms επεζαρει (Phœniss. 45; Rhes. 433) =επεβαρει, ζελλειν=βαλλειν, ζερεθρον=βερεθρον.

556. The existence of such forms as Πτολις, Πτολεμος shews that it would be unsafe to assert in general terms that labials become dentals: we pronounce 'tolemy for Πτολεμαιος from πτολεμος=πολεμος, but in that case no interchange of letters, only an exchange of place, is seen. In agls. for Four are two forms, Fcower out of, and Feþer, Fyþer, in composition: here is no letter change: the mœsog. Fidwor shows that each of them arises from a loss of letter.

ANLAUT.

557. DEEP=agls. Deop = mœsog. Diups=Βαθυς. Sibilation gives βυσσος, whence αβυσσος 'bottomless.'

558. DEER (see 173) =Θηρ=Fera. Virgils use of Ferina for venison, is parallel to our use of Deer.

559. DIP=agls. Dippan=mœsog. Daupyan=Βαπτειν. This group seems akin to Deep. Cf. DIVE=agls. Dufian=germ. Tauchen.

560. FINE=norse Vænn, by assimilation for væn-r, =germ. Fein=dutch Fijn (Kil.). This is to all appearance another form of Tenuis, Thin, Tener, Τερην.

561. PAPS, BUBBIES = Papillæ = ital. Poppe=TEATS=agls. Tyten=fr. Tetons=Τιτθια. I do not know the history of

those english words, but take them to be equivalents of the mœsog. Daddyan ' to suckle,' and so related to Dugs and the sanskrit Duh. Cf. Bubble and art. 1026.

562. Thick = Πυκνος, Πυκινος, Παχυς = lat. Pinguis = agls. þic = germ. Dick = norse þykkr, þungr = erse Tiugh = Fat (πα-χυς) : cf. Thigh.

563. Through = agls. þurh = mœsog. þair = germ. Durch = lat. Per : cf. Thorough. Is it not reasonable to refer to this root Door = (see art. 475) Fores, supposing the sense originally attached to the way, not to what closes the way? thus Gate = mœsog. Gatwo πλατεια = germ. Gasse, cf. Highgate, and still provincially in that sense. Similarly Forare, perforare answer to a dental form in greek and english Τιτραειν, Τρησω, Τετραινειν, Τρυπη ' a hole,' Τιτρωσκειν ' wound,' Τραυμα ' a wound,' especially mœsog. þairko ' a hole,' ' τρυμαλια,' Drill.

564. Toad = lat. Bufo. The agls. Pada, provincial english Paddock, dutch Pad, Padde, swed. Padda, dansk Padde, irish Buaf leave the english dental without parallel.

> Rowgh they weore so a beore,
> They weore mowthed so a mare.
> Evetis and snakes and paddokes brode
> That heom* thoughte† mete gode.
>
> Kyng Alisaunder, 6124.

> As Ask or Eddyre Tade or Pade.
>
> Wyntown, vol. i. p. 15.

565. Warm = agls. Wearm = mœsog. †warms (the verb Warmyan is found) = norse Varmr = lat. Formus (Festus) = Θερμος.

566. Will = Θελειν as well as Velle, βουλεσθαι.

INLAUT OR AUSLAUT.

566 a. In the auslaut of monosyllabic roots or inlaut of longer forms the change of labials and dentals is not rare, Suet is lat. Sevum, Sebum. Card wool is Carpere ; for Carduus a thistle, a teazle, seems to be but carpens, and the existence of Carere alters nothing.

* Heom, dat. pl.   † Thoughte used impersonally.

> Another thing is yet greatly more damnable
> Of rascoldo poetes yet is a shameful rable;
> Which voyde of wisdome presumeth to indite,
> Though they have scantly the cunning of a snite*.
>
> Barclay, Percy Soc. XXII. lxvii.

567. BEARD=agls. Beard=isl. Barð=welsh Barf=breton Baro, Barv, Barf=lat. Barba.

568. CLOD=lat. Gleba=germ. Kloss. Cf. danish Klode 'a globe, sphere, ball,' and lat. Globus, Glomus, CLUE.

568 a. LENDEN=lat. Lumbi: see 873.

569. NEPHEW = agls. Nefa. Cf. lat. Nepos 'a nephew, grandson, descendant,' Ανεψιος 'a nephew,' with mœsog. Niþyis, συγγενης=norse Niðr 'descendant.' It seems akin to NETHER=norse Niðr 'below.'

570. RED, RUDDY=agls. Read, Red, Rud=norse Rauðr= germ. Roth = Ερυθρος (cf. Ερευθος redness)=lat. Ruber, Rufus. Cf. the sibilate forms Russus, ρουσιος, and Rosa (with ροδον).

571. SIEVE=agls. Sife=germ. Sieb. Cf. the verb Σηθειν: a sieve is mostly κοσκινον, but Hesychios has Σηστρα, κοσκινα. Σηστρον is for σηθ-τρον.

572. THUMP=lat. Tundere, which ejects N to make Tutudi. The participial Τυμπανον supposes a verb †τυμπειν an exaggerative of Τυπτειν.

573. TREAD=Τραπεειν? Buttmann (Lexil. II. 154) says "I am firmly convinced that the idea of turning a press did not lie at the foundation of this word (η. 125, Hesiod. Sc. H. 301). By the constant tradition of the grammarians it was used of treading the grapes, which is also the only suitable notion in the passage of Hesiodos. And so far from having their thoughts fixed on the press, the grammarians derived it from τρεπειν, on account of the turning the must into wine. I doubt not in the least, that the greek language, in this verb, retained the Treten, Trappen which runs through the european tongues." So far Buttmann. The agls. Tredan = norse Troða =mœsog. Trudan which translates πατειν and also τρυγαν making us suspect this word may be of the same family. Foot = welsh Troed = gaelic Troidh = erse Troidh, Troigh. Cf. TRIP.

---

* Snipes are reputed foolish.

574. Udder=agls. Uder=Ουθαρ=lat. Uber.

575. West = agls. West = lat. Vesper? = Γεσπερος. This can hardly be a latinism, since the prose term is Occidentem (acc.). But it may be that the words ought, when compared, to be separated.

576. Womb ' belly,' see 892=lat. Venter. Observe how MB, NT go together, and the T of the latin is not always found. Limp=Lentus, see 872. Beard=Barba; Gourd=Cucurbita; Word=Verbum; Loins=Lumbi: see 873. The following will shew that Womb is belly :—

> Wat seiste, quath this gode erl, wan Richard the marshal
> Upe is stede iarmed is, and atiled thorn out al
> And toward is fon in the feld hath is wombe ywent
> Scolde he turne hom is rugh? He was neuere so yssent*.
> > Robert of Gloucester, p. 525.

> For when he was arayde, then gan he first be wrothe ;
> For his womb lokid out and his rigg both.
> > Urry's Chaucer, Additional Tale.

> Of whiche the end is deth; womb is hir† God.
> > Chaucer, C. T. 12457.

> > Poul, after his prechyng,
> > Paniers he made
> > And wan with hise hondes
> > That his wombe neded.
> > > Piers Ploughman, 10195.

577. Word = agls. Word = mœsog. Waurd = norse Orð = lat. Verbum.

578. Write = Γραφειν=lat. Scribere. That Γραφειν was Scratch see 664; and agls. Writan is used for cut, Beowulf 5106=2705: both words refer to graving on wood or stone, not to pen painting.

GUTTURALS WITH DENTALS.

579. That gutturals are exchanged with dentals is not so familiar a doctrine as the interchange of gutturals with labials, or of labials with dentals : nor, when it does occur, will the observer so readily acknowledge and admit to his conviction

---

* Atired, foes, turned to them, back, shamed. † Their.

this fact. Thus Ahrens is not content to believe that τηνος = κεινος, κηνος, but refers the former to the demonstratives in T. That Quattuor = Τεττερα, Quinque = Πεντε, Quis = Τις, Que = Τε, is usually supposed to be due to a labial form, as Πισυρα, Πεμπε, intervening between the two. These doubts appear to deserve due consideration, and it must remain hard to believe that a K can become a T. In the anlaut the following may be compared: Τεττιγα (acc.) = Cicadam, a strong example; Κινναβαρι = Τιγγαβαρι; Γνοφος = Δνοφος; Γνοφερος = Δνοφερος; Ἑπτα = Τεπτα (Hesych.); Γα = Δα?; the welsh Crych, 'rippled, wrinkled,' probably is a remain of the original form producing Rugæ = Wrinkles, often in textures called Crinkles, and is to be compared with Τραχυς,'Rough. Our Peep, Chaucer's Pike, scotch Keek is also Toot.

> A mirrour of glasse that I may toote therein.
> Skelton, Speke Parrot, 12.

> Now ryse up, maister Huddy peke,
> Your tayle totyth out behynde.
> The Four Elements, p. 43.

Forby gives Copple crown = Topple crown, 'a fowls crest;' Coppling, 'unsteady, in danger of falling' = Toppling; Twilt = Quilt. So Topenyere = Copenere (paramour). Δρεπειν = Carpere, Χωρα = Terra, Kittlish = Ticklish, and so germ. Kitzelig; germ. Kichern = to Titter; germ. Kippen = to Tip (over). Τεκειν = Quicken? that is, 'bring into life,' which seems a more seriously true idea than the german notion that Τεκειν = Τευχειν. Is Τολυπενειν connected with Globus, Glomus? The agls. Ticcen = Kid.

580. Jamieson says "Ruddiman has observed that to the west and south whole counties turn W, when a T precedes, into QU, as que, qual, quanty, bequeen for two, twelve, twenty, between, etc." (Jamieson on Quinter). Here is rather a change of the T to the K sound. In the introductory matter to Outzens Glossarium der friesischen Sprache, p. xxiv., is good information. "T is in some words spoken for K, as Tjär = Kjær, palus (the Carr of Yorkshire) = isl. Tjörn; Tjoler = south danish Kjolder, 'a cellar.' So also a crane = ein Kranich = danish en Tranc = isl. swed. Trana. In some places T is used

for Q, as Twicl for Quicl 'slaver;' Tweg or Tweig for Qweg, Qweig, 'yeast.'"

581. In the inlaut compare ορνιθα = ορνιχα; Ocriculum = Otricoli; Poscere = Postulare; Ποκα = Ποτε; Αλλοκα = Αλλοτε; μελιτος, μειλιγμα; siccus, sitis; caccare, κεχοδα; kittlish, ticklish; Forby gives ast = ask; mink = mint ' to aim at;' Sir Fred. Madden holds that in english Make is another form of Mate, Cake of Cate, Wayke of Wayte, Lake of Late (R. Hood, i. 106). Bakke is an old spelling of Bat, as in the Promptorium Parvulorum, Bakke, vespertilio. Wait and Wake, or Watch, are then connected, Wake produces Wachten; and, the vocalisation of the guttural giving I, this becomes Wait; Christmas Waits are Watchers. In this instance the guttural and dental do not change their nature but only by extrusion their place; as was forewarned, we are not prepared to distinguish carefully such instances always.

> Whose golden gardens seem th' Hesperides to mock
> Nor there the damson wants nor dainty apricock*.
> Drayton, Polyolbion, XVIII.

Make is older than Mate, which in Genesis as Helpmeet for Helpmate is usually misunderstood. Needle must be Nagel, as norse Baðmr = mœsog. Bagms.

582. In anlaut conjecture might suppose a relationship among Θυμος 'rage,' Fumus 'smoke,' Ευειν 'burn,' Θυειν 'sacrifice,' Tus 'frankincense,' θυειν, θυνειν (homeric) 'to go raging about,' suffire, suffimentum, and the sanskrit, Hu 'sacrifice by fire.' Sir F. Madden on Havelok the Dane (line 31),

> Erl and barun, dreng and kayn,

calls the last word "evidently a provincial pronunciation of thayne:" an opinion to which, though it would support my thesis, the dutch Kwant 'a young fellow, a blade,' with our Swain, makes me hesitate to subscribe.

583. These instances are not numerous, nor is the conclusion they seem to offer plainly proved. Some of the words

* The usual spelling of his time.

compared may be parallel forms and yet it may not be a law
of language that gutturals can change places with dentals
unless exceptionally. An argument more trustworthy, and
to my perceptions sufficient, arises from observing the use of
the demonstrative pronominal words in the mœsogothic and
the anglosaxon with a relative sense. The same thing is found
in old english and in greek; but as these are languages acquired in our early days, what is familiar is rarely critically
examined. Upon the mœsog. and agls. I rely, to prove that
the demonstrative, interrogative, and relative pronouns are
originally from one root.

584. Thus mœsog. þan=Then=Tunc, occurs often in the
sense of When, translating ὅταν, ὅτε. Take the example first
in order, Matth. vi. 2, þan nu tauyais armaion: 'when now
thou doest mercy,' ὅταν ουν ποιῃς ελεημοσυνην. Similarly in
vs. 5, 6, þan bidyaiþ, þan bidyais, ὅταν προσευχησθε, ὅταν
προσευχῃ. The examples are numerous; but it is not desirable to treat too much at large on the usages of a language
little studied in England. In like manner the mœsog. þe is
τοτε, or ὅτε. This idiom is different from that which forms
relatives by adding -ei to the demonstratives, though the origin
of both may lie in the identity of the two sets of pronouns.
The agls. þær=There, means also Where, " passim apud
omnes" as Lye says. Matth. vi. 19, Nellen ge gold hordian
ców goldhordas on corþan, þær óm and moðþe hyt fornimð,
and ðeofas hit delfað and forstelað: gold-hordiað ców soðlice
gold-hordas on heofenan, þær naþor óm ne moðþe hit ne for-
nymð and þær ðeofas hit ne delfað ne ne forstelað: witodlice,
þær þin goldhord ys, þær ys þin heorte. Be ye not willing to
hoard to you gold hoards on earth, where rust and moth fortake
it, and where thieves delve it and forsteal: hoard to you
soothly gold hoards in heaven, where neither rust nor moth
fortake it, and where thieves delve it not nor forsteal: truly
where thine gold hoard is, there is thine heart. So the various
cases of the pronoun demonstrative or article have the same
sense of qui, quæ, quod. Thus Matth. ix. 9, þa se Hælend
þanon ferde he geseah ænne man sittende æt tollsceamule,
þæs nama wæs Matheus. As the Saviour thence fared,

he saw an man sitting at the toll-bench, whose name was Matthæus.

585. In like manner þanon = Thence, is also Whence: Matth. xii. 44. Ic gecyrre on min hus þanon ic ut eode. 'I will return into mine house whence I outyode.' So also þænne 'Then,' is used as When; Luke xviii. 8, þænne mannes sunu cymð, gemét he geleafan on corþan? 'When mans son shall come, shall he meet with belief on earth?' So þær is There and Where. John xi. 30, Þa gyt ne com se Hælend binnan þa ceastre, ac wæs þa gyt on þære stowe þær Martha him ongean com. 'As yet came not the Saviour within the town, but was as yet in the place where Martha him against came.' It needs not, methinks, pursue the illustrations further. Though in our modern english we employ for our relatives forms in WH, it was not so in the saxon, which reserved the HW for indefinites and interrogatives.

586. The homeric language had the same use. In the same way demonstrative forms in T, that is forms afterwards demonstrative exclusively, are read in the sense of the aspirate forms with 'O, and conversely in some cases, as ὡς = Τως = Thus. The custom continued down to the later poets; and in the attic tragedies την is capable of representing quam, and τῳ, quo. To give an example, Il. K. 12, θαυμαζεν πυρα πολλα τα καιετο Fιλιοθι προ, 'he wondered at the many fires which were burning in front of Troy.' Here we should by no means rest satisfied with the obvious and familiar statement that τὰ is put for ἅ, but we should accept as philological instruction the clear and remarkable fact that τὰ, ἅ, quæ, are varied forms of the same word. And so of all the cases of the pronoun ὁ, ἡ, το.

587. Here then in the mœsogothic, the anglosaxon, and the hellenic are instances in which, without the intervention of labials, we find gutturals and dentals changing places with one another. The interrogatives also are sometimes found in this form, but it cannot so certainly be said that no labial had intervened, since π is the interrogative initial in most words. Thus, for instance, Nubes, 22: τοῦ δώδεκα μνᾶς Πασίᾳ; 'for what do I owe twelve minæ to Pasias?' These are cases of

L

Τίς = Quis. The sanskrit seems to give us no assistance in explaining these changes: the sanskrit relative is nom. Yas, Yâ, Yat; the interrogative Kas, Kâ, Kim: see art. 251.

588. These parallels in the pronouns, added to the examples adduced before, seem to me sufficient to support the proposition that dentals may be exchanged with gutturals. That so it is has been believed in a few instances in various languages by the students of them; but it was not desirable to quote everything which has been alledged.

ANLAUT.

589. Coomb = agls. Comb = welsh Cwm = Τεμπη. Campus is likely to be of the same origin. Dingle? which is written Dimble (Drayton, Polyolb. xxvi.).

590. Cough = Tussim a sibilate form, like Host (o short). See art. 524.

591. Dear = agls. Deor = norse Dŷrr = lat. Carus, in both senses of dear, both loved and high priced. Erse and gaelic have Cara 'a friend,' breton Kâr 'love,' etc.

592. Dry under its original shape germ. Dörre, Dürre = Ξερος, Ξηρος, with Χερσος, Χωρα. See 1006, 1033.

592 a. Screw, see 13. Cf. Στρεφειν. They are sibilate forms of the circle syllable CR: see art. 1026. Wring is another name for the same process, and compares with Στρογγυλος, †στρεγειν = Στρεφειν. The Cheesewring in Devon is a screw-shaped pile of rocks.

593. Till = agls. Tilian = Colere. Words of so special a meaning and so near in form can hardly be of separate origin. Plough, germ. Pflug, sanskr. Fal-au, Fâl-an, hebr. פלח. Cf. Toil.

594. Tinder = germ. Zunder, seems to belong Candere, Accendere. See art. 1025. Erse Teinne, fire.

595. Top with its diminutive Tip = Cop = Caput, etc. = germ. Kopf.

>Gy toke him by the top with that
>And that houed he dede* of † ſlo.
>
>>Sir Gy of Warwicke, p. 138.

---

* Dede = caused to.   † Of = off.

GUTTURALS EXCHANGED WITH DENTALS.

> Sire Simond de Montfort hath suore bi ys cop.
> > Richard of Almaigne, 38.

> Upon the cop right of his nose he had
> A wert and theron stode a tuft of heres.
> > Chaucer, C. T., Prologue, 556.

> But syr James had soche a chopp
> That he wyste not, be my toppe,
> > Whethur it hyt were day or night.
> > > Sir Tryamoure, 764.

> All the stored vengence of heaven fall
> On her ungrateful top.
> > King Lear, ii. 4.

> This white top writeth min olde years.
> > Chaucer, C. T. 3867.

In confirmation see, of Topple, Tumble, 1026. Germ. Kippen = Tip (over) (579) is the diminutive. In Laȝamon (i. 30) where the earlier text has Bi þone toppe he hine nom, the later has Bi þe coppe he him nam : see also the index; also Seinte Marharete, fol. 46 b, 14.

596. TRUE under its mœsogothic form Triggws, πιστος, deserves comparison with the epic Κρηγυος, and Credere.

INLAUT OR AUSLAUT.

597. BLEAT = agls. Blætan. Cf. Βληχη. Scep blætt says Ælfric. Οἰῶν τε βληχήν, Od. μ. 266. Cf. Balare, Balatus.

598. BRITTLE as a derivative from Break, Frangere, is = lat. Fragilis. The agls. has Brecan = Breotan, Bryttian = germ. Brechen = norse Briota. In the earlier english, Brickle as well as Brittle.

> Right in the midst the goddesse self did stand
> Upon an altar of some costly masse,
> Whose substance was uneath to understand;
> For neither pretious stone, nor durefull brass
> Nor shining gold nor mouldring clay it was;
> But much more rare and pretious to esteeme
> Pure in aspect and like the christall glasse,
> Yet glasse was not, if one did rightly deeme,
> But being fair and brickle, likest glasse did seeme.
> > Faery Queene, IV. x. 39.

599. Cushot, Cowshot = agls. Cusccote 'palumbus, ring-dove,' is a derivative (a participial) from Cusc=germ. Keusch =lat. Castus. These birds are ever seen side by side, and have the same mutual affection as turtle-doves. That a verb existed see κοσκινον.

600. Fat = Παχυς = agls.Fæt = germ.Fett. Thus, in Beowulf 1750: Fætte beagas 'thick bows,' collars, armlets of gold. Not to exclude Thick as another form of the root.

601. Flat, art. 442, seems a modern change for †flak, as πλακα (acc.).

602. * * lat. Futuere. Among other testimonies to the antiquity of the words existing at once in the english, greek, and latin, we observe this, that such as lie under the ban of society now were equally shameful in the days of Aristophanes and Horace. Φυτευειν as a subderivative has no connexion with the latin.

603. Lie=agls. mœsog. Leogan, seems to be the active form of Latere, Λαθειν, agls. Lutian; for the mœsog. middle voice ga-Laugnian expresses Λανθανειν. Although the mœsog. writes no initial H, yet the radical syllable is probably Kal, Celare.

>   Thou mon be ded, es noght at laine*.
>   Ywaine and Gawin, 703.

604. Little = agls. Litel=nors Lîtill (litlu)=Ολιγος, see art. 137.

604 a. Lot=agls. Hlot=mœsog. Hlauts=norse Hlutr. Cf. Λαχειν.

605. Need = lat. Necesse = Αναγκη = agls. Neod, Nyd = mœsog. Nauþs = norse Nauðr = germ. Noth. Perhaps the same as Knot. The norse in the plural means bands; Vissi ser â höndum höfgar nauðir (Völundar Kviða, 11), 'He wot (sibi) on hands heavy knots, bands, manacles.' And this confirms the parallel; for Knot is Nectere: it explains also how Necessitudo, Necessarius have the same form yet mean relationship.

606. Nuts=Nuces, art. 333.

* Conceal.

607. QUAKE = agls. Cwacian, is to be compared with lat. Quatere having an active sense. It seems to be equivalent to the labial form agls. Bifian, to Bever, shake. "Es lips bevered agen," Devonsh. Dial. p. 17. Cf. Quagmire, QUIVER.
607 a. ROD, ROOD = agls. Rod in either sense = mœsog. Hrugga, translating ῥαβδος 'a rod.' But Hrugga is evidently allied to Crucem which means Rood, the old english word for the Saviours cross. CRUTCH, CROSS = agls. Cruc, Cric, are found in all the teutonic languages and are probably native: with double g they remind us of the erse Cran ' tree.'
608. TEAT = Τιτθιον = erse Dîd, see art. 209, seems to be allied to erse Dighin 'suck the breast,' DUGS.
609. TICKLE = agls. Citelan, Tinclan (Ælfric) = isl. Kitla = lat. Titillare. Cf. KITTLISH.

Quhen new curage kitillis all gentil hertes.
Gawin Douglas, p. 403. 14.

610. TURN. See the words of latin and greek origin, as Τορνος = Tornus 'a lathe,' Torquere 'twist,' Turbinem 'a whirlwind, a top,' Τορυνη 'a pestle' for a mortar (δοιδυξ), Τρεπειν 'turn,' Τροπις 'keel,' Τορνος also εργαλειον τεχνικον ᾧ τα στρογγυλα σχηματα περιγραφεται 'a tool for drawing circles, compass;' to be compared with the derivatives of the old root †kwer; Quern 'a hand mill' = mœsog. Kwairnus, Vertere, Vorticem, Vertiginem, Gyrum, Carinam, Curvus, Circulus, Whirl.
611. WRINKLE = lat. Ruga (on the N, see 893) = Ῥυτις. The adj. Ῥυσσος bears a sibilate form, Theokr. xxix. 28.

DENTALS WITH L.

612. The dentals, D especially, exchange places with L. Thus Ulysses = æolic Υδυσσευς (Quintilian, 1. 4) = Οδυσσευς. Adipem (acc.) compared with Λιπα and Αλειφειν is clearly for †talipem. Δοχμιος is perhaps Λοξος with sibilation. Σελμα, 'a rowers bench,' is marked by its termination for a verbal; it comes probably from Sedere, as †σεδμα; but, since a dental does not easily stand before μ, so σελμα. Cf. Scandere with Scalæ, art. 1015: agls. Tacur = Δαηρ = lat. Levir. It is not

unreasonable to suppose Δαφνη = Laurus. Θολος may well
be Loligo; Meditari 'practise'= Μελεταν; Θωρηκα = Loricam
(acc.). Are we not hence to conclude that Λαρυγξ, Θωραξ
are the same word, and how can we refuse Φαρυγξ? For
'people' germ. Leute, the agls. had Leode and þeod, the
mœsog. þiuda, whence Ðeodric. Pulverem = Powder; Puddle
= Pool; Cardoel, a word very common in the romances of
Arthur, = Carlisle; coins have CARDU: the spelling is established in Ingrams Saxon Chronicle (note, p. 385). Cauda
becomes spanish Cola; Medius makes engl. Mullion 'the stone
shaft of a window.' Digentia is Licenza, the people of Madrid
are Madrilenos. In Festus " Delicare ponebant pro dedicare."
"Melicæ gallinæ quod in Media id genus avium corporis amplis-
simi fiat; L litera pro D substituta." "Rediviam quidam, alii
Reluvium appellant, cum circa unguis cutis se resolvit, quia
luere est solvere, etc." "Seliquastra sedilia antiqui generis
appellantur, D litera in L conversa, ut etiam in sella factum est,
et Subsellio et Solio quæ non minus a sedendo dicta sunt."
" Mediusfidius compositum videtur et significare Iovis filium,
id est Herculem, quod Iovem Græci Δια et nos Iovem; ac
fidium pro filio, quod sæpe antea pro L litera D utebantur, etc."
" Odefacit dicebant antiqui ab odore pro Olefacit, vetere qua-
dam consuetudine immutandi literas, etc." Cf. Odor, Olet.
Varro de Re Rust. iii. 9, agrees with Festus concerning the
fowls, "quod antiqui ut Thetin, Thelin, sic Medicam, Meli-
cam vocabant."

ANLAUT.

613. TEAR = agls. Tear in cod. Exon. Teagor = mœsog. Tagr =
erse Dear = welsh Dagr, Deigr = Δακρυ, Δακρυον = lat. Lacrima.
With the old forms of Tear seem connected the old forms of
DEW = agls. Deaw = germ. Thau = norse Dögg. Cf. also Leak,
art. 136 a. Mr. Thorpe (note, Cod. Exon. to 182. 23) thinks
the G an insertion!

614. TEAR = agls. Teran, probably for Tehran, since the
mœsog. is Tahyan, representing †tag-yan, and akin to latin
Lacerare. Cf. Lancinare. Δακνειν belongs not to this group,
but to Οδαξ, Οδοντα (acc.).

615. Tongue = lat. Lingua = agls. Tunge = mœsog. Tuggo (where gg sound as ng) = norse Tunga = erse, gaelic Teanga. Here a comparison of the semitic, the sanskrit, and of the verb Lick with its equivalents (art. 139) shews L to be older than T.

INLAUT OR AUSLAUT.

616. Bath = agls. Bæð = isl. Bað = lat. Balneum = Baλaνειον. We may take Bathe to signify 'subject to the moderate action of fire.' The agls. seems to be used properly of warm baths; 'Thermæ' in the glossaries. " To Beathe in provincial english is to heat unseasoned wood by fire for the purpose of straightening it. Tusser has the word and also Spenser. Meat improperly roasted is said, in the midland counties, to be beathed" (Halliwell). " The german Bähen, to warm, may be another form of the same root." Holz bähen, ' to warp or beathe wood ;' Brot bähen, ' to toast bread.' Hence, probably, may be explained the name of Baiæ, as signifying warm baths, to which that spot owed its celebrity. It is difficult to separate isl. Baka ' to heat,' baka sig vip ella ' to warm oneself at the fire:' prov. engl. to beak, platt deutsch, sich bakern, swiss Bächelen ' to bask to warm oneself'" (Wedgewood). So then Bake, Bask. There are several other such words. Bacon is always subjected to the action of moderate heat, and in farmhouses, with wood fires, was hung up in the chimney in the smoke. Is βαλανειον to Calidus as βαλανος to Glans?

> And ligges bekeand in his bed
> When he haves a lady wed.
> Ywaine and Gawin, 1459.

> To beyke his boones by.
> Bone Florence, 99.

> Yokes, forkes and such other let bailie spie out
> And gather the same as he walketh about:
> And after at leasure let this be his hier
> To beath them and trim them at home by the fier.
> Tusser, December.

I have met with the verb in an unpublished agls. MS. with the sense clearer than can be found in Lye. Seo corþe ys call gebeðod mid þære sumorlican hætan (and then again cooled by winter). I would be understood only to suggest, however, that Beþan may be the root of βαλανειον; for a tolerable explanation may be found in בלל (oleo) perfundere. With βαλανος 'acorn,' no connexion in sense is visible.

617. ELEVEN = lat. Vndecim = 'Ενδεκα = agls. Endlufon, in the Heliand Ellevan = mœsog. Ainlif = norse Ellifu. This is of Bopps keen sight: it is the more remarkable since agls. An 'one' and Tigun 'ten' would make a convenient compound.

618. MEAD, METHEGLIN, and their relatives in 511 are immediately connected with lat. Mel = Μελι = erse, welsh Mil. MAD in the sanskrit is to 'to intoxicate, or madden,' and might be supposed akin to the english, but that examples of the early use of the word in the teutonic dialects are rare: agls. gemæd, gemaad 'amens' is from Ælfric, while Wud = o. engl. Wood is the usual term.

619. MUZZLE seems related to the germ. Maul 'mouth of an animal' mœsog. †mul, found in the comp. verb faurmulyan, φιμουν, 1 Kor. ix. 9. And this seems to be another form of the mœsog. Munths = germ. Mund, which is probably related to lat. Mandere, Manducare 'to chew,' and Mouth.

620. SMILE = Μειδιαν. Smile is not extant in agls., mœsog. or norse; but dan. is Smile = swed. Småle = dutch Smylen. In the same sense the agls. uses Smeorcian = to Smirk. The sanskr. has the root Smi and Smerah 'ridens.'

621. SULTRY from SWEAL 'be hot' = agls. Swælen = sanskr. Swid, which signifies both 'sudare' and 'adurere.' The isl. at Sveita is 'to sweat' actively, and Svid is 'heat.' So that Sudare seems connected with Swælen. Eudoxos adds Sweltering heat, which I had overlooked, and Swealing candle, which I never heard. See Halliwell.

> Anon the candent thunderbolt delights
> That tears the bosom of the sultry cloud,
> And from its watery lap prone deluge sheds.
> Let the tempestuous Angel quit his hold
> Upon the SWEALING fork and pour sublime
> His thundering volley through the deep of heaven.
>   Hurdis, Favourite Village, iii. p. 76.

Sweal may be taken, however, in a different light as a sibilation of the agls. Weallan 'be hot,' Wellian, with Wylm 'heat,' derivatives of an old root Gel, and equal to Olescere in Adolescunt ignibus, and Oleum.

622. TWELVE = lat. Duodecim = Δυωδεκα = agls. Twelf = norse Tólf = mœsog. Twalif. Like Eleven.

623. WOUND = agls. Wund = mœsog. Wunds = norse Und = ? lat. Vulnus.

S WITH R.

624. The agls., greek, lat. had but one S. The english SH, though now of a sound distinct from S, always has its origin in SK. In the term sibilants, however, I wish to include the english and sanskrit J, the english and sanskrit CH, and all hissing combinations as ξ, ψ, ST, SK, SP, KSH.

625. Among the various sibilations of letters, the substitution of S for R or R for S stands upon special grounds and is most generally acknowledged: it is frequent in the latin.

626. In the Eleian inscription occur τοιρ for τοις, τιρ for τις. Ahrens in his treatise on dialects gives 35 examples of S, R interchanged; but they are not worth transferring. Gubernator = Κυβερνητης, Arator = Αροτης, and in general the termination -tor = -της. Puer is the same word as παῖς in two syllables, and then by contraction παις in one. Blossom is nearly Flos; but the cases have R, as Florem. The sabine Flusare is explained Florali. The desideratives in -σειειν are in latin desideratives in -rire. The Romans from their monuments mention instances of S becoming in later times R. Cic. ad Fam. ix. 21. Sed tamen, mi Pœte, qui tibi venit in mentem negare, Papirium quenquam unquam, nisi plebeium fuisse? fuerunt enim patricii minorum gentium, quorum princeps L. Papirius Mugillanus, qui censor cum L. Sempronio Atratino fuit, cum antea consul cum eodem fuisset, annis post Romam conditam CCCXII: sed tum Papisii dicebamini. Post hunc XIII. fuerunt sella curuli ante L. Papirium Crassum, qui primum Papisius est vocari desitus. Here Cicero tells us that the Papirian gens was of old the Papisian, and marks the

man in whose name the altered spelling was first used. The
abbreviator of Festus says, "R pro S litera sæpe antiqui
posuerunt, ut maiosibus, meliosibus, lasibus, fesiis, pro maioribus, melioribus, laribus, feriis." Festus in his own words,
"Quæso, ut significat idem quod rogo, ita quæsere ponitur
ab antiquis pro quærere, ut est apud Ennium libro secundo;

<blockquote>
Ostia munita est: idem loca navibus pulcris
Munda facit, nautisque mari quæsentibus vitam:
</blockquote>

et in Cresphonte (frag. 644),

<blockquote>
Duxit uxorem sibi liberum quæsendum causa:
</blockquote>

et in Andromeda [the text is defective],

<blockquote>
Liberum quæsendum causa familiæ matrem tuæ."
</blockquote>

This letterchange explains the S in quæsivi, quæsitum.
Again says Festus " Pignosa pignora eo modo quo Valesii et
Ausclii, Pinosi Pilosi dicebantur:" that is, Pignora, Valerii,
Aurelii were once Pignosa, Valesii, Auselii: the other words
are corrupt. The abbreviator of Festus again, " Plisima,
plurima." So Ausum is the sabine for Aurum (Festus).
Quintilianus, i. 4, to the same effect, "nam ut Valesii et
Fusii in Valerios Furiosque venerunt, ita Arbos, Labos, Vapos
etiam, et Clamos ac Lases ætatis fuerunt." So Asa for Ara:
as in a law reputed of Numa " Pellex asam Iunonis ne tagito;
si taget, Iunoni crinibous demissis arnum feminam caidito."
A. Gellius, IV. iii. 3. So Ausones = Aurunci. Eram is for
†esam. In lat. Mures; other languages have S. Hare =
germ. Hase. Forlorn is for-losen. Lose is sometimes written
with R.

<blockquote>
In what maner, sayd Robyn,
Hast thou lore thy ryches?
A Lytell Geste of Robyn Hode, 200.
</blockquote>

<blockquote>
Sibriht, þat I of told, þat þe land had lorn,
Þat a suynhird slouh under a busk of thorn.
Robert Brunne, i. p. 14.
</blockquote>

Our language at one time had Ure for Use.

<blockquote>
No way to it but one, steep and obscure,
The stairs of rugged stone seldom in ure.
W. Browne, B. P. I. v.
</blockquote>

627. Berry = Bacca: for the mœsog. Basi 'a berry,' Matth. vii. 16, is a sibilate form of Bacca, and at the same time the equivalent of our Berry=agls. Berige, Berie=germ. Beere=isl. Ber=dutch Besje.

628. Chesil is the old english word meaning 'sand'= agls. Ceosel 'glarea, sabulum, arena' (Ælfric)=germ. Kies, Kiesel, Kiesling. This would admit the form, lat. Fasena= Arena. The Chesil bank connecting Portland with the land consists of pebbles. Fasena is found in a passage of Velius Longus cited by Voss in his Etymol. "Nonnulli harenam cum adspiratione, sive quoniam hæreat, sive quod aquam hauriat, dicendum existimaverunt; aliis sine aspiratione videtur enuntianda. Nos non tam per illas causas, quas supra proposuimus, quam propter originem vocis; siquidem, ut testis est Varro, a Sabinis Fasena dicitur: et sicut S familiariter in R transit, ita F in vicinam adspirationem mutatur."

629. Hear=agls. Heoran, in the Heliand Horian=norse Heyra, has S in the mœsogothic Hausyan, which seems to represent the first syllable of lat. Auscultare, and the second of ανηκουστειν, ωτακουστειν. So Ear=lat. Aurem=mœsog. Auso. The greek Ους is not fairly compared, the comparison should be with the full form as in Ουατα.

630. Hoard = agls. Hord is in mœsog. Huzd, in several passages translating θησαυρος, as Luke xviii. 2, thou shalt have treasure in heaven; and this is very near to Γαζα, which belongs to later greek only, and which Hesychios gives as Persian. Cf. גִּזְבָּר 'treasurer.'

631. Nose is akin to lat. Nares as well as to Nasus.

632. Purse is the agls. Pusa=lat. Pera, 'a wallet, a bag.' The islandic Puss is by assimilation for †pusr, pus with the masculine termination; so Âss, for †âsr, an As, a god.

633. Sister=lat. Soror. Some analogy exists, as to the termination, with lat. Vxor=probably Yokester. I suppose the agls. termination -stre to be the sanskr. strî 'a woman :' a conclusion confirmed by the agls. verb Strynan, Streonan 'to beget,' with the sanskr. Strain 'produced from or by a woman.'

For though thyselfe be noble in thy strene
A thousand fold more noble is thy quene.
The Court of Love, 370.

The termination -estre, in agls., says Rask, denotes feminine nouns of action, and though our modern dialect has made Tapster masculine, and has invented Seamstress for agls. Seamestre, yet the examples of -stre as agls. masc. are rare; there is one in Genes. xl. 1. Sister=agls. Sweostor=mœsog. Swistar = norse Syster (dropping w) = germ. Schwester = sanskr. Swasri, which like the latin has no T.

634. SPARROW = lat. Passer. It will be seen that the radical idea is found in ψαρος 'brown ash coloured.'

635. WEAR. The agls. Werian is applied to clothes, and probably therefore should not be compared with Gerere, which by Gerulus 'a porter' etc., differs not from Ferre. Wear then may be mœsog. Wasyan=sanskr. Was 'tegere, inducre'=lat. Vestire, and akin to WEED.

636. WEASEL=lat. Viverra, of which another form is our FERRET, Feruncus. Weasel = agls. Weosul, Wesla = germ. Wiesel=swed. Vessla=dan. Vœsel. MART=agls. Mearð= germ. Marder is equivalent, with M for labial mute.

SIBILATION.

637. Letters receive or lose sibilation; sibilants become non-sibilants, or nonsibilants become sibilants; and it is mostly difficult to determine whether were the older form. That question sometimes meets its solution in the history of a word, but it is always attended by whatever amount of uncertainty is mixed up with the several steps of the inquiry. Thus Tegere with its teutonic relatives, when compared with Στεγειν, looks like a more widely dispersed and more strongly supported form: but when Στεφειν is shown=Στεγειν, and the sanskrit forms are found to have the sibilants, the former conclusion is untenable. Whatever light may be thrown upon that point will spring from the investigation of the descent and far extended use of a word, and can scarcely be conveniently treated separately.

638. Compare then the following sibilate and nonsibilate

forms. And first in anlaut. Μαραγδος = sanskr. Marakatas, Maraktan = Σμαραγδος ' Emerald.' Tegere = Στεγειν. Αυλακα (acc.) = Sulcum ' furrow' with Sulh ' plough.' Κεδαννυναι = Σκεδαννυναι. Κορδινεισθαι = Σκορδιναςθαι, Μαραγνα (Rhesus, 817) = Σμαραγνα. Φωνη = Sonus for †suonus. Μικρος = Σμικρος. Funda = Σφενδονη; †screre 'to say' = Ϝειρειν, ερεῖν (fut.): Si = Εἰ: sanskr. Su = Ευ, as is commonly supposed; the disyllabic homeric form, however, has not been accounted for. Serum = Ορος. Sternutare = Πταρνυσθαι. Πτυειν = Spuere. Spuma 'foam' cf. with Pumex 'a porous stone,' also with Σπογγος? Σπογγος with Fungus. Succus = Οπος. Σμυραινα = Muræna. Segesta = Egesta. Somnus, properly Sompnus = Ὑπνος, not forgetting Sopire and agls. Swefan to SLEEP. Pike with Spica 'an ear of corn' pike shaped. The mœsog. †swairban in the compound Biswairban, Luke vii. 38, 'She wiped them with the hairs of her head,' shews the common original of Verrere and Σαιρειν 'to sweep.' Cf. Sweep with Wipe. Scythæ with Goths. Snottingaham is the saxon name of Nottingham, from the norse Snottr, wise, producing Snotting, the retainers of Snott, and Snottingaham, their ham or dwelling place (what authority had Skinner for his statements?). Scintilla produces Etincelle and Tinsel. Sneeze in dutch is Ik nies, niesde, geniesd. Knapsack in germ. is Schnappsack. Quattuor produces Square and Squadron. Γραφειν is akin to Scrape. Weak = germ. Schwach. Scratch = germ. Kratzen.

> So gret a weping was ther non certain
> Whan Hector was ybrought all fresh yslain
> To Troy, alas! the pitee that was there,
> Cratching of chekes, rending eke of here.
>
> Chaucer, C. T. 2837.

"He began to howle and to braye and cratched with the hynder feet," Reynard the Foxe, p. 16. "Cratched and scraped with my feet," Id. p. 50. "And he was there cratched and byten," Id. p. 141. Lick, Λιχνος, Λιχνευειν, Lickerish with germ. Schleckern. Melt with Smelt, germ. Schmelzen. Cry is represented in germ. by Schreien, in old high germ. by Scrîan: germ. Specht = lat. Picus ' woodpecker.'

638 a. With gutturals first the changes often result in a substitution: as Con=$\xi \nu \nu$=$\sigma \nu \nu$, but the middle step is frequently overpassed. Thus SLY=CLEVER=agls. Gleaw=isl. Glöggr (B. H.)=germ. Klug=norse Slocgr=germ. Schlau. In the substantive SLEIGHT we retain the G.

> And in the craft of weving wonder sle.
> Gawin Douglas, p. 137. 12.

> Weil at ane blenk sle poetry not tane is*.
> Id. Prolog. Book I.

> Sche was in Develin
> The fair leuedi the quene
> Lovesome under line,
> And sleiyest had ybene
> And best couthe of medicine.
> Sir Tristrem, p. 81.

So Havelok the Dane, 108 l, Sley. The lat. Sonus (for †suonus) =$\Phi \omega \nu \eta$=sanskr. Swanas is also found as sanskr. Kwan. $\chi \epsilon \iota \rho o \nu \rho \gamma o \varsigma$ has produced Surgeon. Camel in coptic becomes Samoul, and $\kappa \iota \beta \omega \tau o \varsigma$ is rendered acceptable to a sahidic car as $\sigma \iota \beta \omega \tau o \varsigma$. Germ. Säule=o. h. g. Sul=norse Sûl. Sûla 'a pillar' seems akin to the radical syllable in Columna. Germ. Schlüssel, 'a key'=o. h. g. Slog belongs to Claudere. Setà=$\chi a \iota \tau \eta$. Silex=$\chi a \lambda \iota \xi$. Sweet=welsh Chwys. Swan=$\kappa \nu \kappa \nu o \varsigma$.

639. As H is a guttural, any case in which H and S are interchanged belongs to this class. It is commonly taken, that the H is a substitution for the S, which may be in some instances true; but it is certain that, as analogy suggests, both H and S are mostly substitutes for a stronger guttural, as K: and this will be shewn in some instances which have been regarded as undisputed examples of the putting of H instead of S. To speak plainly, I admit with reluctance, and till better information only, any example of H having its origin in S. Zeuss concludes from the old Sabrina and the new Hafren, 'the Severn,' that the H of the Welsh in place of S is a recent feature in the language. This argument has force; but until the signification of the word is understood, it

---

* Not understood at a glance.

is not wholly conclusive. The Phœnicians trading with Britain, then all keltic, may have lent a name to its greatest river, like the Guad-al-quivir of Spain : the hebrew equivalent of quivir is כַּבִיר; or Hafren may represent Gafr ' a goat.' To the subsidiary argument of Zeuss that Salusa is a brine spring in Gaul (Mela, ii. 5) little weight can attach when we observe that it was in Narbonensis and may have a roman name. 'Εξ = Sex; but the welsh has preserved a guttural form in Chwech 'six,' harmonizing with what is found in the tables of Herculanum, Fεξ, and apparently of high antiquity. Silva = 'Υλη, but these are represented in sense by the english Holt germ. Holz, welsh Celli = gaelic Coill = erse Coill, rendering it probable that ξυλον belongs to the same family. 'Αγνος = Sanctus, and 'Αγιος = Sacer; but these may have had an earlier form; the mœsog. Weihs, ἀγιος, seems likely to be a relative. 'Ολος = old lat. Sollus I shall shew to come from a guttural form in K-L. 'Αλλεσθαι = lat. Salire from an early K-L. 'Ερπειν = Serpere from a root †kwer, as in lat. vermis, sanskr. krimi. 'Επτα = Septem is rendered an unsafe ground for argument by the form τεπτα (Hesych.). 'Υπερ = Super; but the hebrew has a guttural in עֲבַר. Συς = Sus = 'Υς; but Prichard has already compared welsh Hwch = persian Khauk خُوک. Sub = 'Υπο, but cannot be of different origin from ὑπερ. Sui = Οὑ, Sibi = Οἱ, Se = 'Ε have, they say, a guttural in the zend. 'Αλες pl. = lat. Sal, where there is some slight reason to suspect a guttural, to be found in Al-kali قَلِي, which according to Freytag is Cineres qui ex salicornia similibusque combustis herbis conficiuntur, vegetable salts obtained by burning saliferous herbs. It may have been that vegetable salt was known before the mineral. In Sudor = 'Ιδρως, Sudare = Ιδιειν, the welsh Chwys is probably older than the sanskrit. In 'Εκυρη = Socrus = germ. Schwieger = sanskr. Swashru, the welsh Chwegr 'mother in law' seems to justify the greek aspirate, although the initial of the sanskrit here be, as in some similar instances, the simple sibilant. That Sister has commenced with a guttural is evident from welsh Chwaer = breton Choar = armenian Khur = persian Khwahar, Khuhar.

Some hold that welsh Cader, 'chair' = erse Cataoir = breton Kador are taken from καθεδρα; but I hope it will be considered whether they do not display the old unsibilate form of 'Εδρα, Sedes. 'Ημι- = lat. Semi-. 'Υπνος = lat. Somnus, Sompnus. 'Τραξ = lat. Sorex. 'Ισταναι = lat. Sistere. The last of these examples seems to exclude all argument about a guttural. The comparison of the welsh with the other keltic languages testifies also to the commutability of H and S. Lhuyd has given about thirty words which have in irish S, in welsh H. Eudoxos thus: "I often think that S is the strongest phase of the aspirate. An aspirate is the passage of air through a tube; now, when water is coming in, the air driven before it produces in its escape first an aspirate, and it gradually becomes stronger till it ends in a hiss."

640. Sometimes the prefixed S is a distinct word, as in Scorch∗, from ital. Scorticare = lat. Discorticare. Skirmish, Skrimmage is the ital. Scrimaglia, Scherma, Schermire 'to play with the foils,' from lat. Discrimen, Discernere: the word was early introduced, even into the frankish. Sdeign in Spenser is Disdain for Dedignari; Scald is italian Scaldare from Calidus as if Excalidare; king Arthurs sword Escalibur seems formed from the name of the steel makers the Chalybes.

641. Χορος is most likely connected with χαιρειν, of which the original sense was, I presume, 'leap,' whence only the homeric χαρμη of the battle, the springing to and fro, the "hoving and foining," the fight play or sword dance, the Feoht-lac of the saxons: it will be another form of Σκιρταν, Σκαιρειν. Thus Hesychios has Χυρβιασαι, σκιρτησαι, and the welsh Chware is 'to play.'

642. Con = ξυν: Κοινος = Ξυνος: Χηρος probably = Χερσος = Ξερος = Ξηρος. Κειρειν, Ξυραν are recognized as substantially the same by Buttmann (Lexil. ii. 264). The welsh Hweg, Chweg should be compared with Sweet, Suavis: welsh Ffer 'an ancle' with Σφυρον: welsh Chwi = Vos with Σφωι: welsh Chwefr (sound f as v) 'violence, rage' with Severus; welsh Chwerw, 'bitter, sharp,' gaelic Geur 'sharp, acrid.'

* That Scorenedd occurs in the Ormulum is remarkable.

latin Acerbus, with gaelic Searbh, 'sour.' Crus = Sura? Carpere = Sarpere; Κελῦφος = Siliqua.

613. The sanskrit exhibits countless examples of the change of gutturals to sibilants, sh, j, ch.

644. Dentals in anlaut exchange with S. Thus Σειος = Θειος, Σιώ=θεώ, τῷ σιῷ σύματος (Thukyd. v. 77) = τοῦ θεοῦ θύματος in laconic. Οἱ Λακωνες ειωθασι προσαγορευειν ὁταν αγασθωσι σφοδρα του, σειος ανηρ. Aristot. Eth. ad Nicom. vii. 1. They swore ναι τω σιω. In Alkæos σαλασσομεδοισαν for θαλασσομεδουσαν, σαλεσιν for θαλεσιν, σαλλει for θαλλει, εσηκε for εθηκε, Σεραπνας for Θεραπνας. In the Lysistrata σελει for θελει, σετω for θετω, σηροκτονε for θ., σιγην for θιγειν, σιος for θ., σια for θεα. In late inscriptions Σειδεκτας, Σειμηδης, Σειπομπος, Σειτιμος for Θεο-, Σηριππος for Θ. The Thebans put τῦκα for σῦκα, Strattis ap. Athen. xiv. 621. Τυ=Συ; Tuus=Σος; Tibi=Σοι; Ταργανη = Σαργανη; Σευτλον = Τευτλον; Σητες = Τητες; Θεραποντα = Servientem? Θεασθαι = SEE ? = mœsog. Saiwan. Tacere and Σιγαν may be of one origin. Tacere = mœsog. þahan = in the saxon of the Heliand þagian, þagon = norse þegia = swed. Tiga = dan. Tie. Σιγαν = agls. Swigan = germ. Schweigen: Silere, Σιωπαν may be not far off. The german Z is in many instances a derivative or corruption of a dental. Graff (V. 555) gives examples from the old high german: I select from the common dictionary Zahl = Tale (number); Zahn = lat. Dentem; Zahm = Tame; Zehe = Toe; Zehn = Ten; Zeit = Tide (as in Whitsuntide); Zelt = Tilt = Tent (as in the tilt of a cart); Ziegel = lat. Tegula by contraction Tile; Ziehen = Tug; Zoll = Toll; Zu = To; Zug = a Tug; Zwey = Two; Zwischen = be-Tween; Zwilling = Twin; Zunge = Tongue; Zähre = Tear; Zimmer was Timber, Zwitschern = Twitter.

615. The following deserve a separate place: Διωκειν = mœsog. Sokyan = Seek? Ζητειν = Διαιταν? Ζητητης = Διαιτητης? Ζα- = Δια; Ζυγον = Iugum for †diugum? Ζεα = sanskr. Yava for †diava: yava is the twostalked barley, and gives name to Java: see on the omission of D, 790.

616. I have noted, I find, no examples of the sibilation of

labials: see Sharddh (ç) in the sanskrit index, arts. 619, 655, 656, 666, 671, 679, 680, 682, 695. Συκη = Ficus. For myself, however, I am unable to separate the change of S with F from the other similar changes: Festus, through his abbreviator, says that Falerii was so called from salt, "Faleri oppidum a sale dictum;" nor does Ovidiuses account much differ,

> Venerat Atrides fatis agitatus Halesus
> A quo se dictam terra Falisca putat.

Hal was Sal, but Hal could become Fal. See 656 a.

647. The sibilants seem sometimes to be confounded one with another. Buttmann has observed that in the transfer of the alphabet from Phœnicia to Hellas the sibilants have been confused. "In the oriental alphabet were four sibilants, Tsain, Samech, Zade, Sin, and four also in the greek down to T, namely ζ, ξ, σ, Σάν. The names Samech, Zade, Sin answer clearly to Σιγμα, Ζητα, Σαν, and consequently the Tsain falls to ξ. As plainly also in the characters still in use, ζ, σ, ξ, we recognize the forms of Zade, Samech, Tsain of the usual hebrew alphabet. It is therefore plainly seen that the four sibilants, in their travels from race to race, were altered and confused, and exchanged even their places in the alphabet, yet so that for every sibilant of the phœnician alphabet a sibilant stands also in the greek. The place then of the old Σαν was between Π and Κοππα." These observations are somewhat to be modified by recent discoveries. In the alphabet of the hebrew coins as published by Gesenius (Lehrgebäude, p. 8), no equivalents for Tsain, Zet, Kaf, Samech, Pe were given; but the phœnician alphabet is now known from phœnician inscriptions, especially one, the epitaph of Eshmunezer אֶשְׁמֻנְעֶזֶר king of Sidon, discovered in Phœnicia; and the shapes of the characters Tsain, Samech, Sin are sufficiently like Z, Ξ, Σ (Journal Asiatique, 1856). Neither the powers nor the places of the names are, however, the same in the semitic and hellenic alphabets.

648. The confusion of the sibilants seems to be exemplified in anlaut by Spatium = Σταδιον; Συλον = Σκυλον = Spolium = שׁלל; Splendere = Στιλβειν; Stillare with the sanskr. Sal

(obsolete) 'water.' The gaelic has Sil 'to drop;' but this, I suspect, might be an adaptation from Stillare; the keltic nations dislike a concurrence of consonantal sounds; so that the old welsh Steren 'a star' has become now Seren (Relliq. Antiq. p. 93; Zeuss, p. 1100, give the old glossaries); Stimulus is welsh Swmyl. Archdeacon Williams makes welsh Gorsaf 'a station, a stand' contain Stare. So with ξηρος, sterilis. Sand = ψαμμος? Spica = Σταχυς. Stepfather, etc., become in friesic Sjapfaaer, Stink becomes Sjonke. The hellenic σπειρειν, with the heavy vocalization of the imperfect tenses, agrees, when the short vowel of the aorist is employed, in such a manner with the hebrew זרע that σπ stands for ts, and with latin so that σπ stands for S. The great antiquity of the hebrew books, in which this word is employed both literally and metaphorically, seems to warrant the R as radical. The hebrew represents also Spargere, which the same confusion of sibilants exhibits in saxon as Stregdan, from which we draw Spread.

649. BAR, SPAR, BARRICADE. Of these Bar is (teutonic? in Kilian) french and keltic, Barricade french and spanish, Spar teutonic. Somner gives Sparran 'to bar' as agls. = germ. Sperren. Swed. Sparre 'a bar' = germ. Sparren. The greek Φρασσειν, Φραγνυναι may be allied. The norse Barr 'a tree' is probably allied.

"When thou art past the door, shut it, by sparring it with the great bar, or at least the bolt."—(Janua Ling. 542.)

So Spenser Shep. Cal. May, 234.

> For when he saw her doores sparred all,
> Well nigh for sorow adoun he gan to fall.
> Chaucer, Troilus and Creseide, V. 455.

> And rent adoun bothe wall and sparre and rafter.
> Id. Cant. Tales, 993.

> At nyght to chambur sche hur ledd
> And sparryd the dore and went to bedd.
> Bone Florence, 1774.

650. CREEP = agls. Creopan = germ. Kriechen = lat. Repere = Ἑρπειν = Serpere. The radical was †kwer, giving Worm = lat. Vermis, etc. Crimson, etc. Cf. Crawl, Wriggle.

651. Crop = lat. Carpere = (nearly) Sarpere.
652. Deck = lat. Tegere (with Τεγος) = Στεγειν: further, art. 518.
653. Dough = agls. Dah (Ælfric) = mœsog. Daigs = Σταις.
654. Drite = agls. Drihten 'lord,' had a shorter Driht, 'army,' with mœsog. Driugan, στρατευειν, Drauhtinon, στρατευεσθαι, Gadrauhts, στρατιωτης. The same root may lie in Στρατος.

    The ordre fer* the accolyt hys
      To bere tapres aboute wiʒt † riʒtte ‡
    Wanne me § schel rede the gospel
      Other ‖ offry to oure Dryte.
          William of Shoreham, p. 19.

654 a. Farm seems agls. Feorm, ' victus, hospitium,' which is undoubtedly the participial substantive (art. 943) of agls. fercian, 'to sustain, support,' with food (Homil. i. 488), and so related to lat. Firmus, but, as life giving, related also to agls. Feorh, 'life,' to Breathe, and to lat. Spirare.

655. Finch = Spink = Pinnuc = agls. Finc = germ. Fink = lat. Fringilla = Σπινος, Σπινθιον, Σπιζα. 'Οτι συνειρων τους σπινους πωλει καθ' ἑπτα τοὐβολου. Aves, 1079. The birds offer a reward for bringing in Philokrates dead or alive because he strings the finches and sells them at seven for three half pence. Similarly Pax, 1118. Athenæus, p. 65.

    Pinnuc golfinc rok ne crowe.
         Owl and Nightingale, 1128.

656. Foam = agls. Fam, Fæm = germ. Faum (Wachter) = lat. Spuma.

656 a. Fry used of young fish is, I think, the mœsog. Fraiw, 'seed' = isl. Frio, Friof = dan. Frö. In suggesting a root signifying 'swallow' for Frumentum, Fruges (art. 423), an alternative supposition that Fraiw, of the same family as Serere is the true root may be allowable. Fructus belongs to Frui in its usual sense of enjoy, and is the produce of anything, as, of a house, the rent, according to roman law. It was therefore with surprise I observed that Mr. Thorpe con-

---

* Fer, for.   † Wiʒt, with, a false spelling.   ‡ riʒtte, right.
§ Me, man.   ‖ Other, or.

nects Fructus with Frigg, who to my mind is a personification of Friyon, ᚠᚱᛁᚷᚷᚾ 'to love,' the base of Friend. The Æsir are surely but personifications, Woden is Wittend, 'knowing,' Loki 'lie,' Thor 'thunder,' etc.

657. GLOW, GLEAM with their relatives, art. 322, in greek, sanskrit, welsh, seem related to Σελας 'bright light,' Σελήνη 'the moon,' Σελαγίζειν 'to flash,' erse, gaelic Solus 'light,' Soilbheim 'thunderbolt.'

658. A GRAVE with to GRUB from agls. Graban 'to dig,' is the lat. Scrobem (acc.) 'a ditch.'

659. HALL, SAL, Saloon = agls. Sal = norse Höll = germ. Saal = lat. Aula = Αυλη = sanskr. Shâlâ, where the sanskrit initial testifies to the existence of an earlier guttural K.

> With helm on hede and habergoun
> With brondes both bryght and broun
>   Thei went into that sale,
> And all that thei there lafte
> Grete strokes there thei caufte
>   Both grete and small.
>   Amis and Amiloun, 2451.

660. HOLT = lat. Silva = Ὕλη = Ἀλσος (Grimm, Gesch. D. Sp. p. 1019) = Ξυλον = welsh Celli = gaelic, erse Coill = norse agls. Holt.

661. NIBBLE, the frequentative of NIP = germ. Kneiben = Σκνίπτειν. Hence Σκνίψ, a worm that nibbles into figs and wood.

662. SAME, SAMN, Ξυν, Συν, Con, Ganz, Παν, Ἅμα, Ὁμος. The agls. has Sam 'with' as a prefix, Same 'alike' (adv.) Samnian, 'assemble,' Samod 'together.' Sinscipe 'coniugium,' which Lye, etc. erroneously explain: Schmeller has observed Sin = συν in the Heliand: his first example is sufficient, Sinhiun, 'coniuges,' from our Hive 'a family.' The mœsog. has Sama, with Samana, ἅμα, επι το αυτο, and Samaþ, επι το αυτο; the lat. has Simul (same while) Similis (same like); the sanskrit also has Sam συν, Samas 'equal, like,' and countless derivatives: as a prefix Sam denotes perfection like παν and con. Add probably Some = agls. Sum, and Ἕνα. The germ. has Zusammen, and we Assemble.

> Thy lyoun and i sal noght twyn*;
> Owther sal we samyn lende†,
> Or els wil we hethin‡ wende.
> > Ywaine and Gawin, 2223 (so 3176, 3532).

> Twa and twa ay went thai samyn.
> > Id. 3336.

> Miche semly folk was samned there
> Erls, barouns, lasse and mare
> And lenedis proude in pride.
> > Amis and Amiloun, 415.

663. SCORE = Κειρειν, Ξυραν = CARVE = SHEAR with SHARE, SHIRE, and SHORT, the passive participle = lat. Curtus, equally a passive participle. See Curve, art. 264. A SCAR, a SCORE at an inn, the SHORE, Plough-SHARE, a SHEARD or SHRED, SHEARS, SKIRT, SHIRT. At Lowestoft the alleys from the hill to the dene are called Scores, being small deep cut watercourses. The sanskrit also has the sibilation in Kshuras = Κουρευς. Shear in east Anglia is reap. "Betty is a good shearer: she is a fine strong docked wench" (Forby).

> In the mene qvhill tho gan Eneas hold
> Souirly his cours throw the gray fludis cald
> His navy with north wyndis scherand the seyis §.
> > Gawin Douglas, v. 1.

> She found and gadreth herbes suote
> She pulleth up some by the rote,
> And many with a knife she shereth
> And all into her char she bereth.
> > Gower, lib. V. p. 261.

> The laird o Drum is a wooin gane
>   A in a mornin airly,
> And he did spy a weelfaured may
>   Was shearin at her barley.
> > The Laird o Drum.

> As Morgan his brede schare.
> > Sir Tristrem, p. 48.

664. SCRATCH, SCRAPE, Scribere, agls. Screopan are but one with germ. Kratzen 'scratch,' GRUB, GRAVE, Engrave,

---

* Twyn, part.   † Lende, remain.   ‡ Hethin, hence.
§ Interea medium Æneas iam classe tenebat
Certus iter, fluctusque atros aquilone secabat.

Γραφειν, Χαρασσειν, Write = norse Rísta, with the numerous derivatives of the root in the semitic languages. Γραπτυς 'scratches' in Odys. ω. 229.

664 a. Scream = agls. Hreman, Hryman, has for its radical letters CR, which are the base of Garrire and Queri, art. 267, also of Grunt = agls. Grymetan = lat. Grunnire. That Scream in that selfsame form does not appear in agls. is only because we possess but a portion of that tongue.

665. Scut (of a hare) = Cauda? Cf. isl. Skuts 'a tail,' Skutr 'the stern of a ship' (Edda).

666. Seely (happy) = agls. Sælig = norse Sæligr = lat. Felix. By a change of meaning Silly.

> For seli child is sone ilered, ther he wole beo god.
> Thomas Beket, 158.

667. Sere, agls. Scar = erse Searg = Ξηρος = Ξερος (Od. ε. 402, ῥοχθει γαρ μεγα κυμα ποτι ξερον ηπειροιο), with χερσος 'dry land,' Χωρα 'region,' Χηρα 'widow:' see the semitic forms in 1006, and Dry, Terra in art. 592. Sterilis = mœsog. Stairo, Στειρα, shew the confusion of sibilants.

668. Shake = agls. Sceacan = norse Shaka = lat. Quatere. This is the sibilate form of Quake, which see. Germ. Schüttern, Schütteln is nearer to Quatere.

669. Shine = agls. Scînan = norse Scîna seems to be a sibilate form of Candere, in which D is not radical, as Canus and the welsh Gwyn shew.

670. Slacken = Χαλαν = lat. Solvere = Laxare, Luxare, Lucre = Λυειν = agls. Slacian. So to Slack lime, the Slag of a furnace, Luxus, Luxuria, Loose.

671. Slay = †πλαγειν, Πλησσειν = lat. Plectere, as in Plectuntur Achivi = agls. Slagan, Slean (with p. pl. Slogon) 'to strike, to kill,' = germ. Schlagen 'to strike' = norse Slâ (with part Sloginn). Derivatives Sledge-hammer, Slaughter, Plague: in mœsog., Mark, v. 29, Slaha is plague. See þlahsyan by art. 554. Flog, Lick.

> A scharpe wepen ther forth he drough
> And the lyoun ther with he slough;
> The lyoun afrayd up stert.
> Gy of Warwike, p. 152.

A loge of bowes sone he made,
And flynt and fir-yren bath he hade,
And fir ful sone thar he slogh
Of dry mos and many a bogh.
Ywaine and Gawin, 2036.

A ware dede* ma na man tak
Ðan to be slayne into the bak.
Wyntown, II. p. 114.

672. SLIDE is but another form of SLIP=lat. Labi=agls. Slipan=norse at Sleppa, in the sense of 'to give the Slip, to Slip away'=mœsog. Sliupan 'to slip on clothes,' and in the compounds 'slip away,' clabi. SLIPPERY=Lubricus. The earlier forms seem GLIB, Glaber with perhaps Glacies (which however may have Gelu for origin) and Coluber 'a snake.' Perhaps the active voice of Labi may be hid in the danish Slæbe 'to drag, to trail;' and its secondary sense, 'to toil, to drudge,' may be the source of Laborem (acc.), since SLEDGE work must be the earliest toil of a wandering race. The norse Slettr, 'æquus, planus, glaber' (B. II.), is the origin of agls. Slæd a SLADE, a plain, in names of places, as Portslade near Brighton. The semitic languages have the root. Slade is the same as Glade, and in names of places it is now and then applied to high grounds, as in some Oxfordshire Slades: it means level turf:

> "The thick and well grown fog† doth matt my smoother slades."
> Drayton.

> A dronken man wot wel he hath an hous
> But he ne wot which is the right way thider
> And to a drouken man the way is slider.
> Chaucer, C. T. 1264.

"She anoynted‡ alle his body wyth oyle of olyve. And thenne was his body al so glat and slyper that the wulf sholde have none holde on hym."—Reynard the Foxe, p. 144.

673. SLIME = agls. Slîm = germ. Schleim = swed. Slem. With this compare Limax, 'a snail with a shell or a slug without one,' and Limus 'mud.' Λαμπη.

673a. SLINK=agls. Slincan, with germ. Schlange 'a snake,'

* Death.　　† Fog, aftergrass.　　‡ Printed "annoyted."

is probably related to Lentus, art. 872, and perhaps to Slide, 672. I find the agls. form Selincan.

674. SMEAR, cf. agls. Smêru, Smeoru, 'grease, butter'= mœsog. Smairþr, πιοτης = isl. Smiör 'butter, oil' = gaelic Smior 'marrow.' If we look to the means of men in rude life, we shall not object to connect these words with MARROW =agls. Mearu=welsh Mer. Cf. isl. Mör, 'fat, suet.' Hither may be referred μυρον 'sweet smelling ointment,' μυρουν ' to anoint with perfumed substances :' cf. on Marrow. It does not at all appear that myrrh, μυρρα, formed this ointment; and the spelling differs. Myrrh is hebrew and arabic. Μυρεσθαι ' to shed tears' in Homer, with welsh Merin 'dropping, trickling,' may be allied to both, but is probably distinct.

675. SMUGGLE belongs to danish Smug 'secret,' norse at Sminga, ek Smug, 'creep, sneak.' Cf. Μυχος, 'a retired corner,' Μοιχος.

676. SNEEZE, in the north NEEZE. See word families, 1042, and Nose, Nasus.

> So neesing and coughing
> That my ghost fell to scoffing.
> Quoted by Dyce on Skelton, ii. 156.

So Job xli. 18:

> "By his neezings a light doth shine."

So also in Kilian.

677. SNOW = agls. Snaw = mœsog. Snaiws = norse Snió̂r (dat. Snió̂fi)=germ. Schnee=lat. Nivem (acc.) with Ningere = Νιφαδες (pl.), Νιφα (acc.) with Νιφετος, Νιφειν = gaelic Sneachda. If we suppose S represents a guttural, we apply the sanskr. Himan 'frost, snow,' as in Himâlaya, Χιων 'snow,' Χειμα, Χειμων 'winter,' Hiems. Is Can, 'white,' the common notion of all?

678. SORE=agls. Sar seems to be originally 'heavy ;' the agls. Swær is 1. gravis, onerosus, 2. tristis : in the Heliand Swâri 'heavy'=germ. Schwer. Thus "a sore burden too heavy for me to bear." "Slept marvailously sore all that night," Mort d'Arthure I. lxv. (heavily). The mœsog. is Kaurs, which seems to represent lat. Gravis, and this to connect

itself with Gerere = Ferre = Φερειν = Bear, whence Burden, Φορτιον. Hither refer SORROW = germ. Sorge = norse Sorg. The latin Cura offers itself for admission to this group. To the mœsog. Sair, οδυνη, norse Sâr ' a wound,' the substantive a Sore is to be referred, and it seems not to belong to this place.

679. SPARE = agls. Sparian = norse Spara = germ. Sparen = lat. Parcere. The mœsog. Freidyan seems to arise from the same root as the latin, and is like Φειδεσθαι.

680. SPARROW = lat. Passer, from a root represented by Ψαρος 'brown-ash-coloured.' From Ψαρος come also by confusion of consonants Ψαρ = germ. Staar = STARLING = lat. Sturnus. By a like confusion Sparrow is in greek Στρουθος, which is identical with lat. Turdus = THRUSH, THROSTLE = isl. Prostr = dan. Drossel. The teutonic forms of Sparrow are agls. Spcara, Spearwa = isl. Spöre = germ. Sperling, Spatz = = swed. Sparf. What we now call the sparrow hawk is not specially a sparrow hunter, but a brown ash coloured hawk: the agls. is Spear-hafoc, Sperhauk in Piers Ploughman, 4192, and in Spelman, as late as 1687, Sparhawk (voce Sparverius), french Epervier. A Starling, also called a STARE, is in agls. Stær, translated by Ælfric Turdus, Sturnus; and in the Lindisfarne Gospels, Matth. x. 29, Luke xii. 6, sparrows are Staras. It is then plain that the sparrow, the starling, the thrush, and the sparhawk being all of one colour derive their english, greek, and latin names from one root.

681. SPEER = agls. Spyrian = norse Spyrja = swed. Spörja may be Quærere, Quæsere. The signification of the agls. is of wide scope; perhaps the first sense was 'to track,' with SPOOR = norse Spor = germ. Speer = swed. Spår. Does Vestigium arise from Quæsere? The harder form Iscire 'inquire' is extant in agls. (Laȝamon, 17129).

    Min will, min harte and all my wit
    Ben fully set to herken and spire
    What any mon woll speke of hire.
        Gower, lib. ii. p. 226.

    At morn the childe cald seriantes twa
    And bad thai sold his errand ga

Preuely into the towne,
And spir in stretes, up and downe,
Efter a mon of strange cuntre.
Sevyn Sages, 3813.

682. SPIN=agls. Spinnan=mœsog. Spinnan=norse Spinna
=germ. Spinnen= Πηνίζειν. Homer has Πηνιον, Iliad Ψ. 761,
for the thread on the shuttle : very similar to this is the use
of the word by Aristoteles (Hist. A. V. xvii. 5, 6) for cocoon.
He treats there of χρυσαλλιδες, νυμφαι, πηνια, and ὑπερα : it
is plain from the context that these are all grubs in the pupa
state ; the chrysallides are of a gold colour, the nymphæ are
those of the bee tribe, the πηνια such as SPIN themselves
coverings.

683. SPIT=Πτυειν, see art. 202.

683 a. SPUR is not only agls. Spura ' calcar,' but 'calx,'
heel, appearing in Sperlira, ' the calf of the leg,' making ' heel
muscle.' This is Πτερνα ' heel,' and Perna, on which something was said, art. 300, where the teutonic forms are given in
their unsibilate shape. Cf. Fersna in Schmeller. SPURN is
' calcare' and SPOOR ' vestigium :' the agls. Spirigan is ' inves-
tigare,' SPEER; and Spurnere is ' a fuller,' like Walker 'a fuller,'
from the treading the clothes in water, a conculcando.

683 b. SQUEAMISH seems connected with Vomere, Εμεῖν,
see art. 221.

684. SQUINT belongs to Quoin, Κανθος ' corner of the eye,'
see Kent, art. 130.

685. STAR, notwithstanding Αστερα (art. 204), should be
further compared with the sanskrit Târâ. Some trace of this
form is in Σ. 485, of the shield of Achilles, 'Εν δέ τε τείρεα
πάντα τά τ' ουρανὸς ἐστεφάνωται. In the word Septemtriones,
rejecting of course the common explanation as too lame, it
may perhaps be not sufficient to suggest this word as a root,
septem-trio. For myself I prefer another explanation : see
numerals, art. 1000.

686. STEAKS. What are Steaks? The younger Junius
explained them as fried mutton chops, " Segmenta lateris
ovilli cum costis frixa in sartagine." Lye declared they are
also veal cutlets, " etiam bubulæ ac vitulinæ nec minus in

craticulam [-a?] tostæ quam in sartagine frixæ;" that is, also of beef or veal, and either broiled on a gridiron or fried in a pan. These opinions seem borne out by the cognate languages, and even with more latitude: in the isl. Steik is 'assum, caro frixa,' 'meat roast, boiled, or fried '=danish, swedish Stege: the swedish has Stekpanna, 'the frying pan,' Stekspit, 'the steak spit, roasting spit,' Stekugn 'the steak oven.' These senses seem related to Τηκειν 'melt as fat or wax,' Τηγανον 'frying pan.' Beru hold steikja; 'bears flesh to cook:' Var á lægi litt steict etit: 'was on the sea little cooked (food) eaten' (Edda). The agls. Sticce, 'offa, frustum' = germ. Stück 'a piece,' are possibly secondary notions.

687. STEER. Cf. lat. Taurus, Ταυρος. In mœsog. Stiur translates μοσχος; in agls. Steor is 'iuvencus, anniculus:' Schmeller gives the old saxon Stier as 'taurus:' germ. Stier is 'taurus,' even so masculine that Stieren is 'to bull;' in islandic Tiur is 'taurus,' þiór 'bos castratus post aliquot annorum admissuram.' Steer is, I believe, among our farmers, an ox castrated after full growth. These variations in sense do not prevent the words being of one origin: our word Wether is the mœsog. Wiþrus, which signifies lamb. John i. 29. שׁוֹר.

687 a. STEVEN=agls. Stefn=mœsog. Stibna may represent Φωνη (for †σφωνη) and lat. Sonus=sansk. Swanas, with the N participial. The agls. Sweg may be of the same origin. The word is frequent in old english.

> The vois of the peple touched to the heven
> So loude crieden they with mery steven.
> Chaucer, C. T. 2564.

687 b. STINK, which in agls. has an indifferent sense, Stincan 'smell ill or well,' is perhaps not unconnected with Scent, Sentire (with an active sense olfacere, as against olere) Sentina, as if †stink-ina.

688. STIR = agls. Styrian = germ. Stören = lat. Turbare = Ταρασσειν, Θορυβειν. In the saxon and german resides the same sense as in the latin and greek. Lye cites Beda, 646. 4, " Swa monigum and swa myclum styrnesse wiþerweadra

Singa*," 'by so much and so mickle disturbings of adverse things.' So corð styrung, 'earthquake,' Chron. Sax. 196. 1. STORM 'tempest' appears by the agls. to be derivative of this verb: also to take by Storm. See Trouble.

689. STOCKADE is evidently from Stick, Stake, Stock, agls. Staca, Stoc. It seems probable that Stockade was the first notion of Τειχος, just as Sticks set Στοιχηδον are the first elements of Τοιχος. Ξυλινον τειχος, by which I understand a stockade, is mentioned Xen. Hellen. I. iii. 4; Herodot. VII. 142, 143, VIII. 51, IX. 65, 70, etc. Hesychios gives Τειχιον, Αττικοι τον περιβολον τοις χωριοις, 'the fence on farms,' all from Stare, Stehen. Eudoxos says "And what of Στειχειν?" It is a problem for any greek scholar, to say what is the connexion between Στειχειν and Στοιχηδον. But I would suggest that as A Stalk is related to To Stalk, so A Stick to Στειχειν.

690. STRIDE = agls. Strǽde (Somner), with STRADDLE, appear generally with SC: agls. Scrið 'a course,' Scriðan 'vagari,' germ. Schreiten, dansk. Skridt, Skriden, norse Skríða are sibilations of the root which appears in lat. Gradus.

691. SUL, SULH, 'a plough,' with lat. Sulcus, Αυλαξ, may belong to Colere, Culter. Αργυρεα ευλακα ευλαξειν, Thukyd. v. 16.

692. SWALLOW = agls. Swelgan = norse Svelgia, I assume to be a sibilate form of a lost root †kw-l, from which by vocalization comes Gula; also the sanskrit Galah.

693. SWALLOW similarly may be χελιδων = agls. Swalewe = germ. Schwalbe = swed. Svala.

694. SWAN = agls. Swan = norse Svanr = Κυκνος, which is a reduplicate form of †kwan: this word must have once existed; it meant 'white,' and is found in lat. Canus, Candere, welsh Gwyn, Can, breton Gwen, Kann.

695. SWAY = germ. Schwanken = lat. Vacillare = WAG, art. 371, with WAVE, from the swaying motion = with labial, germ. Schweifen = norse Svífa = lat. Vibrare.

696. SWEEP, SWAB, WIPE I believe to be = mœsog. Swairban,

* This passage is apparently ungrammatical. It is however the distinctly written reading of the MS. in the public library at Cambridge. Kk. iii. 18, which I consulted.

the compounds of which translate εξαλειφειν, εκμασσειν (Kol. ii. 14; Luke vii. 38, 44; John xi. 2, xii. 3), the R being omitted, as in Παρδειν = Pedere, etc. The greek is Σαιρειν, and the latin Verrere. Possibly a harder form is found in SCOUR and in Κορειν, usually thought 'sweep,' an inadequate sense in Od. v. 149, 'Αγρεῖθ', αἱ μὲν δῶμα κορήσατε ποιπνύσασαι; whence Νεωκορος. Scour = germ. Scheuern = swed. Skura = dan. Skure.

697. SWEET = lat. Suavis = sansk. Swâtu = Ἡδυς = agls. Swæs, Swête = norse Svâss = germ. Süss.

698. SWERE = agls. Sweor = welsh Gwar = lat. Cervix. Since I doubt not but that Vertere is for †kwertere, I have no difficulty in deriving these words from the power of the neck to turn.

> þi bodi is short, þi swore is small.
> Owl and Nightingale, 73.

> With that upon a grene bough
> A ceinte of silk, which she then had,
> She knette, and to herself she lad,
> That she about her white swere
> It did and hange her selven there.
> Gower, lib. IV. p. 30.

699. THOU = agls. þu = mœsog. norse þu = lat. Tu = Τυ, Συ = sanskr. Dwam. So with its cases and derivatives.

700. TIN = agls. Tin = swed. Tenn = germ. Zinn = lat. Stannum. I know they insist that Tin is not Stannum. Καττιτερος, says Boeckh, non stannum est (stannum enim compositum ex argento et plumbo nigro), sed plumbum album, Zinn. But this does not prevent the names being the same, as in Honestas, Honesty, Pietas, Pity, Mustum, Mustard, and countless others, there is a variation in the sense. Ælfric certainly translates "stagnum," that is, stannum, by "tin" and "stagneus" by "tinen." Is Tin related to the homeric Τιτανος? In the sanskrit Kastiran I seem to trace the hebrew word for silver כֶּסֶף.

701. TOKEN, Δεικνυναι, Dicere, Indicare, art. 496, with sibilation become Signum, Sigillum, SEAL.

702. WHEAT = agls. Hwæte = mœsog. Hwaiteis? Hwaiti?

= isl. Hveiti = Σιτος. Though σιτος be used for 'food,' it was properly some kind of grain, and probably, as given in the lexica, Waizen, 'wheat.' As the whitest of the corns, wheat is probably from white; so in welsh Gwenith 'wheat,' Gwyn 'white.' In the sanskrit many of the words for white begin with sibilants, as Swachchh, Shwet, Sit.

703. WILLOW = agls. Wilig = welsh Helyg = Salicem (acc.).

INLAUT OR AUSLAUT.

704. The various classes of mutes receive sibilation in the middle syllables of words, or inlaut. Of gutturals Φυγη = φυζα (poetic); σφαζειν and φασγανον change twice; δικειν gives δισκος; cf. ταγος, τεταγμαι, ταξις; δοκειν, δοξα; μιγηναι = misceri, and here the S is found in the sanskrit, hebrew, and syriac; nocere gives noxa, noxius; parcere produces parsimonia; Αρκος, an old form (Hesych. Etym. Mag.) of Αρκτος, produces Vrsus; if the sanskrit Rikshas 'bear' be the same word, it has also, as often happens, received a foreign sibilation: Equus is in sanskrit Ashw-as; Lingua = γλωσσα; Λεγειν, cf. Λεσχη, Αδολεσχειν. Vivere produces Viscera and Vescor; maculæ measles and mesel 'a leper;' "And take ye kepe now, that he that repreveth his neighbour, either he repreveth him by som harme of peine, that he hath upon his bodie, as mesel, crooked harlot; or by som sinne that he doth."—Chaucer, Persones Tale*. Laqueus produces Lace, Lasso, Latchet; Throat-latch is a tie about the throat, the Toplatch in a horse collar is the thong which ties the sales (wooden parts) together (Forby). The agls. Bugan 'bow,' gives Bosom = agls. Bosm. The mœsog. Kukyan gives Kiss: Pugnus and Fight give Fist; Buccina = Basoon = dutch Basuyne 'trumpet,' as in the dutch bible, Matth. xxiv. 31, = swed. Basun. Legere, Lesson. Ambactus = mœsog. Andbaht has been traced by Grimm to Ambassador. So Rust from Ruddy, Red. True = mœsog. Triggws = Trusty. Dregs, Draff give Trash. Crack gives Craze.

* That Misellus is not the true explanation may be seen in Kilian under Maeschelen and its compounds.

I am right siker that the pot was crased.
Chaucer, C. T. 16401.

Break gives fr. Briser, "Brised his speare upon Sir Tristram," Mort. d'Arthure, II. lxxxiii. Tergum, Dorsum seem only a variation. Picem, Pitch. Licere 'leisure;' germ. Kitzeln = †kittle=Tickle. Lizard is a sibilation of Lacerta, which seems to derive its name from λεγεσθαι 'to Lie, to Liggen,' from its basking in the sun. Bask is a sibilation of Bake.

705. The dentals are in inlaut sibilated, or sibilants turn into dentals. Thus Kæso, Cæsar, Cæsaries are to be explained by the sanskrit Kêsh-ah, Keshar-ah = erse Cas 'hair of the head '=Χαιτη, used by Homer of the hair of the head, by later authors of the mane = Seta ' bristle :' the sanskrit sibilant indicates a previous guttural, Kêk, so that we have in this case the former guttural become a sibilant, the latter a sibilant and a dental. Besides the change of Θ, Σ, given above, we have in inlaut παρσενοις for παρθενοις, Ασαναια for Αθηναιη, Ασαναιων for Αθηναιων in Alkæos, αγασος for αγαθος in the Lysistrata, μυσιδδω for μυθιζω, μυσιξαι for μυθισαι, ελση, ελσοιμι, ελσων for ελθη, ελθοιμι, ελθων, κυρσανιος for σκυρθανιος, i. e. μειρακισκος, ορσα for ορθη (Ahrens). Ποτειδαν for Ποσειδων. Ἐξεσθαι with Ἑδρα, Sedere; Ῥοδον, Rosa; Medius, μεσος; esurire, esca and edere; ordiri, orsus; οσμη, οδωδεναι, οδμη, οζειν; resina, ῥητινη; βαθος, βυθος, αβυσσος; Προτι=Προς=sanskr. Prati. In this preposition the latin Prodesse retains the dental before a vowel : no "stop gap to a hiatus" is known. Τεσσαρες, τετταρες, πισυρες (Ψ. 171) = Quatuor. Piscis probably = Ιχθυς. The latin In may be easily, in its government of an ablative, reconciled with the greek Εν : in its government of an accusative also In=Εις=ενς=old latin Endo, so that the sigma is a sibilation of the D. In greek one dental does not stand before another (except τθ), nor does a dental easily stand before μ: hence εδειν became, on intrusion of θ, εσθιειν; the theoretic †Fιδεθι became ισθι; †Fιδατε, ιστε; †αFιδτος, †απυθτος became αιστος, απυστος; cf. επιλαθεσθαι, επιλησμων; πληθειν, πλησμονη; κορυθα made κορυστης; οιδαμεν=ισμεν; οσμη=οδμη; and regularly. It seems also that, notwithstanding the affinity of N the

dental liquid for the dental mutes, yet it changes to S in πεποσθε for πεπονθατε, τετασθην for τετανθην, Iliad Ξ. 404. Γαστερα = Ventrem = Κενεωνα = Κυστις, Κυστη, and the teutonic forbidden form of the word which is wide spread all over Europe = Κυσθος in the aristophanic use. Ἱμασθλη from Ἱμαντα (acc.). Μυσταξ seems best to come from the teutonic Mund or Munþ, a Mouth. Cf. Μασασθαι with Manducare. The latin also makes Æstus, Æstas from αιθειν, Monstrum from Monere †mondere. It seems thus that Mamma may = Μαστος, Μαζος. Does βλαστεῖν belong to Planta? Κεστος from κεντειν; χασμα from χανειν; πεφασμαι for †πεφαν-μαι. Lazy is shewn by the mœsogothic to be related to Let 'hinder,' and hence to Late. Bequeath makes Bequest. In Cassia the hebrew has in one form D, Kiddah. Season = ital. Stagion from Stationem. Throssel, Thrush = Turdus: Attonished = Attonitus: Wise and Wit in agls. Wisian is the causative of Witan.

706. The german as it was before shewn to turn T into Z, that is, TS, in the initial of a word, so it affects SS and other sibilants in the middle and towards the end of words. This is most common with the dentals. In the imperfect tenses of verbs, past and present, the greek also largely uses this change. Seat = setzen; sit = sitzen; spatiari = spatzieren; bite = beissen; norse nióta = geniessen; fluere = fliessen; agls. geotan = giessen; agls. etan = essen; agls. spreotan = spriessen; split = spleissen; agls. witan = weissen; agls. greotan = grüssen; agls. hatan = heissen, and we also have Behest; shoot = schiessen; blow = blasen; legere = lesen; let = lassen; plant = pflanzen; fangen = fassen; bleuch = blassen; fart = furzen; melt = schmelzen; agls. frettan, fret = fressen; foot = fuss; gasse = gate (road, street); white = weiss; wheat = waizen; spiess = norse spiot; sweet = süss; wort = wurzel; curtus = kurz; swart = schwarz; holt = holz; stilt = stilze; kater masc. a cat, fem. katze: heart = herz; salt = salz; kettle = kessel; emmet = ameise; besser = better; self = selbst; nettle = nessel. Thus τασσειν for †ταγειν, ορυσσειν for †ορυχειν; πρασσειν, πρησσειν for †πραγειν, †πρηγειν; χαρασσειν for †χαρακειν; φρισσειν for †φρικειν; απομυττεσθαι for †απο-

μυχεσθαι; φρασσειν for †φραγειν; φραζειν for †φραδειν; ταρασσειν with ταραχη; σταλασσειν for †σταλαγειν; ελισσειν for †ελιγειν; αινισσεσθαι, αινιγμα; αρασσειν, αραγμα; αμαρυσσειν, αμαρυγμα; μειλισσειν, μειλιγμα, μειλιχιος; αλλασσειν, απαλλαγηναι; σπαρασσειν, σπαραγμα; αμυσσειν, αμυγμα; αιμασσειν, αιματος; κορυσσειν, κορυθος; πτερυσσεσθαι, πτερυγος; κηρυσσειν, κηρυκος; πτυσσειν, πτυχη; ανασσειν, ανακτος; πλησσειν, πληγη; οσσε from †οππε; οσσομαι for οπτομαι; ρυσσος from Rugæ; εχειν, ισχειν; εοικασιν = ειξασιν; αυξειν, augere, agls. ecan; ερυθρος, ερυσιβη, and so Red, Rust; docere, διδασκειν; λεγειν, λεσχη; οπισω, οψε; γαλακτα = colostra?; facere, faxit; gobio, gudgeon; rationem, reason; pipionem, pigeon; coagulum, caseus?; πλατεια, place; racemus, raisin; probrum, reproach; prope, approach. Examples of sibilation with labials are Grip, Grasp; nephew, ανεψιος; gape, gasp; οπτεσθαι, οσσεσθαι; vocem, Foπa, Foσσα which allows the vau in all the homeric passages. In βλασφημειν for βλαβ-φημειν, the concurrence of medial and aspirate was contrary to the laws of utterance.

706 a. The following differ somewhat. Grind, Grist; Like, Lust, mœsog. Leikan, αρεσκειν, Lustus, επιθυμια; Feed, Foster; Break, Burst = agls. Berstan = norse Busta.

> The neighboures bothe smale and grete
> In rannen for to gauren on this man,
> That yet aswoune lay both pale and wan,
> For with the fall he brosten hath his arm.
>
> Chaucer, C. T. 3194.

Bolster from mœsog. Balgs 'a bag,' Bolster is an ancient saxon word occurring in Beowulf. Mistletoe = norse Mistilteinn is a compound of Mist 'dung' and agls. Tâ = mœsog. Tainr 'a twig' = norse Teinn (for †tein-r). The plant is supposed to be propagated by birds, which deposit the berries in or on branches; this Mist with Mixen is but Muck; mœsog. Maihstus is κοπρια 'dunghill;' agls. Meox, Mix 'dung.' Testa from Tegere; Testis from Dicere = δεικνυναι, indicare; Pestis for †plestis = plague = πληγη; erse Caig, Caidh = agls. Cuse = Castus; lucem, illustris; bladder, blister; λειπειν, λοισθος; κομμω, κοσμος?, χανειν, χασκειν.

707. Examples of sibilants in inlaut confounded are κοσ-συφος = κοψιχος, εσχατος for εξ-τατος; thrush, throstle; texere, tissue; fox, fuscus; ιξος, viscus; Dross=Trash; Ask= Ax=agls. Acsian; Hasp is more correctly Hapse from Keep, like Hoop, the agls. is Hæps.

708. CHASTE, see 599 = agls. Cusc. (as ' clean ')= Καθαρος.

709. EASE, agls. Eaðe, cf. lat. Otium: the mœsog. has the adv. Azetaba, ἡδεως, subst. Azeti ' ease,' 1 Tim. v. 6, but the root †azets, is not found.

710. ETHEL ' noble,' in proper names as Ethelbert = agls. Æðele, norse Aðal (subst.), germ. Adel is compared with dor. Εσλος=Εσθλος.

711. FLASH, BLAZE, FLUSH, BLUSH = Φλεγειν, see 410 and 322.

> Thik drumly skuggis dirkinnit so the heuin,
> Dim skyis oft furth warpit fereful leuin,
> Flaggis of fyre and mony (a) felloun slaw,
> Sharp soppis of sleit and of the snyppand snaw.
> Gawin Douglas, Prol. Book vii. (p. 200. 52.)

712. FREEZE, FROST. Cf. lat. Frigus=erse Fuaire; welsh Ffer ' congealed;' agls. Freosan ' freeze ' = germ. Frieren = isl. Frera.

713. KISS=Osculum if for †kosculum: the verb in mœsog. is Kukyan, καταφιλειν, φιλημα δουναι, and the latin seems to have added a sibilant to the second guttural while removing the first: akin may be Os, Ostrea, χαος, χασκειν.

714. LIST is but Likes impersonally=Placet. On the loss of P see 809. List in the norse is always impersonal.

> And doth with Phillis whatso* that him lest.
> Legend of Good Women, 2467.

> Strong was the win and wel to drinke us leste.
> Chaucer, C. T. Prolog. 753.

> Shote on, boy, quod the frere,
> For that me listeth to see.
> The Frere and the Boye, 230.

---

* Whatso=whatsoever, what is indefinite.

715. Lust also is a relative of List, Like, Placet, with loss of P and labial, Lubet, Lubido.

716. Meed = Μισθος. The agls. is Meord, on the omission of R see art. 901: the Heliand gives Mêda, Mioda, Mieda=mœsog. Mizdo, translating Μισθος.

717. Mid=Μεσος for Medius, see before, 151.

718. Midge = agls. Micg, Muggia = dan. Myg = swed. Mygga=dutch Mug=germ. Mücke: these lie between Μυια, which has converted the guttural into a vowel, and lat. Musca, which has added a sibilant. Sanskr. Makshikâ, Makshîkâ, Mashkas; french Mouche. A parallel for the latin and greek is seen in Μυων, Μυιων = Musculus; where μυια = musca is likely to overthrow the derivation which describes a muscle as a little mouse, for it makes the radix, mug, not mus.

719. Nest=lat. Nidus=sanskr. Nîd masc. or neut.= agls. Nest. The notion of the native sanskrit grammarians notwithstanding, I believe the greek Νεοττια makes this word find its origin in Novus, New, Νεος, Νεοσσος.

720. Out = Εξ = lat. Ex = germ. Aus = mœsog. Us = agls. Ut=norse Ut. Therefore was Ex the original form, as in εσχατος, ξενος, εξω, and εκ was introduced to avoid the concurrence of three consonants.

721. T the termination of the latin third person singular, found a parallel in the agls. as Lufiað = Loveth, also in the mœsogothic as Sokeiþ, Sokiþ, Sokaiþ, Secketh, and originally in the greek as εστι; this is now Loves, Seeks. That τυπτει was †τυπτετι is evident from the analogies, †τυπτετι, τυπτοντι, τυπτεται, τυπτονται, ετυπτετο, ετυπτοντο.

722. Rake = agls. Racc = lat. Rastrum. To Rake = lat. Radere, the swedish Raka is to shave, shear, like Radere: and Rad-trum is by the rules of euphony changed to Rastrum: if derived from the supine as they call it, Rasum the process is the same. Rake = germ. Harke, with transposition = Harrow.

723. Thrush = Turdus = Throstle = agls. Þrisc, Þrostle, Þrosle.

724. Weed = lat. Vestis = Εσθης, Ϝεσθης = agls. Wæd = isl. Fat = mœsog. Wasti. Ϝεννυναι may be taken either for

Fεσ-vvvαι or Fεδ-vvvαι = mœsog. Wasyan. Cf. sanskr. Vas 'wear clothes.' The following lines shew that weed is not limited to the attire of a widow.

> Syre bissop, wy ne ȝyfst us of þyne wyte brede
> Þat þou est þesulf at þy masse in þyne vayre wede.
> > Rob. Glouc. p. 238.

> Richard aros and toke hys wede
> And lept on Favel his gode stede.
> > Richard Coer de Lion, 6907.

> They halp him up and his stede*
> And anon chaungeth† his wede.
> > Kyng Alisaunder, 4273.

> The Erl of Naverne com to this thede ‡
> Wel atired, in riche wede
> With my lonerd for to plai;
> And so he dede, mani adai.
> > Seuyn Sages, 1081.

> > Sir, at the yate ther is a knyght
> > The feyryst that euer I sey in syght
> > > Maskyd under mone;
> > Sir, on a mylke whyte stede,
> > The same color his is wede
> > > That he has aboue.
> > > > Sir Amadas, 614.

725. WASP = lat. Vespam = Σφηκα, sibilant twice altered, and guttural for labial. Equivalents, art. 225.

726. WHISKY, the rivers EXE and USK are the keltic Uisge water, which is a sibilate form of Aqua: also erse Easc. USQUEBAUGH is Uisge beatha, aqua vitæ. Eudoxos objects: "Was the letter X the hieroglyphic for a river, hence Ax, Ex, Ox, Ux, as picturing the mouths or Deltas? The Achelous was fabled as a horned animal: see also the myth of the Bosporus, Æsch. Prom. Vinct."

727. WICK = Fοικος = Vicus = Fαστυ = sanskr. Vâsah, All 'dwelling.'

---

* He swims a river on his horse.   † Chaungeth is plural.
‡ Thede properly people.

728. Wıþy = agls. Wiþie, Wiþige = Ιτεα, supposed Fιτεα. Then Οισυη. Odyss. ε. 256: of the raft.

Φράξε δέ μιν ῥίπεσσί διάμπερες οἰσυΐνῃσιν.

With O compensative for the digamma.

LIQUIDS.

729. Between S and R a D is inserted, Ezra = Esdras, cf. Hasdrubal (Gesenius, Lex. p. 753).

729 *a*. R frequently shifts its position; compare Agrigentum, Girgenti; δερκειν, εδρακον, δρακων, supposed to be so called from the fascination of snakes eyes; erse Dearg 'eye;' Frantic = ital. Farnetico; agls. Cræt = Cart; agls. Gærs = Grass, Cress.

On the grene gers sat down and fillit tham syne,
Of fat venison and nobill old wyne.
Gawin Douglas, I. (p. 19. 39).

Agls. Ers = isl. Rass; cf. Oar with Row; Arm with Ramus, 'a branch,' an arm of a tree (Grimm, Gr. iii. 411, note): perhaps this is doubtful; the erse Craom is Ramus, Cran = welsh Pren is 'tree.' Fromage french for 'cheese,' J. Grimm derives from the "Form" in which it is squeezed; the agls. glossaries translate Cyse = Cheese by Formaticum, Formellum; germ. Harz = Resin; germ. Ross = Horse, as in Walrus: Ἕρση, ἔρση, ἐέρση = Ros. Persona may be an alteration of Προσωπειον 'a mask,' or Προσωπον 'a face.' Περθειν, επραθον; Ἁμαρτανειν, ημβροτον; κραδιη = καρδια; Κραπαθος in Homer for Καρπαθος; δρατος for δαρτος, Il. Ψ. 169; αταρπος = ατραπος; βαρδιστος from βραδυς; cf. καρτα, καρτιστος, κρατος, κρατιστος; τεταρτος, τετρατος. "Tinca Placentinus, si reprehendenti Hortensio credimus, Preculam pro Pergulam dixit," Quintil. i. 5. The custom of transposing R prevails much in Oxfordshire, a Thorpe is there a Thrup, so Calthrop, Heythrop; Althorp is pronounced Althrop, and on the Spenser tomb at Yarnton is so written. At Pakefield in Norfolk they call Warts, Wrats; the old spelling of Bird was Brid; Brent = Burnt, as Chaucer, C. T. 2165. Crull = Curled, and so islandic Krulla𐌃 hâr, 'curled hair;' Cruddes = Curds. Trundle is the frequentative of Turn. I have hesitated to insert Raucus = Hoarse, since the agls. has Hás, and the R seems an insertion, a burr upon the vowel. Traces exist in greek and latin of the sanskrit root Gaur ' yellow ' (see art. 308), and χρυσος seems to be a transposition for †χυρσος, the yellow metal, from this root: χοιρος may be 'the yellow one,' as wild boars are of a yellowish brown.

> I grant that from the dede* myself I fred
> The landis I brest and syne away fast fled.
> > Gawin Douglas, II.

> A lover and a lusty bacheler
> With lockes crull as they were laide in presse.
> > Chaucer, C. T. 81.

> Crulle was his here and as the gold it shon.
> > Chaucer, C. T. 3315.

> His hed was crolle and yolow the here
> Broune thereonne and white his swere †.
> > Kyng Alisaunder, 1999.

> I have no peny, quod Piers,
> Pulettes to bugge †
> Ne neither gees ne grys §,
> But two grene cheses,
> A few cruddes and creme.
> > Piers Ploughman, 4361.

730. BRENN, BRIM as in Brimstone, are forms of Burn, Fire, Πυρ. A sow in heat is said to be Brimming.

> As brimme as blase of straw yset on fire.
> > Troilus and Creseide, IV. 157.

731. FRAME = ?lat. Formare = Μορφωσαι = agls. Fremman = norse Fremja.

732. OAR, Row = Ερετμειν, Remus for †retmus. See art. 169.

733. ROB = Ἁρπαζειν = Rapere = agls. Reafian = mœsog. biraubon. See art. 287.

* Dede, death. † Swere, neck.
† Bugge = buy. § Grys = pig.

734. TRIM = agls. Trum seems allied to Turma, for in Ælfreds Orosius we have "butan truman" without order, and Lye shews Trum to be 'firm, stable,' so that Turma is a well ordered compact body. Hy hi getrymed hæfdon, 'had set themselves in array' (Ælfreds Orosius, IV. ii. = p. 286. line 7. ed. Thorpe).

> Of senne ich wot by thyse sekyle
> That ther hiis wel great host;
> And for the fend imut* so felet
> Therof hys alle hys host†.
> And he arayeth hare§ trome
> As me ‖ areyt men in fy3t.
> William of Shoreham, p. 108.

> The king gan fle with alle his trome.
> Gy of Warwike, p. 201.

> Helle hundes, lauerd, habbeð bitrumet me.
> Seinte Marharete, fol. 42. line 5.

735. TROUBLE may come to us through the french, but the origin is teutonic: in the Heliand we have Drôbi, Druobi, 'turbidus, tristis,' Drôbian 'turbare;' mœsog. Drôbyan, translating ταρασσειν: germ. Trübe. Compare therefore Turbare, Ταρασσειν, θορυβειν, and the words collected under Stir.

> Ah duieri ant darie drupest alre þinge.
> Seinte Marharete, fol. 50. b. 13.

736. L, N are interchanged as Bononia = Bologna; Anima = span. Alma; Panormus = Palermo; Naupactus = Lepanto; Canonicus = ital. Calonico; Venenum = ital. Veleno; λιτρον = νιτρον; πνευμονα = πλευμονα; Bulldog is in the Promptorium Parvulorum, Bondogge, Molosus. The dutch kinderen with a double plural termination seems = children, and so germ. Kind = child = agls. cild. The epitomator of Festus has these two passages, "Luscitio vitium oculorum quod clarius vesperi quam meridie cernit." "Nuscitiosus qui parum videt propter vitium oculorum, quique plus videt vesperi quam meridie."

* Imut = agls. Mot = must (be).   † Fele, many.
‡ Host read perhaps bost, boast.   § Hare, of them.
‖ As man (or one) arrayeth men in fight.

Hence Luscinia may be from Nocte Canere, like Nightingale = germ. Nachtigall, from agls. Galan ' to sing.'

737. Tilt is now applied to the covering stretched over a cart; the german Zelt, with initial sibilated, is Tent. At first sight it seems a latinism, Tentorium; but Wachter argues that germ. Kind = agls. Cild = Child, and the verb is genuine teutonic, germ. Dehnen, agls. þenian. If a latinism, the english would have been formed on the usual prose word Extendere, but we find Tel.

> A pavyloun yteld he sygh.
> Sir Launfal, 264.

> His her to his fet tilde of berde and of heved.
> St. Braudan, p. 30.

> The schurte tilde anon to his thies, the brech to his to.
> Thomas Beket, 1478.

738. L, R are interchanged as Amsterdam on the Amstel; Sericum, Silk; Sulcus = span. Surco; Morus = Mulberry; Morari = ?μελλειν; μελος = Membrum in sense, and Membrum is a reduplication of μερος; hence μελος = μερος; Strigilis = στλεγγις; Pellitory = Parietaria (Skinner), Paritorie in Chaucer, C. T., 16049. Colonel is only ostensibly an example, for the pronunciation retains the R.

> To scuse ourselves and coronell withall
> We did foretell the prince of all these needes.
> Gascoigne, Fruites of Warre.

Procobera (Orelli, inscript. 3121) is now Polcevera, a river; ulmus = fr. orme; floccus = fr. froc; luscinia = ital. Rossinuolo; Arborem = ital. Albero; alchemy = ital. Archimia, from arabic al ' the,' chem ' black ;' applied to Egypt, Χημια, the land of Ham; (Humboldt); ululare = ital. Urlare; pallidus = span. Pardo; palpebra = span. Parpado; Apostolus = fr. apôtre; titulus = fr. titre; epistola = fr. epitre; capitulum = fr. chapitre; ital. navile = fr. navire; miraculum = span. milagro; periculum = span. peligro; Marble from Marmor, Turtle from Turtur. The agls. Didrian becomes our Diddle; laurer as in Chaucer, C. T. 1030, and Dunbar = fr. laurier = laurel; κιθαρα = Citol (Chaucer, C. T. 1962); tenebræ = span. tinieblas; peregrinator = pilgrim; mœsog. Wairilo = agls. Weler, 'a lip.' In the appendix to Tattam's Coptic dictionary it is stated, with what accuracy I know not, that the Colocasia, the egyptian Arum, is in coptic Corcasi : also Culex = coptic Koris. The Etymologicon Magnum declares Κρυπτειν to be an alteration from καλυπτειν, and since the root in Kal, celare, is traceable in many languages, but κρ in that sense, not, the teaching seems correct (col. 542) : "κρυπτω εκ του καλυπτω, καρυπτω και κατα συγκοπην." With Αγελη 'herd,' cf. αγειρειν 'assemble.' With Freckle cf. germ. bleck. Corylus makes Colurnus (Servius). Michaelis says that the aloe, Agallochum אֲהָלִים is called by the inhabitants of Malacca and Sumatra where it grows, Garro (Lex. Syr.), and so the sanskrit is Agaru, Aguru.

739. DEAL I have argued to be Τελος. Terminus appears to be τελομενος 'divider.' Usually τερμονες is applied to fields; but Iliad, Σ. 544: Τελσον αρουρης.

740. PLUM = Prunum. Plum from its relation to Πελ (see 535) 'of lead colour,' seems the more genuine spelling.

741. Between L and R we occasionally find a dental inserted; the old english Alderbest, Altherbest is for Aller-best, Alra being the genitive plural of the agls. Al, Eal. Chaucer exhibits the earlier form.

> Up rose our hoste and was our aller cok*.
>
> C. T. Prol. 825.

742. To L a D easily adheres, as in Cold compared with Chill, Gelu; Field compared with the norse Völlr and rather removed in meaning lat. Vallem; in these two however an assimilation may have found place; Mould (454). To grow MOULDY is in islandic, at Mygla akin to Mucor, Mucescere, the G produces a long vowel in english and the D is accretional. MUSTY is a sibilation of the original form. Dan. Mugne. The germ. Moderig, swed. Mudderig use the same root with a dental, MOTHERY. Cf. Muscus, Moss.

743. M, N are interchanged, Πεντε, Πεμπαζεσθαι; Longo-

---

* Cook of us all. Another example in 735.

bardi = Lombardi, Generum = γαμβρον for †γαμερον from γαμος.

744. CAMP (see art. 1026) = germ Kämpfen = ?lat. Certare. M, R must be as much interchangeable as N, R.

745. N, R are interchanged. Dunholm = Durham. Herbergeour (Chaucer, C. T. 5416) = Harbinger, properly from germ. Herberge = french Auberge, 'shelter,' one who looks for lodgings, for shelter. Pampinus = fr. Pampre; ordinem = fr. ordre; diaconum = fr. diacre; sanguinem = span. sangre; stamen = span. estambre; selinum = ital. celeri = celery; hominem = span. hombre; famem = span. hambre; nomen = span. nombre; carchesia = conchæ? The phœnician root found in Minah originally part, is to be cfd. with μερος, membrum; donum = δωρον; δεινος = dirus; καπνον = vaporem; viscera = viventia = †quickend-ia = agls. cwiccnde: murus = ?mœnia, αμυνειν, munire: leporem = leapend = leaping; fulgura = fulgentia; vomerem = vomentem; pecora = pascentia; obscœnus nearly = obscurus, from isl. at Skyggia, whence Sky, properly cloud, and σκια; μινθος = merda; μειων, minor; μειζων, maior; πλειονες, plerique; πλειονος, pluris; ἱνες = ϝινες = ?Vires. A suspicion arises that the latin infinitive in -ere = the greek in -εναι, the old termination reduced to -εν, and strengthened to -ειν: compare dicere, δεικνυναι, μειουν, †μειοεναι, minuere. Something similar seems to occur in saxon derivatives from verbs, as player = agls. plegere = agls. plegiende = playing; eater = agls. etere = agls. etende = eating: lover = agls. lufiend = lufiende = loving. From these are to be separated derivatives from substantives, which answer to the mœsogothic termination in -arcis, as agls. bocere = mœsog. bokareis.

746. MIN, MEAN, see art. 153, lat. Memor, must be a reduplication of this root as seen in Monere.

747. MOUTH represents agls. Muþ = mœsog. Munþs = norse Muþr, with genitive Munns, dat. Munni. The danish, german are Mund, dutch Mond: the saxon of the Heliand gives Muþ, Mund. These words seem connected with Mordere. Nations are so lax in the application of descriptive terms, especially when roots become antiquated, as Chin = Gena, that

I suppose Mentum 'chin,' to be the same word as above. On Mund in greek see 705.

748. OPEN=Aperire; see art. 173 and 1037.

749. SHEER = agls. Scir, is identical originally with Shine =agls. Scinan, which is one of the sibilate forms of Candere. I can testify myself, that the Norfolk fishermen say " the sea is sheer," that is ' clear.'

> Now let us passe skere.
> Lybeaus Disconus, 297.

> Her kercheves* were well schyre,
> Arayd wyth riche gold wyre.
> Sir Launfal, 246.

> Therfor they seyden alle
> Hyt was long on the quene and not on Launfal
> Therof they gonne hym skere.
> Id. 703.

> Some dampnede Launfal there
> And some made him quyt and skere.
> Id. 880.

> þarof þu, wrecche, most be skere,
> ȝif þu wult amang manne beo†.
> Owl and Nightingale, 1300.

A sheer fall, sheer nonsense, sheer off. In the mœsogothic another application is made, the explanatory paraphrase of St. Johns gospel is called Skeireins, and ga-skeiryan is ἑρμηνεύειν.

750. The dentals which adhere to N often are employed, intrusively and euphoniously, to separate it from R: as ἀνέρος, ἀνδρός; genera, genders; generum=fr. gendre; tenerum = tender; reddere = render; Veneris dies = fr. Vendredi. Cinder (Cinerem) is perhaps misspelt: it should be Sinder (see Outzen); a child however addresses another in the language of the sunday school with 'O! you wicked sinder !'

751. But sometimes instead of a D a T or Θ seems possible: as Τενθρηδών 'a wood boring bee' compared with Τερηδών 'a wood boring worm;' Ἄνθρωπος perhaps for †ανερωπος:

* Covering of her head.
† Be. So Robert of Gloucester, p. 334. ult. 335 quinquies.

Ανθρακα compared with the sanskrit Angâr-as masc. or neut. Country=agls. Cynrice? and the norse words Maðr, Sviðr, on the formation of which see 859.

752. Between M and R a euphonic B (a fulcrum for the voice, Eudoxos*), as akin to the labial liquid M, is inserted; numerus=number, camera=chamber; cucumerem=cucumber; humerus=spanish hombro; ponerem=span. pondre; μεση ημερα = μεσημβρια; βροτος is a derivative of mors, βροτος = †μβροτος a form existing in Στησιμβροτος, Κλεομβροτος, φθισιμβροτος, τερψιμβροτος, and=†μοροτος 'mortal' from Mors: γαμβρος = †γαμερος from γαμος. Timber has no B in german Zimmern 'to build' = dutch Timmeren = danish Tömre=mœsog. mostly Timryan: cf. germ. Zimmerman 'carpenter.' Fr. tonnerre=thunder.

753. Between M and L a euphonic B is inserted. Βλωσκειν the compounds of which occur in Homer is for †μβλωσκειν and that for †μολωσκειν from μολειν, with εμολον. The homeric μεμβλεται as in T, 343. ἡ νύ τοι οὐκέτι πάγχυ μετὰ φρεσὶ μέμβλετ' Ἀχιλλεύς, is for μεμελετο, μεμελεται. Even Lobeck agrees that βλαξ is rightly derived from μαλακος. Βλιττειν 'take honey' is from Μελι, or Μελιττα. Humilis=humble; tremere=tremble; cumulare=fr. Combler; simulare=fr. sembler, resemble; Camaracum=Cambray (Pott); grommeler = grumble; dutch wammelen = wamble (Craven gloss.) = wabble.

FINAL N.

754. A final N represents in greek sometimes an S, as attic κοπτομεν=doric κοπτομες, latin cædimus; it represents a dental in κοψον for †κοψαθ, †κοψαθι; εκοπτεν for †εκοπτετ, 'cædebat.' The accusative imparisyllabic terminations in N seem to be for dentals; thus εριν is for †εριδ from εριδα, χαριν for †χαριτ from χαριτα, γελων for †γελωτ from γελωτα: earlier forms doubtless be †εριδαν, †χαριταν, †γελωταν, answering to lapidem, gratiam.

* So Varronianus, p. 191.

LABIALS TO R.

755. The labials, and hence the gutturals, change into R. This was first observed, as far as I know, by Graff, who compared the old high german Birumes 'we are,' that is, Be adding the greek and latin termination -ομες, -imus, Beimus, with the sanskrit equivalent Bhavâmas. So Shwas, Cras. So the old latin in-seco appears in asserere Sermonem (acc.); ειπειν, επος in ειρηκα, ερειν. Barm = bosom from agls. Bugan, bow, form of a bow, bay. Δερειν, Δεφειν, cf. Διφθερα; Καρα = Κεφαλη.

756. BERRY = lat. Bacca, see 627.

757. SHAVE = SHEER: agls. Scafan = Sceran = Κειρειν = Ξυρειν. With Shearing then a SHEEP may be connected etymologically * = agls. Sceap = Κριος כר = erse Caor = gaelic Caora, welsh Corlan, 'sheepfold,' and perhaps by dropping the guttural Αρνειος, Αρνες. An old english form is SHIVE often used of cutting bread into slices.

> She asks one sheave of my lords white bread
> And a cup of his red red wine.
> Lord Beichan.

Hence of the eucharistic bread transubstantiate

> Ac wen nauȝt that Cryst be to-schyft.
> William of Shoreham, p. 27.

> Thys manere senne nys nauȝt ones
> Ac† hys ischyt in thry,
> In thouȝt, in speche, in dede amys
> Thys may ech man ysy‡.
> Id. p. 107.

From this verb comes a derivative SHIVER (as I maintain a passive participle for Shiven), a piece Shiven off.

> It was na wapen that man might welde
> Might get a shever out of their shelde.
> Ywaine and Gawain, 3177.

---

* This suggestion rather more strongly expressed, was doubted by Eudoxos. His doubts may be taken as denials: it is well there have been so few.

† Ac, but.   ‡ Ysy, see.

Which we still use, "all in shivers," "break to shivers," and a new verb "Shiver to pieces." SHAFT=agls. Sceaft, SHEAF =agls. Sceaf, SHAPE=agls. Scapan, agls. Sceadan with numerous derivatives are all very near, and all perhaps depend on Secare which appears in the teutonic Seax 'a sword,' and the skythian Σαγαρις.

758. Sow with lat. Sevi is thus connected with Serere. Sow = agls. Sawan = mœsog. Saian = norse Sâ. Observe mœsog. Saian for †sawan, and lat. Semen for †sev-men. This letter change reconciles ירע with Sow, Sevi, Serere.

758 a. SPEED, Σπευδειν, art. 201, the agls. Speowan being nearer the root, may be compared with Σπερχειν, supposing Δ and Χ not radical. Holding P to belong to the later phases of the teutonic, I look for a purer aspect of the root in Swift, which bears traces of a sibilate form of Vivere, Quick.

759. WHITE=agls. Hwit=sanskr. Shwet has for its feminine lat. Creta.

759 a. WEIGH. A little apparently out of place, but in analogy with Bacca, Berry, Sage = Saw = Serra, will stand Weigh=Φερειν=Ferre=Vehere. Wegan in agls. is 'bear, carry' as well as 'weigh;' take an unpublished illustration "wegan þin winsume geoc" 'to bear thy winsome yoke.'

V TO L.

760. V as it changes to R so it must also change to L. Thus our SLEEP, is the sanskrit Swap; thus the mœsog. Slawan is the german Schweigen. Su-ovi-taurilia = Soli-taurilia; agls. Swaþe=Slot=gaelic Slaod. Compare SLING, Σφενδονη, Funda, so named from the Spon which forms the bed in which the bolt lies. Of this change I shall say no more here. I assume it from the preceding, and shall give some examples as suggestions in word families.

760 a. The change of R and D seems clearly to occur in Καρυκειον Caduceus and in HEAR = lat. Audire. Ar=Ad, see the article on Ar in Forcellini, so that Ar-morica, on the sea, ad mare, is equally significant in keltic and latin.

GUTTURALS TO M.

761. Let those who take an interest in the history of words decide for themselves whether a guttural does not sometimes become an M. Part of the proof depends upon a proposition not yet fully worked out, that, namely, the semitic languages are, in a measure, radically allied to the european. I shall content myself with submitting instances. Χιλιοι = Mille? Kal the root of ἁλες, sal, salt, as changed in hebrew, etc. to mal, in מֶלַח? Mill, Μυλη, Molere are to be referred ultimately to κυλ in κυλιειν? but see art. 45. Gall, Gold, Yolk, Yellow, Χολη, Χλωρος are connected by the idea of Yellowness; but Mel is also inseparable from yellowness and must have affinity to the other words, cf. welsh Mêl 'honey,' Melyn, 'yellow.' In this case the labial forms Fel, Bilis, Fulvus, Flavus are found, and these are known to be exchangeable for M.

762. MILK seems another form of Γαλακτ-ος (gen.) = agls. Mile, Meole = mœsog. Miluks.

763. HAND, if connected with Κονδ-υλος, may be lat. Manus. That Manus was †mandus becomes quite evident from Mandare.

764. MOUTH = germ. Mund may be connected with Χανδανειν. These instances have in them a large measure of doubt.

ASSIMILATION.

765. Of two concurrent consonants the latter commonly exerts some influence on the former.

> These noble Saxons were a nation hard and strong
> On sundry lands and seas in warfare nuzzled long.
> Drayton, Polyolbion, XI.

So Muzzle, Stirrup, Maggot, Scabbard, Bless, Daffodil, Blossom, Accelerare, Assimilare, Assensus, etc. Tusser retains the older form of the first syllable of Maggot, "Sheep wriggling tail Hath mads without fail," p. 145, like Mite, Meat. In greek κ, γ, χ give a preceding N the sound of NG, as εγκλημα, εγγελαν, εγχειν, τυγχανειν; π, β, φ turn N into M

ASSIMILATION. 193

as εμπαλιν, εμβαπτειν, εμφυναι; λ, μ, ρ assimilate N to themselves as ελλειπειν εμμενειν, συρραψαι. In the formation of verbs a dental takes κ for its guttural, a μ takes γ, an aspirate takes χ: as λελεκται, διειλεγμεθα, ελεχθη, and these changes are constant; γται, κμαι, κθην are impossible combinations. Two mutes of different organs can come together only when the second is a dental; here the preposition εκ forms an exception. Before a tenuis only a tenuis can stand, before an aspirate an aspirate, before a medial a medial; thus ἑπτα, ἑβδομος; οκτω, ογδοος; κρυπτειν, κρυβδην; γραπτος, γραβδην, γραφθηναι; πλεγδην, πλεχθεις: here the foreign word Εκβατανα is an exception and the same aspirate is not doubled as Σαπφω not †σαφφω. An M changes a preceding labial into M as γραμμη for †γραφμη λελειμμενος for †λελειπμενος. An M changes a preceding guttural generally into a γ, as τευχειν, τετυγμαι, πλεκειν, πλεγμα; but some exceptions as ακμη, εχμα, τεκμωρ are met with. An M often changes a preceding dental into an Σ, as ᾳδειν, ᾳσμα, πειθειν, πεπεισμαι. Here exceptions occur as ιδμων, κευθμων, ποτμος. This rule shews that ισμεν, ιστε, ισασιν are for ιδμεν, ιδετε, ιδασιν, and equivalent to οιδαμεν, οιδατε, οιδασιν. Dentals stand only before liquids. Dentals before other dentals change to Σ, as ἡδεσθαι, ἡσθην; πειθειν, πειστεον. On this change with N see art. 705.

766. The latin is subject to some of these rules as in combibere, comminari, corruere. Officere is ob-facere, officium is opi-ficium, officina is operi-ficina. The old lost leg 'lic' as in λεγεσθαι produces Lectus, Tegmen but Tectum : Lugere but Luctus. Quamquam Vmquam are nearer to the usual simple forms, but euphony requires Quanquam, Vnquam. So Longobardi = Lombards, Amita = Aunt, Emmet = Ant.

767. Of αμφιεννυναι the root, if ascertained by the sanskrit, was Fεσ and Fεσνυμι became by assimilation Fεννυμι. The same assimilation is found in the old ionic Εμμι, 'I am,' as in the vase, where a charioteer drives without reins by means of a rod; ΤΟΝΑΘΕΝΘΝΑΘΛΟΝ : ΕΜΙ, των Αθηνηθεν αθλων εμμι and in Αμμες 'we' compared with the sanskrit oblique cases in Asm, as accusative Asmân.

o

768. An S succeeding changes P to K in Proximus from Prope, G to K in Maximus from Mag-nus, μεγ-ας, and in Buxom for agls. Bengsam, 'compliant.'

769. Navel = Ομφαλος. This appears probable on separating the labials †οναφαλος.

770. Hemp = Κανναβις = sanskr. Shan-an.

771. More rarely in assimilation the latter consonant takes the sound of the former; thus ολλυμι is for †ολνυμι: the æolic οππατα is for †οπ-ματα in attic ομματα; Mollis = μαλακος μαλθακος, Bully for †balg-ig.

772. Hoard = agls. Hord may be thus Horreum; that it is not from Far is evident, since it stores grain not meal or flour.

LETTERS LOST.

773. The suppression of consonants exhibits some remarkable examples. Syllables, single letters are dropped from the beginning, from the middle and from the end of words. Consonants before vowels or before other consonants disappear: nothing preserves a word from change. From assimilation it is very easy to pass to omission; thus it is a rule in spanish to write but one consonant, so that Ad, Con, Modus being placed in latin under the influence of assimilation produce Accommodare, but the spanish writes Acomodar. The same process has worked itself out in other languages, where the spoken not the printed language has been acted on. Custom and the influence of german philology impose upon us a necessity for methodical treatment even in the fantastic changes we shall now consider. We therefore first take the anlaut, or initial letters of words.

774. An imperfect assimilation half reaching suppression may be observed in course of operation with the spanish: thus Flamma = span. Llama; Clamare = sp. Llamar; Planus = sp. Llano; Planctus = sp. Llanto; Clavis = sp. Llave; Plenus = sp. Lleno; Plorare = sp. Llorar; Pluere = sp. Llover. The welsh presents occasionally similar phænomena. Llan 'a village with a church, also an area' is Planus; Llawn 'full' is Plenus; Llyg 'a shrew mouse' is Glirem; Llawr

is Floor; Lliban is Glib. Of these the two first are probably borrowed from the latin. The french also has altered Glires into Loirs.

775. The loss of letters in the life of words is as the loss of limbs in the life of men, not to be accounted for by any one cause. Within our own time the word Omnibus has been inventively applied to a new carriage, and it has been cut down by almost general consent to Bus. Fender, Fencing, Fences are for Defender, Defencing, Defence, Drawing room for Withdrawing room, Livery for Delivery, Tender for Attender, Stress for Distress, Story for History, Spend for Expend, so we find Spense for Expense (Thomas Beket 1388), Scomfit for Discomfit, Spise for Despise, "Idil speche I rede thou spyse" (Songs and Carols, p. 1), Kever for Recover, Recuperare. " Several verbs even at this day are used sometimes with and sometimes without the vowel, as Espy, Escape, Establish," etc. (Guests English Rhythms, I. p. 36, where the subject is illustrated.) Thus the old grammarians take τραπεζα 'table' to be †τετραπεζα 'a four foot,' κατα αποβολην της τε συλλαβης, εστι γαρ τετραπεζα (Zonaras). Pott (Etym. F. II. 108) thinks plausibly that Culina is †coculina from coquere. Κτεις, Κτενος 'a comb' is so like to Pecten, Pectinis that it must be supposed to have lost the two first letters and to be a participial substantive from Pectere. The perpetual application to the study of latin has checked the disposition shewn in our early writers to cut off the heads of latin words, of which countless examples might be given.

> Therfore iloren is this luytel faunt *.
> Kyng of Tars, 563.
>
> When that lady fayr of face
> With mete and drynke kevered† was.
> Emare, 374.

776. Some examples have already been given of initial vowels existing here, deficient there: apis=bee, aper=boar, episcopus = bishop, acerbus = herbe (germ), Ariminum = Rimini, adamanta = diamond, la Poule = Apulia, amaracus = marjoram, αριθμος = ρυθμος, εθελειν = θελειν = velle, αστερα = star, stella.

* Infant. † Recuperata.

777. LEAD appears to be the causative of the verb †ελευθειν. The agls. is Lædan. The mœsog. Leiþan by its compounds translates the compounds of ελθειν, and it=agls. Lîðan. LET, 'missum facere, sinere' appears also of the same group. On the other hand Let, 'impedire,' belongs to Late, and agls. Latian 'tardare.' Whether the phrases 'lead corn, lead hay,' customary in most counties, belong to this seems doubtful; they are rather to be referred to Load=agls. and mœsog. Hlaþan.

778. RED, REDDEN, ροδον are to be compared with Ερευθος 'redness,' Ερευσαι 'redden,' Σ. 329, Ερυθρος 'red.'

779. RIME (rhyme) is the agls. Rim 'number,' which is doubtless equivalent to 'Ρυθμος, Αριθμος. In these words I imagine the θ to be radical and the μ afformative; so as to make the agls. Rim stand for †riðm. In support of this view observe that the mœsog. Raþyan in the compound Garaþyan translates αριθμειν. If rightly explained, νηριτος ὑλη in Hesiod (Works and Days)=νηριθμος ὑλη. In welsh Crif is 'a row of notches,' Eirif 'a number, a counting.' Behind all these forms must lie a root such as we see in χαρακ, giving χαραγμος, indicating the SCORINGS, or SCRATCHES, the γραμμαι, by which numbers are marked; or else such an arabic root as Carat, (four grains), properly Kîrât, a berry of the κερατιον order, connected possibly with Grit, with Margarita, and with arabic Gharaz-un, 'sphærula vitrea, a talisman,' Gharazah-un 'gemma, omnisque res in seriem coniuncta,' חֲרֻזִים‎ series margaritarum.

GUTTURALS LOST IN ANLAUT.

780. ROOF = Οροφη = agls. Hrof = mœsog. Hrot. Here the H marks a lost guttural, which is found probably in Carpere; Καθυπερθεν ερεψαν, λαχνηεντ' οροφον λειμωνοθεν αμησαντες, Ω. 451. Οροφη, ερεφειν, ερεπτειν are closely allied.

781. Of the loss of gutturals whether before vowels or consonants examples have been already given, κηπος=ape; καπρος =aper, carpere = ερεπτειν, χαραγμος = αριθμος, con-lectus gives αλοχος, con-vulva gives αδελφος, χηνα=anserem, γαια = αια, corvus = raven, gnoscere = noscere, γλυκυριζα = li-

quorice, Clanius = Lagno, glires = loirs (fr.), κλεπτειν = lift, κλινειν = lean, clump = friesic Klomp = Lump, creep = repere, κνιδη = nettle, knot = nodus, knit = nectere, κονιδες = nits, circulus = ring, gleam = lumen, λαμπειν, κλυειν = listen, come = kwiman = venire, quean, cunnus = Venus, glad = lætus, quick = vivus, grab = rapere, gloria = laudem. A good example may be seen in Amulet a word of arabic extraction and signifying ' a thing carried ;' we have the same root in Camel ' the carrier :' all the intermediate steps are lost to the english, and we observe nothing but the falling away of the guttural.

782. CHOP ' barter' is probably akin to old and good latin Cambire : which was perhaps a form of Αμειβειν, of which the forms αμευσασθαι (Pind. Pyth. i. 45. xi. 38), αμευσεσθαι testify that †αμεβειν, †αμενειν were possible spellings.

783. GRIN = agls. Grinan = dan. Grine = swed. Grina = germ. Greinen. Cf. Ringi; " grin like a dog" says our version of the bible, Ps. lix. 6. 14. Rictus then is formed by ejecting N, art. 860. The gaelic Drein converts G to D, art. 579.

784. LOIN = Clunis = FLANK. In friesland Lunk is ' hipbone,' otherwise ' upper thigh,' (oberschenkel). See Loin = Latus.

786. MARROW perhaps Mucus, Μυελος : see art. 902.

DENTALS LOST IN ANLAUT.

787. Of the loss of dentals in anlaut we have examples well established, as Bonus from Duonus dropping the D and changing the vowel to B : DVONVS is still extant in the epitaph of L. Scipio. etc. Bis in the same manner from †dnis, Bini for †duini, Bellum for Duellum, Billii for Duillii (Quinctilianus, I. iv.). It is clear also that Iterum is for †duiterum = Δευτερον. The Twinkling of the stars is a frequentative of the Winking of the eyes. " Twink with the eye" occurs in Wit and Folly, 21 (Percy Soc.).

> Not suffering the least twinckling sleepe to start
> Into her eye, which th' heart mote have relieved.
> F.Q. V. vi. 24.

We retain the old form in " the Twinkling of an eye."

788. The anglosaxon Begen 'both' is in the same manner formed from Twegen 'two,' and the whole declension of the two corresponds: thus,

	M.	F.N.	M.	F.N.
N.	Twegen.	Twâ.	Begen.	Bâ.
G.	Twegra.		Begra.	
D.	Twam.		Bam.	

The mœsog. Bai 'both' stands in the same relation to mœsog. Twai, 'two.' Whatever the termination be, the origin of the initial B will be the same, and BOTH = mœsog. Bayoþs is a derivative form of Two.

789. An immediate result of these observations is a suspicion that lat. Am-bo, Aμ-φω, sanskr. Ubhau, are compounds, of which the second syllable is a disguised Duo, Δυω, dwau.

790. Some words in sanskrit and latin beginning with I we may conjecture to have dropped a D, as Ianus for †dianus, Iuglans for Διος βαλανος, and of these some were apparently derivatives of Duo, which was capable of the form Di as in διακοσιοι. Thus the island of Java (Yava) is so called, says Humboldt, from the two stalked barley, called in sanskrit Yavah. This is the greek ζεα, where ζ answers to Di, not, I think, to I, as in Ζευς, Διος, ζητητης, διαιτητης itself perhaps from δυο. In the same way

791. YOKE = Iugum = sanskr. Yug-an = Ζυγον are all for diugum.

792. TWIN = sanskr. Yamas = lat. Geminus = Διδυμος which has reduplication.

793. †yokester probably = Vxor. And Iecur = sanskr. Yakrit is for †dia-krit, two-formed, dis-creatus, on account of its two lobes, which, I am assured, would be noticed by a common observer. The syllable Car as representative of the sanskr. Kri 'make' is found also in Carmen. ‛Ηπαρ, ηπατος belongs rather to the hebrew כָּבֵד and the arabic. Lassen has observed that sanskr. Yam-, meaning in the neuter 'a pair,' in the masc. 'a twin,' is the chief syllable of Geminus, Γαμειν. Of Yam it must be conceded that it is a derivative of Two in some of its forms, but of Γαμος it may be doubted whether

the marriage feast is not an earlier sense, and we should otherwise expect an initial Z as in ζυγον.

794. T is omitted before a vowel. Τηγανον in ionic was Hγανον. Athenæos vi. 229. Χωρις δε του Τ στοιχειον Ιωνες ηγανον λεγουσιν ως Ανακρεων· χειρα τ' εν ηγανω βαλειν. So also in the plural article, οι, αι had an older form τοι, ται frequent in Homer and the dialects. It is reasonable to suppose that the singular nominative was τος, τα, τοδ; but historical evidence is not thought to support that view, since the mœsog. is Sa, Sô, þata, the agls. is Se, Seo, þæt, and the sanskr. is Sah, Sâ, Tad or Tat. To say in face of this evidence that the S has arisen from a T is disapproved as too presumptuous. We have however in Τοιουτος a fresh proof of the omission of T, for a combination of τοι and τουτον makes τοιουτον, and so through all cases, reserving only the nom. sing. m. f. For myself I believe that Vnde=†eunde, requires us to take Inde as =tinde, Vbi=†cubi, requires Ibi=†tibi with the demonstrative T. So ὡς=Τως=Thus. If T before a vowel can be omitted, it may be that Ακην=Tacenter, οργαν =Turgere.

795. To this place it belongs to observe that Spenser uses many words in which Dis is reduced to S, as Seerne for Discern, Scryde for Descried, Sdeign for Disdain, Stresse for Distress. The italian has many similar formations as Sballare, Sbandare, Sbarazzare, Sbarbare, Sbarcare 'disbark,' Sbilanciare 'throw out of balance,' Sboccare 'debouche,' Sborsare 'disburse,' Sbrogliare 'disembroil,' Scalzare=discalceare, Scapestrare= discapistrare, Scapigliare=discapillare=Dishevel, Scaricare= Discharge, Scatenare = Déchaîner, Scendere = Descendere (losing De), Scernere = Discernere, Schermire = Discernere 'fight,' whence Schermaglia, Scrimaglia, Skirmish, Skrimmage = Discrimen. Scorticare = Discorticare ' to unbark,' whence probably our Scorch. This list might be much extended.

796. Dim = agls. Dim = norse Dimmr = provincial english Dunch=germ. Dunkel. Buttmann (Lexil. II. 266) finds "a very striking, but certain and long recognized example of a word which in the same language appears in five different

forms passing into one another; ζοφος, δνοφος, γνοφος, κνεφας, νεφος." Tenebræ seems the latin representative of these forms and Dim, Dunch seem to be the original root preserved. If so, νεφος, νεφελη, nubes, nebula with agls. Nip 'darkness' have lost an initial dental. Has also Night? Of Dunch, Halliwell gives, Dunch passage, 'a blind dark passage.'

> What with the zmoke and what with the criez
> I waz amozt blind and dunch in mine eyes.

797. REAP = Δρεπειν = agls. Ripan = mœsog. Raupyan used of plucking the ears of corn. Δρεπανον, Δρεπανη is a reap hook. Carpere, Sarpere may be not radically distinct. Cf. agls. Drepan 'strike,' mœsog. ga-draban 'cut' (as, out of a rock), norse at drepa 'strike, kill,' drubbing. Cf. 780.

798. RIDGE 'back.' The lat. Tergum, Dorsum, also ῥαχις the spine, also Τραχηλος 'the neck,' should be considered as allied to this word. Possibly Τραχυς may be the essential idea, as the spinal processes of the neck and back are very rough, especially to a rider. " Smote the boore on the ridge," Mort d'Arthure, vol. i. chap. xii. Agls. Hrycg = Hryggr = germ. Ruck = scotch Rig. " Spina dorsi totius structuræ fultura est, ut erecti stare possimus: constituitur autem e triginta quatuor vertebris = The chine or backbone is the prop of the whole frame or pack; that we may be able to stand bolt up-right: now it is made up of four and thirty rack bones." Janua Linguarum, 259.

> Hit berth on rugge grete semes*
> An draȝþ bivore grete temes.
>   Owl and Nightingale, 773.

> She helped him opon his hors ryg.
>   Ywaine and Gawin, 1834.

799. ROUGH = Τραχυς? = agls. Ruh, for †rug. In the mœsog. cf. þruts-fill 'leprosy,' rough skin; also Τραγος 'the he-goat' with his rough shaggy coat: a long or short vowel makes no conclusion. The welsh Cryg 'rough' may be another form and may explain the H in the previous word, Hrycg.

 * Of the horse. Semes = loads: cf. agls. Syman.

800. Rub = Τριβειν = lat. Terere (with Trivi) = germ. Reiben = dutch Wryven, which last helps nothing.

INITIAL LABIALS LOST.

801. Of the suppression of labials we have examples in the æolic Βροδον = att. ῥοδον; æol. Βρυτηρ = att. 'Ρυτηρ; æol. Βρακος = att. 'Ρακος (Greg. Kor. etc.); æol. Βρητωρ = att. ῥητωρ (Priscian). Compare Βρυχησασθαι ὡς λεων (Hesych.) with Rugire. The emperor Geta was so far given to philological study as to say Agni balant, Icones rugiunt (Spartianus in Geta). At the end of Valcknaers Ammonios are some similar lists, and they give Λεων Βρυχαται. Rogare represents doubtless the active of Precari, and germ. Fragen. The germ. Löschen ' extinguish ' is in Kilian Bluschen. Ριγος = Frigus, see by way of confirmation, T. 325, ῥιγεδανης 'Ελενης ' that one shudders at.' So old eng. Rach = Brach ' a hound,' Lin = agls. Linnan (Andreas, 2277) = Blinnan = old engl. Blin, ' cease,' " The heart never lin's panting or throbbing " " sine requie palpitat." (Janua Linguarum, 274: the word is of frequent occurrence in old english.)

> The pipe went so meryly,
> That I coude never blynne.
> The Frere and the Boye, 306.

As in pronouncing Two, Sword, Greenwich, Woolwich, Warwick, Berwick, we drop the w, so also sometimes in greek. The change of kw or koppa to k or kappa has been already mentioned. Δωδεκα for Δυωδεκα Δις for Twice = Bis; Δοιος seems to have a compensative O, as in the aristophanic κοαξ = qwack.

802. Belch. Βρυχασθαι, Rugire ' to bellow ' are very similar in form to Ερευγειν ' bellow,' Σ. 580, ταυρον ερυγμηλον εχετην ' were holding a bellowing bull,' Υ. 404, ηρυγεν ὡς ταυρος, and this has the very letters of Ερευγεσθαι ' belch,' e-ructare. An initial B appears in irish and gaelic Bruchd ' a belch ' = breton Brengeud. These forms we presume to have a common origin: compare Bray, Βρεμειν, Fremere, welsh

Breferad 'a bellowing,' Brefer 'to bleat, bellow.' But since
L, R easily interchange, Βλεμεαινειν (in Homer), Belch, Bellow, Bull, Balare, Bleat, Βληχη, Bell (of a stag) are also at
no great distance.

803. BLEAK (a fish) = Λευκη. The family to which Bleak,
Blank, fr. Blanc, belong has been recounted in art. 529.
The latin name for the fish Alburnus is translated Bleak
with the remark "call'd so because it is of a palish white."
(Janua Linguarum, 166.) The affinity of these groups is
strongly seen in the agls. Blæcern = Lucerna. The white
mark on a horses face is a BLAZE. In the germ. Augenblick
exists the sense 'look, glance,' as in Lumina 'the eyes.'

> The lyoun bremly on tham blist.
> Ywayne and Gawain, 3163.

804. BREAK, WRECK = lat. Frangere = 'Ρηξαι, 'Ρηγνυναι =
agls. Brecan = mœsog. Brikan = isl. Braka.

805. BROAK, BROCK, 'belch' in east Anglia according to
Forby. The agls. is Roccetan (not as Forby gives it) = lat.
e-ructare = Ερευγεσθαι. Cf. Rumen for †rugmen. Referring
to the remarks above, Brook, art. 423, the greek words for
throat come into immediate connexion, Βροχθος, Βρογχος,
etc., and it seems ρυγχος 'snout,' Ronchi 'snoring.'

806. FISH = lat. Piscis = agls. Fisc = mœsog. Fisks is suspected to be Ιχθυς with loss of labial and sibilation. The
welsh Pysg compared with the gaelic and irish Iasg affords
some confirmation.

807. FRAYNE = agls. Fregnan = germ. Fragen = mœsog.
Fraihnan = norse Fregna = lat. Rogare. Other forms sibilate
the guttural as mœsog. Fraisan = norse Freista = agls. Frasian.

> I frayned him if he wolde fight.
> Ywaine and Gawin, 272.

> And if ani man the oght frayn,
> Seeke now lely* that thou layn†.
> Id. 579.

---

* Lely = loyally.   † Layn = conceal. So also 2195.

808. Fresh = lat. Recens = agls. Fersc = .germ. Frisch = swed. Fœrsk.

808 *a*. Lick (give him a licking) has not yet been found in agls. It appears however to be of the true breed: it probably = mœsog. Bliggwan = lat. Plectere = Flog, etc. †fligere in Affligere, Profligare, Configere.

809. Liketh = lat. Placet = agls. Licað (as, me licað = mihi placet) = mœsog. Leikan (inf. = placere, as Guþa galeikan ni magun 'cannot please God,' Romans vii. 8). Libet seems = Placet with loss of P and substitution for guttural. See on List, Lust which then matches Libido, and Pleasure. Observe that welsh Blys = Lust, which reminds us of Bliss, Bless = agls. Bletsian, Blithe, Blandus, Blandiri, which may be duplicates of Placere.

> My gayest gelding I thee gave
> To ride wherever liked thee :
> No lady ever was so brave,
> And yet thou wouldest not love me.
>   Lady Greensleeves in Ellis, ii. 395.

> My fader, it hath stonde thus,
> That if the tresor of Crœsus
> And all the golde of Octavien
> Forth with the richesse of Yndien
> Of perles and of riche stones
> Were all togider min at ones
> I set it at no more accompt
> Than wolde a bare straw amount,
> To yive it her all in a day
> Be so that to that swete may
> It mighte like or more or less.
>   Gower, lib. v. p. 285.

> Quod Achab thanne : There is one
> A brothel, which Micheas hight ;
> But he ne comth nought in my sight
> For he hath long in prison laien ;
> Him liked never yet to saien
> A goodly word to my plesaunce.
>   Gower, lib. vii. p. 172.

> I make myn avowe, sayd Lytell Johan
> These strokes lyketh well me.
>   A Lytell Geste of Robyn Hode, iii. 87.

> Ac* therof liked him nought to take.
> Sir Gy of Warwike, p. 157.

> Most goodly persone, most leve and dere
> That hir best likethe.
> Lydgates Minor Poems, p. 34.

810. Lisp (verb) = lat. Blæsus (adj.) = agls. Wlips Wlisp (adj. in Ælfric gloss.) = germ. Lispeln (verb) = swed. Læspa = dan. Læspe.

810 a. Lock of hair = agls. Locc = Πλοκαμος. See 442 a, 447, etc.

811. Rain. Βρεχειν 'to moisten' seems to be an old form of germ. Regen = agls. Regnan, Rinan 'to rain.' So in the Anakreontica Βρεχομαι δε κἀσεληνον κατα νυκτα πεπλανημαι 'I am getting wet with the rain.' See Lobeck Phrynich., p. 291. Rigare is very close. See 841.

812. Wort (an herb) = lat. Herba = agls. Wcort, Wyrt = mœsog. Waurts. (B and T as in Womb = Venter, Lumbi = Lenden.) That the latin should have lost the W, generally retained, may seem surprising: it is equally so that the mœsog. is also deficient, for our Or-chard = mœsog. Aurtigards, 'a wort garden,' κηπος, and Aurtya is a gardener. W is generally preserved in the mœsog. Another example of the loss with a compensative A is probably found in Airus; see 383.

> And ȝyt he hakkyt hem smallere
> Than wortes to the pot.
> Songs and Carols, p. 101.

813. Of the omission of initial L the following example is found in greek Λειβειν = Ειβειν, (as Od. θ. 531, 532). The remainder are very far from convincing: Ιγδη = Θυεια compared with Λιγδος (the same), Λαιψηρος = Αιψηρος (? cf. Αιφνιδιος). Λαφυσσειν = Αφυσσειν, Λαχνη = Αχνη. Ihre thinks that the swed. Läka 'to cure,' akin to Leech 'a physician,' = agls. Læce, is the scandinavian form of Ακεισθαι: but I am disposed to compare welsh Iach, 'sane, sound, whole' with ιασθαι (for †ιακεσθαι) and ακεισθαι. Ihre also compares Lamb with Αμνος, Liver with Ηπαρ, but I see no

---

* Ac = but.

reason to follow him. An example of lost L in friesic Jacht for Ljeacht=germ. Licht=Light (Outzen).

Of the two examples I am about to produce nothing beyond a possibility that they are valid can be alleged; that Famelicus contains a teutonic termination appears very uncertain, and that a lost letter in Homer is a Vau rather than an L is to be presumed, since L was familiar to the scribes while F was not. The first might even be put thus: such a word as Ϝεικειν began primitively with an additional initial, Like also had a lost initial, and in those circumstances V and L are interchangeable. Art. 760.

814. LIKE. Is εοικεναι = †λελοικεναι? εικως = †λεικως? No evidence for †ϜεϜοικεναι, beyond the scansion, which would equally admit †λελοικεναι, has yet been discovered. The agls. Lic occurs in numerous derivatives and = mœsog. root †leiks in derivatives = norse Líkr. Such lines as β. 283, Τηλεμαχῳ δ' εικυια κατα πτολιν ῳχετο παντη are reconcileable with Bentleys theory about the digamma, that δε was capable of becoming δ before it, but some other doctrine must be invented for δ'λεικυια. Let us mark by the way, in confirmation of Bentley, that in the teutonic languages the negative Ne coalesces with a W following, so that Ne wot=Not; Ne were=Nere. They frequently occur in all our old english.

815. OTTER = lat. Lutra? = agls. Oter, Otyr = norse Otr = sanskr. Udr-as. The greek is a compound Ενυδρος.

816. An L sometimes falls away when it is the second letter, a consonant preceding. This is something more than Piano from Planus, ital. Pianto from Planctus, ital. Fiato from Flatus, but ital. Bestemiare = Βλασφημειν is sufficient. Buttmann (Lexil. 1. 76) considers εκπαγλος for †εκπλαγλος, πυελος for †πλυελος from πλυνειν, λελιημενος for †λελιλημενος. Γυμνος must be participial, the welsh Llom 'bare, naked,' helps us to †γλυμνος akin to Glubere and to בגלנ. Obliquitas = breton Beskel = fr. Biais = eng. Bias. I believe Fistula to be for †flistula from flare, like blast: perhaps with R inserted it appears in the unexplained

With trompes, pipes, and with fristele.
Ywaine and Gawin, 1396.

Pestis to be for †plestis from Plectere=$\pi\lambda\eta\sigma\sigma\epsilon\iota\nu$, in the hebrew we find the same word for 'blow' and pestilence: Fons I suppose to be Fluens. So Pucker is not saxon and seems to be Plicare, Pleach, Plash.

817. Blow = Flare is $\Phi\upsilon\sigma\alpha\nu$ for †$\phi\lambda\upsilon\sigma\alpha\nu$. Homer has $\Phi\upsilon\sigma\alpha\iota$ 'bellows.' This seems quite clear from Bladder, Blister=$\Phi\lambda\upsilon\kappa\tau\alpha\iota\nu\alpha$, Vesica, Pustula.

818. Flap appears with loss of initial in agls. Læpe, ora, fimbria, germ. Lappen, which are the source of Lap, Lappet: so overlap. Fimbria appears to me to be for flimbria and akin to the agls. *Flaxa*.

819. Flask = agls. Flasc = welsh Flasg. Cf. Basket = lat. Fiscus = welsh Basged. Flasket is in Kersey, a great sort of basket, Flask is properly now bottle inclosed in a plaited covering: both are from mœsog. Flahta, $\pi\lambda\epsilon\gamma\mu\alpha$, root $\pi\lambda\epsilon\kappa\epsilon\iota\nu$.

820. Flee = agls. Fleogan, Fligan, Fleon = $\Phi\epsilon\upsilon\gamma\epsilon\iota\nu$ = lat. Fugere = isl. Flya = germ. Flichen. The mœsog. is þliuhon with θ. Does the welsh Ffoi 'fugere' our Fowl, and the german Fügel argue against this comparison? Filix 'fern' argues in favour of it, for Filix like Fern and $\Pi\tau\epsilon\rho\iota\varsigma$ should mean Feathery, like Pluma.

> He that byfleke wel lecherye
> Bivlekth foule continuance.
> William of Shoreham, p. 36.

821. Glad = lat. Lætus. Cf. $\Gamma\eta\theta\epsilon\iota\nu$, $\Gamma\epsilon\gamma\eta\theta\epsilon\nu\alpha\iota$, Gaudere.

822. Key = agls. Cæg. Cf. Clavis = $K\lambda\epsilon\iota\varsigma$.

823. M. Buttmann (Lexil. I. 195) desiring to prove that $Ου\lambda\alpha\iota$, $Ο\lambda\alpha\iota$, are represented in lat. by Mola, parallels the loss of M by $M\iota\alpha$ = $I\alpha$; Mars, Mas, Maris = $A\rho\eta\varsigma$, $A\rho\rho\eta\nu$; $M\alpha\lambda\eta$, $M\alpha\sigma\chi\alpha\lambda\eta$ = Ala, Axilla; $M\ο\nu\theta\ο\lambda\epsilon\nu\epsilon\iota\nu$ = $Ο\nu\theta\ο\lambda\epsilon\nu\epsilon\iota\nu$; $M\ο\sigma\chi\ο\varsigma$ 'branch' = $Ο\sigma\chi\ο\varsigma$ Helladius ap. Phot. cclxxix. $\ο\tau\iota$ $\tau\ο$ $A\lambda\epsilon\upsilon\rho\ο\nu$ $\kappa\alpha\tau\alpha$ $\pi\lambda\epsilon\ο\nu\alpha\sigma\mu\ο\nu$ $\tau\ο\upsilon$ μ $\epsilon\sigma\tau\iota\nu$ $\epsilon\upsilon\rho\epsilon\iota\nu$ $M\alpha\lambda\epsilon\upsilon\rho\ο\nu$. So $A\lambda\phi\iota\tau\alpha$ will be †$\mu\alpha\lambda\phi\iota\tau\alpha$, $A\lambda\epsilon\sigma\alpha\iota$ †$\mu\alpha\lambda\epsilon\sigma\alpha\iota$, and belongs to Mill.

824. N. That initial N may be dropped appears from Adder which is agls. Nædre = norse Nadra = welsh Nadr = gaelic irish Nathair, but dutch Adder. Apron seems to be

for Napron like Napkin, Napery. So in Promptorium Parvulorum Barmclothe : napron.

> And with her napron fair and white ywash
> She wypid soft hir eyen for teris that she out lash *.
> History of Beryn (initio).

Nombles was later spelt Humbles, Umbles.

> They wasshed togyder and wyped bothe,
> And set tyll theyr dynere ;
> Brede and wyne they had ynough
> And nombles of the dere.
> A Lytell Geste of Robyn Hode, 124.

"We eat the humbles or bowels as a delicate meat" (Janua Linguarum lit. v. 25). The french has Nombles, ' partie du cerf qui s'eleve entre les cuisses.' pumle is in the agls. dictionaries.

825. R. At least when another letter precedes, R is omitted, sometimes, it is inserted. So Tremere=Tremble= span. Temblar. Fimbria = Fringe, Fanny is for Frances, that Bust = Breast, always probable, one may be convinced by the friesic Bostsä'l = germ. Brustsicle, ' horse collar,' in this case Borst becomes Bost, before R is lost; so in english " Fust of all." The agls. Grantabrycge=Cambridge.

> . . . . . . And for my subject chois
> To sing the Ryel Thrissill and the Rose.
> Dunbar, Thistle and Rose, xxvii. so xix.

Tug=Drag. Ducere=Trahere=for †tragere, Beck = Brook ? mœsog. Freidyan = Φειδεσθαι? Cremare = spanish Quemar, Pinguis = span. Pringue, germ. Sprechen = Speak, sanskr. Kramel = Camel. Is τρεχειν akin to ταχυς? Προτι=sanskr. Prati=Ποτι. Δρυφακτοι the barrier between the court and the audience is a change from †δρυφρακτοι. The welsh Coch ' red ' answers to the erse Croch ' red ' also 'saffron ;' hence Coccus may be of one origin with Crocus; a deep yellow becomes a red. Tabula I scarce doubt, is the diminutive of Trabs. Timere which is without corresponding forms in other languages may be Tremere, which has teutonic equivalents. And Temere ' rashly ' is only Trepide ' hurriedly ' otherwise

* Out lash is ut-leccan sibilate, ' let drop out,' see Leak, 136. Cf. Lusny.

†tremide; so Temerarius. Dumus, Dumctum for †drumus, †drumctum answering to the sanskrit. The scotch say Prin for Pin.

> She prinned the dishclout to his tail
> And cooled him wi' a waterpail.
> Song.

And this to be seen in the agls. Preon, 'a fibula, brooch,' that is, pin, also Ear preon 'inauris' 'ear ring' that is, ear pin. We seem here to have a participle of Prick, pricend, which = Breakend = Piercing, so that Preon = Brooch.

826. FINCH = lat. Fringilla. For the other equivalents see 655.

827. DRAG = DRAW = lat. Ducere? = Trahere.

827 a. GROOM = agls. Guma = Homo, see 943 a. Bridegroom is agls. Bridguma. See the dutch in 368.

> Ant bring me to þi brihte bur*
> Brudgume of wunne †.
> Seinte Marharete, fol. 52. b. 8.

LETTERS LOST IN INLAUT.

828. In the middle syllables of words, or in the Inlaut, gutturals, dentals, labials, and S are omitted. As examples of the omission of gutturals take $\Sigma\pi\epsilon o\varsigma$ = lat. Speeus, $\Delta\rho\upsilon o\psi$ 'woodpecker' for †δρυ-κοψ, the compounds in -πλους, -πλοος from πλεκειν, ψιαδας (Il. II. 459) = Ψεκαδας, Πρωϊ 'early in the morning' compared with the sanskrit Pråk. Ωον, art. 543, if compared with Egg, etc. has lost a guttural. Frigus is perhaps the labiate form of Κρυος, Facere perhaps = Ποειν, Ποειν, Τεθνεως = τεθνηκως, τεθναναι = τεθνηκεναι, εστως = εστηκως, εσταναι = εστηκεναι, εσταμεν = εστηκαμεν. Hence Grimm compares germ. Schweigen with Σιωπαν. Dodrans for dequadrans. Before a consonant also; Limen from λεγειν 'to lay,'? Quini from Quinque, Deni from Decem, Duodeni from Duodecim, Aranea from Αραχνη, Lana if it be Λαχνη, Σημα must be connected with Signum, Planus for †placnus, Examen from Exigere, Contaminare compared with Contagium, Pinus if, as Buttman holds, it be †picnus, Rumen from ερευ-

* Bur = bower. † Wunne, joy.

γεσθαι, Sumen from Sugere, Lumen from Lucere, Vita for †victa from Quick. If Vanus be †vacnus it is related to Vacuus. Struere is for strucere as appears from Struxi, Structum. Fluo is for †fluco as appears by Fluxi, Fluctus. Hill = germ. Hugel, Seal = lat. Sigillum, Wain = Wagon, Wainscot = Wagen-scot = wall-shide, a thin shive of wood for the wall, Rail = germ. Riegel, Sail = germ. Segel, Nail = germ. Nagel, Frail = lat. Fragilis, Tile = lat. Tegula, Sure = lat. Securus, Strait = Streight = lat. Strictus = fr. Etroit; Flail is from Flog (not Fliegen). Tain or Tane is old pronunciation for Taken; Made is for Maked = agls. Macode, french Larme = Lacrima, Faire = Facere, Taire = Tacere, Dîme = Decima, Paresse = Pigritia, Entire = fr. Entier = lat. Integer. Fain, Disdain have lost a G. We drop G in pronouncing Sign, Reign. Beam = mœsog. Bagms, Bristol = Brig-stow 'the bridge place.' Digitus = fr. Doit = ital. Dito = span. Dedo. Vagina = span. Vaina. Vigilare = fr. Veiller = span. Velar. With sibilation added to the guttural, Maxilla = Mala, Axilla = Ala, Taxillus = Talus, Paxillus = Palus, (Cic. Orat. c. 45, § 115). Vexillum = Velum, Seni from Sex, Tela probably and Mantile and Subtilis and Subtemen from Texere, Male from Masculus, Μαλη with Μασχαλη.

> Hire shoon were laced on her legges hie
> She was a primerole, a piggesnie,
> For any lord to liggen in his bedde
> Or yet for any good yeman to wedde.
> Chaucer, C. T. 3267.

Piggesnie seems to make by contraction Pansy: the heartsease has marks like a pigs nose.

LOSS OF GUTTURALS IN INLAUT.

829. AILS = Αλγει = agls. EgleÐ, cf. mœsog. Aglo, translating θλιψις, μοχθος, οδυνη. It is here presumed that there has been a transposition for easy utterance of the liquid as in Σιγμα for the hebrew Samech.

830. DAY = lat. Dies = sanskr. Dyu = agls. Dæg (pl. Dagas) = mœsog. Dags = norse Dagr = germ. Tag = erse Dìa, Dìe, Dè. In Norfolk the Y is still pronounced.

P

831. Draw = Drag = lat. Trahere = agls. Dragan = norse Draga=dutch Trekken. That Trahere was †tragere appears by traxi, tractus. The mœsog. is doubtful.

832. Laugh. No doubt Γελαειν is for †γελαγειν and laugh for †glaugh: compare Giggle. Laugh=agls. Hlihan =mœsog. Hlahyan=germ. Lachen, לעג. Cf. Χλευη, Χλευαζειν.

833. Lock meant originally only 'shut.'

> That standis loukit about and obumbrate
> With dirk schadois of the thik wod schaw.
> Gawin Douglas, Æn. Book VI. 44.
>
> The chiftanis al about him lowkit war.
> Id. XI. 45 (p. 359, ed. 1710).
>
> Gif ich me loki wit the bare*
> And me schilde wit the blete †.
> Owl and Nightingale, 56.
>
> The paleis was beloken al
> Aboute with a marbel wal.
> Rembrun, 959.

So did agls. Lucan, as Ge belucað heofona rice beforan mannum (Matth. xxiii. 13) Ye shut up the kingdom of heaven against men. In the Heliand Bilucan, Belucan 'to shut,' and Antlucan 'to open.' Mid enu felisu belucan, 'closed (the sepulchre) with a stone.' (Hel. 170. 20). In the mœsog. Galukan 'to shut,' Uslukan 'to open' (Luke v. 6). Galukun managein fiske filu 'they inclosed a great multitude of fishes.' In the norse also Luka, Lykja are 'shut,' as þá er sókn lokit. (Sœm. Edda, Helgakwiða, I. ult.) 'There is closed the contest, is a close to the contest.' From analogy the presumption is strong enough that L was not originally the initial letter, and this presumption is strengthened by the forms, Cliket, 'a latch key,'=breton Kliked, Liked, by agls. Cleofa, which means cubiculum or prison (Elene. 1419) and therefore generally 'Clausum quid;' by agls. Clusa 'a prison.' Hence it is probable that Claudere is for †clac-idere: in Clavis a labial represents the lost guttural, which appears again in agls. Cæg if it be put for †cleg, as conjectured

---

* Bare=agls. Bearu, grove. † Blete=agls. Blæd, leaf.

before. The Tab. Heracl. II. line 107 has actually ποτι-
κλαιγον 'closing.' (Mazochi).

> And the dore closed
> Keyed and cliketted.
>
> Piers Plowman, 3735.

> This freissche May, that I spake of so yore,
> In warm wex hath emprynted the cliket
> That January bar of the small wiket,
> By which into his gardyn ofte he went;
> And Damyan, that knew al hir entent
> The cliket counterfeted prively.
>
> Chaucer, C. T. 9990.

The verb is used in old english in the sense 'decide,' 'conclude' which is a natural derivative from Lucan Claudere, though obscure as long as Lucan is believed to be 'obscrare.' Sibilate forms in Kilian under Slot.

> Al þe help and loking ys in oþer monne honde.
>
> Robert of Gloucester, p. 100 *.

> Sertes, lordynges, hyt ys so
> I am a redy for to tho †
> All that the court wyll loke.
>
> Launfal, 781.

834. MAID = agls. Mægð, in the Heliand Magath, where Schmeller observes, "etiam pro experta virum, adultera" in John viii. = germ. Magd = mœsog. Magaths: derivatives of the verb, to MAY = agls. Magan = mœsog. Magan 'to be able to be strong,' δυνασθαι, ισχυειν. Compare MAIN = agls. Mægen, and MIGHT = agls. Miht, Macht = germ. Macht = mœsog. Mahts. The teutonic significations of strength and power compared with Μεγας 'great' and the participial Magnus make it evident that the verb once meant 'to be full grown,' and Maid is 'one grown up.' So we have Hu mæg he? (Genesis xxix. 6) How mays he? how does he thrive? The sanskrit Mah 'to grow, increase,' amplificare with Mahat-as 'great' is of the same old stock. In the radical syllable nothing feminine is implied, the agls. Mæeg, masc. is 'man,' Mago, Maga, masc. 'a relation :' the mœsog. Magus is 'son.' Cf. gaelic Mac.

---

* So p. 339. 4. 359. 28. 360. 4. 562. 5. 14.   † Tho for Do.

835. Midge = agls. Mygga = Μυια (with g become y) = germ. Mücke=sanskr. Makshikâ (with sibilation, see 718) = lat. Musca (sibilate).

836. Mingle = agls. Mengian, Mængan, Menegan = Μισ-γειν with Μιγηναι = lat. Miscere with hebrew and sanskrit.

> Al his lyf his * here imengde
> With sorwe and eke with sore.
> William of Shoreham, p. 1.

837. Mole (on skin) = agls. Maal, Mæl, Mal (Lye quotes, Ful maal on rægel, 'foul spot on garment' = mœsog. Mail (ρυτις) = germ. Maal = lat. Macula. The latin preserves the guttural. The sibilate forms agls. Mesel 'leper,' and Measles seem latinisms.

838. Nail (in both senses) = agls. Nægel (in both senses) = germ. Nagel (in both senses) = sanskr. Nakh 'nail of the finger' (masc. or neut.) = lat. Vnguem (cf. Vngula) = Ονυχα (acc.). From the nails of birds and beasts of prey the iron nail may have taken its appellation.

839. Naked = Nudus = agls. Naced, Nacod = mœsog. Nakwaps. In the last the guttural was lost and the W vocalized, then by contraction was produced Nudus. In the same manner Klag-id produced Cludere, Claudere, and we shall see Plak-id Ludere. The erse has Nochdaighim 'I make naked.' [Eudoxos "can't quite follow this:" I am much for it, it is due to Germany. The agls. often writes and of course pronounced Hnacod, where a past participle of a verb is evidently seen: the mœsog. þ is also participial, and it will be shewn shortly that Timidus is as much a participle as Monitus.]

840. Play. Ludere is a contraction of †lakidare. The mœsog. Laikan 'to leap,' σκιρταν with its subst. Laiks, χορος, Lax, Leax the norse and agls. names for the salmon, the river leaper, Locusta the latin for the locust, insect leaper, also Locusta the lobster, the sea leaper (leaping, I am told, by its tail), the latin sibilate form Lascivus†, the greek Λα-

* Life is.

† Skylarking is believed to be from agls. Lacan, so that Lasciva puella is 'Larky girl:' "Malo me Galatea petit, lasciva puella."

γως, the hare, all keep the guttural. The Aristophanic words Λαικαζειν, Λαικαστρια may also be conveniently referred to this root. The agls. Lacan does not occur very often, and is used rather more loosely, like Ludere. The poetical compound Fcoht-lac retains the old sense referring to the leaping in the sword and spear combat, the fight leaping. A good latin dictionary will afford several passages which must seek their explanation in the root now suggested as, Continuo cor meum cœpit artem facere ludicram atque in pectus emicare (Plautus). One of the english forms is LEAP=agls. Hlaupan = mœsog. Hlaupan taking a labial for a guttural and it produces LOUSTER=agls. Loppestre, and ELOPE, which has, like the german Laufen, the sense of running. So also INTERLOPER and the latin Lepus 'hare.' Hence becomes clear the origin of Eludere 'escape,' for it is 'run away, elope.' In old english Leap may occur as run:

> þe flagetes* he let falle and gan to flo ȝerne
> þe liȝtliere to leap his liif for to saue.
> William and the Werwolf, fol. 27.
>
> On hors lopen† tho kniȝhtes prest
> And lopen togider til schaftes brest.
> Sir Gy of Warwike, p. 359.
>
> "The blode lepe‡ over his eyen."
> Reynard the Foxe, p. 19.

Now it is always to be considered probable that an initial L has lost a previous consonant. Let us therefore believe that PLAY is a fuller form=agls. Plegian, Pleogan, which evidently signifies to leap in Boeth. xxxv. 6 = p. 101. 5 : þa sceolde cuman þære helle hund ongean him * * * se sceolde habban þrio heafdu, and ongan fægenian mid his steorte and plegian wið him. 'Then, say they, came the hound of hell over against him (Orpheus), which they pretend had three heads and began to fawn with his tail and leap against him.' So also Lye quotes from the Cotton MS. in Matthew xiv. 6: plegge 'danced' before Herod, and xi. 17, we have piped unto you and ye have not danced. The identity of the words is

* Flagetes=flaskets. † In two senses, leapt, ran. ‡ Ran.

further illustrated by the passages quoted below. FLEA=agls. Fleo=germ. Floh is probably a remnant of a more thoroughly gothic form, with the aspirate F: another saxon name for the flea is Loppe from its leaping. Pulex is nearly the same word and certainly from the same root. With the constant tendency to sibilation Pulex or Flea becomes Ψυλλα. By a similar sibilation Plegian=lat. Salire=Αλλεσθαι. Salmonem (acc.) is then again participially 'the leaper.' For the P a guttural is also found in GALLOP = Καλπαζειν, and in the mœsog. Hlaupan=agls. Hleapan the guttural is reduced to an aspiration: so norse at Hlaupa 'run, leap;' isl. at Hleypa 'to gallop a horse' (act.). The recent surmise that Gallop is gahleapan would require †gellop; for the mœsog. Ga is the agls. Ge. With the customary change of G to W we have WALLOP in the sense of gallop (William and Werwolf, Prompt. Parv. Forby). The erse sibilates the closing consonant, Cleas 'game, play,' Clisead, 'a skip or jump,' Clisim 'I skip or jump.' The greek has some forms in PL as Od. ζ. 318: ευ δε πλισσοντο ποδεσσιν. Acharn. 218: ελαφρως αν απεπλιξατο. Here πλικ=laik. The sanskrit has Plu 'go by leaps, gallop.' The mœsog. Plinsyan 'dance,' which has the rare initial P. Ελαφος 'a stag' is perhaps 'the runner,' though it may be 'the light.' Now since these tracings back have brought us to a monosyllabic root, we must certainly compare Celer: and still earlier than that hebr. קל 'swift.' Here as koph represents KW, we obtain by loss of K the latin Velox. There is I suppose no reason to doubt but this notion of leaping or hopping gives rise to the forms Claudus (as if Ludens), Χωλος, and HALT. Clokke 'limp' is found in Piers Ploughman, 1420.

> It was non so litel knave
> For to leyken ne for to plawe
> That he ne wod with him pleye.
> The children that yeden in the weie
> Of him he deden all here wille
> And with him leykeden here fille.
>
>   Havelok the Dane, 949.
>
> And layked him long while to lesten þat merþe.
>   William and the Werwolf, fol. 1.

So lovely lay that ladi and ich layking to gaderes.
Id. fol. 10. B.

Her* lovelaik thou bihald.
Sir Tristrem, p. 118.

Theune were set and bord leyd
And the beneyson was seyd
Biforn him come the beste mete,
That king or cayser wolde ete
Kranes, swannes, veneyson,
Lax, lampreys, and gode sturgun.
Havelok the Dane, 1727.

The strau‗der†, the lekere
The wild der, the lepere.
Names of the Hare in Reliq. Ant. I. 133.

To continue the investigation into a region of more doubt. To CLAP hands is in agls. Plegian (Lye) which brings us to Plaudere. Further we find agls. Clappan, Palpitare, Clæpete, Palpitaret, Clæpetung Pulsus. That is, the galloping motion of the pulse is expressed by a word in saxon of the Gallop family, and in the latin by the syllable Palp, so that palpitare =†gallop-itare and by Pul, as we had it in Pulex. Pellere, pepuli has in itself some signification of leaping beats, as " Pelle humum pedibus," " Fugiens pellit vada remis." " Pectora pellite tonsis " (Ennius, of drawing the oar upon the chest). " Tunc has pepulisti fores?" " Pepulisse lyram." Pulsare in the same way. It may, therefore, be conjectured that Pellere is a causative form of, say, the sanskrit Plu, and in its most frequent sense means ' cause to leap away ' so ' drive away.' Of Plaustrum I can only guess that it was originally a thespian dancing wagon (Hor. Art. P.).

841. RAIN may have relationship to 'Ραινειν. It has been shown that Rain is probably Βρεχειν, and it is by no means impossible that ραινειν may be further †βραχ-ενειν. We see certain examples of gutturals omitted in greek words, as above, and N is not radical in Σημαινειν from Σημα, Λαν-θανειν, Μανθανειν, Αλγυνειν, Κρατυνειν, etc. Between the

* Her, their. † Der=deer=θηρ.

ideas 'wet with a shower' and 'sprinkle' is a close approximation.

Διοσημια 'στιν και ῥανις βεβληκε με.
Aristoph.

The connexion of Ραινειν with a radix ραδ αρδ as suggested by Pott is undeniable; but surely βρεχ— and ραδ must be originally identical.

842. Slack. Comparing Laxus, Λυειν, Solvere, Χαλαν a suspicion arises that the first letter in Slack is a sibilation of the first in Χαλαν, and that the most ancient form of the word would be †χαλακειν, †χαλυκειν. A passage of Hesiodos Theogon. 521 seems to shew that λυκειν was an old form of λυειν.

Δῆσε δ' ἀλυκτοπέδῃσι προμηθέα ποικιλόβουλον.

842 a. Shake = agls. Sceacan = Σειειν? We had before Shake=Quake, so that Σεισμος=a Quaking, an earthquake.

843. Streak=lat. Stria? The agls. Strice=moesog. Striks is used of a stroke to form a letter, κεραια.

844. Struggle the frequentative of Strive seems to be from agls. Strec, and Strive = germ. Streben to have a labial for a guttural. Mannings quotations will shew that Strec is used for 'fortis, violentus' and it may represent lat. Strenuus for †streenuus. The στρηνης of Hesychios is a false light here.

844 a. Seam interpreted by Kersey "a measure of eight bushels: of glass the quantity of 120 pound," by Halliwell " 1. a horse load of wood in Devon. 5. a horse load in Cornwall" is properly the agls. Seam 'a load for a pack horse;' the agls. Seamere is our Sumpter, the low latin Sumerius, Sagmarius; and since horse loads must be packed in Sacks, the verb Σαττειν and Σαγμα are evidently derivatives of Sack. In art. 943 we shall see that the agls. had the participial termination μεν, μα or μη, and it had also the root: there is therefore no reason for pronouncing Seam a borrowed word.

   An hors is strengur þan a mon
   Ac for hit non iwit ne kon,
   Hit berþ on rugge grete semes.
      MS. Cott. Caligula, A. IX. fol. 235.

815. Ten = agls. Tigun = lat. Decem.

816. Tug = Ducere = —ducre. Since the sense is one, since also the greek and agls. omit gutturals in the inlaut and since Virgilius uses Inducitur as if Induit se, it seems fit to conclude that Inducre, ενδυσασθαι is Inducere. Exuere may be †ex-ducre, †ex-ducere.

817. Way = agls. Weg = lat. Via. Vehere = sansk. Vah was †vegere as shewn by Vexi, Vectus; Wagon, Wain may be the participle.

DENTALS LOST IN INLAUT.

818. That dentals in middle syllables are omitted appears by Ma'am = Madam, Other = Or, Parais in old english = Paradise, Catena = Chain, Pater = fr. Pere, Mater = fr. Mere, Frater = fr. Frere = engl. Friar, Matrona (fluvius) = Marne, Radicem = fr. Racine, whence Race, Scaturiginem = Source, Latrocinium = Larceny, Desiderium = Desire, Benedictionem = Benison, Maledictionem = Malison, Nativus = Naive, Predicare = Preach, Natalis = fr. Noel, Claudicare = fr. Clocher, Nidificare = fr. Nicher, Maturus = fr. Mur, Iudicare = fr. Juger. Confidence = span. Confianza, Credere = span. Creer, Iudicium = span. Juicio, Cadere = span. Caer. Fœdus may be Putidus. Ruina compared with Rudera may be †trudina. Σπαν, †σπαειν for †σπαδειν as appears by the derivatives Σπαδων, etc. Πρωτος for †προτατος.

819. Fern = anglosaxon Fepern = Πτερις from its feathery shape.

850. Float = Πλεειν. Herod. ii. 156 uses Πλεειν, Πλωτος of a floating island. Agls. Fleotan 'to float,' Fleot, as in Northfleet, Purfleet 'a place where vessels float,' Flot 'a float, raft' and Fleet. In isl. at Flôta 'to float,' causative, Fliôt 'the deeper parts of a river.' Πλοιον 'a boat or ship.' With these Fluitare, Fluere, Flow, Flood have some connexion.

851. Four = agls. Feower = mœsog. Fidwor = lat. Quattuor = Τετταρες, Τεσσαρες. Πισυρες = Petor in Petorritum.

852. Gush, Gout (a sewer), Gutter. Cf. lat. Gutta, 'drop;' agls. Geotan 'pour' = mœsog. Giutan = Χεειν, with

Χυτλον, Χυτλαζειν. Χειν is used of the foundery of metals; and so Geotan: art. 280.

> Thah mi tonge were mad of stel
> Ant min herte yʒote of bras,
> The godness myht y never telle
> That with kyng Edward was.
> Percys Reliques. Vol. II. Death of Edward I. 81.

852 *a*. YODE, YEDE a frequent word in old english=agls. Eode 'went' is according to Grimm from the mœsogothic Iddyan ' to go,' which appears in greek as Ιεναι for †ιτεναι and in latin Ire for †itere comparing ιταμος, Iter, Equitem, Peditem, Comitem. The agls. has also Yting a journey. Welsh Addu ' go.'

> Well weened he that fairest Florimell
> It was with whom in company he yode.
> F. Q. III. viii. 19.

853. LEWD was originally ' people,' agls. Leode ' people.' Cf. Λαος. The agls. has two forms; the other is þeod=mœsog. þinda ' people,' and the dental has evidently become L. The change of signification in this word has been quick. Acts xvii. 5. Certain lewd fellows of the baser sort. Των αγοραιων ανδρας τινας πονηρους.

> Yet lewdly darst our ministring to upbraid.
> Milton, VI. 182.

> For gold ne passeth noʒt in bounte so much leode*, iwis†,
> As dignete of preosthod passeth the lewed man that is.
> Thomas Beket, 1031.

854. MADDEN=Μαινειν. The sanskrit form of Mel ' honey' changes L to D, Madhu, used also to denote spirituous liquor, one of the earliest intoxicating beverages being MEAD, METHEGLIN, Μεθυ. The sanskr. verb Mad ' to madden or intoxicate,' with several derivatives shews that Mead Maddened. The greek may be referred to this root as easily as to MOON.

LABIALS LOST IN INLAUT.

855. The labials are often omitted in middle syllables. Lark=Laverock, Kerchief=Coverchef ' cover head,' Poor=

---

* Leode=Lead. † Iwis=I know.

Povero = Pauper, cf. Impoverish; Rout = fr. route = ital. Rottura=span. Rotura=lat. Ruptura. Doubt (with B sunk in pronunciation) = fr. Douter = span. Dudo(s) = Dubitare, from Duo. Lord = agls. Hlaford; Lady = agls. Hlæfdige, City = Civitatem. Ditia, Ditare, Ditissimus for †divitia etc. Novus makes Nuper by vocalisation. Nubilis = †nubibilis. The greek omits a Vau, in Οις, Ωον, Λειδειν = ᾁδειν, Αηδων, Αργειον. Δαηρ = sansk. Devri = lat. Levir. Super = fr. Sur, Supercilium=Sourcil, Septimus dies, or Sabbath day= Samedi. Appropinquare=Approach. Θαυμα is by vocalisation from Τεθηπα, Θαμβειν.

856. CRAFT (cunning)=germ. Kraft (strength)=Κρατος?

857. HEAD = agls. Heafod = mœsog. Haubiþ = lat. Caput. Κεφαλη answers in the first syllable and the agls. has Hafela 'head.' Sansk. Kapâl 'skull,' masc. or neut. The german has two forms, Kopf and Haupt.

> For so astonied and asweved*
> Was every vertue in my heved.
> House of Fame, 42.

The scotch use the word for the side of the head, and so a man has two haffets.

> She fand him ance at Willie Sharps
> And, what they maist did laugh at,
> She brake the bicker, spilt the drink,
> And tightly gowffed his haffet.
> Song.

858. That S is omitted in initial and afformative greek syllables is established. Some examples of its omission in middle syllables may be found. Thus sansk. Snushâ=agls. Snoru=lat. Nurus=Νυος. One might conjecture the first syllable to be engl. Son=sansk. Sunu. In Μιγηναι=Misceri the S appears radical, if we compare the semitic languages: the hebrew has מסך and the arabic, syriac, sanskrit correspond.

LIQUIDS LOST OR GAINED IN INLAUT.

859. The liquids are omitted in middle syllables. M and N are inserted in some words, omitted in their cognates.

* Asweved=sopita, put to sleep.

Many word hunters believe in the insertion, we shall learn to believe also in the omission. To avoid solving or failing to solve hard problems, these shall all go together. Consobrinus (for †consororinus) = Cousin, Mansio = fr. Maison, Messager (Chaucer, C.T. 4426, 4743) = Messenger; Nightingale = germ. Nachtigall, Χελιδονια = Celandine (Skinner), Αποστημα = Imposthume, Eleven = agls. Endleofan (for An-tigun) = Ἑνδεκα = Undecim, Tithe = Tenth, Month = mœsog. Munths, Tooth = mœsog. Tunthus, Sooth = mœsog. Sunya, Wish = germ. Wunschen, Blank = fr. Blanc has verb Bleach, Splinter (from Split) = germ. Splitter, Tongs with Take, Covent garden for Convent garden, Coblentz for Confluentes, Us for Uns, Twitch with Twinge, Switch with Swinge, Μεις with Μην (Il. T. 117, 118), Τυπτειν with Τυμπανον, Timbrel, Tambourine, Ταφη with Τυμβος, Τεθηπα with Θαμβειν, Nubere with Νυμφη, Κικιννος (Vesp. 1070) = Cincinni, Αμφαδον = Αναφανδον, Στρομβος with Στρεφειν, Στρογγυλος with †στρεγειν = Στρεφειν, Λαμβανειν with Λαβειν, Οικαδε with Οικονδε, Μανθανειν with Μαθειν, Ἁνδανειν with Ἡδεσθαι, Ομφην with Οπα, Densus with Δασυς, Hirundo with Χελιδων, Pinguis with Παχυς, Fat, Ταθεις for †τανθεις, Κλιθεις for Κλινθεις (Hom.), Γεγαως from Γεγονα, Μεμαως from Μεμονα (not μαω). Quotus says Forcellini ponitur pro Quantus 'Quota pars:' it is formed by ejecting N. Frangere with Fragilis, Fregi, Break; Findere with Fidi; Pangere with Pepigi; Sigillatim with Singillatim; Pandere with Πετασαι, Patere; Impingere with Impegi; Tangere with Tetigi, Integer and Contagia. Piscre, Pinsere, Pistor; Nubes, Nimbus; Scindere, Scidi, Nuncupare has only been explained as Nomen capere (†nominicupare), so Dominus = span. Dueño, Locusta = span. Langosta, Coniunctura = span. Coyuntura; Laterna with Lantern; Brachium with Branch, the welsh Braich is both; γναμπτειν and καμπτειν, with γαμψος, γαμψωνυχος. Averruncare with απερυκειν?, agls. Sið = mœsog. Sinþs = lat. Semita = fr. Sentier = span. Senda; the agls. often loses N in formation of verbs as Hehð pl. Hengon, Onfehð pl. Oufengon. Bind = sansk. Bandh, Badh = mœsog. †widan found in compounds, so that Pawn = germ. Pfand, and Pound (for cattle) and Pinder (who keeps it), agls. Wed (pledge) = mœsog. Wadi, seem all of one race. Housel = mœsog. Hunsel, Croup = Rump?, Nipe in old engl. = Ninth (Rob. Gloue. p. 269, line 19) Ensample = Exemplum; the gaelic for Potatoe is Bantáta.

Spider is from Spin, Spinner, Spinder, Spider. The D is an appendage only of the N as in Spindle, and N is withdrawn. Thus is the norse word Maðr formed, first the root, Man, or Mann, then with the nominatival R, †mannr, then †mannðr, then Maðr. Sviðr would seem formed in the same way. Haldorsen spells Brnðr 'a burn,' Brunnr, and Muðr 'a mouth,' Munnr.

860. Consider Adversus; here we have 'to' and 'wards' and no opposition: it must therefore be for †and versus from ante, αντι. The mœsog. expresses εμπροσθεν, εναντιον by Andwairþi an exact equivalent. Mundus (muliebris) is perhaps to be referred to sanskr. Mad, 'to ornament,' making third sing. Mandati. It may be connected with Monile, 'necklace' = sansk. Mani = norse Men = Μανιακον.

861. Blithe = mœsog. Bleiþs, οικτιρμων = lat. Blandus?

862. Bottom = agls. Botm = Βενθος = Βαθος = Βυθος = Βυσσος, and Βενθος = Fundus. If Βαθυς = Deep, very unlike words are of kin to one another. This is sometimes to be believed, and it is also to be held that one language may contain twofold, threefold and fourfold shapes of one root.

863. Chafer seems = Κανθαρος, φ for θ. Agls. Ceafor = germ. Käfer. The erse has Canda, 'a moth.'

864. Chop (barter), Chaffer, Cheap, Cheapen, Chep-, Chippen or Chipping in proper names, agls. Ceap 'a bargain, something for sale,' Ceapan 'to buy,' Ceapian 'to traffic,' Copeman 'a trader,' mœsog. Kaupon πραγματευεσθαι, norse Kaupa 'to buy,' germ. Kaufen 'to buy' Καπηλος 'a retailer' probably belong to Cambire which is a word of good antiquity. Cf. Αμειβειν.

865. Cup. From the sanskrit Kumbh-as 'a water jar,' Κυμβια 'vessels, pots' (Demosth. in Meidiam. 133), Cymbia lactis I would eject N and obtain Κυπελλον, Cup. Capiduncula, Capedinem, Capides (Cic. Nat. D. iii. 18).

866. Five=agls. Fíf=mœsog. Fimf, Fíf, Fim=Πεντε for †πεμπε=Quinque=etc.

867. Goad=Κεντειν? If we suppose the hellenic the older then N before a dental will change to S, and mœsog. Gazds=κεντρον=agls. Gad. Those who compare Gerte, Yard confuse the handle with the spike. The mœsog. occ. at 1 Korinth. xv. 55, 56, O death, where is thy sting?

868. Great=agls. Great, Grete=lat. Grandis. From the latin?

869. Hump I am unable to trace in the teutonic; the agls. is Hofer; in sense it='Υβος, which belongs to Κυπτειν, Gibbus, Κυμβια, etc.

870. Hundred='Εκατον=Centum=sansk. Shatum.

871. Lick=Λειχειν=Lingere: sanskrit and semitic also.

872. Lip=lat. Labium are related to Lambere. Virgil Catalect. v. 32, lambis suaviis, 'lip with kisses' that is 'kiss with lips.' Æneid viii. 632, Ludere pendentes pueros et lambere matrem, 'lip their mother,' 'apply lips to.' Yet also Lambere Lingere.

872 a. Lithe = agls. Liþ = lat. Lentus. Also = Limp, Limber. Cf. germ. Lind 'lenis,' Lenken 'to bend.' As Lentus is used for 'clammy' so is Lithe. "Visco et pice lentius," "The sweet lithe honey." Affectionate Shepherd, p. 17. Lithing, 'thickening for the pot:' to lithe the pot is to put thickenings into it (Wilbraham). So Brockett and Jamieson. Lentus is also lazy, "Lentus in umbra." Lither 'lazy, sluggish,' (Kersey). So Carr in Craven Glossary.

> My ladde he is so lither, he said
> He will doe nought thats meete:
> And is there any man in this hall
> Were able him to beate.
> King Estmere, 203.

> Some litherly lubber more cateth than two
> Yet leaveth undone what another would do.
> Tusser, p. 260.

> Ceis man, scho said, I se ȝe do bot tyre,
> And wax lidder lang or [ȝe] werk begin.
> Stewart, Cronielis of Scotland, 131.

Quheþer he war worth til have þe crown
Dat had be vertu þe renowne
Of manhod helpe and of defens
And þare-til couth gyve diligens
Or he þat lay in lythyrnes
Worth to makyn besynes.
                            Wyntown, I. 160, 69.

Lentus is also 'tender' = agls. Illiðe; nor is it a derivative of Lenis but a different form of the same; so agls. Liþenes is Lenitas. See 1021.

The 'bacco was strang and the yell it was lithe*.
                        R. Andersons Cumberland Ballads.

They gafe him metis and drinkis lythe.
                        Sir Isambras, 494.

873. LOIN, LEND = agls. Lend = lat. Lumbus = also Clunis. But by rejection of N we get Latus mostly in the sense of Flank, so as to reach the Clunis. Virgil thus describes an eastern dancing girl,

Copa Syrisca, caput Graia redimita mitella
Crispum sub crotalo docta movere latus.

that is, lumbos, flank, clunem. To FLANK belong FLITCH, FLANGE, germ. Flanke 'flank,' Lanke 'side,' swed. Flank 'flank, side.' With Lumbus compare Λαπαρη in Homeros and Λαγονα. LANKY is akin and = Λαγαρος.

A barme† cloth as white as morwe‡ milk
Upon her lendes ful of many a gore.
                        Chaucer, C. T. 3236.

The agls. Lend is correctly given in the lexica Clunis. I supply an example from an unpublished MS. Oxan tægl on lendinum : 'tail of ox on the clunes.' Latus = norse Hlid, with a trace of the guttural.

874. MIND as a purely teutonic root has been already asserted in art. 153. MOOD, MOODY are other forms, in the two senses of reflexion and anger; agls. Mod 'mens, animus,' Modig 'superbus, contumax, animosus,' mœsog. Mods 'θυμος,

---

* The ale was soft.
† Barm cloth = lap cloth, apron.   ‡ Morwe = mornings.

οργη' = norse Moþr = germ. Muth. METTLE compare agls. Geanmætan 'encourage:' agls. Mynegian = admonere. This root may be inferred to exist in lat. Meditari 'meditate' as distinguished from Meditari 'practice,' which is to be deduced from Μελος, Μελεταν. METTE 'dream' is a frequent old english word = agls. Mætan (with impersonal construction).

> And fast I slept and in sleeping
> Me mette such a swevening*
> That liked me † wondrous well.
> Chaucer, Romaunt of the Rose, 25.

To this same root I wish to refer Μανθανειν and to hold that Μαθειν has thrown out N : the same also of Μηδεσθαι. And perhaps the Μηνις anger of Homeros is not to be set far off.

> Therto me aneleth the wyttes fy3f
> And fe3et and breste and lenden †.
> William of Shoreham, p. 43, on extreme unction.

875. MOUTH = agls. Muð = mœsog. Munþs = germ. Mund seems related to Manducare.

> Thy mone pynnes§ bene lyche old yvory,
> Here are stumpes feble and her are none.
> Lydgate's Minor Poems, p. 30.

> Mary stod stylle as ony ston,
> And to the amgyl che seyde anon,
> Than herd I nevere of manys mon.
> Songs and Carols, p. 84.

Mund passes into Mumble which is expressed in swedish by Mugga and so we come towards the despised word Muᵷ, which is in sanskrit Mukh-an.

876. PAIN, PINE, agls. Pin, Pinan, isl. at Pina to torture. Pœnitet, Punire, Pœna and perhaps Αποινα (Yes, says Eudoxus). With these words of no genuine teutonic descent, marked by the P as importations I am so far here concerned as to point out, that it is by rejection of the N in

---

* Swevening = dream. † Liked me = placuit mihi.
† Fy3f for Fif, five, and Fe3et for Fet, feet are misspellings. Me = man. P. 44 also, Lenden.
§ Monepins = Teeth = (I suppose) Mouth pins, a trace of the old form.

Πενθειν, Πενθος, Πεπονθα, Πεισομαι (for †πενσομαι) that we obtain Παθειν, Πασχειν (†παθισκειν). And let me add that the second aorist of the greek verb does not always exhibit the ancient root, as we here see. Thence μανηναι may be really †μαδνηναι, and Μανθανειν Mind.

877. RIDDLE (a sieve) = agls. Hriddel with Hridrian (Luke xxii. 31) 'sift' = erse Riobhar 'a sieve' = lat. Cribrum 'sieve.' With these compare agls. Grindlas (in Cædmon, 24. 27. Th.) = GRATINGS = isl. Grind 'gratings;' a GRID-iron, to GRIDDLE, lat. Crates 'any wattled texture,' especially HURDLES, in the Edda, Grind, Craticula 'a gridiron' (in Martialis). Hurdle work is in Devon called RADDLING. These all contain the notion of crossbars as seen in the sieve. Cradle I would willingly add: and without hesitation I offer Cancelli for †crancelli, Κιγλιδες for †κριγλιδες. An earlier foundation for all these words is in Κρινειν 'to separate' hence 'to sift' hence 'to judge.' The GROIN is the line that separates the thigh from the belly, and such a line is still a Groin in architecture and carpentry. Similarly germ. Groenze 'border, limit.' In islandic at Greina, discernere, etc. In latin Cernere, which even when supposed to mean 'see,' is really 'distinguish.' "A line across meadows where has formerly been a hedge or a road is called the RAIN." (Hallamsh. Gloss.) I should hardly be excused for entertaining even momentarily the notion that Inguen contains †gren, and indeed the first letter should be C; unless we be allowed to plead that C G are really in latin one character and represent sounds sometimes confused as Cains, Gains. The agls. tongue was long since remarked as easily dropping N, therefore Hriddrian = Κρινειν, and resembles the formation of Spider, being put for †grindrian. By the light of these words I would explain the provincialisms Grindel, Grindlet for a ditch, drain.

> The pryst demyed them devylles both, wyth them he wolde not mett,
> He sparyd nother hylle nor holte, bnsche. gryne nor grett *.
>   Lydgates Minor Poems, p. 113.

The verb RID = agls. Hreddan is therefore = Cernere, and is

* Grett = stone, I presume.

used for separate. A sibilate form of Riddle is SKREEN, which is properly a standing, leaning sieve, as for skreening coals.

> A skuttle or skreen to rid soil from the corn.
> Tusser, p. 14.

878. STING, STICK (to stab), STITCH, cf. agls. Sticce 'punctio, incisio, a stab, a stitch,' Sticel 'aculeus, stimulus,' Stician 'pungere, transfigere, iugulare,' Stingan, Stimulare, pungere, mœsog. Stigkwan $\sigma \upsilon \mu \beta \alpha \lambda \lambda \epsilon \iota \nu$ and in compounds $\pi \rho o \sigma \kappa o \pi \tau \epsilon \iota \nu, \pi \rho o \sigma \pi \iota \pi \tau \epsilon \iota \nu$, etc., norse Stinga, german Stechen $= \Sigma \tau \iota \zeta \epsilon \iota \nu, \Sigma \tau \iota \gamma \mu \alpha$ with Stimulus. That the radix lies in the instrument, the Stick, Stang, agls. Stenge, Stynge, with which the wound is inflicted seems clear. These belong to the numerous relations of Set, Stare.

> Stongen with a spere.
> Erle of Tolous, 645.
> Many a stede there stekyd was.
> Id. 97.

879. SWAY, SWING = agls. Swingan = lat. Vacillare, or with labial Vibrare. Olaus Wormius gives a runic word Sveiger 'vibrator.'

880. SWEVEN = lat. Sompnium, erroneously spelt Somnium = agls. Swefen from a verb Swef-an = norse Sofa = $\Upsilon \pi \nu \epsilon \iota \nu$ actively Sopire. Sweven = the compound $E\nu \upsilon \pi \nu \iota o \nu$: sanskr. Swap 'to sleep.'

> Many menne sain that in swevening es
> There nis but fables and lesinges *:
> But menne may some sweven scene
> Which hardely that false ne been.
> Chaucer Romaunt of the Rose, 1.

881. THINK = $\Delta o \kappa \epsilon \iota \nu$ = agls. þencan, þincan = mœsog. þagkian = norse þekkja (by assimilation). These teutonic verbs eliminate the N in the course of their conjugation as Think Thought þencan, þohte, þagkyan, þahta. Like $\Delta o \kappa \epsilon \iota \nu$ the verb signifies also 'seem:' the phrase remains ME THINKS, $\delta o \kappa \epsilon \iota \; \mu o \iota$, 'to me it seems.' In the agls. a page and a half

---

* Lese is a sibilation of the old Liugan, Lie.

of examples of this sense may be found in Lyc. To express videtur the mœsog has þugkyan, (þuhta) and the german Dünken. Perhaps lat. Ducere in the sense of 'think' is identical. THANK is a form of THINK.

> The more ydropesy drinketh
> The more him thursteth *, him thinketh
> That he may never drink his fille.
> Gower, lib. V. p. 135.

> Thame thocht thay mocht haif wyn with labour licht.
> Gawin Douglas, Æn. p. 135. 17.

"This was king Arthurs dreame: Him thought that there was comen into this lande many gryffons and serpents and him thought that they brent and slew all the people in the land." Mort d'Arthure.

> Ho was þe gladur nor þe rise
> And song a nele cunne wise;
> Het puȝte þe dreim þat he were
> Of harpe and pipe þan he nere †.
> Owl and Nightingale, 21.

> If love be good, from whence cometh my wo?
> If it be wicke, a wonder thinketh me,
> Whan every torment and adversite
> That cometh of him, may to me savery think.
> Chaucer Troilus and Creseide, 1.

> So that wo seȝe ane lond, thiderward oure schip drouȝ
> Briȝttere hit thoȝte than the sonne, joye ther was ynouȝ.
> St. Brandan, p. 2.

> The see as he fal adoun thoȝte ek al afure ‡.
> Id. p. 22.

882. THRONG = agls. þringan = isl. þrengia = mœsog. þreikan = germ. Drucken. To be compared with lat. Frequens, having labial F for dental þ. Creber is similar in form. "Matlock will be thrung." (Derbyshire dialect.) Premere is perhaps another form.

---

* Thursteth also is here impersonal, as in the mœsogothic, þaurseiþ mik, where the verb is never personal.

† Ho, she; rise = agls. Hris = the spray or fine twigs of trees; nele = much; Het puȝte, it seemed; dreim = sound, thrum? mœsog. Drumyus? He is masc. since Dreim is masc. Nere = ne were, were not.

‡ Seemed all on fire.

883. THUSTER dark = agls. þeostre = germ. Finster with labial F and N. With this last compare Fenestra, taking it, as it is sometimes to be taken, for the double shutter, which closed the loophole. Our Window itself seems to have been Wind-door: it is often pronounced Winder by those who speak ancient words and I find it expressly spelt Windore, "windows (windores)" in Janua Linguarum, 550, where this derivation is pretty much confirmed by the expression Draw windows = shutters. "A draw window (a shut) being shut in darkneth the room." Jan. L. ibid. But the cognate languages are for Wind-eye which has its difficulty: is it for wind-eye-thirl?

> Vor euerich þing þat schuniet rizt
> Hit luueþ þuster and hatiet lizt;
> And enrich þing þat is lof misdede
> Hit luueþ þuster to his * dede.
> Owl and Nightingale, 229.

> An mai eft † habbe to make ‡
> Hire leofmon wiþute sake §,
> An go to him by daies lihte
> þat er stal to bi þeostre nihte.
> Owl and N. 1426.

884. TINDER remains in our language from the agls. Tendan, Tyndan, 'to set alight' = mœsog. Tandyan = isl. Tendra = germ. Zünden a sibilate form. It answers to lat. Tædam = Δᾳδα (acc.). But N was part of the original root, see 1025: the welsh has Tan 'fire'=gaelic Teinne; and the tree Tædam (acc.) is in german Tenne. Ἡ με κεραυνῷ διατινθαλέῳ σπύδισον ταχέως Vespæ, 329. Οἴναδι καὶ γλυκόεντι ποτῷ κεκαφηότα πιμπλάς Τινθαλεῳ, Nikandri Alexiph. 441. "Jist bevore candle teening" Devonshire Dialogue, p. 18. The Beltan of the Highlands which some make the god Baal, is only Bal, a pyre, a pile of wood for burning, a bonfire, rogus, with this word 'to light' and means the bonfire lighting. "As ver ys herte tende." Robert of Glost. p. 206 (as fire his heart inflamed). The match boxes of Sweden are stamped Tandstickor, 'tind-sticks."

885. THUMP = lat. Tundere. It is commonly thought that

* His=its. † Eft=again. ‡ Make=mate. § Sake=rebuke.

the radical form of Tundere is seen in tud-, tutudi, and that the N is an insertion to strengthen the present. If however Thump be a vocal representation of a sound, tund, and not tud must be the representation of the same sound; Tap gives a less noise answering to τυπτειν. And whether Thump have an historical traceable pedigree or not, tund is to Thump as, venter to womb, lenden to lumbi, lentus to limp. Hence it follows that tutudi has thrown out the liquid. הפת that is הת הת τυμπανον.

885 *a*. THURSDAY. The god of our pagan forefathers known as Thor takes his name I believe from Thunder = agls. þunor then þunr, þorr, þor: his hammer is the thunderbolt. Cf. lat. Tonitru. The R in Thor is radical not accidental; hence the full nominative is þorr.

886. TOOTH = lat. Dentem (acc.) = Οδοντα = agls. Toþ = mœsog. Tunþus = norse Tönn = germ. Zahn (sibilate). On the participial origin see 925: welsh is Dant = erse Dead, Deat.

887. TUMBLE, STUMBLE = agls. Tumbrian = isl. Tumba also Trumba. Cf. lat. Titubare 'stagger.'

888. TWENTY = lat. Viginti (for †dviginti) = æol. Ϝεικατι = Εικοσι. Similarly Διακοσιοι = Two HUNDred = lat. Ducenti with the other hundreds, and Τριακοστος (for †τριακοντατος) = lat. Trigesimus.

889. WEND, 'go,' may be Vadere and Βαδ-ιζειν.

890. WHEN was shewn art. 343 to be the english representative of Quando, Quum, and in our old language it was used indefinitely as the lat. Aliquando, Siquando; so mœsog. Hwan, ποτε, indefinitely. The same indefinite sense appears in Quotidie, Quotusquisque, and quoti answers to ποτε: this conclusion is fully confirmed by the mœsog. (Luke ix. 23). Daghwanoh 'cotidie.' That Quotus also = Quantus = ποσος (like εικοσι) see 914.

891. WINTER, WEATHER, WET, WATER, the sanskrit Und 'to wet,' Ud-an 'water,' Ambu 'water,' Ap 'water' in compounds Apa, welsh Afon = gaelic Abhaim = irish Aban, Aman 'river,' 'Avon,' gaelic Abh 'water,' welsh Ach 'fluid,' Ὑει 'it rains' (with loss of dental for †υδει), Ὕδος 'water' (in

Hesiodos, Works and Days, 51, γαιαν ὑδει φυρειν), Ὕδωρ 'water,' Ὕετος 'rain,' Ομβρος 'shower,' Vnda, 'wave,' Aqua 'water,' Vdus 'moist, wet,' Imber 'shower,' Amnis 'stream,' agls. Winter, Weðer or Weder, Wæt, Wæter, mœsog. Ahwa 'water, stream,' Wintrus 'winter,' Wato 'water,' norse Vetr 1. 'winter,' 2. 'storm,' with R radical and retained in all the cases *, Vatn 'water,' Unn 'wave,' Udi 'moistness,' arabic Wâdi 'river,' Waþaa 'fluxit aqua,' Wâþi 'fons,' are all varieties of a root in Und, Wamb, two forms related in the same manner as Venter, Womb, Lumbi, Lenden. As the saxons counted years by winters, so it appears the early greeks did, for Ετος, originally Ϝετος as in the Eleian inscription, ἑκατον Ϝετεα, must be referred to this root: the presence of the digamma entirely disproves any connexion with the mœsogothic Aþn, for that language very rarely fails to preserve its Vau, Uuinne. But Vetus old can scarcely be referred to Ϝετος since the exaggerative termination -osus is wanting. Possibly WIND, Ventus is to be added, though it rather seems to be a participial from mœsog. Waian 'to blow' = sanskr. Vâ. Grimm, Gr. iii. 391, quotes the slavonic Vjetar, Vitr for Wind and observes that the ideas wind and weather touch each other. In Weather gage, [Weather side (Eudoxos)] weather seems to be wind. Jamieson gives for the Roxburghshire use, Weather a fall of rain or snow accompanied with boisterous wind; also Weatherie, Weatherfu, stormy. Also Weddyr, wind.

> And there be a tempest fell
> Of great weddrys scharpe and snell †.
> Wyntown, vol. I. p. 387. v. 184.

Thus I would understand such a passage as,

> The birdes that han left hir song
> While they han suffred cold full strong
> In wethers grille and derke to sight,
> Ben in May for the sunne bright
> So glad, etc.
> Chaucer Romaunt of the Rose, 72.

---

* Vetr may be found in the same paragraph, both as storm and winter, in the Landnamabók, p. 6.

† Snell = swift.

But ere he it in his sheves shere
May fall a weather that shall it dere *.
    Chaucer Romaunt of the Rose, 4302.

And ride through ween and weather.
    The Clowns Complaint (Percy Society, III. p. 3).

With weders wakend him of rest.
    Ywaine and Gawin, 411.

Ne non other tempest of wynd and wedirs grct.
    Myrour of Lewed Men, 1059.

Weder is often storm in Laʒamon and Ormin. In the four places of Cædmon quoted in the index Weder signifies 'tempest.' The first Weder-wolcen 'the storm cloud' Mr. Thorpe has set down as 'cloud' only: the second 'holmegum wederum' he has given 'with its raging storms,' in the two next though falling drops and a shower are mentioned he does not say anything of tempest, but prefers weather and skies. Tempestas is used in the same way: it is 'tempest,' or mere 'weather,' for it must be conceded that the agls. can be indifferent and even fine weather, but this is not the place for instances of the opposite kind.

892. WOMB=lat. Venter as in 576=lat. Vterus by rejection of N=Vter=Ουθαρ=UDDER. So it is also in sanskrit Udar-an 'belly' Udhas 'udder.' The latin words Venter, Vterus had the same sense, see Forcellini and Virgil Æn. xii. 811. Lupus .... caudamque remulcens Subjccit pavitantem utero. Vtrem must be also Vterum.

893. WRINKLE = lat. Ruga = erse Grug = welsh Crych = agls. Wrincle = germ. Runzel (sibilated) = swed. Rynka, Skrynka, which suggests a connexion with SHRINK = agls. Scrincan and by ejection of N, with guttural changed for labial SHRIVEL. Connected also with ROUGH, Τραχυς, Ρυτις, and Ρυσσος. CRIMP in Crimping irons, RIMPLE are labial forms of Wrinkle with, I suppose, the exaggeratives CRUMPLE RUMPLE=agls. Hrympelle. Cf. RIPPLE, RUFFLE. CRUNKLE is in Jamieson. A CRANK is a simple form: the root is in CR.

  There is set to keepe, foule her befall
  A rimpled vecke ferre ronne in rage.
    Chaucer, Romaunt of the Rose, 4495.

---

   * Dere = damage.

That is so wrympled as a mase.
　　　　　　Lydgates Minor Poems, p. 203.
Rympled liche a nunnys veylle.
　　　　　　Id. p. 200.
Base quean and riveled* witch.
　　　　　　Drayton Polyolbion, III.

And for the house is crencled to and fro
And hath so queint waies for to go,
For it is shapen as the mase is wrought, etc.
　　　　　　Chaucer Legend of Good Women, 2008.

See how this river comes me cranking in
And cuts me from the best of all my land
A huge half moon, a monstrous cantel out.
　　　　　　I. Henry IV.

But Wye, (from her dear Lug whom nothing can restrain,
In many a pleasant shade her joy to entertain)
To Ross her course directs and right her name to shew
Oft windeth in her way as back she meant to go.
Maeander, who is said so intricate to be,
Hath not so many turns nor crankling nooks as she.
　　　　　　Drayton Polyolbion, VII.

894. YOUTH = lat. Iuventus. (properly Yungþ.)

895. The liquid L is omitted in the inlaut; as mœsog. Balgs = engl. Bag, art. 394. Grimm thinks FILM = $'T\mu\eta\nu$ (Gesch. D. S. 681). Salvus = Safe; Outrage from Ultra; Put from Pult; Push = fr. Pousser = Pulsare; span. Alma = fr. Ame; fr. Ecouter = span. Escuchar = Auscultare; fr. Maudit = span. Maldito = Maledictus. As is a compound word = Alswa = Also = Als = As; Sir F. Madden against Singer has copiously traced the word. Savage = Salvage = Silvestris. Season = germ. Salzen to salt. In pronouncing Should, Would, Calm, Embalm, Psalm, etc. we sink the L. Halsberg 'neck protection' = Hauberk = Habergeon = ital. Usbergo. The dutch often omits L, as Goud = Gold, Bout = Bolt, Oud = Old, Bout = Bold. In $\Sigma\alpha o\varsigma$, $\Sigma o o \varsigma$, $\Sigma\alpha\omega\zeta\epsilon\iota\nu$ compared with Salvus, etc. an L seems dropped.

897. SUCH from mœsog. Swa-leiks, whence also lat. Sic. Such = germ. Solch-er = old engl. Swilk, Swich, Slike.

898. R is omitted or inserted in the middle of a word as
　　　* Agls. Gerifled, Somn.

Massilia = Marseilles; Ebudæ = Hebrides; agls. Pusa = engl. Purse; Αιγαιον πελαγος = Archipelago; Umbrella = Umbella in Martialis and Iuvenalis; κυκλος for †κυρκλος circulus, for the Cir syllable is radical in both tongues; μαπεειν is the aorist of μαρπτειν (Hesiod Scut. 232, 252, whence εμμαπεως E. 836. ζ. 485). Hos = Hoarse, and the former is commoner in old english; as

> Ofte he criyede and ofte he ros
> So longe that he wox al hos.
> Kyng of Tars, 598.

Gnash = dutch Knarren, Knersen. Gawin Douglas writes Hale, Harl, " Lo the ilk tyme harland unto the king | Troiane hirdis with gret clamour did bring | Ane ȝoung man."

899. Δεχεσθαι besides its signification 'receive' in which it is related to Dextra, Dicare, Dicere, indicare, Δεξια, Δειξαι, the Deccan, etc. has a second meaning 'look' in which it is akin to Δερκεσθαι. The lexica give 'await' but the sense is not generally that of manere, ὑπομενειν, though the passage Ψ. 273 spoken of inanimate things Ἱππῆας τάδ᾽ ἄεθλα δεδεγμένα κεῖτ᾽ ἐν ἀγῶνι comes up fully to that. For the most part 'look' is the purport of the word.

> Φείσατο δὲ φθογγὴν τᾶ Πριάμοιο Πολίτῃ
> ὃς Τρώων σκοπὸς ἷζε, ποδωκείῃσι πεποιθώς,
> τύμβῳ ἐπ᾽ ἀκροτάτῳ Αἰσυήταο γέροντος
> δέγμενος ὁππότε ναῦφιν ἀφορμηθεῖεν Ἀχαιοί.
> Β. 794.

> ὡς δ᾽ ὅτε τίστε κυῶν συὸς ἀγρίου ἠὲ λέοντος
> ἅπτηται κατόπισθε, ποσὶν ταχέεσσι διώκων
> ἰσχία τε γλουτούς τε Fελισσόμενόν τε δοκεύει.
> Ο. 358.

> Ἄρκτον θ᾽, ἣν καὶ ἄμαξαν ἐπίκλησιν καλέουσιν
> ἥτ᾽ αὐτοῦ στρέφεται καί τ᾽ Ὠρίωνα δοκεύει.
> Σ. 487.

> αὐτὰρ ἐπ᾽ ἀκταῖς
> ἧστο ἀνὴρ ἁλιεὺς δεδοκημένος· εἶχε δὲ χερσὶν
> ἰχθύσιν ἀμφίβληστρον, ἀπορρίψοντι ἐοικώς.
> Hesiod, Scut. 203 (Λελοικως?).

In δοασσεται Ψ. 339 where the guttural has been rejected, the same sense is found. It is therefore to be concluded that Δεχεσθαι = Δερκεσθαι, Προσδοκαν = Προσδεχεσθαι = Προσδερκεσθαι. The antiquity of Δερκεσθαι is illustrated by the irish Dearc 'an eye,' Dearcaim 'I see,' welsh Edrych 'look,' sanskr. Drish 'see,' Drishti = Drik = Drishâ = Drishi 'the eye.' The irish has also another form without R, Diuicain 'the eyes.' Whether Look and Think belong to this family I dare not say.

900. CHAFF=agls. Ceaf. Cf. Καρφος?

901. ** = Παρδειν = lat. Pedere, cf. 430.

902. MARROW = agls. Mearh, Mearg = norse Mergr = germ. Mark = sansk. Majjâ. Hence apparently by sibilation SMEAR. See art. 674. It would be useless to compare Mucus 'snivel,' Macerare 'reduce to a pulp,' Απομυττεσθαι 'wipe away snivel,' sanskrit Manj, Enmungere, but that in the semitic languages these words meet, מֹחַ is 'marrow' and so arabic, מחה is 'wiped away,' and similarly in arabic. The process seems R = N and either is rejected. Μυελος has rejected the guttural, see art. 786, 828.

903. MATE (dead, half dead) = agls. Mcδig (defatigatus) = germ. Müde (wearied out) = dutch Mat (defessus). Cf. Checkmate 'king dead.' This appears to me = lat. Mortem, Mortuus, Morbus, Mori. The hebrew and arabic write death מות without R: and hence comes the spanish name for the bullkiller Matador. That the sanskrit Mri, the greek Βροτος and the latin have a common MR is clear to all; but it is also not unlikely that the semitic words may be reconcileable with the rest, nor that the latin may be possibly Vau = R.

> And then he bar me sone bi strenkith
> Out of my sadel my speres lenkith.
> For mote i lay down on the grownde
> So was i stonayd in that stounde*.
>   Ywaine and Gawin, 421.
>
> Aswogh he fell adoun
> An his hynder arsoun †,
>   As man that was mate.
>   Lybeaus Disconus, 1171.

---

* Stound = hour.
† Arson, the rise of the saddle. Thus Le Bone Florence, 771.

904. Meed=agls. Meord=lat. Mercedem (acc.)=Μισθος.

> Phelyp of hem took ransoun:
> For mede he sparyd his foon.
>
> Richard Coer de Lion, 3873.

905. Purse=agls. Pusa=lat. Pera=Πηρα, which in Od. v. 437 is 'wallet.'

906. Sup, Sip=lat. Sorbere=agls. Supan, Sipan. Cf. isl. Sopi, 'a sip,' Soppa, a Sop. From Persia the latin form comes back to us as Syrup and Sherbet. Sherbet شربة is 1. 'one drink or sip,' 2. 'sherbet or syrup.'

907. Sweep, Swab are in sense Σαιρειν, Verrere, art. 696, and in the mœsogothic †swairban, found in compounds, the two forms seem to meet: but †swairban is 'wipe,' not quite 'sweep:' further however Sweep, Wipe=agls. Wipian, Wisk as with the tail (Whisk is erroneous spelling), a Wisk or small broom for making trifle, the germ. Wischen 'to wipe'=swed. in comp. Viska, a Wisp of straw, Scopæ 'a besom,' are it seems varied forms of the same root.

LETTERS LOST IN AUSLAUT.

908. The omissions of letters in the auslaut or final syllables of words are even more numerous than losses at the beginning or in the middle. Horne Tookes neat remark that "Letters like soldiers are very apt to desert and drop off in a long march" is most applicable to those in the rear. The final M or N is often omitted in greek, thus lat. Septem=Επτα and Εβδομος retains the M. Similarly Decem becomes Δεκα. Εκει must be for †τεκειν as seen in Εκεινος 'that man there' and = the english Yon = mœsog. Yains = germ. Jener. The sanskrit proves Εγων to be older than Εγω. The final M or N of the accusative is omitted in some varieties of the greek declension, Feram=Θηρα, Gratiam=Χαριτα, Vocem=Fοπα, Noctem=Νυκτα, Patrem=Πατερα, Matrem=Ματερα, Pedem =Ποδα, Corvum=Κορακα, Vnguem=Ονυχα.

909. Few remains of the accusative in N are found in agls. There had not been much in the mœsogothic, where Hanan (cock)=Χηνα (goose), Swaihran=Socerum ='Εκυρον. But

Hine is the accusative of the saxon pronoun of the third person, and the acc. masc. of adjectives ends in -ne. (See on þone, 207.)

> To ham* that hine baptizeth.
> William of Shoreham, p. 68.

> Bot oither he sold hymselven sla.
> Ywaine and Gawain, 377.

> Tharefore have nou godne day.
> King Horn, 731.

910. Every one knows that N before Σ is omitted with a compensating vowel, as τυφθεις for †τυφθενς, χαριεις for †χαριτενς. Sometimes there is no compensation as in Αφρονα, Αφροσυνη, Ελεημονα, Ελεημοσυνη. In the moesogothic the accusative plural ends for the most part in ns, and this is sufficient evidence that Αγγελους was †αγγελονς, Pisces was †piscens = moesog. Fiskans. The sanskrit also testifies to the N for the accusative Ignes = Agnîn, Socios = Sakhîn, while the N does not appear in the nominative plural. As in other instances so here the vowel sometimes is found short as in the doric acc. in -ος.

> Καὶ τὺ δ' ἐπεὶ κ' ἐσορῆς τὰς παρθένος οἷα γελεῦντι.

and in the imparisyllabics Θηρας, Κορακας, etc. The termination of the dative plural Τυπτουσι for Τυπτοντσι, (Bopps protest notwithstanding,) the third person of the plural verb Τυπτουσι for Τυπτοντι, the doric ending, like the latin -unt, are other examples. The contracted comparatives also omit N, as Πλειους for Πλειονες, Πλειονας.

911. N final in greek represents S in the first person plural as Κοπτομεν = dor. Κοπτομες = latin -imus. It represents T in the third singular as Εκοπτεν, Εκοψεν as compared with εκοπτετο, εκοψατο and with the latin third singular in T, the moesogothic and agls. in þ. In the dative plural as Ναυσιν, the latin is Navibus and the sanskrit Naubhyas, so that N may be a substitute for S.

912. A valuable word for the comparison of latin forms with the greek is Εικοσι as compared with Viginti. Ginti

---

* Ham. them, em.

here is the termination of the tens -ginta, κοντα and Vi is Duo, so that the latin termination is the older. Viginti appears in æolic as Ϝεικατι by rejection of the N, and then, subsequently, by sibilation changes to Εικοσι. Now it is quite evident that it is on this model we are to make Τριακοσ-τος out of Τριακοντα, Τεσσαρακοσ-τος out of Τεσσαρακοντα, Πεντηκοστος out of Πεντηκοντα and so on: the additional syllable -τος being the ordinal adjectival τος as in Ἑκτος, Sextus, Six-th, Δεκατος, Ten-th, Thirti-eth, Forti-eth, Fifti-eth. It is also evident that the same changes shew the identity of Ducenti Διακοσιοι, Trecenti, Τριακοσιοι etc. If we look round we find on the same principle Quantus=Ὁσος and interrogatively=Ποσος, Tantus=Τοσος.

913. A converse change is detected in the latin adjectives in -osus, for as Χαριτα=Gratiam, so Χαριεντα for †χαριτεντα=Gratiosum; and if Ιχθυν=Piscem, Ιχθυοεντα=Piscosum.

914. If we stop at the rejection of the N we find Quando= Ὁτε; and Quum, When may be esteemed abbreviations of Quando. The mœsog. þanuh=agls. þanne=Then, together with Τηνικα prove the existence of a similar base †tan, and render it probable that Tum might be †tando = Τοτε. In supposing a base †tan=†tand, it is assumed that the sanskrit adverbs of time have rejected N. The elimination of this liquid throws a full light upon the nearly similar senses of Tanti, Tot, Quanti, Quot, Quotus, Quoties, Τοσοι, Ποσοι, Ὁσοι.

915. An important part of this investigation belongs to participles and participial nouns. It is well known that many substantives were of old participles, as Friend from mœsog. Friyon ' to love,' and Fiend from Fiyan ' to hate.' So in latin Parens, Adolescens, Serpens, Kalendæ, and the words ending in -men, -mentum, as Tegmen, ' a covering,' Alimentum, ' what is nourishing.' It has not been so closely observed that some adjectives in -os, -us are participial, having rejected the N. They are, it is true, declined apparently on a different set of inflexions, but there are reasons for supposing the latin and greek and sanskrit, and less clearly the gothic

declensions to have been all one. Postponing this part of the
subject, observe that since Maledicus, Magnificus make Ma-
ledicentissimus, Magnificentissimus it follows of probability
that Maledicus is Maledicens, with the vowel long or short,
Magnificus is †magnificens, Magnificans, the conjugation
being variable. Grandiloquentia shews that Grandiloquus is
†grandiloquens. Nescius is Nesciens. Cernuus is †cernuens
of a lost conjugation in U=cernens, ' striving to distinguish,'
and so stooping. Vivus=Vivens; Clypeus=Καλυπ—ends;
Colonus=Colends? Tolleno=Tollends? Torrens, Potens, Secundus, Rotundus = in the A conjugation Rotans, for †ro-
tands, rotants; Fluentum, Crepundia, Benevolus, Oviparus,
Omnivorus, Inscius, Coquus, Lupus, Incubus, Mergus, Vagus,
Veridicus, Reliquus, Pedissequus, Portentum, Continuus, Con-
spicuus (=Conspiciendus and passive), Contignus, Congruus,
Deciduus, Irriguus, Nocuus (Ovidius) Occiduus, Perspicuus,
Residuus, Vacuus, Sompnus, Bonus = Duonus (=duends,
giving) Assiduus (ab asse dando), Oriundus, Gladius, ' glitter-
ing,' Argentum are participial, Carduus ' thistle, teazle,' is
for carpens (otherwise carens Varro, Plautus) ' teazing' wool:
our word Carpet made of the refuse is the passive participle.
(Wedgewood.) Procax however shews that Procus is not
Precans. The adjectival termination in -εις, -εντος, as in
χαριεις, χαριεντα is not distinguishable from this participial
in ους=ων, ans, ens, but habit makes us speak of it as participial. Derivative forms are often found with this affix.
Thus from a root discoverable in the semitic languages the
hebrew imperative גל ' roll,' written in the dictionaries under
the triliteral form גלל ' he rolled,' comes a verb conjugated
with iota, κυλιειν; but this verb was pretty much out of use
in the common prose language of the attic age, and its place
was occupied by κυλινδειν formed upon a participle of the
earlier. Thence also the derivative substantive αλινδηθρα.
Ταλαντον is a participle of the root Tul, Tol common to
greek, latin, english, sanskrit, which in the last of these
tongues signifies ' weigh.' Γεροντα (acc.)=sanskr. Jarat for
jarant is from Jri ' to become or be old.' Ακοντα (acc.)
seems rather adjectival than participial. Λεοντα is meta-

morphic as is clear from Leonem, Λεωνιδας. Ἱμαντα is participial from Ἱμᾶν and not the converse. Ακανθα 'a thorn,' Ακανθος = Ἐχινὸς 'a hedgehog;' with insertion of R, Urchin, are like ακοντα from the root Ακ- belonging to the Edge, acute. Κεντειν 'to prick' is a derivative of Ακανθα, or Ακοντα, having lost its initial vowel. Κοσκινον 'sieve' is properly 'cleaning,' the agls. form of lat. Castus is Cusc = germ. Keusch = dutch Kuisch 'clean, neat' with Kuischen, 'mundare, reinigen' to keep clean.' See art. 599. Stand (203) seems participial. So Shred which is properly a substantive = passive participle of Shear.

> Oft takes a leg or wing, oft takes away the head,
> And oft from neck to tail the back in two doth shread.
> Drayton Polyolbion, XX.

Pecten, Pectinem has dropped the D = T: so has Plenus: Craven in old english Crauant = Precant, Rogant. Τεκτων, Τεκτονα is evidently from Tegere, Τεγος, Στεγος and means a roofer. Βροντη seems participial and may be formed on the root †mur, the reduplication of which gives Murmur, Μορμυρειν, and which lies at the foundation of Σμαραγειν. Sanguinem with nom. Sanguis, Sangueu, that is, †sanguens is probably related to Sacer, Ἁγιος; Currus is most likely Currens.

916. The following exhibit an additional element, not yet satisfactorily explained, interposed between the termination and the root; fœcundus, rubicundus, iracundus, incundus, verecundus, cogitabundus, deliberabundus, errabundus, gemebundus, gratulabundus, hæsitabundus, esuribundus, fremebundus, furibundus, lacrimabundus, populabundus, ludibundus, minitabundus, mirabundus (vanam speciem) lascivibundus, meditabundus (bellum), nitibundus (Gellius), pudibundus, vitabundus (castra), tentabundus, venerabundus, sitibundus. See 923, 935. In Temulentus, Truculentus, Turbulentus, Fraudulentus, Pulverulentus, Esculentus, Violentus, Opulentus, Sanguinolentus, Vinolentus, Corpulentus, we have probably two adjectival terminations, one in L as in Vigil, and other used by the participles.

917. Some of these derivatives reject N, as Πυρετος =

Burnand, Ερπετον = Serpentem = Creepand, Βιοτος = Vivendum = Quickand, Αροτος = Arandum = Earand, Εμετος = Vomendum, Αλετος = Molendum, Αμετος = Mowand, Ποτος, Τρυγητος, Προβατον, ὑλοβατης, κωκυτος, αλοητος, θανατος. Fervidus, Gravidus (from a neuter †gravere, gravescere answering to Gravare), Algidus, Splendidus, Aridus, Calidus, Callidus, Frigidus, Humidus, Lucidus, Madidus, Pallidus, Rubidus, Tepidus, Turgidus, Rapidus, Cupidus, Trepidus (from Tremere), Validus, Candidus. Insubidum = apparently, Insipientem. Solidus, Roscidus, Rabidus are adjectival, formed on substantives. Vvidus seems to come from the root Und, Amb, by rejecting the liquid, †ubidus. Some have T as Tacitus, Vegetus, Digitus (δεικ), Segetem, Æstus (αιθειν), and the numerous verbals of the fourth declension as Fluctus (a flowing) Gradus (a striding).

918. Before proceeding, however, the examination of participial forms will require an investigation of the original form of participles. The ending of the active participle is in latin NT, regentem, monentem, etc.: in greek NT, κοπτοντα, κοψαντα, etc. but in the perfect T without N, κεκοφοτα : the mœsogothic of the strong conjugation, present ND, anbindands 'binding,' of the past N, gabundans, 'bounden,' of the weak conjugation present ND, sokyands 'seeking,' of the past D or þ, sokyiþs, sokyids, seeked (=sought), in the norse of the strong conjugation present ND berandi 'bearing,' past N borinn, 'borne' (where the second N by assimilation stands for the nominatival R), of the weak conjugation present ND kallandi 'calling,' of the past þ, kallaþr, 'called,' in agls. of the strong conjugation present ND, berende 'bearing,' past N, boren 'borne,' of the weak conjugation lufiande 'loving,' lufod 'loved.' The old english had a literal agreement with the saxon and the change of the termination to NG is recent.

> This dredand Juno and ferthirmare alswa
> Remembrand.   Gawin Douglas, I. 42.
>
> I hold my toung for schame bitand my lip.
>   Id. Preface, 36 (p. 7).

The affinity of the teutonic terminations with the latin is as regards the present plain enough, and as to the past we observe that the þ, T, D forms are common to the active and passive: also in latin the deponents have the past participle in -tus, in either sense; the passives have it as a past. If the story about Iuno Moneta were possible, Moneta must have an active sense; observe its archaic formation, Moneo, Monevi, Monetus. Patratus is active in the old latin Pater Patratus. A further view is afforded by a due consideration from the greek active perfect of the form κεκοφοτα. Κεκοφοτα is formed by rejecting Ν in †κεκοφοντα. It has been said there is no trace of the Ν. I don't know but that scholars may be able to urge something against manuscript readings and traditionary spellings, but I do know that the analogy of all the participles of the active, at least, goes far to prove that †κεκοφοντα is the ancient form. Ν appears in some MSS. Eumenid. 706. εγρηγορον φρουρημα. Agam. 346. εγρηγορον το πημα. That the form was used ' a recentioribus ' is to be explained, maybe, as a reversion to the old analogy which must have once been universal. In Homer we have εγρηγοροων (Od. v. 6) and κεκληγοντες (Il. II. 430 etc.) which Bekker writes κεκληγωτες like τετριγωτες (B. 214). In Pindar Pyth. IV. κεχλαδοντας ήβα, where κεχλαδειν = κεχλαδεναι and is in my favour. Some evidence, then, has been adduced for the form †κεκοφ-οντα.

919. If we consider the two teutonic forms of which Broken and Called are representatives, we shall see that they may be derived from one early common termination in ND, in the first case by rejecting D as †brokend, Broken, in the second by rejecting Ν as †kallend, Kalled. Again Broken = Fractus = 'Ρηκτος and these may be reconciled by supposing an early †brokends. If there be anything startling in setting down the same forms as the original of the active and passive, reflect that in the earliest elements of instruction we learn Regendus to be passive, and Regendi to be active, Conatus to have an active sense, and Conata, as a plural substantive, to have a passive: Professus is active, but " arma professa" is passive: Ultus is active, but Inultus passive. And in Oriundus, Rotundus, Secundus etc. we have an

R

active sense. The greek verbal adjectives in -τος, as χριστος = greased, στρωτος = strewed, γνωτος = known, ζευκτος = iunctus = yoked, had then, I suppose, of old, the termination ND. Of these also many are capable of an active sense. (Buttmann, Gram. 102. 6.)

920. The greek verbals in -τεος seem also to be formed out of this same termination ND, so that Δοτεος = Dandus and is formed from it by rejecting N. Ασκητεος = Ex-ercendus, (giving us by the way, the information that -ercere = ασκειν): and so of the rest. The E is of no account, for some of the adjectives in -τος are found retaining the sense of what is to be done, ου βιωτον εστιν, non est vivendum, τοις ουκ εξιτον εστιν, quibus exeundum non est, Hesiod. Theog. 732, where the latin is verbally the equivalent of the greek, αρα γρυκτον εστιν υμιν Lysistr. 636, θαυμαστος 'admirandus.'

921. The sanskrit presents the same phenomena as those already explained. "The present participle," says Bopp truly, "forms the strong cases with the suffix ANT but in the weak cases rejects N, which is retained by the kindred european languages, as also, for the most part by Zend." For example the masculine participle of Tud ' to vex ' has

	Sing.	Dual	Plural
N	Tudan	Tudantau	Tudantas
G	Tudatas	Tudatos	Tudantâm
D	Tudatê	Tudadbhyam	Tudadbhyas
A	Tudantam	Tudantau	Tudatas
Ab.	Tudatas		Tudadbhyas.

Participial substantives are declined in sanskrit in the same manner.

922. The middle and passive participles of the greek, first, had the same final letters as the active and the same changes. Κεκομμενος, Κοπτομενος are short forms of †κεκομμεντος, †κοπτομεντος. This is evident enough from the latin participial substantives in -men, -mentum. Bopps idea that -mentum is a lengthening of -men, is disproved by the forms that result on the rejection of N, and can only be so far true as that N often draws a D after it. It arose from taking

the sanskrit as a touch stone to try other tongues and is no more true of -mend than of -end, -and, -ant. In the same manner as Loved for †lovend, Fractus for †brokend, γνωτος for †knowend, Tudatas for †tudantas, we get 'Ρηματος for †brokendes. Compare

Fragmentum = 'Ρηγμα for brokend
Fragmenti = ῥηγματος ,, brokendes
Fragmento = ῥηγματι
Fragmenta = ῥηγματα
Fragmentorum = ῥηγματων
Fragmentis = ῥηγμασιν.

An instructive example is Ομμα, 'eye,' which has of course the active or middle sense, 'the seer,' the root being Οπ so that ομμα = †οπμα = æolic οππα. In latin this root was Oc, and the corresponding participial substantive would be †ocmen, that is, Omen, but taken in the passive sense 'a thing seen;' the active or middle sense however is discoverable in Abominor, 'I turn my eyes from.' So little has the true theory of participial forms been understood, that these two words have never till now been truly explained.

923. We have now I hope arrived at a point where we may look back at words of the form moribundus. The B has ever proved a difficulty, but it turns out, I think, to represent an M, as in Hibernus for †himernus. Moribundus is Mori-μεντος = Mori-μενος, and it is a middle participle. Looking, however, at the list of words ending in -bundus, they are seen to be not all middle verbs. This point at art. 935.

924. In τεκτων, τεκτονα = deckend = decking = thatching, and in saugnen, a passing allusion was made to those active participials, which are written without the T or D. The sanskrit declension of the participle affords us a sufficient parallel in its nominative. Instances within the scope of the latin and greek languages are numerous enough : consider the word Tendon. This is an english latinism from Tendinem, Tendonem (Bailey's Auctarium), and the greek etymological equivalent which as a substantive occurs in the Medea, is Τενοντα, though it be not the medical term νευρον = purer latin nervum. Here evidently Tendinem = Tendentem. So

R 2

also Pectinem = Pectentem, and so also Κτενα = †πεκτονα = Pectinem = Pectentem, the word having lost its first syllable.

925. Tooth = agls. Top is the participle of Eat, and = Eatend, Etend: the mœsog. is Tanpus = lat. Dentem (acc.) = Οδοντα = æolic Εδοντα (Greg. Kor. 22) = lat. Edentem. The english and saxon reject the N. The german on the contrary refuses the T and writes Zahn, sibilating the initial. The sanskrit forms offer no impediment to this reasoning: the notion that the N in sanskr. Dantam (acc.) is a nasal augment, may be, I suppose, due to the Brahminical grammarians, but Bopp's view is correct, the N is rejected not inserted, and the word is a participle of the same verb agls. Etan = lat. Edere = homeric Εδειν = sanskr. Ad, of which the actual participle is Adat; nom. masc. Adan, acc. Adantem. Let this word be an instructive lesson to convince us that the changes of letters are as widely spread as is the human race. The Saxons and the Indians form this word upon the same principle of rejecting N, much as in μειζονα, μειζω. Then we see the Germans making it look like an old root by refusing to pronounce the T: here they are accompanied by the Hellenes, who had another derivative which equally wrote only the N: for Οδυνη = æolic Εδυνη = Εδοντ-η. The Tines* of harrows and of a deers antlers are in agls. Tindas which is evidently a less altered form than Tooth of the ancient form †tetend.

926. As in χαριτεντ, the root is not always a verb. In english Stiffnecked people, Lightfingered gentry, Horned cattle are both usual and correct. In latin Barbatus, Alatus, Fimbriatus, Cordatus, Nasutus, Cincinnatus, Auritus, Turritus, Verutus, Astutus, Cristatus, Dentatus.

927. Among those which retain N only I have gathered Κτενα, Οδυνη, Αγανος, Πτηνος, Σπερχνος, Στιλπνος, Στρυφνος, Τερπνος, Ακονη, Δαπανη (δαπτειν), Ὑπνος, Λιτνη (αιθειν), Φασγανον (σφαζειν), Ἱκανος (ἱκειν 'reach'), Ταλανα (polian), Αγχονη.

928. Deem by its old participle Deemend may produce

---

* Tines of antlers might come from Tein, twig, as if branch, but not so of harrows.

Dominus, for domus neither describes the relation truly nor explains the N. So Pema (πετεσθαι), Tignum (Tegere 'roof') Luna, (lucere). Sometimes with a long vowel Concubina, Fodina, Rapina, Ruina, Lucina (liggend).

929. The examples in which a passive sense attends these participials are rare: since for the most part N is rejected. We have Στυγνος, Σεμνος (σεβειν), Regnum.

930. A little further on I shall endeavour to shew that in terminations of verbs N and R are interchangeable and that frequently: hence will arise an inquiry whether some substantives in R are not changed forms of participles in N. Thus Pecora, Pecudes may be Pascentia, Pascentes, βοσκοντα. So of Genus, Frigus, Pondus, Nemus (νεμειν), Clamorem, Fragorem, Amorem, Favorem, Timorem, Furorem, Pallorem, Ruborem, Splendorem, Terrorem. But as letters change more and more the recognition of forms becomes more difficult. Αργυρος, Φοβερος, Ισχυρος, Αερα from the homeric αημι, theoretically †αεμι with infinitive αηναι theoretically †αεναι. Αιθερα from Αιθειν. I have already mentioned the parallel between the keltic Iach, 'sound, in good health,' and Ιασθαι; and have shewn that dentals can exchange for gutturals, so that Ιατ-ρος is this root with (I submit) a participial termination.

931. Rymorem seems to be the participle of the agls. Reomian cf. germ. Ruhm, norse Rôma 'noise' as of battle. That the word is pure teutonic is in itself probable: Reomian = dutch Roepen 'call' = agls. Hræman, Hreman = agls. Hrepan = mœsog. Hropyan, κραζειν, κραυγαζειν, βοαν. The norse has Hrôp, and the isl. at Hrôpa 'clamare.' If the letter change of W to R be recollected it may be mœsog. Wopyan. Provincial english retains Roop in the sense of hoarseness, cf. Croup, Crow: a crow is in agls. sometimes Hræm (Ælfric). Cf. therefore Corvus, Κραζειν: with sibilant Scream, Fremere and art. 359.

932. There may be entertained also a suspicion that as Αροτης = Earand, so Agricola = †agricolens, †agricolans, Advena = ad-kwimands = †advenens = advenicus. Boreas = †frigends = Freezing. Conviva = †convivens, Transfuga = †trans-

fugens = transfugiens. Paterfamilias has the termination of an old genitive for familiais. Some are unconnected with this theory; Primores for example. Marmor is a reduplication of the root seen in μαρμαιρειν, αμαρυγη.

933. Having endeavoured to show that all participles had their terminations in ND, NT, I now venture upon a train of somewhat speculative induction, with a view to explain some apparent anomalies of the derivative forms. First it seems to me probable that the infinitive mood had the participial termination, or nearly so. Doubtless as concerns the greek the earliest form of the infinitive, as κοπτειν, was †κοπτεναι, then †κοπτεν, as seen in the contracted χρυσουν conjugation, then κοπτειν. Κεκοφεναι, Τιθεναι, κοφθηναι, κοπηναι are still preserved: κοψειν will follow κοπτειν. To say the same of the passives requires a presumption, which will perhaps be not conceded by any but those who have observed how nearly alike are the inflexions of the passive and active. I assume then that κοπτεσθαι is for †κοπτενθαι, κεκοφθαι for †κεκοπ-ενθαι, †κεκοφνθαι; κεκοψεσθαι for †κεκοψενθαι; κοφθησεσθαι for †κοφθησενθαι, and so forth. The change of N to Σ before the dentals has been illustrated by examples art. 705.

934. In the lat. the infinitive Regere is equivalent to Regεναι = Regend- for N and R interchange much in inflexions, or auslaut. This supposition is necessary to the declension of the verbal substantive.

N. Regere
G. Regendi
D. Regendo
A. Regere or Regendum
Ab. Regendo.

The verbal substantive is in modern english a participle as "Rowing is a fine exercise," in modern german the infinitive mood. These are all one. The verbal substantives of the german in -ung, as Forschung, and the agls. as Halgung 'a hallowing,' are of the same origin, the termination in ND whether of participle or infinitive.

935. In the old greek writers we find an active infinitive in -εμεναι, and this, if we admit the approximation of infinitive and participle, will recommend us to entertain a supposition that there was an old active participle of the same form. It is thus I would explain the actives in bundus as Vitabundus, and the active derivatives in men, mentum, as Tegmen, Alimentum.

936. Verbals of either an active or passive sense, thus formed from active, passive or middle verbs are, Amentum, (from ἅπτειν 'tie,' or Habere?) Armamentum, Alimentum, Adiumentum, Argumentum, Atramentum (Atratus is found), Cæmentum (rough stone, from Cædere), Capillamentum (Capillor, Plinius), Crassamentum, (Crassare, Apuleius), Complementum, Condimentum, Documentum, Elementum (from Val?), Experimentum, Fermentum, Figmentum, Firmamentum, Fomentum (Fovere), Formamentum (Lucretius), Fragmentum, Frumentum (Βρωματα from the form Βρυκειν see Brook art. 423), Fulcimentum (Celsus, Vlpianus), Ferramentum (Ferratus is found), Honestamentum, Iumentum, (Iungere, Yoke), Imitamentum, Indumentum, Iuramentum, Invitamentum, Instrumentum, Lamentum (†clamentum?), Lutamentum, Levamentum, Libamentum, Legumentum (Gellius), Lenimentum, Lomentum (bean meal used for a wash, Lavere, Lavare), Momentum, Munimentum, Medicamentum, Molimentum, Monumentum, Mollimentum, Nocumentum, Nutrimentum, Ornamentum, Operimentum, Omentum (a contraction of the preceding?), Purgamentum, Salsamentum (cf. Salsarius; no verb is recorded), Sedimentum, Solamentum, Sacramentum, Tegumentum, Tormentum, Tomentum (from —?), Velamentum, Vimentum. Abdomen (from —?), Acumen, Albumen, Agmen, Bitumen (πιττοειν?), Cælamen, Cacumen (from —? Iovi Cacumo occurs in Orellius), Columen, Culmen (both from KAL in the sense of thatching: Columen according to the grammarians cited by Voss, is the 'ridge piece' and Columna the kingpost or its equivalent), Certamen, Curvamen, Crimen, Carmen (from Car to make, a latin sanskrit and teutonic root), Documen (Lucretius), Examen, Fragmen, Ferrumen, Flamen, (a priest said

to be Velatus, Pileatus or Filatus) Foramen, Fulcimen, Fulmen (fulgere), Farcimen, Frumen, (Feminis the genitive of Femur with e short is not perhaps a verbal at all), Flemina (burst veins in the ancles, from —?) Flumen, Formidamen (Apuleius), Germen (for †cermen? crescere?) Gramen (from γραειν = sansk. Gras, devorare; Kallimachos has και μονος αιζηων εγραε κηδεμονα) Glomeramen, Lumen, Lætamen, Lutamen, Libamen, Legumen, Levamen, Medicamen, Molimen, Munimen, Nomen, Nutrimen (Ovidius) Omen, (see 922), Putamen, Purgamen, Præfamen, Sagmen (vervain may be ἁγιωμα), Solamen, Stamen, Sumen (Sugere), Semen, Stramen, Sedimen, Tegumen, Tegmen, Tentamen, Velamen, Volumen. Salmonem can be nothing else than the leaper from Ἀλλεσθαι, Salire. Sermonem from †serere in asserere, disserere. Cf. Querimonia, Parsimonia (Parcere), Germanus? Some however in -mon are not formed on verbs as Ægrimonia, patrimonium, matrimonium.

937. Alumnus is from alere, Terminus seems to be from Deal, Theilen, Ignominia is rather an anomaly since we know of no instance in latin in which the prefix Un = In is applied to verbs, Femina (φυειν), but Auctumnus, Vertumnus, Neptunus, Lamina look doubtful.

938. In the greek, Θεραποντα is I think Servientem. Κτενα has been explained as Pectinem = Pectentem. Τερηδονα, Teredinem is TREE EATING. By insertion of N and Θ see art. 751, Τενθρηδονα, which has the same sense but is applied to a wood boring bee instead of a worm. Πεμφρηδονα seems only another form of the same word. Tree, δρυς occurs again in Θριπα (acc.) made up of the word Tree and ιπα, a worm. That Θριψ is a woodworm is established by Hesychios in Θριπποβρωτος, Θριπηδεστον in which last word is the passive participle Etend, with Σ for N (see art. 705) Ανθρηδονα, Ανθηδονα is 'flower eater'. (Eudoxos marks these statements with a query.) Was Σαρπηδων an eater of the fish of ill repute Σαλπη, Σαρπη, fr. Saupe, Stockfish? Not however all words in -ηδων can be explained from Edere. Those three stand alone. Ανθρηνη, Τενθρηνη may be contractions. Lobeck has something of the other words of the

termination -ηδων, comparing them with the latin -edo, -udo, as in dulcedo, multitudo. (Butt. Gr. II. 407.)

939. Πνευμονα, Γνωμονα, Δαιμονα, Στημονα, Κηδεμονα, Ἡγεμονα, Ποιμενα (related to Πωΰ, Ποα, Pascere?), Αϋτμενα (cf. Ἀσθμα), Ἀηδονα, Εγκυμονα, Ἰχνευμονα.

940. Ποιμνη, Βελεμνον, Μεδιμνον, Κρηδεμνον.

941. Lobeck (Paralip. p. 391) has a list of words in -μα found in Homer. Αγαλματα, Αθυρματα, Αἱματος (for ἁγματος and = sanguinem?) Ακηματος, Ἀλματα, Αργματα (απαρχαι), Ἁρματα, [currere?] Ασθματος (Αἰσθειν homeric) Δειματος, Δερματος, Δεσματα, Δηληματα, Δραγματα, Δωματα (δεμειν, a remarkable vocalization), Ειλυματα, Εἱματα (=œol. Ἑμματα Greg. Kor.), Ερισματος, Ἑρματα (from?), Ερυματα, Ευγματα, Εχματα, Ἱματα (ἱεναι), Θαυματα (τεθηπεναι), Ιθματα (ιεναι, mœsog. Iddyan), Καλλυμματα, Καταπαυματος, Καυματος, Κτηματα, Κυματα (κυπτειν rather than κυειν), Κυρματα, Κωματος (κεεσθαι, Quies), Λαιτμα (from?) Λυματα, Μειλιγματα, Μελεδηματα, Μνηματα, Νηματα, Νοηματα, Οιδματα, Οιματα (from?) Οιμηματα, Ονομα, Ομματα, Ὁρμηματα, Πεισματα (πειθειν? vix.) Πηματα (παθειν?), Πωματος (' cover,' from?) Πτυγματα, Σελματα (sedere), Σηματα (=δειγματα), Σπερματα, Στεμματα, Στομα (εσθειν), Σωμα (from?) Τερματα, Τφασματα, Φλεγματα, Χαρματα, Χειματα, Χευματα, Χρηματα. Lobeck whose temper was admirably suited to such toil, would have done well to have collected all words in -μα of which the radix is obscure. Πελμα is very like the agls. for 'a sole,' Welm, which retains life in our cobblers word Welt. Λημα from Λω for †Fλω = †βλω = βολω = Volo.

942. Some have a long vowel, as the participle in sanskrit. Χειμωνα (root sansk. Him 'frost, snow,' verb?), Πλαταμωνα, Κενθμωνα. Τελαμων is from THOLE, it was a strap to support the shield about the shoulders. Salmonem (acc.) the leaper.

943. Among the throng of new views I set before the reader it has almost escaped my thoughts to note down instances of the termination -mentum in the more ancient forms of our own language. At art. 163 it has been observed that the m of Name is participial and that the agls. verb re-

tains further the N so that Nemned as compared with Nominatus has all the consonants except that of the case ending. And this is true though the sanskrit have also dropped the N. Gleam with Leme, comparing welsh Llumon 'a beacon' must also have the participial M. The agls. has other examples as Flyma 'a fugitive,' Fleam 'a flight,' Beorma, BARM, Ferm-entum. GUMA GROOM may still be Hominem though the N be lost. In the norse plural the N remains; sing. Gumi G. D. Ac. Guma; plur. N. Gumnar, G. Gumna, D. Gumnum, Ac. Gumna. Now since man is distinguished from most brutes by the absence of a natural coat, that is, by being naked, it is probable that both Guma and Hominem are identical with γυμνος. Not only the neuters in -μα, but the feminines in -ma, -μη, and verbs as Clamare, are participial. The number of verbal derivatives in agls. with m is very large. Bosom from Bugan, Seam 'a load' from to Sack, Seam from to Sew, Stream from Strican, Halm (art. 292) Blossom (412), Bottom (419) Warm of which θερειν represents the verb, Foam from Spew, Spit, Spuere, Πτυειν, cf. Spuma, Slime and Clammy (1044) Breme, Dream are examples.

914. The declensions of the latin and greek however various appear to be from a single original and common model. One of the most striking varieties is in the datives plural in -ibus and in -οις = -is. This however is certain that Τοι = Tibi, Οἱ = †σφοι = †suibi = Sibi, Poematis = Poematibus, etc., Quis = Quibus = Οἱς. Filiabus = Filiis, etc., Domibus = Δομοις, Funibus = Σχοινοις, Humilibus = Χθαμαλοις, Mollibus = Μαλακοις. There are also some datives in οις of the imparisyllabic declensions, known to us from the grammarians and inscriptions, γεροντοις, μειονοις, φυλακοις, παθηματοις, αγωνοις, εντυγχανοντοις, Λαμεοις, πωλεοντοις, οντοις, and the bœotian datives in -υς. In the sanskrit the termination is regularly -bhyas, shewing the antiquity of the latin -ibus; thus if Sakhi, 'a friend,' be assumed to be Socius, Sociis is Sakhibhyas: if Οστεον be assumed to be Asthi, 'a bone,' Οστεοις is Asthibhyas = Ossibus.

915. A comparison of the whole system of inflexions will render this conclusion stronger.

	Sanskr.	Lat.	Gr. (old).
N.	Naus	Navis	Νηυς
G.	Nâvas	Navis	Νηϝος
D.	Nâvê	Navi	Νηϝι
A.	Nâvam	Navem or -im	Νηϝα
Ab.	Nâvas ⎫	Nave or -i	—
Instr.	Nâvâ, Nâvayâ ⎭		

N.	Nâvas	Naves	Νηϝες
G.	Nâvâm	Navium	Νηϝων
D.	Naubhyas	Navibus	Νηϝεσσιν
A.	Nâvas	Naves	Νηϝας
Ab.	Naubhyas	Navibus	—

946. From this comparison one cannot escape the conclusion that Ναυσιν = Navibus as regards termination as well as radix: that Brevibus = Βραχεσιν, Lapidibus = Λιθοις, Pellicibus = Παλλακισιν, Pinguibus = Παχεσιν, Umbonibus = Αμβωνεσιν, Clavibus = Κληϊσιν, Nubibus = Νεφεσιν, Tribus = Τρισιν, Pulmonibus = Πλευμονεσιν, Unguibus = Ονυξιν, Leporibus = Λαγωεσιν, Draconibus = Δρακοντεσιν, Spicis = Σταχυεσσιν, Suibus = Ύεσιν, Canibus = Κυνεσσιν, Noctibus = Νυκτεσιν, Pedibus = Ποδεσσιν, Bobus, Bubus, †bovibus = Βουσιν = sansk. Gobhyas. Παιδεσσιν = Pueris, Χιτωνεσιν = Tunicis, Δᾳδεσιν = Taedis, Βραδεσιν = Tardis, Δελφινεσιν = Delphinis, Σφηκεσιν = Vespis, Χαριτεσσιν = Gratiis. Hilaris may be compared in all genders and cases with Ἱλαρος.

915*. This comparison, broad and reiterative as it is, comes short of the whole accessible truth. For an older form than -οις existed in -οισιν, and it is not the traditional Φυλακοις but an earlier †φυλακοισιν which is to be compared with Φυλακεσσιν. It would be doubtless a bold assumption to speculate on any thing older than the sanskrit -bhyas, but how can we avoid thinking that it might have been preceded by -bhyusin: so that †lapidibusin may = Λιθοισιν?

916*. No case offers so great difficulties as the dative. That the genitive singular has for its termination in general S preceded by a vowel is evident as in Navis, Νηϝος. That this inflexion is in some way reconcileable with those of the parisyllabic declensions is probable from the comparison of the parisyllabic and imparisyllabic datives plural and from what we shall see of the genitives plural. The sanskrit does not present a full solution but some hints and anomalies. Bopp refuses to compare the two first declensions of the latin with the sanskrit in the genitive case singular, and says " that in latin the two first declensions together with the fifth have lost their old termination and have replaced it by that of the old locative." With these he joins mei, tui. Bopps reasoning is often faulty out of too much affection for the sanskrit. Mei, Tui appear in the older greek as Εμειο, Σειο, and there exist traces of a form still further back, †εμειος, τειος : thus

Εὗδον δ', αἴκε μόνον τὸ καλὸν στόμα τεῦς ἐφίλασα.
Theokr. II. 126.

Ait illam miseram cruciari et lacrimantem se adflictare Quia tis egeat, Quia te careat, Plaut. Mil. Gl. IV. ii. 42. Olli enim et Quianam et Mis et Pone pellucent et adspergunt illam, quae etiam in picturis est gratissima, vetustatis inimitabilem arti auctoritatem. Quintil. VIII. 3, where is some doubt about the reading. Apollonios Dysc. p. 95 gives Εμεος as doric, Εμευς dor. from Epicharmos with other forms from Rhinthon. Τεους as in Ἡρακλῆς τεους καρρων ην from Sophron. Περι τεους Ἑρμας ποτ' Ἀρηα πυκτευει from Korinna. Εκπεφηναντι τεος αἱ δυσθαλιαι from Sophron. Τευς from Epicharmos εν Κωμασταις η Ἀφαιστῳ

ουδεποτ' ιοι γινετ εγων τεος αξιω

where is some error : και ποκ εγων παρα τευς τι μαθων. He says it is also Bœotian plainly Τευς γαρ ὁ κλαρος, which they have set down to Korinna. Priscianus also XIII. p. 955 is cited to the same effect. Were we concerned with the latin and greek only it would be appropriate to conceive the genitive full inflexion to be -yus, -ιος, ·ius ; we should thus obtain Qui, Quoius; Ille, Illius ; Is, Eius ; Ipse, Ipsius ; Vnus, Vnius ; Alius, Ali-ius ; Hic, Huius. Priscianus (p. 679) quotes some genitives of the first declension in -as, from Livius (Andronicus), in Odyssea, " Escas habemus mentionem :" " Nam diva monetas (for monetae) filiam docuit :" " filius Latonas :" from

Nævius " filii Terras;" "Et venit in mentem hominum fortunas" for fortunæ. There is also Paterfamilias, Materfamilias. These combined with Pictai, Aulai, give us a termination in -aïs. If we suppose the final S to be laid aside we understand at once the ancient forms Εμειο, Σειο, Ἐο and the long genitives in -οιο, as πολεμοιο, πολοφλοισβοιο. Appended to a consonant -yus would become easily -is, -ος, as †nomen-yus, Nominis; ανερ--yus, Ανερος. This is clear against Bopp that Cuicuimodi is cuiuscuiusmodi (Priscianus p. 959). It is fairly to be presumed that as Θηρα is not far from Feram, so Θηρος is not far from Feræ; as Αλλος, Αλλον are Alius, Alium so Αλλου is Alius (ali-ius) and Λυκοιο is Lupi.

917. It is so strange for any one to maintain Λυκοιο to be Λυκου and not Lupi that I quote Bopps words from the translation. " I cannot however believe that the i of the second declension is an abbreviation of οιο, of which the ι [say οι] alone has been retained; for it is clear that lupi and lupæ from lupai rest on the same principle; and if lupi proceeds from λυκοιο whence can lupai be derived as the corresponding greek feminines nowhere exhibit an αιο or ηιο?" This statement has been already answered from the ancient latin; that the form is not known in the greek is remarkable perhaps but cannot negative the proof from another source. But let us ask out of the sanskrit; Is it any way surprising that both Μουσης and Musaï should be deduced from -âyâs the genitive termination of the first declension feminine?

918. The sanskrit in most of its declensions exhibits nothing inconsistent with what I have said above: but in the masculines terminated in a short, the genitive ends in -sya, so that as Bopp developes it, Tasya = †τοσιο = τοιο. I apprehend that this termination in -sya, claims to be separately examined. This sanskrit declension must be identified with Κυβερνατας = Gubernator; gen. Κυβερνατας = Gubernatoris; Αροτας = = Arator; gen. Αροταο = Aratoris: and whatever may be the result as regards the S of the sanskrit genitive = R of the latin, this is plain that in Shiva, and Δεσποτα, and Agricola, the short a represents an older âs with a long. As regards

Agricola I hold that it renders more probable my deduction of the word from a participial formation †agricolands.

949. In old english the saxon genitive in s is often to be observed: and it remains in the modern form. "A Devonshire Dialogue" presents us with "can tern her hand to any kindest thing." "Why I'd ne'er the heart to hurt thee nor any kindest thing in all my born days." Here the T is an error of the writer or speaker, the word is Kinnes=agls. Cynnes, and any kinnes thing is 'a thing of any kind.'

> Hose and shose and alkins gear.
> *Ywaine and Gawain*, 3108.

> But of o thing, sir knyght, i warne thee
> That thou make no bost of me
> For no kennes mede.
> *Sir Launfal*, 361.

> With nones kunnes speche.
> *Kyng Horn*, 964.

950. The dative singular as in Tibi, Sibi (for Tuibi, Suibi, twibi, swibi) must have ended in -ibi, having close analogy to the plural in -ibus, -bhyas, and the sanskr. dual -bhyam = οιν, αιν. Then †lupibi = ΛΥΚΟΙ = Λυκῳ = Lupo.

951. In the genitive plural, such forms as Μουσων are contractions of Musarum, and the intermediate Μουσαων is extant. Famarum = φαμαων = φαμῶν = φαμᾶν. Though we have no uncontracted form between Equorum and Ἱππων, and though the accentuation denies the contraction yet it is to be believed. It accounts for such forms as Vectigaliorum. The consonant between the vowels, in latin R is in sanskrit N. It is also N in the mœsogothic weak declension of adjectives. Blind, makes gen. pl. Blindane, Blindono, Blindane, and in some substantives, as Hana (=germ. Hahn = Hen but masc.) makes gen. pl. Hanane. Tuggo (=tongue), gen. pl. Tuggono. It is also N in agls. in some declensions of substantives as in the well-known word Witena-gemot 'meeting of the wits,' and in the definite declension of adjectives as þara godena 'of the good.' But S appears in pronouns of the third person in sanskrit, and the demonstratives in mœsogothic have Z, in agls. R. Some remains of this R are found

in old english, as in Allerbest, Alderbest, Altherbest 'best of all.'

> And that was with thair bother will.
> Ywaine and Gawain, 3556 so 3759.

where the R in Thair, and in Bother belongs to the genitive plural.

> And siththe wosch here* alre fet here mande† to do.
> St. Brandan, p 17.

> Ne mai no man clene telle of here ‡ beire § durne ‖ wo.
> Thomas Beket, 128.

Of the genitives plural in N examples are less frequent in old english.

> To wrostle with that foule thyng
> That wes the geaumdene kyng.
> Chronicles of England, 53 Ritson (King of the giants).

Consider whether the agls. Twegra 'of two,' be the real source of the comparative termination -ter, = -τερος.

952. That the accusative plural in sanskrit and greek ends sometimes in a short syllable and so contrasts with Lupos, Naves has been already explained. Bopp goes a different way to work and thinks ποδας to be †ποδνς comparing †τετραφνται, τετραφαται.

953. Not all the phænomena of the cases have been made clear. In the genitive plural we expect to see applied the rule which makes the nominative (Wilsons Sansk. Gr. 457), dative, accusative plural out of their singulars by adding S : this we do not see. Yet in general it is made good that the greek and latin declensions are in substance one.

954. In verbs, allowing a not unreasonable freedom to the deductions from analogy we shall find that the inflexions

S.	-μι	-σι	-τι
D.	—	-τον	-τον and -την
P.	-μες	-τες	-ντι

will explain the greater part of the paradigma. Κοπτω for

---

* Here alre = of em all.

† Mande = the work of Maunday Thursday, the commandment of the Lord, to wash feet.

‡ Here, of them. § Beire, of both. ‖ Durne, secret.

†κοπτωμι for †κοπτομι; εκοπτον for †εκοπτομ, †εκοπτομι, which cannot be admitted by those who appeal to the sanskrit as of the last resort, for they must take εκοπτον, εκοπτες, εκοπτετ to be original, even while they would obtain a plural with a termination -âm, -at, -an, shortened from εκοπτομες, εκοπτετε, lat-tis. Κοψω in like manner for †κοπ·εσομι; εκοψα for †εκοπεσαμι; κεκοφα for κεκοφαμι; κοπτοιμι, κοψαιμι, κοποιμι in their ancient form. The verbs in -μι as they are called retain the short vowel in the passive-middle, τιθεμαι; whence †τιθεμι as more ancient than τιθημι receives support. The barytones are in the optative verbs in -μι still, while τιθειην for †τιθειημι forgets that it is a verb in -μι.

955. The passive for the most part so differs from the active as to have a heavier final syllable -μαι for -μι. So

κοπτομαι, κοπτεσαι, κοπτεται
κοπτομεσθα, κοπτετεσθε?, κοπτονται.

The dual seems to be †κοπτετενθον, †κοπτετεσθον, κοπτεσθον, or if Σ be the original final letter, †κοπτετες first in the active. In the perfect κεκοφθε has rejected Σ from the group of three concurrent consonants, †κεκοπ-ετεσθε, †κεκοπ-σθε, †κεκοφσθε, κεκοφθε. Εκοπτομην is plainly the correlative of †εκοπτομι, which, as a theoretical form, is sustained by the parallelism. So Κοπτοιμην to Κοπτοιμι, Κοπτωμαι to Κοπτωμι, homeric. Κοπτεσθαι if for †κοπτενθαι hardly differs from the active.

956. The latin verb shows a willingness to accept such an account of its parentage : thus in the moods †regomi, †regebi, †regami, †regenai, †regents, becomes Rego, Rege, Regam, Regere, Regens. The latin passive drops the terminations and writes R for M or N, as Regor for †regomai, Regar for †regamai, Regier for †regentai, Amari for †ama-entai, †amanai; Moneri for †mone-entai, †monenai, Audiri for †audientai, †audinai.

957. -LY the termination of numerous words in english comes from the agls. -lic, and was originally LIKE, so that Lovely = agls. Leoflic = germ. Lieblich = mœsog. Liubaleiks. This is to be compared with the latin -lis, in regalis, legalis, coningalis, hiemalis, carnalis, auguralis, civilis, hostilis, invenilis, virilis, puerilis, senilis, anilis, servilis, similis, humilis,

vitalis, bestialis, amphoralis, fatalis, infernalis, liberalis, esurialis, fidelis (from Bopp). Agilis, fragilis, docilis and the like cannot be classed here. The english also presents some exceptions. Thus Only=agls. Æulipig, the former element of which is the numeral One, and the latter the verb Leave in a form more close to λειπειν.

958. There is some shew as if the ending of the plural verb in the indicative -þ, we habbeþ, ye habbeþ, they habbeþ found frequently in old english and an established part of agls. grammar were drawn from the proper form of the third plural in -οντι, -unt, κοπτοντι, regunt by rejection of the N. The past tense of the indicative and the whole subjunctive in agls. had the plural ending in -N, we habdon (Heliand) hæfdon (usually) ge habdon, hæfdon, hig habdon, hæfdon. This point is not clear enough for any more to be said about it. The old english turning as we all know Hath into Has, changed also the plural at the same time, so that such forms as "we haves, ye haves, they haves" are not at all uncommon; they are quite as truly grammatical as "he has."

> Calves younger than other
> Learns one of another.*
> Tusser, p. 81.

959. Has=lat. Habet. The agls. was in the Heliand Habad, Habed, Habit, usually Hæfð, whence Haveth, Havth, Hath, Has. The same with other verbs in the third singular indicative present.

960. These results are so scanty that it may be as well to set out a comparison of the more perfect forms of the mœsogothic, with the latin.

Kwima = Venio	Kwimam = Venimus
Kwimis = Venis	Kwimiþ = Venitis
Kwimiþ = Venit	Kwimand = Veniunt

The comparison would be more fairly made if Venio were of the simple conjugation †veno, †venis, venit, †venimus, †venitis,

* Where Mavor who reprinted the work says "this anomaly in syntax is not uncommon in Tusser." He would find the same "anomaly" in all our old writers of that age.

s

†venunt. The terminations of the aorist are not so distinct in the mœsogothic.

Kwam = Veni	Kwemum = Venimus
Kwamt = Venisti	Kwemuþ = Venistis
Kwam = Venit	Kwemun = Venerunt

961. The termination of the second person plural imperative as in Habete, Regite, is often retained in old english, and the process of changing the T to S is repeated here also. The mœsog. gives -ciþ, -iþ or -yiþ, the agls. -aþ.

> He said, Sirs, if ye be agast
> Takes the beste and bindes him fast.
> *Ywain and Gawayne*, 3177.

> Come ȝe my fader blissed and haves the reume of hevenne.
> *Myrour of lewed men*, 1080.

962. In art. 914 etc. I have shewn that the pronominal derivatives, as Quotus, Quot, Quoties, Tot, Toties, Ποσος, Ποτε, Ὁτε, are deduced from a base in †quand or †quond, which is at the same time the origin of When, Quanti, Tanti, Tunc, Πηνικα, Ἡνικα, Τηνικα. I shall now shew that this base is the neuter of the demonstrative and interrogative pronouns, and Quid was once †quand, What was once †whant. The agls. pronoun indefinite neuter had two forms Hwæt, and Hwon, Hwan. It is true that Rasks grammar does not give us any information about this double form, but turn to the examples in Lye. He begins with Bed. II. xvi. Cwæþ þat he wære lang on bodige and hwon forþheald, which is thus in the latin Referre solitus quod esset vir longæ staturæ, paululum incurvus. Here, as a lexicographer, Lye did his devoir, paululum is the equivalent and the proper version of Hwon. But to translate by the equivalent in form it would be necessary to employ Quid indefinite. His next example is þanon hwon agan Marc. i. 19. Inde paullulum præteritus [l. prætergressus]. Here the same observation applies. Us hwon restan. vi. 31. Nos paulisper reclinare. Lye uses a different word, but the saxon is still Quid. Gif hi on hwon agyltan Bed. III. v. Si illi quantulumcumque deliquerint. To arrive at this translation he treats On hwon as a phrase.

On is a preposition and should be followed by a case, it takes the accusative or dative, and Hwon is governed by it. So For hwon, and in the construction with the genitive as Hwon gecarnunge 'quid meriti.' Bed. IV. xxix=608. 1. And so forth. It is certainly not to be denied that any dative in -m could according to custom be also written with -n, and that both Hwam and þam were occasionally written Hwon, þon. So that On hwon may be On hwam in the dative. It may however be added that Hwonlic, 'little,' and Hwæde 'little,' contain a common element, the root †hwant : the termination -lic can, it is true, be affixed to a dative as in dæghwamlic, or to a genitive as þæslic, but it is usually added to the base without case ending. Mindful that I am discussing the modern english language, I shall make a quotation or two, shewing the existence of the form as a recognizable substantive in our old writers : the glossaries also will give it.

> Out at his window set he
> Brede and water for the wode* man
> And tharto ful sone he ran
> Swilk† as he had, swilk he him gaf
> Barly brede with al the chaf
> Tharof ete he ful gude wane.
> Ywaine and Gawain, 1680 and so 1666.

> Mid his forthere fet he brouȝte a fur-ire and a ston,
> Forto smyte fur therwith, and of fisch god won.
> St. Brandon, p. 30.

> He askyd when maner jugement ‖
> That sche worthy were.
> Octavian, 215.

963. The same form occurs in the same way in the mœsog. and is called in the glossaries an adverb; it is sometimes adverbially used, like Somewhat, but the glossarists commit a grave error in confounding it with When. One passage is not to be got over. Hwan lagg mel ist, ποσος χρονος εστιν : the substantive Mel is neuter, and the construction is What long time is it? Hwan is here plainly a neuter pronoun adjective, as in the citation from Octavian.

---

* Wode, mad.   † Swilk, such.   ‖ What sort of sentence.

964. The sanskrit neuter answering to Quid is Kim and the form Kat is considered obsolete; Kim in certain positions is Kin: thus answering to mœsogothic Hwan.

965. We have then the latin forms continually rising before us as †quand, †quant, the saxon, mœsogothic and sanskrit require †quad or †quan, and the conclusion is, it seems to me, inevitable, that Quod, What, Τι are instead of †quant, †hwant, τινδ. I propose to identify these forms by and by with the numeral Ἑκα 'one.' Let me say in confirmation that we now see explained the N, in the declension of Τις, for Τινες = †τινδες. We may think also the two forms of the neuter τοσουτον, τοσουτο, for every one knows that Ἀλλο = Aliud, To = That, are to be explained by the aversion of the Achivi to a final dental, so that τοσουτο was †τοσουτοδ, and with τοσουτον makes †τοσουτονδ.

968. In making †quant the pronominal base and neuter, I am aware that I must be taken to suppose the masculine under whatever form it appears, say †τος, τις, or quis to stand for †quant-s, and the genitive του, (be it) or cuius, to represent †quant-yus. To this difficulty I can only reply by the suggestion that the loss of letters especially in terminations has rendered such a supposition rational, and that τινος retains one of the letters. In arguing that Magnificus = †magnificens and Agricola = †agricolens, I was arguing that Magnifici = †magnificentis, and Agricolæ = †agricolentis: and I think it possible.

969. According to my notions, for which reasons will tacitly present themselves hereafter in treating of the numeral One, this form †quant was the earlier, and the demonstrative †tant was an alteration of it. It is clear enough from the discussion above, that the forms †quan †than as neuters had been pretty well obsolete in the gothic tongues for a thousand years before the age of our saxon literature, and remained, as words remain now, only in a few phrases.

SEMITIC.

970. Religious sentiments led the older wordfinders to hold that the original of languages is the hebrew. Like other widely received opinions this teaching had a portion of truth in it; but how much no man ought to say, for we know very little of the affinities of the arabic stock of languages with those of Europe. A thousand years passed between the earliest and the latest writings of the old testament, and in that time foreign words were introduced. I shall be able to shew, that some words of the mosaic writings had changed their original form, and on the whole I am convinced that the hebrew even of the Pentateuch had undergone much of the same attrition and alteration which is detected in other tongues. We know historically that much was borrowed by Europe from Palestine. Phœnician commerce carried to the shores of the Mediterranean many useful manufactures, many asiatic productions, which were unknown and nameless to their distant purchasers. And not so only; the same skill and industry which wove rich robes for foreign princes or worked in brass and silver vessels of unrivalled beauty, had nursed arts of high importance to the life and well-being of man. While the people of the north got mad on mead, or drunk on beer, the more luxurious Wine appears among the southern languages; and while wandering hordes with their families in wagons searched the skythian wilds for pasturage, the art of sowing corn is traceable to the south. Among the tongues called semitic the hebrew is the best guide in tracking words and in watching the advance of the arts. It is of unsurpassed antiquity in its records and is free from all trace of attic and roman terms. I have never taken much interest in the disputes about κιθαρις, σαμβυκη, συμφωνια, ψαλτηριον supposed to be discoverable in the book of Daniel, (Bunsen, III. 217) nor do I think that much can be made of that argument. It is not however, in looking at the hebrew roots, to be understood that words placed by the side of hebrew words, represent ideas or things coming from Judah to Italy or Hellas, but more from some one of the kindred

nations and especially rather from Sidon and Tyre than from Jerusalem. The hebrew vocabulary is taken, as far as my investigations are concerned, for that of the semitic class most free from recent admixture.

971. We find then that our alphabets in the names of the letters, are of hebraic or phœnician origin; and the forms of the characters can in many cases be certainly recognized; the Θ, which was before missing, is now seen on the sepulcral stone of Eshmunetzer. Balsam, Ape, Nard, Nitre, Sapphire, αρραβων, παραδεισος (after the captivity), Χιτων = Tunica, Ξιφος, Μνα = Mina, Σκορπιος (without initial sibilant), Κυμινον, Λιβανωτος, Καδος = Cask, Casia, Canna, Cinnamon, Sack, Tympanum or Timbrel, Manna, Myrrh, Carbasus, Jasper, Aloes, Turtur, 'Αρπη (the weapon of Bellerophon), Vermillion, Fucus, Cypress are words borrowed, imported and carried into Europe out of some part of Asia and the east. For sowing the latin and greek are both very near to זרע which occurs in the earliest hebrew books freely used in its literal and in metaphorical senses: the Ain of this word stands for the G in Spargere: on Serere alone not much could be grounded, see art. 758. Cf. the cognates זָרְמָה‎, זרק‎, זרה‎. For Ϝοινος rather Ϝινος, WINE, we have יין‎ where the initial Yod is substituted for Vau according to a well-known law of hebrew utterance. On Cask it may be remarked that Rebeccas pitcher at the well is Cad; and of כַּרְמִיל‎, a borrowed word it is true, that it also gives Carmine and Crimson. Navis also appears in hebrew with prefixed aleph, and yod for vau, אֳנִיָּה‎, the usual word for ships of Tarshish. This fact seems to have escaped the lexicographers. Add also that Haruga the etruscan word for victim is the passive feminine participle of Harag, 'he killed;' it is the former element in Haruspex. Αραχνη 'a spider' illustrates the proposition, that we are dealing with the semitic languages in the whole and not specially with the hebrew: it is undoubtedly a derivative, a participial derivative of Arag 'wove,' and it means the 'webster,' the female weaver; yet to express spider the he-

brew uses עָבְרִיּשׁ which is a contraction of the arabic quadrisyllabic equivalent, and of origin unknown.

972. The importation of the foreign names of foreign products and foreign arts or legends, does not, however, tend in any the smallest degree, to justify us in holding other portions of the greek latin or english languages to be identical with some part of the semitic vocabulary. This question must be discussed on separate grounds, and as a comparison with the hebrew or its neighbours is of value to my present purpose, I propose to say a few words on the subject. To give a list out of a lexicon comparing european words with semitic would not be satisfactory. The parallels already drawn by good oriental scholars are occasionally strained and forced beyond acceptance. Thus the usual guide of students at present, Gesenius, declares רפא to be the representative of ῥάπτειν: but ῥάπτειν means 'sew' which רפא never does, but only 'cured, sanavit.' שׂרף means 'combussit' but the lexicographer compares it with Sorbere, where the arabic goes for nothing, being taken from the persian: סלף 'pervertit, evertit' he declared to be Slip.

973. Another fault exists in our hebrew books of instruction: though they greedily compare roots or what are supposed to be roots, they exclude the general principles of wordshaping, which as long as man has a mouth will be found prevailing all the world over. Thus the hebrews have two words for the moon לְבָנָה which means white, the pretended root for which לבן has no existence in the hebrew language, and is not the true root at all: and יָרֵחַ which when it signifies moon appears in large letters as a primitive, or is a derivative from an arabic word meaning 'maduit:' whereas in truth it is but another form of יָרָק with kôf for kheth 'greenness,' which with its derivative יְרָקוֹן 'paleness' shews that in hebrew the two names of the moon signify severally 'white' and paleness. So גְמֹרָה Gomorrha shall be derived from something wholly alien rather than from הֵמָר, bitumen. It is an admitted principle that

kôf caf and kheth will interchange but the system of inventing trilitteral roots, where no real roots can be found is an impediment to an enlightened study of the language. Thus again it is laid down as regards quadrilitterals, that 'Lamed in fine additur,' yet the trilitteral method throws such a mist before professors eyes that no connexion is recognized between עָרְלָה (orlah) 'prepuce' and עוֹר 'skin.' Then sometimes the learned, whose real scholarship none can dispute, open a little wicket for a certain bilitteral theory, which appears very charming to some minds. It is not reasonable to suppose nor is it according to experience true, that the hebrew can be reduced to bilitteral roots any more than any other tongue, and to attempt to carry out the idea within the limits of the language itself is to build sand pies upon the shore. Dissatisfied with the ordinary systems Professor Jarrett has printed a lexicon in which all the Heemanti initials and finals are thrown out of the roots. The heemanti letters are those which are used in the construction of the grammatical forms; and what a monstrous assumption it is to presume that none of these letters formed part of a root. It may be seen by the criticism now to follow on the first numeral, that the probabilities are wholly in favour of the supposition that aleph was the first letter of the root in that case.

974. Having given a hint to the same effect I will say distinctly that as L is an afformative letter, mostly adjectival, in greek as in $\mu\epsilon\gamma\alpha\lambda\omicron\iota$, from our May, $\acute{o}\mu\alpha\lambda\omicron\varsigma$ from One, in latin as Vigil from Wake, in english as Girdle from Gird, so it is also in hebrew as in גָמָל 'camel' which is so called from its Hump as if thumple, and the arabic verb 'carry' is a denominative. בַּרְמִיל has just been mentioned, it is a derivative of Krim which produces Worm, and which is the same word as Creep, and the afformative is Lamed.

975. From curiosity and from a desire to test my own proficiency within a defined room and on an appointed task, convinced also that I should best win the confidence of the reader by treating of well-known words and a few of them I set myself to examine the numerals and some proper names

of common occurrence. That I am surprised at the results would be a small thing to say; though they are imperfect and partial, I trust they will win the assent of all scholars in Europe : and if so, they cannot fail to lead on to an application of the ordinary principles of philology in the case of the hebrew, and to bring it more or less within the reach of illustration from other tongues.

976. ONE. The hebrew for one אֶחָד Ekhâd, all linguists know is found in the sanskrit: in that language it is declinable as Ekas, Ekâ, Ekan in three genders. It appears in the greek words Ἑκάτερος 'one of two,' and Ἕκαστος 'one of more than two.' So much has been already established. It would instantly occur to any one engaged upon such a problem as I have had before me, to examine whether Each were not the same word, but that comes from agls. Ælc by throwing out the L and it shall not detain us. The greek and sanskrit form is found in agls. Æg, a prefix, meaning 'one,' as in Æg-hwa ' unus-quisque,' Æg-hwær 'each-where,' Æg-hwile ' each-which,' indefinitely and in Æg-þer, EITHER which is the same word as Ἑκάτερος and the sanskrit Ekataras = erse Ceactar = lat. Vter for †euter in the interrogative sense, Vterque in the indefinite.

> For mani man seyt ay whare*,
> That Tristrem bi me lay.
> Sir Tristrem, p. 117.
>
> For he ne may Ysonde kisse,
> Fight he sought aywhare.
> Id. p. 130.

977. The homeric versification afforded to the scholars of the last century, good reason for supposing that ἕκαστος had been written Ϝέκαστος and yet there were many passages which seemed to refuse the vau and to be incurable by any tolerable method of emendation. It will clear up both these points to observe what occurs in the semitic languages. The arabic, besides the form اَحَدٌ, corresponding exactly to the hebrew, has a collateral form with vau, وَاحِدٌ, wâkid in the

* Says everywhere.

sense of 'one only.' By the change of vau to yod common in the semitic tongues this word answers to the hebrew יחד with its derivatives. And since the same word commences with aleph held to possess an imperceptible aspiration, or with vau the digamma, there is no need to doubt but that this was also the case in the Iliad and that the true writing was ἕκαστος or Ϝέκαστος indifferently.

978. From this harmonizing process it will be observed that the hypothesis which represents Homers language to have been in a transition state, and therefore not always consistent with itself, has now been deprived of one of its chief supports. It must further be urged, that it would be wholly contrary to philological experience in the main, to entertain the idea that the sanskrit root of two letters is older in word descent than the hebrew with three. Should it turn out that we can fix on an extinct form older than either and consisting of four consonants, it will still remain true that the sanskrit may in some instances fail to solve all possible questions.

979. If reflecting on the phænomena before us as we do in solving all problems, we attempt to generalize the ideas contained in the group of words Con, Ἅμα, Ὅμος, Παν, Συν we shall find that they meet best under the notion of One. Were it possible that our investigations should bring us up to the conclusion that Con is really = One, then the aspirate in Ἕνα would be explained. We are then invited to look for some connecting link, for a trace of this sense, and of the connexion between the forms in some shape that shall speak as a witness with open mouth and put down the gainsayers. This witness appears in Ἅπαξ. Hesychios says that the kretan form of Ἅπαξ was Ἄμακις, the tarentine Ἄματις. This Ἄμακις is an adverb formed on the same method as πολλάκις, τετράκις; hence it follows undeniably that in the word Ἄμακις, Ἄμ meant One. But if Ἄμ meant One so also did Ὅμ, and we no longer scruple at turning ὁμὸν λέχος ἀντιόωσαν by 'sharing one bed;' 'together' is no longer the first notion in Ὅμος. These words bring all the rest of the group with them, Con, Sincerus 'one hearted,' Simplex and the rest. Ἅπαξ itself is produced by contraction from Ἄμακις, by

turning the labial liquid into the labial mute. It affords collaterally an explanation of the termination in Λαξ Οδαξ and any others like them.

980. The next step I take will prove to the capable observer very full of linguistic instruction. The sanskrit word for one as declined Ekas, Ekâ, Ekan is evidently the same with the mœsogothic old form as exhibited in art. 963 Hwas, Hwo, Hwan, and with the agls. Hwa, Hwon as similarly determined. The same I mean both in form and in sense, Hwas and Hwa being taken indefinitely; so that Vnus, Vna, Vnum in the sanskrit is Some one in the teutonic. The latin Quis, Quæ indefinite corresponds very well, but Quid Quod is only explained by the theory proposed before, that the neuter was †quant. It was argued before that as magnificus, magnifica, magnificum, stands for †magnificents, †magnificenta, †magnificent so Quis, Quæ, Quid stand for †quants, †quanta, †quant; the mœsog. Hwas, Hwo, Hwan, stand for †hwans, †hwanta, †hwant and the agls. Hwa, Hwon or Hwæt for the same. This argument being based upon investigations wholly independent of the numeral 1 am now treating, comes to be here applied, and it appears that all these pronouns as well as the sanskrit numeral must have had an earlier form

   †ekants †ekanta †ekant,

or rather †ekwants †ekwanta †ekwant.

With the hebrew Ekhâd, throwing out the N, this result agrees perfectly. Now recollecting that we have just proved the group of words, Con, 'Αμα, 'Ομος, Παν, Συν to be forms of the numeral One, we turn to them and ask whether they preserve any trace of this theoretic †ekant beyond what was before noticed. The reply is that Παντ not Παν is the radical form: and here we have a new confirmation. I would not be accused of overlooking the full form Ekant in the sanskrit with the adjectival terminations, Ekantas, Ekantâ, Ekant, meaning 1. ' solitary ' 2. ' excessive,' but the argument would have been very weak had it not comprehended a large number of forms.

981. It is evident that the word 'Εκα ' one ' must be contained in 'Εκατον. The sanskrit has lost the initial vowel

and has sibilated the guttural, Shatan. The latin Centum and the agls. and mœsog. Hund shew that the greek and sanskrit have rejected an N before the T. Hence we obtain an old form †hekanton, which in the compounds sometimes is seen 'Εκατοντα, †hekantonta. Whatever the termination may be, the first element One corresponds with the preceding statements. One signifies that a new reckoning by HUNDreds begins here.

982. The comparison of the pronominal forms and such words as Quondam of which I am about to speak, shews that when the teutonic nations and the latins parted from the common stock the form of the numeral was not †ekant, but †ekwant, and the greek, sanskrit and hebrew afterwards threw away the koph and adopted the kheth, ain or kappa. I shall cite some hebrew words with KWD. (986.)

983. As Tu, Thou seems to match Duo, Two, so I, Ic, Ego, Εγων, sansk. Aham appears to be †ekant.

984. When we turn from these purely numerical words to others less confined in sense the reasoning becomes much weaker, we must then rely upon similarity of forms on which every one holds an opinion tinged by the state of his own mind. This will be said however, that if the numeral One really is of the same origin in hebrew and latin, then some of the kindred significations will appear in the shorter forms. The pure hebraists do so insist. עם 'together,' having a different guttural, is they say akin to Cum, Con. This, after them, I hold. Further I suspect that in the unexplained word עִמָּדִי ' with me,' we possess remaining the dental of the root, with the suffix of the first person. Perhaps the following have also some affinity to Con; כן the demonstrative adverb, כי the relative, כנס 'he collected,' כנע, 'he gathered,' כנש ' he assembled,' כנת ' collega, fellowslave.'

985. So much has been formerly said about the changes of form presented by the derivatives of this root, that I will now drop that subject and try to collect them under their changes of signification. The sense One is retained in ὁμος, ἁπαξ, ἑνα, ἑκατον, ἑκατερος, ἑκαστος, uter, uterque, either, one, an, a, unus, some, semper, simplex, sincerus, semel, quondam, uncia?.

In Quondam we have nearly the original numeral. If we combine Quondam and sanskrit ekadâ both meaning Once, we arrive in a moment at the root †ekwant with suffix â. H. Etienne objected to αδελφος that if made up of ἁμα together and δελφυς it would signify 'twin,' but that objection is now removed; it and words like it, as αγαστωρ explained by Eustathius ὁμογαστριος, come from a in the sense 'One:' so Ἀμαζονες having one breast as far as the old legend shews; αγαλακτες 'brothers;' αταλαντος 'of one weight.' In the sense of 'every,' in Quotidie, Παντα with τινα, Πας τις. In the sense of 'in one, together,' Con, Ξυν, Συν, Ἁμα, Ὁμου, Ἁμιλλα, old engl. Samn, κοινος, ξυνος, agls. ge-, ακολουθος, etc., Atonement. In the sense of 'as one,' Same, ὁμοιως, Similis, Simul. Milton P. L. VI. 163, illustrates the transition of sense:

> At first I thought that liberty and heaven
> To heavenly souls had been all one*.

In the sense of 'oneness,' integrity, Παν with παντ-, the compounds of παν, and some compounds of Con, Sound, Sanus, welch Iach, Ἀκεισθαι. In the sense 'at one,' Al-one, Lonely, Sunder=agls. Sundrian with mœsog. Sundro, Only, Vnicus, Any, Singuli, Sigillatim, Sine?, the greek Ἀν?=lat. In?= engl. Un? of privation. The essential idea lies in the numeral, as in these lines on the ten commandments

> The man that Godes hestes† halt ‡
> And that myd gode wylle;
> And nauȝt one byfore men,
> Ac both loud and stille §.
> William of Shoreham, p. 90.

From these no one would think of separating Ὁμαλος, and to it, I believe, belongs Even=agls. Efen=mœsog. Ibns=norse Iafn, the labials in which are to be explained as the labial in ἁπαξ, by the change of M to F, since in compounds the agls. had another form in the same sense, Emn-, and Emn-christen for fellow-christian is not uncommon in old english. What

* That is, all the same.
† Hestes, orders. ‡ Halt, holds.
§ Loud and stille, in all circumstances.

shall we say to Æquus? Απεδον in the sense of ισοπεδον shows the same loss of letters as in other senses. 'Αμαλος 'smooth' and 'Απαλος, Αμαλδυνειν, Αμαθυνειν with Αμαθος the sand of the desert as distinguished from Ψαμαθος the sand of the shore, go with 'Ομαλος.

986. Besides those forms of the root there are some the meanings of which do not seem so readily to connect themselves with the rest. It is not quite easy to see the thread that joins Con with Contra, and even after shewing that originally the sense One resided in Con, it is not full satisfaction to the curious inquirer, if we plead that One is ever in front, a head, over against. Yet the words קדם 'in front of,' קדם 'the east,' קדד 'fall down before,' Εκεινος, Εκει, Yon, Yonder, Contra, Ante, Αντι, 'Εκας, 'Εκατηβολος, Again, Gainsay, Against, Αγων, belong apparently to the radix.

987. If it should be decided that gutturals can become M, then probably Μονος is a derivative: and this would fully account for the use of μοναδα (acc.) as 'unit,' and help us towards Μια. We see the same relation between Εγων and Εμε, as between 'Εκα and Μια.

988. There is, I apprehend, no doubt but that †ckwant was the origin of the demonstratives in T; the letter change, the community of sense has been already treated of; we find the change already complete in τις=quis whether indefinite or interrogative. In the period at which we have arrived we observe the making of pronouns; the pronouns of the first and second persons, the pronouns interrogative, the pronouns indefinite, and now, the demonstratives are provided from one root. The demonstrative Εκεινος Yon, was deduced direct; †τος, he, †τη, she, †τοδ, that, indirectly from quis, quæ, quid indefinite but emphasized. The S of She and its proper masculine was a change from T. The pronoun Σφεις, †σφος Sui, is a sibilation of the root: Sponte, 'Εκοντα (acc.) have little difference of form. Self=mœsog. Silba, Αυτος come in a foreign garb, and are not recognizable. Since Soon=agls. Sona=mœsog. Suns, must be placed with the other derivatives, Ευθυς offers itself by the side of Αυτος. But these points are very dark.

989. The explanation of the first numeral here given will bring the keltic languages within its reach, welsh Cynt 'first' as adv. 'before,' in composition Cyn 'before,' Cyd as prefix 'together,' Cant a hundred; erse, Céad 'first,' Ceadna 'the same,' Cead 'a hundred' etc.

990. Two other conclusions must be drawn from this inquiry which will, it is feared, seem to pass the bounds of cautious investigation. The mœsogothic Wiþra is the teutonic representative in sense of Contra, and it is of the same origin. In assuming a numeral †ckwant, Contra is to be supposed to take the vowel O from a vocalization of the W, and to be equivalent to †kwantra, reject the guttural as we have so frequently seen, and the N which is very often done, and we have †watra, mœsog. wiþra. Even the þ will some day be explained. Wiþra = germ. Wider = norse agls. engl. With : the english retaining the sense of the agls. in Withstand, fight with, etc. This statement might not have arisen of itself, but it forces itself upon us after the comparison of the other words. The next perhaps incredible, perhaps erroneous, conclusion is, that Mid, Medius, Μεσος with their kin, are also of this family. For whether we change K or W into M, perhaps K for μονος on account of the round vowel, and W for Mid, mœsog. Miþ, 'cum,' we do but add one link to the changes seen in With. And here is in a measure cleared up what ought always to have seemed an anomaly, that the teutonic languages use Wiþ in two so different senses: these senses are at least the teutonic representatives of Con, Contra.

991. TWO. The word Twins, Διδυμοι is traceable in תאוֹמִים=תְּאׇמִים, which at first sight has no hebrew affinities. The proper name Thomas is a remnant of the old testament word, and many a boy is called by his parents Thomas, who was no twin.

992. From what I can gather of the ancient language of the world we live in, the agls. Twegen is a near approach to the oldest form: for this supposition I shall give some reasons when speaking of the termination of the numerals art. 999. The M of the hebrew, we find in the

sanskrit Yam, the greek διδυμ and the latin Gem-elli: it seems to stand for the N in agls. Twegen: and I shall dare to express the opinion that the hebrew is a contraction of Twegenîm.

993. Before I approach the usual hebrew word for two, which is so unlike the teutonic that no one has yet spoken of any resemblance, let me speak of the syriac and chaldee, which may be represented by the consonants TRN. ܬܪܝܢ, תְּרֵין. Now I suppose that no one who has studied philology by the aid of the sanskrit can doubt but that W may be changed into R. I have already applied the principle which I first learned of those who treat of the relations of sanskrit to other languages, and have expanded what I had read by the addition of examples hitherto unremarked. This change I make no doubt to have occurred here, the R in TRN is changed out of the W in Twain. The statement must unavoidably seem at first strange and rather to be rejected, but it will, I hope, be accepted.

994. In treating the arabic I have now the advantage of having proved two branches of the semitic stock to have contracted the old numeral, safe by some strange course of things in the anglosaxon, into a form scarce recognizable. If the argument was valid of the two, it ought to hold good of the third. The arabic for two is îthnain اِثْنَانِ Which is îthn with the suffix of the dual. It is the custom of the arabic to throw out a vowel and prefix an initial, as in ibn = hebrew Ben, 'son,' so that the letters which are radical in the arabic numeral for two are þn, and those who can believe what has here gone before will be able to believe that these two letters are a contraction of Twegen. The english has in like manner made Ten out of the agls. Tigun.

995. Now every one who has looked even cursorily at the relation of the hebrew to the other semitic languages knows that of all the group it has a singular love of sibilations. Not to give a doubtful example, I will only say Batanæa = Bashan; we shall come to another immediately. The hebrew form

therefore of the arabic is שְׁנַיִם, which had its original in some word very near to Twegen.

996. At the results thus arrived at I confess I am myself startled. Of the authenticity and antiquity of the hebrew writings I long ago, by an inquisitive and unhasty examination, convinced myself: and I have no doubt when I declare, quite needlessly too, except for this present occasion, that any other opinion is totally untenable. More examples will appear, not many perhaps, in which the teutonic or scandinavian forms are evidently older than the mosaic. It is no part of my present study to reconcile these apparent contradictions: but I think that a fair and sufficient solution may be found in the consideration that the rude life, rough minds, and hard mouths of the northern people retained forms which rapidly disappeared before the smoothing influence of civilization. For an illustration this word may suffice; if as I assume and am convinced Twegen was nearly the old name for the numeral, it remained down to the conquest of William, a thousand years after the birth of Christ, wholly unaltered, while the sanskrit, old as it is, the greek, and the latin, all southern languages, had curtailed it a thousand years at least before that era. We should not forget the great changes which in these later days of comparative tranquillity have happened in the language spoken by ourselves. To how few among us the easiest anglosaxon, as we call it, is intelligible, how many are the stumbling blocks in its harder poems to the most skilful. One small advantage perhaps may accrue to the cause of truth from what here is set forth: that the incredible and scientifically unacceptable doctrine of a half a dozen pair of parents for mankind will derive less imaginary countenance from linguistic mistakes. If the semitic languages have in them a european element, copious, old, and mostly further back than the other, it will no longer seem impossible that all men are cousins, and their words from one wellhead.

997. THREE. The hebrew three was compared with the european forms by Dr. Prichard, but his was only a timid comparison, two letters of the word seemed to correspond,

T

while the third remained unexplained and constituted an element of hesitation and doubt. I shall now drive the nail home. A suspicion first arises that in Three, Tres, Tria, we have not the full root by looking at the sanskrit ordinal, but here the authorities hold that Tri is the root, and I am not able to shew out of that language that they are wrong. When we turn to the latin and compare tertius with quartus, quintus, sextus, there is visibly something unusual. Why not †tritus or †tertus? The greek ancient ordinal answers the query and solves the difficulty.

998. The homeric ordinals were Τριτατος, Τεταρτος, Πεμπτος, Ἑκτος, Ἑβδοματος, Ογδοατος, Εινατος, Δεκατος; and it is at once evident that the last is a shortening of †δεκεματος. The final syllable the mark of the ordinals is common to the latin and the modern english, as well as to the earlier sanskrit and the teutonic languages. Take away ατος and the third numeral is Τριτ. This form may be suspected to be the real base of the sanskrit ordinal; let sanskrit scholars decide. We may now understand the -ius in Tertius, for T has fallen away and †tertitus corresponds to τριτατος. The word Tritavus also supports the conclusion, for the Romans do not compound with tertius as the first element, trit is therefore three. The double T in the agls. for Thirty, þrittig, is a trace of the lost letter. Now the root Trit when compared with the arabic, syriac, and chaldee presents no difficulty: these tongues have L for R, which neither Dr. Prichard nor any other student of the affinities of words could hesitate to accept as a common letter change. From the semitic t-l-þ, or þ-l-þ ݠݠݠ palaþ, ܐܠܬ þloþ, תָּלָה tlaþ, comes by sibilation the hebrew form.

999. At this point we will consider the evidence regarding the antiquity of Twegen, for a good deal was built upon it. Let it be remembered that as a hypothetical origin for the numeral two, it did in a manner account for the M in Thomas, the N in the semitic numerals, the M in gemelli with the sanskrit, and the N in twain, twin. My proposition is that the oldest form of most of the numerals in the languages

before us had for a termination -em, -en. One, if †ekwant, †ekwand, easily became †ekwan, as in Ἐνα, Unum, One, An. Two, was Twegen. Five has its proper termination in the sanskrit Panchan, which shews that quinque is for quinquem, πεμπε for πεμπεμ. Seven was Septem. Eight will be denied and rejected, for the learned world is pledged to its being a dual. My theory is that the sanskrit ordinal Ashtamas exhibits the original cardinal numeral †ashtam = †octom; that the latin Octavus was really of old †ογδοματος; that like septimus for ἑβδοματος and somewhat like tertius it rejected the T syllable and thus became †ογδομος, and that the change of M to V produced Octavus, with a long vowel which might arise from the altered form of the cardinal, or from compensation. In †octom with V for M and vocalized we without difficulty discover the sanskrit, greek, and latin numerals, false duals. The learned world is not called upon to acknowledge the probability of this account: it is, I confess, a bit of systematizing, a forcing of this numeral to match others. But before they openly condemn it, let me ask them to account for the M at all: it will not do to talk of comparing latin and sanskrit ordinals and to pretend that -mus is, at option, occasionally, or what not, an ordinal termination: the homeric forms distinctly shew that these endings in -mus are shortened from older ones in -ματος and the M of Ashtamas cannot be accounted for in that way. Till better taught I shall hold by †ashtam, Eight; sanskrit radix Ashtan, of which I have not availed myself as it is not the actual nominative. Nine is Novem, agls. Nigun. Ten is Decem, agls. Tigun. We have then †ekwan, Panchan, Septem, †ashtam, Novem, Decem; and these six out of nine are the testimony to the superior antiquity of Twegen.

1000. While upon this branch of the subject let us examine whether there were any probability of an older form in -NT like †ekwant. The problem is too difficult for me: but there are many learned men whose curiosity may be further excited if they read these pages on numerals. The word Twenty, Viginti, Εικοσι is perhaps best to be understood of any. It consists of Twegen -tigun, two tens, which by loss of letters

T 2

contract into †twain-ty, Twenty. If Viginti were thus formed, which seems very likely, it then retains the two syllables of Twegen, the oldest form of two, in all these dialects, and Twegen-tigun contracts to Vigin-ti. But what is to be done with Triginta? If we divide similarly Trigin-ta we shall have to begin with something not quite †trit, as just proved. Should we assume a guttural G for the T we should have to suppose †trit = †trig to have been once †trigem and so divide trigem-ti. Passing by forty as more difficult, if we divide Πεντηκον-τα we shall arrive at a form longer and harder than Panchan, and if we divide Ἑβδομηκον-τα we shall have the termination in N or M twice over. These explanations then will be rejected. Perhaps we shall hold fast at the observation that Viginti, Εικοσι end with a different vowel from the rest and are to be differently accounted for. If so, Triginta, out of †trit-tigun, agls. þrittig, will require Tigun to be at least †tigunt if not †tigunta. It is possible, and hardly that, for ἑβδομηκοντα to arise out of septem-tigunt. Should, however, that be established, from †ekwant, †tigunt, with Nundinæ perhaps, and surely with September, November, December, we shall arrive at a termination for the numerals in -NT instead of M. It seems most agreeable to the practice of all languages which preserved their adjectival terminations in three genders, to suppose day and month wholly suppressed in Nundinæ, September, October, etc. The seven stars of the Carls wain, Septentrio, may perhaps be explained from †septent, for neither terrio, nor τειρεα seem quite sufficient: for the termination cf. Ternio, Quaternio, Senio.

1001. FIVE. The feminine חָמֵשׁ is Quinque with the second kôf sibilated. Since Quinque was at least †quinquem, †quinquen, the hebrew word has less of the original root than the sanskrit. In this word some guess at the nature of the names of the numerals may be made. The similarity of the hebrew to Chemosh the evil deity of the Moabites, and to חֵמָשׁ, the belly, is quite agreeable to the theories of word affinities which have offered themselves to me as probable:

see art. 315. The sense however in which these words are taken does not suit very well with the reckoning on the fingers, and I am very far indeed from accepting the idea that the belly was a pars quinta in the human frame: such a mode of affixing names would be better suited to some technical teacher of a modern university than to the rude methods of men in the early stage of society. When speaking of the family to which these words belong I propose to find in the greek language traces not, to my thought, obscure, of a root πεμπ signifying 'hand.' But neither will this content us; for as the two first numerals are evidently the same as Eγων, and Tu, the whole system of numerals must be names not of a number of fingers, but of each finger separately. Now observe how closely Pinguis approaches to Quinque in form: take away the case termination and the word is †pingw. The norse has one of the teutonic equivalents for pinguis in the form þungr, or, without the R of the nom. masc., þung: it means Thick, which is but another form of the same word. All these words I believe to belong to one far extended family. And on the whole I have come to the conclusion that the numeral in all its shapes says THUMB.

1002. Six = שֵׁשׁ. That the welsh Chwech is a very ancient form of the word is evident from all the analogy of letter change, and from the existence of the form Feξ. The word is very similar to Cusc, Castus, take them in the sense of 'clean;' the syriac Shcþ ܐܠ, 'six' the usual arabic Siþþ (fem.) ܣܝ and the fuller form in derivatives out of the ancient language ܣܠܝܫ, S-d-s with the æthiopic of the ancient form Sydis, Sdis ስድስ, 'six,' seem equally to remind us of the welsh Coeth 'pure,' irish Caið 'pure, chaste, holy,' the hebrew קָדֵשׁ 'clean,' much more commonly used in the derivative sense 'holy,' חָדָשׁ 'new,' the chaldee חֲדַת 'new,' the arabic قدس kwadasa, purus fuit, حديث khadíþ 'new,' the syriac ܩܕܝܫ kwadish 'holy,' ܚܕܬܐ khadþô 'new,' the greek

Καθαρος 'pure.' It would seem unlikely that these two sets of words containing but two meanings 'six' and 'clean,' yet varying their form in two ways, having or rejecting the medial dental, can be quite separate in origin. The greek words for sacred are ἅγιος, ἁγνος, ἱερος to which ὅσιος is near: the root ἁγ as compared with welsh Chwech 'six,' has lost only the Van. Ἱερος as compared with Καθαρος has rejected the middle consonant. Ὅσιος is near enough to Cuse. Sacer, Sanctus all admit to be sister words to Ἁγιος, Ἁγνος; and Sanguinem, Αἱμα will have their suitable sacrificial sense 'purifying.' Now this is further worthy of attention, that as regards the hebrew for six, שֵׁשׁ may be the common hebrew sibilation of such a form as we see in the syriac, and in that case the radix will lie in the consonants S-þ: or it may be a contraction of the older arabic and æthiopic forms in S-d-s, S-d-þ, and then still the bilitteral radix is S-d. The same argumentation holds true in the sanskrit. The welsh, which accounts for the aspirate in ἐξ, shews that the initial S of the semitic languages is a sibilation, and that the original letters were kw-d in the numeral. The interchange of the forms kwee, kwed will account for every form of the numeral in all the languages before us. The same is true of all the forms of the expression for clean and holy; kwech, kwaþ will be the roots of every one. These roots look like philological assumptions, and so they were; but they are both actually found in the sanskrit with the well known change to the sibilant; the sanskrit words Shudh 'purificari, lustrari,' Shuchi 'purus, honestus, pius' will be admitted by all readers of the language to have originated in kw-ð, kw-k. The professors of that tongue will hardly be prepared to admit that these two words can exchange one with another; but how will they escape the comparison instituted above? The arabic has also the semitic bilitteral radix in خَدّ khatida 'originem puram habuit.' צדק 'was just, righteous' may stand in nearly the same relation as ὅσιος to this root. In the words שֵׁשׁ 'fine linen,' 2. white marble, שׁוּשָׁן 'lily,' שֵׁשִׁי 'was hoary,' the hebrew seems to contain a root very similar in sense, of the same form as the numeral.

1003. SEVEN, Septem, שֶׁבַע fem. Of the ultimate identity of these words no one entertains a doubt. The greek ἑπτα does not, according to my reading of letter change, answer immediately to Septem, but to such a form as †keptem. The mœsogothic Sibun, agls. Seofon, germ. Sieben do not contain any thing like T.

1004. EIGHT. שְׁמֹנָה may be brought within reach of a comparison with Octo. Setting out with the assumed †octem =sanskr. Ashtan, I find the sclavonic given as Osmy, which is but the hebrew provided with an initial vowel: so that Shemonch = Osmy = †octom = Octo. Doubtless a proper understanding of the word would account for the seeming difference: in the mean time remark that the coptic for 8 has a sibilant like the hebrew, but that 80 gives the ancient guttural ⲡⲓⲉⲛⲉ.

1005. EVE. חַוָּה Khavvâ. The wide ranging affinities of the ancient root Kwikw = in english QUICK have already been partly mentioned. The word above belongs in form and signification to that group, and Eve the latinised shape is related to the hebrew much as Ever is to Quick. Other words of the same sense and letters are חַי 'alive, vigorous,' חַי 'life,' חָיָה 'lived,' חָיָה = chaldee חַיְוָא (giving the vocalisation of Quick) 'a living creature,' חָי 'lived.' They are softer, if not softened, forms, the second guttural being missing or replaced, and they thus approach nearer to the mœsogothic Kwiu-s, than to the saxon: so also the æthiopic. With a softer aspirate appears הָיָה 'was,' not remote from Fuit. If the authorities in the hebrew language would permit the suggestion, to this root might be referred some forms with a Lamed suffix, חַיִל 'strength, vires,' whence חַל 'army,' חִיל 'the pain of child birth,' חוּל '1. to bring forth, 2. to suffer pains of child birth, 3. to be strong.' If a further conjecture should be heard, the words in אִיל, with the softest aspirate, might be mentioned.

1006. ARABIA עֲרָב so called from its dryness and sterility:

עֲרָבָה 'a desert:' of these words the trilitteral root is admitted to be one of those conventionalisms which are supposed to adorn and do really deface our hebrew lexicons. With stronger guttural exists חָרַב '1. was dried up, 2. was desolate,' חָרֵב '1. dry, 2. desolate,' חֹרֵב 'mount Horeb in the desert,' חֹרֶב 'dryness,' חָרְבָּה 'desolation,' חֲרָבָה 'a dry land,' חָרָבוֹן 'dryness.' Under this form we find in the greek Καρφειν 'to dry up,' Καρφαλεος 'dry,' Καρφος 'dried stuff,' Κραμβος 'dry,' Κραμβος 'a shrivelling of the grapes,' with several bye words. To the whole of these belongs I believe as radix a monosyllabic biconsonantal word common equally to the greek and hebrew, חרר that is חר, in Niphal 'was dried up.' חֲרֵרִים 'dry places,' חַרְחֻר 'fever.' With a softer guttural are many words implying bareness and nakedness, the accompaniments of dryness: עוּר, ערר, ערה 'was naked,' עוֹר 'the skin,' that is the naked, the bare, עֲרוֹת the meadows by the Nile bare of trees and bushes, עָרוֹד 'onager,' עֲרוֹעֵר Jerem. xlviii. 6 in a reduplicate form, ονος αγριος LXX. the wild ass of the desert. Between nakedness, bareness, and dryness, barrenness, there is so close a connexion, especially in the semitic countries, that it cannot be well doubted the present words are akin to the former. The greek representatives of this root are Χερσος 'dry land,' Χηρα 'a widow,' with sibilation Ξηρος dry, our SERE with agls. verb, Scarian, and, with, if you will, confusion of sibilants, Sterilis, Στειρα (as Βους Od. λ. 30). It would not be in harmony with the observation we have arrived at, of the community of utterance, did not this root appear in the latin and teutonic; and we are very ready to recognise it in the latin Tor, Torrere, the german Dorr, the english Dry, which by sibilation would give Sterilis. From the forms with the softer guttural proceed probably those which have rejected the guttural altogether, as Arere, Area, Ερημος and an armenian word Airi meaning 'viduus, vidua;' we have also, from the same consonants as in Arabia, Orbus, Ορφανος meaning originally, I suppose, 'bare, destitute.' From ער 'was bare' with עוּר 'skin' we may compare ρινος, our kind, for the original form of ρινος was γρῖνος, Hesychios, Etym. M. 211. 48, where the vocalisation is similar, with yod for waw and ρ transposed.

1007. By the side of Arabia in the hebrew lexicon lies a root having the same letters but a wholly different sense, עָרַב (the sun) 'set,' whence comes al Mogreb 'the west,' the usual arabic name of Morocco: with it עֶרֶב 'evening' and מַעֲרָב 'the west.' In these letters and in this sense we recognize Ερεβος 'gloom,' νυξ ερεβεννη, Ερεμνος M for B, and nine words belonging to Ορφνη 'gloom,' Crepusculum, Creperus. The last word has been wrongly interpreted by the most ancient and reliable authorities: that what is here advanced is more probable may be shewn by the following passages out of Forcellini; Priusquam manifestus dies creperum noctis absolveret: Dumque iter horrendum per opaca crepuscula carpit: the notions dubius, anceps, incertus are only accessory. The homeric ηεριος indicates a root without the Beta: as in Od. λ. 15. ηερι και νεφελη κεκαλυμμενοι. Some of the comparisons above, after making them myself, I saw anticipated in Parkhursts lexicon; and under עֲרָפֶל 'darkness,' Gesenius compares Ορφνη, but as a quadrilitteral he would make it a compound: it has only the addition of the Lamed suffix.

1008. SOLOMON, SALEM. From the letters שלם of the conventional trilitteral radix proceed several derivatives, and the most common of the senses are those of Salvus, Safe, Salutem, Salve, and peace: so that the Salaam of the oriental is but the Salve of the latin; we shall see also that it is the Hail! of the english. In the lexicon a rarer form without the final Mem שלה, שלו will be observed, and this goes some way to shew that there was a bilitteral original שׁל. Now the hebrew language affords us the means of referring these words to their proper family and identifying them not only with those few above, but with a large and illustrative group of a different form. Any one who will turn to שלם and its derivatives will see mixed up with the above senses others, as 'absolvit, perfecit,' from passages where there can be no confusion, and if at all a reader of the hebrew he will soon reflect that 'absolvit, perfecit' are commonly expressed by the various modifications of another radix, like at once and unlike, כלה. So many hundred instances have already been given of sibilation of almost all classes of consonants, certainly of all mutes, that it ought to take no effort to say that של is a sibilation of כל. But here we take a step which in effect had been made before; old latin Sollus='Ολος : Hole (whole), Heal, All, welsh Holl, 'Ολος כּוֹל=Sollus, Salvare, Salvus, etc. But we will not stop where our forefathers did. The hebrew, greek, and latin reduced the ancient Kôf, KW in numerous instances to K. In the hebrew exists another form יָכוֹל,יָכֹל 'potuit, valuit,' and it is at once probable that כל=Val= Well, so that all the derivatives of Valere and of Well are lessenings of an ancient †kwal, and of the same parentage as Heal, All. And if the sanskrit Bal-an 'robur, vigor' belong to this group, it also is a softened form; so Balas 'valens.' Nor is this all; wholeness (holeness), entireness, completion are connected with maturity, full growth, manhood, womanhood; and in hebrew we have with a softer guttural עָלֶם 'a young man,' עַלְמָה 'a young woman,' coptic 'ⲁⲗⲟⲩ for either sex, without the mem, and so in arabic with the derived, not radical, notion of libidinousness, an animal impulse which shews very fierce in Arabia. Of the hebrew words on the trilitteral system, which still holds the best scholars in its slavery, the hebrew root is not discoverable within the language, and recourse is had to the arabic derivative sense. The welsh has Gallu, 'to be able, to may, to can.' In the latin we have derivatives of the same sort without the Vau, Ad-olescens, Ad-olevit, Suboles, Proles, when olescere is valescere, 'begin to be well, hole, entire, mature.' The verb Alere has an active sense like Heal. Is not Καλος=Valens? the first idea of beauty is that of health and strength.

1009. Ham. The latin Amare is now commonly referred to the sanskrit Kam to love, the irish Caemh 'love, desire,' especially since the indian Cupid is Camadeva. Here the hebrew comes near enough : חָם, חָמָא, חָמַד, הֶמֶד, חֶמְדָה,

כָּמַר, יָחַם, חֶמֶר, חֵמָה, חַמָּה, חֲמָדוֹת are words signifying heat, with the subordinate senses of anger, desire, beauty. The arabic حَمَ has a similar sense. That words of burning are natural expressions for love, is evident to all : καιετο μεν Ναννους : ardebat Alexin. If Gomorrha derives its name from the bitumen it supplied, that substance drew its name from its inflammability. We seem to have the same root in Candere, Candle, Kindle.

1010. CHERUBIM are described by Ezekiel and Josephus : every one had four faces, the face of a man, of a lion, of an ox, and of an eagle; and four wings; the wings joined one to another, and two covered their bodies : they kept the gates of paradise, and seemed to guard the ark. In this description and office it is impossible not to be reminded of the composite figures that were doorkeepers at the palace of Nineveh, and of the three headed Cerberus, the doorkeeper of Hades. Κερβερος is made up of nearly the same consonants as כרוב. The orientalists have already compared the Γρυπες, Griffins which guarded gold on fabulous mountains.

χρύσειοι δ' ἑκάτερθε καὶ ἀργύρεοι κύνες ἦσαν
οὓς Ἥφαιστος ἔτευξε Ἰδυίῃσι πραπίδεσσιν
δῶμα φυλασσέμεναι μεγαλήτορος Ἀλκινόοιο :
Od. η. 91.

1011. KIRYAH as in Kiriaþ-arba, 'city of Arba.' קִרְיָה 'a city,' קִיר 'a citadel,' and with softer guttural עִיר 'a city,' קִיר 'a wall,' Kiryaþ-arba, Kiryaþ-baal, Kiryaþ-ye-ârim, Kir-yaþ-khuzoþ, Kiryaþ-sannah, Kiryaþ-sefer, Kiryaþaim, and the phœnician towns, Carthago, Cirta, Carteia, Cartenna, Carthæa, with Tigranocerta, Melicerta, 'king of the city,' the name of the tyrian Hercules, seem all connected with the root Circa and the idea of GIRDING by a wall. כֶּרֶם 'an orchard, a vineyard,' כַּרְמֶל 'a garden,' with lamed suffix according even to the lexica, with some others not so clear, belong to GARDEN, YARD etc. as in art. 272. As regards the sense, Town has a similar origin : agls. Tynan 'to inclose ;' in Devonshire a tun is the farm yard, and in some names of villages as Bishopstone, bishops tun, near Seaford, which could never have been walled.

1012. ALEPPO حَلَب is supposed to be so called from the fatness of the district. The arabic root and similarly shaped words refer to milking, almost wholly, and not at all to fatness; but the conjecture is well founded, the hebrew חֶלְבּוֹן, the ancient name, being referred to a root having the same letters as the arabic root and producing both חָלָב 'milk' and חֵלֶב 'fat.' To perceive a connexion between the two senses it is only needful to remember that the milk of sheep, asses, and goats, chiefly used by the early folk, is full of that fatty substance cream. Now in the sense of milk it is easy in these hebrew words to recognize Γαλακτος Lactis. Among the derivatives is חֶלְבְּנָה Galbanum having a bright white or red yellow tint like rich milk, and among the Romans used as a word to signify yellow.

> Cœrulea indutus scutulata aut galbana rasa.
> Juvenalis, II. 97.

That such a word as this may probably be related to agls. Gealo = YELLOW, GOLD, GALL, Χολη, must be evident, but as these last contain but two consonants of three they may lie further back in the pedigree. Whitish and yellow are nearly the same colour, in gaelic Geal is white; Suetonius assures us (Galba, 3) that the Galli called a very fat man (præpinguem) Galbam, answering exactly to the hebrew. It is somewhat strange to me that no hebraist, as far as I have seen, has observed that the hebrew for white has been formed in the same manner as Lacteus for †glacteus, by dropping the G. This is doubtless due to the grammatical or lexicographical burden they have tied upon their shoulders, and to a strong and rightful sense of the antiquity of the hebrew records. Yet to me it is quite evident that לָבָן 'white' and LEBANON and לְבָנָה 'the moon' and several other words are descended from חָלָב 'milk.' Whether the latin Luna be considered as a word arising within the latin itself for †lucna, or as borrowed from some earlier form of speech, approaching to the sanskrit Glau 'the moon,' or as a near approximation to Lebânâh, the result will be the same, for †gel as in Γελει, the oldest form for Flame, and Yellow, and Gleam, will still be the ultimate source of all. In the word Alabaster we have the hebrew for milk, divested of its ancient guttural but not of the vowel that accompanied it. It is paralleled by Ελπος, ελαιον, στεαρ, ευθηνια; Ελφος, βουτυρον, Κυπριοι (Hesychios). The latin Albus 'white,' is formed in the same manner and retains the vowel which לָבָן has lost. Again, to take the second meaning of the root, we find with sibilation SALVE = germ. Salbe = agls. Salf, Scalf, which gives the mœsog. Salbon, 'αλειφειν, μυριζειν, χριειν,' and Salbons 'μυρον.' We might guess at CALF that it shall signify milker, and compare the irish and gaelic Laogh = welsh Llo 'calf,' with irish Laehd 'milk' = welsh Llaeth. Aleppo, like Alabaster, Albus, has lost the guttural, and retained the vowel; from Kheleb 'fat' take away the guttural and we obtain †alipem which is the latin Adipem 'fat,' with Αλειφειν, Λιπα, Αλοιφη (ὐες θαλεθοντες αλοιφη), Αλειφαρ (homeric), with also the mœsogothic Alew 'oil,' Ελαιον (with yod for wau), Oleum, Oil. In a former place Ελαιον has been compared with agls. Ælan 'to burn;' and herein is no difference of radical, for Ælan is Γελειν with loss of guttural. The sanskrit equivalents of αλειφειν, whether beginning with â or with l, are here of course held to have lost something at the beginning.

PERSIA, see arts. 531, 1040.

1013. MALACHI מַלְאָכִי is, they tell us, and doubtless truly, a shortened form for מַלְאָכִיָה legatus Iehovæ, from the same source as מַלְאָךְ 'an angel,' or 'legatus.' The radix is not itself in actual use in the hebrew, but is recorded in the lexica according to custom, לאַךְ, and compared with latin Legare. That this comparison is well founded can scarcely be doubted by any one who casts his eyes upon Ludolfis æthiopic lexicon under this head: ለአከ LEGAVIT.

הלה 'minister, famulus, LICTOR.' He quotes, for the use of the verb as Legavit, misit nuncium seu hominem, the places Matth. xxvii. 19; Mark iii. 31. It is also a recognized fact that the very common words הלך, ילך 'went' belong to this family; and here it is akin to Legere in 'legere vestigia,' and as 'percurrere, prætcrire, obire.' It seems that while the original, if really original, form of the root had gone out of use in the hebrew, the language retained שלח as its representative, for this word has the sense and embraces the letters of the other words for 'sent.' It might be alledged that the principles of hebrew grammar allow ש to be occasionally a prefix (Gesen. Hebr. Gr. § 54. 6, § 83. 35; Michaelis Syr. Gr. § 38. 7); but this Shaphel conjugation wants discussion; in the example which is sufficient for Gesenius להב, an obsolete root to signify 'blazed,' compared with שַׁלְהֶבֶת 'flame,' there seems to me to be involved a mistaken assumption: a comparison of other languages, Γελειν, Glow, Gleam, induces me to suppose that the original letters GL have in the one instance undergone sibilation as in Σεληνη, Σελας, and in the other have dropped the initial, as in Low, Leem (art. 322), Lumen. On the above example see other theories in Lee Gr. p. 142. It may be then that ש is not in that instance a prefix; and the rule for Shaphel, that ש may be prefixed, was meant in our grammars to manufacture quadriliteral verbs out of trilitteral roots and was not intended to apply to such a case as שׁלח. Considering therefore that this point is doubtful, and that there is much reason to suspect that an initial L has always lost some consonant before it, we may say that in שלח we find a trace of an earlier form.

1014. JERICHO, whether it takes its name from the pale moon, or from the fertile valley of the Jordan and וְרָקוֹן 'greenness,' may, if we trust to our guides, be connected with Virere.

FAMILIES OF WORDS.

1015. Spoon. In the younger or prose Edda near the beginning we read thus, þak hennar var lagt gyltum skjöldum, svo sem spónþak, 'thatch of it was laid with gilt shields so as a spoonthatch,' 'its roof was laid with gilded shields as it were with shingles' (Dasents translation). Here we see plain enough that þak = thatch = τεγος, = στεγος = tectum; but what is this phrase a spoonthatch? Spánn = Spónn in islandic is 1. *ramentum ligni*, 'a chip,' dan. Spaan, 'a chip, a shingle;' 2. 'cochleare,' 'Skje, Skee,' 'a spoon.' Junius reconciles the two significations, for he tells us that the first spoons were but chips of wood. "Cochleari vero inde nomen dedit antiquitas, quod qualecumque ligni segmentum leviter excavatum cochlearis usum præbuerit simpliciore adhuc sæculo atque inculto. Unde agls. Sticcan sunt cochlearia, Herb. xviii. 4. Ipse quoque in illo tractu Hollandiæ, ubi cespites bituminosos ad focum effodiunt, incidi in aliquot familias, quibus cochlear quotidiano sermone Gaepstock dicebatur." He met with some turfcutters in Holland whose name for a spoon was a Gape stick, a Chopstick.

> Or wilt thou in a yellow boxen bole
> Taste with a wooden splent the sweet lithe honey?
> The Affectionate Shepheard, p. 17.

Spon in agls. was 'a chip,' 'astula, putamen.' Gloss. Of þam treowe þæs halgan Cristes mæles sponas and sceafþan nimað. Bede. 524. 30. Lye. 'Of the tree (= wood) of the holy cross of Christ they take spoons (= chips) and shavings.' Spaan, dutch, is 'Splent, Splint,' and Spaander 'a chip,' "Daar men hakt daar vallen spaanders," 'where one hews there fall chips.' In the prose Edda also towards the end, Spænir is splinters.

> By water he sent adoun
> Light linden spon
> He wrot hem al with roun.
> Sir Tristrem, p. 119, ed. Scott.

Hence the phrase Spick and Span.

> Lo I make bothe hovens and erthe alle span newe.
> Myrour of Lewed Men. 1067.

By recollecting how P and K interchange, we see that Scandula, Shingle=germ. Schindel, are of the same root; which removes all that was strange in the expression of Snorri in the Edda. The word is used by him as chips for firing. Dasent tr. p. 86. byrðar af lokarspónum (p. 46. ed. 1848). Shingle I find, is nearly forgotten with the use of it; it is "a lath of cleft wood to cover houses with" (Kersey). Wooden slates is the full sense. Dach-verdekens (Kilian). Σκανδαληθρον is the splent in a bird trap, which falls when touched and brings down the trap (Acharn. 687); later authors use Σκανδαλον, Σκανδαλη in the same sense. Scamnum looks like a derivative of the same root, and if †skand were the rung of a ladder, Scandere would be explained. Scantling is a term in carpentry meaning the size to which wood is cut and seems of the same origin: this word along with Scant is closely connected with the isl. Skamtr 'modus, dimensio, portio,' at Skamta 'dividere, dimetiri,' and to be compared with Σπανιος. The harder forms remain in several words with us, but they mostly reject the N according to custom. Dan. Skinne 'a splint,' Skinne been = Shin bone = agls. Scinban = germ. Schienbein = dutch Scheenbeen = swed. Skenben. Shank = agls. Sceanca = dutch Schenk, Schenkel = germ. Schenkel. Skid for a wheel = isl. Skið 'lamina lignea' also 'snow shoe' = swed. Skid, 'snow shoe' = agls. Scide 'Scindula' (Gloss.), all these words having the notion of the latin Scindere. Schedula, Scheda is of the same origin but used for writing. So Skates. Σχεδη is a tablet, Σχεδια a raft. As consisting of a thin lath of wood, lamina lignea, Sheath = agls. Scæð = dansk. Skede = germ. Scheide = swed. Skida, which is, as it should be, also 'shell.'

> Swithe go shape a ship
> Of shides and of bordes.
>> Piers Ploughman, 5436, 6418.
> Mouth they haveth gret and wide,
> And a tonge as a schyde.
>> King Alisaunder, 6420.
> Myn baselard* ha3t a schede† of red.
>> Songs and Carols (Warton Club) p. 85.

---

* Baselard, long knife.   † Schede, sheath.

Since lamina lignea, a skid of wood, makes a dish, germ. Schotel, Schüssel 'a dish,' = agls. Scuttel = SCUTTLE. The norse Skutill is 'mensa parva,' a small table. Scot in Wainscot is of the same origin, Wain is Wagen, the walls, so that Wainscot is 'parietum lamina lignea.' The mœsogothic verb Skeidan = germ. Scheiden comes in of course along with these. Comparing Skeidan with Scindere the general opinion would be that as we have Scidi, Scissum, which is of course for †scid-sum = †sciditum, the N is inserted to strengthen the imperfect tenses; I have already hinted under πενθος, παθειν, that this conclusion is not always sound, and in the present case we shall find enough of N to shake the theory. In the mean time by side of Scindere, Scintilla, Σχεδη we have in Aristophanes Σχινδαλαμοι 'chips,' also Σχιζειν 'split.' Observe now that for all the most important significations above noticed we have also forms with P, as Spónn 'a chip,' a Spunk 'a spark' = germ. Funke, Σφην 'a wedge,' Σπινθηρ which is either Scintilla or a Spónn in the way of a broach; fibulam in humeris, to fasten the toga, aut armillam significat (Priscianus, V. 616). Σφονδυλος, Σπονδυλος in its various significations is no more. Sponda is a lath that holds the sacking of a bedstead. SPINDLE is usually a rod, as the axis of a wheel, and it seems very possible that the verb SPIN may be a derivative of Spónn. SPIT rejects the N : so SPADE, Spatula, Σπαθη which retain the notion of breadth; so the keltic Spatha 'sword,' for the keltic languages have the root in such a manner that the whole class answers to the teutonic. Some forms drop the S, as Cuneus 'wedge,' *i. e.* 'splitter,' Findere, that is, Scindere, for rude life made no distinction of sharp edges and blunt wedges, Κεαζειν (homeric), wrongly explained by Buttmann Lexil. 1. 12. Some forms terminate in labials, as SHIVE and all its relatives, Fibula, which is but Σπινθηρ or isl. Spensl, Spennill : add Scapula? Some end in L which is convertible with D, T, norse Skilja 'to divide' = agls. Scylan, round which assemble mœsog. Skalya 'a tile,' Skilva 'a knife,' to SKILL as 'it skills not,' an idiom belonging to other teutonic languages, as dutch " Dat scheelt veel," that makes a great difference. SCALE either of fish or balances,

U

being lamina, SHIELD=agls. Scyld, as formed of a lamina, SHELL, SILL=agls. Scel, SLATE for Sclate, SHALE, and more than one needs here recount.

> Was neuer wepen that euer was make
> That o* schel might therof take
> Na more than of the flint.
> Gy of Warwicke, p. 313.

I make no doubt but that Scale were the stails or steps of a ladder. Σκελος is to Skill as Shank to Scindere. SCABBARD =norse Scalpr is of this class, as Sheath of the other. Similarly Schiefer the german for 'slate.' SHAFT of a spear. Skill also becomes SPILL, as in a SPOOL 'a bobbin,' the game of SPILLIKINS, and SPILLS, matches for lighting pipes, =swed. Spjäll=germ. Spille; a spigot in a beer barrel is a SPILE, the verb in swedish 'split' is Spjälka, and the adjective Spjälkig, splintery; this verb is but germ. Spalten, our SPLIT, with subst. germ. Splitter=SPLINTER. Numerous other illustrations of the root may be found in the glossaries and teutonic languages: to pursue them further is not now much to the purpose. Σκολοψ 'a stake' is a derivative of this form; and a curious confirmation of the assertion is found in the use of the other word already discussed in the sense 'impale' which is almost always ανασκολοπιζειν: we have Τελευτων παντα κακα παθων ανασχινδυλευθησεται, Platon. Rep. II. p. 362. A, whence it is evident that σκολοψ=σχανδαλον. Whether the third consonants be considered interchangeable or not, a common root is found in Secare which was teutonic as well as latin. The main object of this article is to bring us round to the conclusion that Spoon and Σπενδειν are related: and hence Fundere. For what is Σπενδειν? To make a libation was to take with a ladle, say Spoon, some wine unmixed with water out of the wine bowl, pour it with the ladle into the hand, and fling it towards the skies, or towards the deity invoked. The significance of Σπενδεσθαι, 'make a truce,' arose from both parties dipping their spoons into one wine vessel and so engaging in a common religious ceremony, which stops hostile feeling. The roman name for the ladle was simpulum,

* o=one.

and "one of the most celebrated vases in the neapolitan collection was found with a bronze simpulum in it; upon the vase itself there was a sacrificial painting representing a priest in the act of pouring a libation from a vase with the simpulum." The ladle in greek is οινηρυσις, spoon μυστρον, the word Spoon I do not know except in the derivatives of Σπενδειν, or that verb itself. It is remarkable that in latin Libare is of religion, Fundere is not, in greek Λειβειν is not, Σπενδειν is. With the older harder K agls. Scencan to pour out drink, seems related to Σπενδειν. See Halliwell in Skink, Skinker for examples.

> To thame he birlis* and skynkis fast but† were†.
> Gawin Douglas, Lib. I.
>
> No sire, ne be þe day so long, þe while heo§ sitteþ o benche,
> And som of the nyȝt nymeþ‖ þerto, þe drinke for to shenche,
> Of an holi prechoures word heo nolde not so ofte þenche,
> As of the muri word, þat hem¶ þinkeþ of þo sely wenche**.
> Robert of Gloucester, p. 118.

Here one cannot help thinking of Rabshakeh, the chief butler, head-skink, and the verb שקה not occurring in kal, is found in hiphil, signifying Scencan. At any rate Σπενδειν cannot be separated in form from σπινθηρ and the other relatives of Spoon, nor can it be denied that a connexion in sense is visible. The shoulder has often taken its denomination from the broad shoulder blade; Shoulder=agls. Sculder=germ. Schulter=swed. Schuldra=dan. Skulder: these are of Skill. Scapula, 'the shoulder blade,' belongs rather to Shive. The sanskrit for shoulder Skandh-ah goes further back to Scindere. For the shoulder of a wild boar the proper form is Shield: "By eating of a sheelde of a wilde bore he got an appetite and after recovered" (Fulk FitzWarine: notes, p. 189). Spand is a rare english synonym for Shoulder, but the shoulders of the arches in architecture are constantly Spandrels. Sir Tristrem having stripped the hide from off the deer according to the right art of venerie, proceeds to cut up the carcase:

* Birlis, is acts the butler, agls. Byrel, pocillator, pincerna.
† But, without.   ‡ Were, wariness.   § Heo, they.!
‖ Nymeþ, take.   ¶ Hem, to them.   ** Wenche, Rowena.

> The spande was the first bredo*.
> P. 33, ed. Scott.

Take out N, and we have another form with the same sense, also our own broad SPADE for digging, and Espada 'sword.' Cf. art. 537.

> By th' shoulder of a ram from off the right side par'd
> Which usually they boil, the spade bone† being bar'd.
> — Drayton, Polyolbion, V.

Besides Shank the leg seems to be also SPANK; Spankers in Jamieson is 'long thin legs;' and the expressions to SPANK along, a Spanking pace, which are as much saxon english as lowland scotch, seem derivative, since the friesic and danish Spanke is 'to strut:' so welsh, Ysponcio 'to jet;' and 'to take long strides' is a fair notion of all.

1016. SAY. No one doubts but that, whatever be the correct spelling, ϵἰπεῖν would come from a lost verb ϵ̔πειν like ϵ̓́πος. The equivalent of this verb in latin was Secere. (Festus) Secessiones, narrationes. Again, Inseque apud Ennium, dic. Insexit, dixit. Gellius, XVIII. 9, dismisses the philological inquiries and quotes both Ennius,

> Inseque, Musa, manu Romanorum induperator
> Quod quisque in bello gessit cum rege Filippo :

and Cato, eiusmodi scelera nefaria, quae neque insecendo neque legendo audivimus : also Plautus Menaechm., Haec nihilo mihi videntur esse sectius quam somnia, which Gellius explains, nihilo magis narranda quam si ea essent somnia. There is another passage not mentioned by Gellius; Plautus, Miles Gl. IV. vi. 6, Cum ipso, pol, sum secuta : and there are some passages of Virgil and other authors which are ambiguous, as Sequitur sic deinde Latinus. To this root we must assign Sector 'a bidder' and Sectio 'a bidding at an auction,' as also Sectio 'a plea,' which Festus makes out as persecutio iuris, and draws from sequi 'follow,' as others from secare 'cut.' The identity of Secere 'to say' with agls. Secgan 'to say' is evident, and this brings us to the german Sagen

---

* The shoulder was the first quickly removed.
† It is lower down "shoulder blade."

and the english Say. Now as an R sometimes displaced a C, as Bacca = Berry, Sage = Saw = Serra, so there was a collateral form of Secere 'to say,' in Serere 'to say,' whence Sermo, Disserere, Asserere. Of Seegan another form was Specan, SPEAK and germ. Sprechen. Observe how another example runs off in the same manner. Sow = Serere = Σπειρειν..

Beyond, however, these clusters of words, others may be traced. Since the latin shows that the original root began with S, and since constant homeric usage and the actual characters of the eleian inscription prove that it was read with the digamma, it follows that an earlier form than any yet spoken of was Swee- Swer-, the latter of which is found in our ANSWER, in the norse Svara ' to answer,' Svar ' an answer,' and, losing the sibilants, in Verbum = Word. We may also conjecture that our own SWEAR = mœsog. Swaran was originally no more than Say. I should wish to add Hortari.

That the attic verb Ερειν, Ειρηκα is for Swer-, will be evident if the homeric form has the Vau. Heyne decided in the affirmative and with reason. The present occurs as Fειρειν: Od. β. 162, μνηστηρσιν δε μαλιστα πιφαυσκομενος ταδε Fειρω: v. 7, similarly; λ. 136, ολβιοι εσσονται ταδε τοι νημερτεα Fειρω. Il. Δ. 182; ως ποτε τις Fερεει: so Z. 162; Il. 91. In I. 56, ουδε παλιν Fερεει. The passage Δ. 176 may be thus amended, και ποτε τις Fερεει. ψ. 793, Αντι-λοχ' ου μεν τοι μελεος Fειρησεται αινος. The other passages are ambiguous. It appears therefore that Fειρειν = agls. Swerian and is the present tense of ειπον, and = †επειν = secere.

In the sanskrit are several words to be referred to this root, and those that mean 'speak' lose the S, answering, as sanskrit words do, to the radix Swee- seen in the agls. Sweg 'a sound.' The greek as early as Homer has dropped a large number of initial sibilants, and the equivalent of agls. Sweg is lat. Vocem = homeric Fοπα. There is not much difficulty in reading all the passages in the iliad and odyssey with the restored Vau. In Λ. 137, δ' Fοπ' ακουσον by Bentleys theory; φ. 92, Σ. 222, λ. 421, Ξ. 150; the hiatus in ευρυFοπα is

removed. Not quite so easy is ε. 61, δαιομενων, ἡ δ᾽ αϝοι-
διαουσ᾽ ϝοπι καλῃ, but restore αειδουσα σϝοπι καλῃ, like
σϝεκυρε in Γ. 172. The verb αϝοιδαειν is of a suspicious
form and may be banished from Homer by writing in κ. 227,
αειδησιν, as now read in I. 519.

By the rejection of SW in Swer, the attic forms already
mentioned, the messenger goddess Ιρις, and our Errand are
almost historically deducible. Hither also refer the Ειρεας
αθανατων of Hesiodos (Theog. 801) and till something better
be brought up Ειρηνη, ϝειρηνη.

The moesogothic presumed simple verb Aikan 'to affirm,'
may come from swee- by rejection of S, and compensation
for Vau. From Aikan reject the guttural and we obtain
lat. Aio, which has an affirmative force.

The hebrew has שִׂיחַ 'to speak,' as subst. ' sermo:' in
semitic vocalization vau=yod, and may represent the consonantal vau in Swee.

The sanskrit forms are वच् 'speak,' वम् ' a speaker,' derivatives of वाक्, वाग् or वाच्, स्वृ, making in 3rd person स्वरति,
and the cognates of Sonus, Φωνη.

It appears likely that further back than all these lay an
earlier root †kwek, nearly Quack, and represented by agls.
Cweðan, which we retain in Bequeath, the norse Cveða,
moesog. Kwiþan, in QUOTH and perhaps Quote. The past
tense survives in Quoth. That words are often imitations of
sounds we know by experience. If quack, quek, seems one of
these, like our quack of ducks, cackle of geese, and Aristophanes Κοαξ of frogs, some perhaps of the words for mouth
may have arisen from it. If Osculum were †kosculum, †kose
was Os; a sibilate form, to be compared with friesic Keek
' mouth,' our CHEEK, very widely applied, like Bucca, Bouche,
and perhaps Gag.

1017. GWAL, GUL in Gula, Glutire, Ingluvies, sanskr.
Gal ' to eat,' Gili-ah, ' swallowing,' eng. GULP=norse Gleypa
= dutch Gulpen, germ. Kehle ' throat,' lat. Collum 'neck,'
agls. Ceolas ' fauces,' may have come from an early Kw-l, giving
by sibilation Swallow=agls. Swelgan, and Swill. It seems

impossible but that Γλωσσα 'tongue' should be connected with it; and if so we must of consequence hold that the following have lost an initial G: Λαιμασσειν, Λαπτειν, Λαυκανιη throat (Ω. 612), Λαφυσσειν, Λειχειν, Λεγειν, Lingua, Lingere, Lambere, Labium, Lick=agls. Liccian = germ. Lecken=mœsog. Laigon (in a comp.), Lip. Χειλος retains the initial. It is very remarkable that the hebrew forms are all read without the G, while the evident similarity of לָשׁוֹן γλωσσα will not permit us to question the affinity. We have לָקַק, לָחַךְ 'he licked,' לוּעַ 'to swallow,' לַע 'gula,' לָעַט 'he gulped, avide edit,' לֶחֶם 'food, bread.' The welsh has Llafar 'speech,' Llef 'a voice,' Llcibio 'to lap or lick,' Llwnc 'a gulp, the gullet,' irish Liobar 'a lip,' Líogar 'a tongue,' Leagaim 'I lick:' gaelic Slugan 'gullet.' Call קוֹל, and agls. Galau 'sing' are not far off. SLOBBER, SLAVER appear, when compared with the friesic and bremish equivalents, to belong to this group: they mean 'lick' about Holland (so Kilian). That γαλακ-τος, the hardest known form for Milk, with its correspondent synonyms in the various languages are related, is probable from the consideration that milk must be in a pastoral nomad life, the chief article to be swallowed, and it should not be forgotten that γαλακτ-ος must have the τ significant, perhaps as a passive participle of a verb, as †gwelgan=swelgan. The identity of the root in G-L with that in G-R has always been asserted by the sanskrit philologues. See the sanskrit index. Thus †gwal = welsh Gwar 'neck,' old engl. Swere, art. 698, analogous to Swallow. The latin has Gurges 'a swallow, a swallower' as in Fabius Gurges; Gurgulio ' the throat.'

The root in R is somewhat antiquated in the teutonic, the islandic has Qverk, Kverk, the friesic Querke 'throat;' the old english has Querken 'to suffocate,' and, dropping the guttural, the german Würgen 'to strangle:' dogs that WORRY sheep, take them by the throat.

1018. GEL as in Γελειν, in Gleam and its group as in art. 322, seems to lose G in Lumen and its group, to take labials in Flamma, Blaze and their group, art. 529, to sibilate the G in Σελας, Σεληνη, to be connected by colour with Gold, Gilvus, Yellow, etc., though these may also be referred to γαλα.

1019. DRY. The numerous derivatives of a hebrew root identical with Χηρ-ος, Χερ-σος seem to correspond so closely with the teutonic Dorr, and the latin Torr-ere, etc., that a commutation of initial letters may be presumed. See § 478 and 1006. That Terra is only a feminine adjective meaning Dry with a fem. subs. suppressed as in patria, appears in a striking way by the swedish translation of Genesis i. 10. Och Gud kallade det torra Jord.

1020. GLABER 'smooth,' GLIB, GLIDE seem to lose the initial in Labi, Lubricus, and to sibilate it in SLIP, SLIDE, SLEDGE, SLEEK, SLUG, SLINK, with germ. Schlange = dan. Slange 'a snake,' קָלַל, קְלַל.

1021. CLAMMY, CLING, CLEAVE, CLAY, Κολλα 'glue,' seem to lose the initial in Limus 'mud,' Lutum 'clay,' Limax 'snail,' perhaps in Linere, in Lentus, Lithe, Limp, and to sibilate it in SLIME, SLOUGH, SLUDGE. This group is near to the preceding: Daub in Gen. vi. 14, is agls. Clæman. Clamm is 'mortar' (Exod. i. 14), 'clamp,' and 'malagma, poultice.'

1022. To FLAG, FLABBY, FLAP, words which are not easily traced historically, Flaccus, Flaccidus seem related to Χαλαν 'to loose,' and as in § 812 to Laxus, Lucre, Luxus, Luxuria, Languescere, with sibilation SLACK, SLOW, SLUT, SLATTERN: whether to Lap, Lappet, Fimbria, Fringe is less clear.

1023. GULL, GOLD, GALL, Χολη, Χολος 'anger,' YELLOW, Gilvus, become Fulvus, Flavus, Fallow, Βαλιος? Badius? Bay? and with sibilation SALLOW.

> His eyen holwe and grisly to behold,
> His hewe fadwe and pale as ashen cold.
> Chaucer, C. T. 1366.

1024. QUICK is more fully written in the norse with two Kôfs: Kvikr, pl. nom. Kvikv-ir, participial substantive Kvikvendi n. pl. Its affinities in Vivere, Βιωναι, Βιος, Βεη, breton Béva = welsh Byw 'live,'

οὔ θην οὐδ' αὐτὸς δηρὸν βέῃ, ἀλλά τοι ἤδη
ἄγχι παρέστηκεν θάνατος καὶ μοῖρα κραταιή.
Il. Π. 852.

in words signifying strength, as Κικυς, Βιη, Ϝις, Vis, with the hebrew developments of the root, have been alluded to before (335, 1005).

ἀλλ' οὐ γάρ Ϝοι ἔτ' ἦν Ϝὶς ἔμπεδος οὐδέ τι κίκυς.
Od. λ. 393.

νῦν δέ μ' ἐὼν ὀλίγος τε καὶ οὐτιδανὸς καὶ ἄκικυς
ὀφθαλμοῦ ἀλάωσεν.
ι. 515.

It affords a home for the ancient root Be, Fuisse, Fore = Φυναι, the causative Φυειν, the sanskrit Bhu. Αιων, Αιει, Ævum, Ever, Æternus, sanskr. Ay-ah have been mentioned: we are told that Αιων seems to be used for spinal marrow, the 'quick' of the body. Farmers and gardeners are vexed sometimes by a grass very tenacious of life; if a single joint of the running root be left in the ground, it springs into growth: it is called in Norfolk Quicken, and elsewhere Couch-grass, a mistake for Quitch. The same word is also Wick, Οικος for Ϝικος, Vicus, places to live in, Hive it appears by the mœsogothic had the same sense, and may be assumed to have the same origin. Αστυ = Ϝαστυ, with the sanskrit, is perhaps a sibilate form. It is also Wax = agls. Wacsian = mœsog. Wahsian = norse Vaxa: and Wake = agls. Wacian = mœsog. Wakan translating γρηγορειν, αγρυπνειν; Vigil, Vigere; and Queo 'I am able.' Do Eke = Augere, Egg on = agls. Eggian = norse Eggja, and Εγειρειν belong to it?

1025. An old root †kwan 'white,' which appears in welsh Gwyn 'white,' lat. Canus, sinking the vau, as in Canis, breton Kann, Gwenn, sanskrit Kan 'splendere,' has many affinities. We have the sibilate form in Swan, the white bird, perhaps in Swoon = agls. A-swunan, in agls. Swinan Swindan 'to languish,' in Wan 'pale,' a loss of the guttural, whence Wane, both agls. On the sanskrit Swan 'dog' = Κυνα = Canem, see 694. On Gander see 1018. Cuniculus 'rabbit' may be 'the little white one,' from the tame variety: the word is like the others, a problem. From the notion of whiteness it seems scarce possible to separate that of burning with a bright blaze, as Candet is near to Incendere, Accendere, KINDLE, welsh Cynneu. The resinous tree that burns brightly is called in the agls. runesong Cen, the german Kien, which, as appears to me, cannot be very different from Κωνος the seed-vessel of the same tree, nor Κωνησαι 'to pitch.' In these I recognize, with softer P, the latin Pinus, hereupon superseding Buttmanns idea of †picnus, which was previously acceptable. Candere (see art. 884), with dental for guttural, appears in the mœsog. Tandyan = germ. Zünden, producing TINDER, erse, gaelic Teinne 'fire.' This form of the root gives by rejecting N the latin Tæda 'a torch' or 'a fir-tree,' and Δᾳδα (acc.) 'a torch.' The following has been misunderstood.

> Tho that weren in hevene
> Token stella cometa
> And tendeden it as a torche
> To reverencen his burthe.
> Piers Ploughman, 12554.

קדח 'kindled fire,' קנא 'burned with jealousy.' It may be that sanskr. Kam 'to love,' erse Caemh 'love,' lat. Amare, hebrew חָם 'hot,' חמד 'he desired,' הֶמְאָה 'thickened milk' thickened by heat probably, חמם 'was hot,' חָמָם 'violence, injury,' as arising from a heated mind, חָמֵץ 'what is fermented,' חֹמֶץ 'vinegar,' as fermented, חמר 'æstuavit,' חֵמָר 'bitumen,' as combustible, Ἵμερος 'desire,' כמר 'was scorched,' are all of this group. Either CLEAN = welsh Glân = irish Glan = agls. Clæne may be obtained by changing V or W to L, or from the root Γελ, GL 'shine,' or else all these are connected among themselves.

1026. Round some such form as the sanskrit Kumbh-ah 'a water jar,' may be grouped a considerable number of words, and one or two of them seem to afford instruction and novelty. Let us consider that a calabash is naturally one of the earliest water vessels, and that the Kumbh would be probably something of the PUMPKIN, PUMPION kind, belonging to the same root therefore as Cucumis 'cucumber.'

The facility with which letters change leads us to believe that Cucurbita = Gourd, germ. Gurke or Kurke (Wachter) 'a cucumber,' with our Gurkins 'small cucumbers for pickling,' and, with initial, Αγγουρον 'a cucumber,' a word of glossarial and late greek, 'water melon?' french Courge 'gourd,' spanish Pepino 'cucumber' are all reasonably referred to the same root. So Κολοκυνθις 'cucurbita silvatica,' dutch Quint Appel (Kilian). To which as gourd shaped add

The stomachs comforter the pleasing Quince.

In this cluster we have a considerable number of forms, and they easily connect themselves with others, too easily, no doubt, to make out much of a proof. Supposing then that we have seen enough of letter changes, we may most conveniently here arrange by significations. It ought to cause no exception if we meet with forms implying an earlier †kwambh, reduced to the sanskrit †kumbh by vocalization of the W. Cup has been already mentioned with its allies at art. 865. Add Αγγος 'a vessel.' Hanap=agls. Hnæp 'a cup,' Hamper, Can, the agls. word Cyf 'dolium, cadus, modius,' an ancient greek word κερ recognizable in Κεραμος and in Κεραμευς 'a potter,' equivalent to mœsog. Kas, 'σκευος,' latin Vas, norse Ker (neuter), danish Kar; Carchesia. With S prefixed Σκυφος, Scoor = germ. Schüppe = dutch Skop, welsh Cafnio 'to scoop.' כב 'a cup.' From the use of all vessels, say originally a gourd, a calabash, for holding and containing liquids, we come to Capax, Capere in the same sense, Χανδανειν, Χαδειν, our Hold (for Hent). From the hollowness, Cavus, welsh Caf, gaelic Cobha. From the hollowness of the hand or the roundness of the fist, Hand, Manus for mandus, as in Mandare, a possible greek root of the same form, a teutonic root of the same form, mand, or mund, a greek root of the form πεμπ meaning hand, Pungere 'to punch,' Pugnus 'fist,' Pugil 'boxer,' the greek adverb Πυξ, Κονδυλος 'fist,' כַּף 'the hand,' חָפְנַיִם 'the two fists,' the sanskrit Pâni-ah 'the hand.' That mand 'hand' was an old greek root there is tolerable evidence in Μαρπτειν 'catch' and in the line, out of Agamemnons oath that he had never touched Briscis,

ἀλλ' ἔμεν' ἀπροτίμαστος ἐνὶ κλισίῃσιν ἐμῇσιν.
T. 263.

The latin Manus is, according to the custom of language (tegmen = tegmentum, lentus = lenis), not different from †mandus: Mandare is to 'hand to one:' Masturbare changes N before a dental, as in the above line from the Iliad. Mund 'hand' is in the agls., in the norse of the older Edda, and in some old teutonic proper names, as Cunimundus, Kuhn Mund 'Boldhand,' Ruodmunt 'Redhand.' That the greeks would have such a form as †πεμπ 'hand' might pretty well follow from pungere and κονδυλος. It seems to be at the base of the verb Πεμπειν, one of the senses of which is 'escort,' most easily first 'take by the hand, lead by the hand, hand.' It is strongly confirmed as affording a good solution of the difficult word δυσπεμφελος in Hesiodos,

καὶ τοῖς, οἳ γλαυκὴν δυσπέμφελον ἐργάζονται.
Theogon. 440*.

μηδὲ πολυξείνου δαιτὸς δυσπέμφελον εἶναι
ἐκ κοινοῦ· πλείστη δὲ χάρις, δαπάνη τ' ὀλιγίστη.
Works and Days, 667.

In the first of these, if πεμπ means hand, δυσπεμφελος is 'hard to handle, hard to deal with,' in the second 'hard handed, close fisted.' Cf. also Pampinus the tendril or hand of a vine (also shoot). Among the rest χειρ may stand, and we need not be frightened at making the verb Kri in sanskrit, the car- in Carmen, a secondary notion. With it Καρπος 'wrist,' Palpere? Palma? GRAB and all its equivalents. GROPE = agls. Grapian is connected with Grasp by the common root signifying 'hand.' After the word Hand should stand some of the notions which belong to hand and Κονδυλος. First HOLD, which I take to be an altered form of the moesog. Hinpan, to Hend, an old english word = norse Henda, in the same way as agls. Cild = germ. Kind = Γονος, lat. Hendere in prehendere, Ansa.

* Cf. Iliad, Π. 748.

Told men whose watchful eyes no slumber bent
What store of hours their guilty night had spent.
W. Browne, B. P. II. i.

Then from a form closer to the hebrew Kaf, Capere 'take,' Habere 'hold, have,' HAVE = agls. Habban, Hæbban = mœsog. Haban = norse. Hafa : KEEP = agls. Cepan ; Hoor : mœsog. Fahan = germ. Fangen = agls. Fon = norse Fa 'lay hold of,' whence FINGERS, FANGS. קָבַץ 'prehendit,' welsh Cafael ' to hold,' gaelic Gabh 'take,' and so erse. If Fast be from holding, then mœsog. þwastyan shews the loss of W in Fangen. Then FIGHT = Pugnare = agls. Feohtan with FIST = germ. Faust, sibilations. Boxing is an artificial olympic exercise, and the word was probably adopted in times when the saxon lips had not yet learned the letter P. Another old teutonic word of the same sense was Camp, whence CHAMPION = agls. Cempa = germ. Kämpfer = norse Kappi by assimilation. Camping with ball is still preserved in the eastern counties; an account of the game may be seen in Moore's Suffolk Glossary.

<blockquote>
In medow or pasture, to grow the more fine,
Let campers be camping in any of thine.
Tusser, December, p. 64, ed. Mavor.

Get campers a ball,
To camp therewithal.
Tusser, p. 56.
</blockquote>

It may well be imagined that in this sense every GAME is a Camping. GRAB with its equals, art. 287. Carpere, Sarpere, Ἐρέπτειν, Crop, Δρέπειν may be another set, but it would seem that Δράττεσθαι, Δράγματα contain the notion of 'hand,' and are very near Δρέπειν : they lead on to Drag, art. 476. As derivatives of Hand, words meaning a handful, עֹמֶר, קֹמֶץ, Pugillus, Manipulus, Merges, like mordere from mund. Κώπη in attic ' handle of a sword or oar ' is negatived by the homeric usage of its cognates. Cf. Garb 'a sheaf' especially with Grab, art. 780.

<blockquote>
Great Ensham's * fertile glebe what tongue hath not extol'd
As though to her alone belong'd the garb of gold.
Drayton, Polyolbion, XIII.
</blockquote>

---

* Ensham = Evesham.

Some names of vessels neither cups nor casks, Cymba 'a boat,' Λμβιξ 'olla;' with initial S, Σκαφος, irish Scafa, Ship, Skiff. In signification near to these are Himmel=Heaven=agls. Heofon = mœsog. Himins = norse Himinn = שָׁמַיִם a dual form, with the æthiopic in the singular, both these sibilating the initial, sanskr. Sûm 'sky' (morn), and we might suppose Cœlum, Κοιλος to have lost a letter as if †cavilus, with adjectival L. Then come several words which have like a gourd something spherical in their form: welsh Camp 'a circle,' with a long list of keltic words its neighbours, our Camp, מַחֲנֶה 'a camp,' the radical syllable being חֵן, which in חנה seems to agree. Κωμη 'village,' Ham. The various senses of גַב '1. back of animals and men, 2. boss of shield, 3. fortress, 4. circuit of wheels,' agree very well with many senses of our varied forms. כּוֹמָז 'globus?' כּוֹבַע 'helmet,' Cincinni, Umbo, Ομφαλος which on this supposition could not be identified with Navel. Γομφος, Ογκος, Ορχις, Αμφι=agls. Ymb=germ. Um, Αμβων 'crest of hills,' Hummock, Hump, with its equivalents (art. 869) and cognates as Κυπτειν, Cam (art. 87), Γογγυλος 'round,' חָמוּק, Hamus 'hook,' Humilis 'humplike, bentlike' rather than 'groundlike,' Mamma?, and possibly with dental "the whirling Top." The coats of a clove of garlic are Αγγλιθες, Αγλιθες, which seems by assimilation to produce Allium. These forms are so like many others here debated, that they may derive their name from the same root, or one of the roots involved, and thus also the sanskrit for garlick is Kand-ah or -an. The names of some animals with round backs as Camel, חֲמוֹר 'ass,' this explanation better agreeing with the equivalent ονος Κανθηλιος with his round back; οἱ δη πιεζομενοι ὑπο βαρους ανω κυρτουνται, ὡσπερ οἱ ονοι οἱ κανθηλιοι, Xen. Kyrop. VII. v. 11. Κανθυλη 'a swelling.' Κανθαρος, Chafer=germ. Käfer. Words implying such a hollowness as to hold in the manner of vessels, as Κυμβαλον, Κενεων, Venter, Womb, and their allies. Words implying hollowness as of a cup, Combe=welsh Cwm=עֵמֶק 'valley' with Campus, if a little distorted in sense. Κενος 'empty;' with the dental, Toom=agls. Tom 'empty'=dan. Tom. Combe is to Kumbh, as the usual welsh word for a defile Bwlch is to Bwlg, which is one with our Bag, Belly, Bulk, etc. art. 394, and why not Vallis? Some which are ring shaped, as Κανθος 'tire of a wheel;' the welsh has Can-fys = Can+Bys = ring+finger, latin Annulus, Αμπυξ, welsh Cant 'rim of a circle.'

The head as gourd shaped, a human calabash, may be compared with the rest. Homer expresses head foremost by Κυμβαχος.

αὐτὰρ ὃ ῥ' ἀσθμαίνων εὐεργέος ἔκπεσε δίφρου
κύμβαχος ἐν κονίῃσιν ἐπὶ βρεχμόν τε καὶ ὤμους.
E. 585.

The same action is expressed by κυβισταν applied to a diver.

ὁ δ' ἄρ' ἀρνευτῆρι ἐοικὼς
κάππεσ' ἀπ' εὐεργέος δίφρου, λίπε δ' ὀστέα θυμός.
τὸν δ' ἐπικερτομέων προσέφης, Πατρόκλεις ἱππεῦ·
Ὢ πόποι, ἦ μάλ' ἐλαφρὸς ἀνήρ. ὡς ῥεῖα κυβιστᾷ, etc.
Π. 742.

It appears, then, that the radical syllable in Κεφαλη, Caput, Κυβη, Kopf, Haupt, præ-ceps, agls. Heafod, Head, might be in Homers time as well expressed by Κυμβ-. The norse has in composition another form, Fimbul, which will be found in the Sæmundar Edda. Top=swed. Topp as related to Cop has been before spoken of. I do not see how we can reconcile Tumble with the popular wandering Tumblers without supposing the verb to signify 'go on the head:' the agls. Tumbian is used to express the dancing of the daughter of Herodias; and I have read somewhere that the tradition of the roman church represents her as dancing on her head. Topple is clearly used for fall on the head, or causatively:

Shake the old beldame earth and topple down
Steeples and moss grown towers.
I. Henry IV. iii. 1.

Though castles topple on their warders heads.
Macbeth, iv. 1.

This sense embraces Titubare and Stumble, nor is it inconsistent with Luthers Taumeln in Ps. cvii. 27; Isaiah xxviii. 7, li. 17. The dutch Tuimelen has the two senses of the english. When the agls. glossaries translate Tumbian Saltare, it is in its wide sense, which embraced every sort of pantomime and buffoonery: so where Aut Satyrum aut agrestem Cyclopa movetur, the prose word was Saltat.

The words for HEAP, HUMP, HUNCH, MOUND, Cumulus, Acervus if the A be a prefix, חָמוֹר, Copia, Montem (acc.), mœsog. Fairguni = agls. Firgen = agls. Beorh, Beorg = germ. Berg = engl. BERG, as in iceberg, and, changing C to a dental, Tumulus, Tumere, Τυμβος, rejecting M, Ταφος with Θαπτειν, a TUMP, may be also inserted. The agls. word Beorg, a BARROW, whence we obtain the verb BURY, is nearly identical with Beorg 'a hill.' DOWN, the keltic Dun, as in London, Lugdunum, Sorbiodunum, is a teutonic word very similar in form to Tum-ulus, and applied in the same manner. In Condés battle of the Dunes near Dunkirk, the Dunes were Sandhills. In the english Downs we have generally chalk: in friesic, where some say Düm (Molbech), sand or snow: isl. Dyngja 'a heap:' old dutch Dwynje 'to swell.' Turgere, Turgidus are not impossible: compare them with dutch Pompoelie 'mater crassa, ventricosa,' and our PAMPER.

The bend of the arms presents a sort of annulus, κανθος; it is expressed by Cubitus, Αγκυλη, Αγκων, whence Αγχου, Εγγυς, Αγχι 'near, at ones elbow.' Οργυια? FATHOM = agls. Fæþm, which signifies also an embrace between the arms, seems to come from Fangen, as isl. Baþmr = mœsog. Bagms. Angulus, and NOOK, which has borrowed its N from the article An, = germ. Ecke = friesic Huk = Hoeck in Kilian: cf. germ. Winkel. Similarly Uncus, Aduncus, Αγχιστρον, Αγκυρα, Σκαμβος, Καμπτειν, Hamus, HOOK, ANCLE, the game HOCKEY or Bandy, played with hooked or bent sticks.

From the notion of sphericity may have arisen Pinguis, Παχυς, Fat, etc., and, with dentals, Thumb = germ. Daum = agls. þuma = swed. Tum = dan. Tommelfinger. THICK = isl. Þungr: DUMPY: Κοσμος: Mundus.

If Venter, Womb be conceded to be from a root †kw-n, or †kw-mb, all the words connected with Gignere, Γυνη will come in: and the dental form which appears in Toom 'empty' will shew itself in this sense by Teem=agls. Teamian.

By the change of V or W to L come in Clump, Lump, teutonic words, with perhaps Glomus, Globus, Plump, Clunis; κλινειν however, Lean seem too distant. The welsh has Clamp 'a mass, a lump,' Clap 'a lump, a knob,' Clob 'a knob, a boss,' Clopa 'a knob, noddle, club,' Clowyn 'a knob, boss.' In connexion with the family of Kin, Gignere, as originally, which may be asserted, from †kwen, the change of W to L produces the erse and gaelic Clan, which expresses welsh Plant 'children.'

Besides all these we shall be able to embrace the large list of words which imply roundness and have K-R or equivalent letters, sometimes with a third consonant, as Circ-um, Corona, Cardines, Circ-a, Curv-us, Gird, agls. Cyrran, whence Ajar,

The auld kene tegir with his teith on char.
Dunbar, p. 50. ed. 1788.

Urbs, Orbis with loss of initial, Ἑρκος, fully in Ἑρκος οδοντων, the teeth set in a circle, Carcer, Ορχεισθαι, Γυρινος, a tadpole from its roundness, Girlond, Garland, Crank as in the citation art. 130, Crook, Crumple, and the semitic words which explain Carth-ago. Of the cornish Gosgordd, Zeuss (1095) says that the irish Cuairt is 'ambitus, circuitus,' the welsh Cordd is 'tribe, circle.' (See art. 272, 1011.) Heart and its equivalents, Kernel, Core. Those also which have KW-R, or its milder forms as Quern, Vertere, Wring, Writhe, Wrist, Screw, Wriggle, Wrinkle (see art. 893, 336, etc.). To these add others of the same sense commencing with a dental as Tornus, Turbinem (acc.), Torquere (art. 610), Στρεφειν, Στρογγυλος, Strombus, Strobilus, with irish Cúar 'crooked, perverse,' cf. agls. þwær, our Thwart. Dwarf=norse Dvergr =germ. Zwerg=welsh Cor, may be referred to this band. Drill, Trundle also, for Trent in friesic is Bezirk, Kreis, and Omtrent = omkring. Round is supposed to be from Rotundus, but the O contributes nothing, germ. Rund, dutch Rond; I suspect it to be for †trund.

In the method here pursued of assembling as it were a number of forms bearing unlike significations in a speculative

manner round some centre I confess to a certain fancifulness.
The reasoning is not cogent. But for any one willing to
compare english with greek and latin, this conjectural method
is the only one which can lead to results; authority wholly
fails us.

1027. TWAIN. Several words seem derivatives of the agls.
Twegen. Tusser calls ewes which bear Twins by the name
Twiggers. Twine=isl. Twinni is with B. H. filum dupli-
catum, dobbelt Garn, doubled yarn. To Twine is isl. swed.
Twinna, duplicare, copulare. The mœsog. Tweifls = germ.
Zweifel 'doubt,' is from this root: so Twill, a kind of cloth.
Twig = germ. Zweig = agls. Twig, is in the danish Tvege, a
forked branch, and one thinks whether Surculus may = †fur-
culus. The friesic Tjug' is a great wooden fork for throwing
straw or hay, and Sveinn Tiugu-skegg was "Sveno furcatæ
barbæ cognomento clarus." Chaucer uses Twinne, 'depart.'

> Now draweth cutte or that ye forther twinne
> He which that hath the shortest shall begin.
> C. T. 837.

Hence, with loss of W, I would draw Tie, cf. friesic Teeg, and
Tether, and as Bini, Bis drop the D, so hence may come Bind,
Vincire, though recorded in the sanskrit; consider also whether
Weave may be a derivative. See sanskr. index.

1028. HEEL = Calcem with λαξ for †καλακις. HAIL =
χαλαζα. HILL = Collis = Κολωνη. These words present difficulties apparently all of the same kind. The dutch Hiel
compared with the friesic Hájel and Hägel, seems to add an
afformative L to the Hacke of lower Saxony and Kilian,
meaning Heel. The isl. Haki is interpreted by B. H. as
extremitas cuinsvis rei, Hann vard í hakanum 'things went
wrong with him:' the german Hackbalk, Hackbort, is part
of the stern of a ship. Hacke, our Hock, is also the midway
joint of a horses leg, in some sense the extremity. If Heel
be a contraction of †hackel how can it be one with Calcem?
Hail also = agls. Hagol = germ. Hagel is less like χαλαζα as
it is traced back. Of Hill = germ. Hügel the root is Hoch,
High, and how can it answer to Collem (acc.)? The isl.
Hialli seems to shew the steps of the contraction, and suggests

that FELL=norse Fiall may be of the same origin. Are we then to suppose that Calx, Collis, χαλαζα are also contractions? Another set of words has a claim to be compared with Calcem. Walking as applied to clothes is the employment to this day of young women in our far off corners of the land; they lay the clothes in a running stream and trample them with their feet; hence the proper name Walker means fuller. In this process, and in the ordinary use of the verb WALK we have a strong resemblance to lat. Calcare. The agls. Welm is the sole of the foot. LUKE if agls. Wlæc, may with Wylm 'heat,' Wellian 'to be hot,' in like manner be compared with Calidus, Calere.

1029. The words Σκεπαζειν, and isl. at Skyggia 'obumbrare,' seem to contain a notion common to many other words beginning with Sc or altered from Sc; SKY was of old 'cloud,' as in the norse, the long vowel representing the two letters -yg-; it is probable that a similar usage of Νεφος for sky occurs in the keltic languages; the first verse of the bible in welsh is, Yn y dechreuad y creodd Duw y nefoedd a'r ddaer, where we recognize "creavit Deus nubes et terram:" in the irish, Sann tosach do chruthaidh Dia neamh agus talamh, "creavit Deus nubes (b=m) et tellurem." SHAW=norse Skôgr, SHADE=agls. Scadan=germ. Schatten=irish Scath= Σκια perhaps for †σκιδη; SHELTER illustrated by isl. at Skýla 'protegere, defendere;' SKIN=agls. Scin, Σκηνη 'tent' both as shelter and as made most easily of the skins of the hecatombs, Obscœnus 'covered up,' Obscurus, perhaps SACK. Shield as ending with the D of the passive participle is better referred to Skill.

1030. The sanskrit Bhrâj 'to shine' is very like to our Bright, and the consonants B-R-G are the old letters of the word, as appears from agls. Beorht=mœsog. Bairhts; the sanskrit J is the usual softening of a guttural. Losing a letter the sanskrit gives in the same sense Râj, which is akin with Αργος 'white,' Argentum, Αργυρος. Observe now that this enables us to say without incorrectness that these last words have lost a B, and are for †Βαργος, †Βαργυρος, †bargentum, a conclusion we should not easily have accepted. The root seems to be visible in Purgare, Φαρμακα, perhaps Purus, the long vowel compensating for the lost G. The hebrew gives us a cognate בָּרָק 'lightning' and ברר for בר especially in the Niphal, Piel, Hiphil and Hithpael, with בְּרִית 'res purgatoria, res purgandi vim habens.' These last exhibit the biconsonantal radix.

The sanskrit grammarians derive Râjah from Râj to shine; but this word is so like to Regem that it cannot be separated. The speculation of these grammarians is of no more value than the conjecture of other people; but it seems very probable that Regem was once †bregem. To what may be seen in the sanskrit index I add here that in welsh Baran is WREN, which is in latin Regulus. The radix, whatever it be, should account for Regere in the sense 'draw a right line,' and Rectus, Arrigere; with this sense Brachium agrees well, and to it I look for the kingly notion.

1031. The element KR=GR, sometimes softened to WR, makes many words relating to the action of cutting tools upon stone and earth, and it is supposed to be a representation of the GRATING sound. These words are secondarily applied to similar processes, where the sound is not so discernible or not perceived at all. To GRAVE, a GRAVE, GRUB, a GRIP=agls. Groep 'ditch,' WRITE, EAR, art. 105; germ. Graben 'a ditch,' Graben 'to carve, cut, dig,' Grube 'hole, pit,' Grübeln, frequentative of our Grub, Gruft 'pit,' Kratzen, to SCRATCH, art. 664, SCRAPE, Kritzeln, to scratch, to SCRAWL; Χαρασσειν, Χαραξ, Γραφειν, Ἀρπη, Αρουν, Ορυσσειν, lat. Scribere, Arare. With L for R, Γλυφειν, Sculpere. Probably Corn, Gravel, Grit, Granum. Κειρειν seems rather to belong to See-arc. The hebrew has several kindred forms, חרשׁ, 1. insculpsit literas tabulæ (once), 2. aravit (often); חָרָשׁ, 1. sculptor (once), 2. faber (often); חֶרֶט 'scalprum, tornus, stylus,' חָרוּץ 'fossa,' חֶרֶב ἁρπη, אִגֶּרֶת 'a letter' in Nehemiah, Esther; כרה 'dug,' כרת 'cut,' מַחֲרֶשֶׁת 'ploughshare.'

Ἀλλ' ἁρπας τε χαρασσεμεναι και δμωας εγειρειν.
Hesiodos, W. D. 533.

חָרוּץ 'gold' seems to be properly coin, κεχαραγμενον. Αγγαρος is a persian letter carrier, and Αγγελος is probably formed out of it.

1032. Sec of the latin Secare occurs in Sax, from which the Saxons are said to take their name : Sax 'a sword, dagger, knife,' " Cultelli nostra lingua Sachs dicuntur" (Witikind). " Usus huius vocis hodie dum in Saterlandia obtinct apud incolas prisci sermonis retinentissimos, apud quos, ut coram audivi loquentes, Sachs cultrum sonat" (Schaten, Hist. Westphaliæ) (from Outzen). Seax, Culter (Ælfrics gloss.), Sithe for †sigþ=isl. Sigþ=friesic Segd. With these cf. the skythian Sagaris. Sickle is a latin provincialism. To this root I refer Shear, Score, and Κειρειν for σκειρειν, Curtus=short for †scurtus, rather than to art. 1031. The Scars, Scaurs of the north as in Scarborough, it is agreed belong to this root.

1033. Ξηρος, Dry. These words have been compared in art. 1006. Hence Terra=Χερσος, Χωρα, and all the words which in greek and hebrew are akin to Ξηρος find expression in the teutonic and latin by a †tor or a †dor : art. 478.

1034. Calculus seems to come from a root identical with the gaelic Clach 'a stone'=perhaps eng. Flag 'a flat stone' =welsh Llech (id.) = irish Leacht (id.) = perhaps Lapis=Λιθος. The root πλακ=flat makes these conclusions doubtful.

1035. Pal in Palma, whence we make old eng. Pawm and Paw, is probably the first element in welsh Llaw 'the hand' =irish Lamh=Loof, Λαμβανειν, or Λαβειν, Λεγειν 'gather,' Legere, Laqueus, Leasing, לכד 'he took,' לקט 'gathered,' לקה 'took.' Palpare is close to Palma. Cf. Feel, Fumble, germ. Fühlen, isl. Falma, dan. Föle, Famle, friesic Famlen, Famplen. Adelung (art. 458) shews that Klammeren is to hold fast with the hands or Claws, which would suggest Clamber and Climb, and a root in Cl. : cf. Glean.

1036. Πλαγ in Πλησσειν=the words collected in art. 118, 671, 414. Add gaelic Slach 'strike,' Slais 'lash,' Slash, Lash. The first syllable may be identical with the first of Palma. Flog, though not found in the printed agls. literature, does occur in the unpublished pieces. I find in the Herbarium Geflogen translating 'percussus.'

1037. כפר in the arabic sense 'texit' semms to be Operire, then Co-operire=ital. Coprire, Cobrire=eng. Cover. Perhaps the guttural lost in Open, Aperire is found in Gape. See art. 351, 317. The required form for mouth is found in agls. Ceaca, dutch Kaecke 'cheek;' for such an uncertainty of sense compare Bucca, Bouche, Gena, Yawn, the mœsog. Kukyan, sibilated into Kiss, with art. 547. On the system of sound imitation Quack will be mouth, and Quek 'say,' art. 1016.

1038. Cheek in art. 522 has been compared with Fauces; compare also Bucca = germ. Backe, Jaw, Choke, Chaff, Beak. Jowl is a longer form.

> He strake the dragon in at the chowyl.
> Ywaine and Gawin, 1901.

1039. To Deck, Thatch, Tegere, $\Sigma\tau\epsilon\gamma\epsilon\iota\nu$ (486) seem related to $T\epsilon\nu\chi\epsilon\iota\nu$, $T\epsilon\chi\nu\eta$, since the art of the $T\epsilon\kappa\tau\omega\nu$ is the earliest. The germans comparing their own use of Zeugen are willing to believe that $T\epsilon\kappa\epsilon\iota\nu$, $T\iota\kappa\tau\epsilon\iota\nu$ are of the same race. For $\Sigma\tau\epsilon\gamma\epsilon\iota\nu$ cf. sanskr. Sthag.

1040. Persia has been above mentioned, art. 534. With a dental for the S, we have it in the german Pferd, and in the name of the successors of the Persians, the Parthians. Such also is the affinity of M and P, that the radix may be not different from the keltic March 'a horse,' the agls. Mear, which is masc. (Marh), the teutonic Mar, sufficiently illustrated by Wachter and remaining in Marshal, literally 'horse-boy,' and our feminine word Mare.

1041. May. Besides the illustrations of this root which have been already given, the continental etymologs have given another, which is at least a pretty conceit. In english May is the earliest of all blossoming branches, a bunch of hawthorn in bloom: and the village beauty was crowned queen of the May. Mey, Meytack, Ramus frondosus (Kilian). At mayo in dan. 'frondibus viridioribus ac floribus ornare.' Hence "Maius mensis a voce May vel Mey, qua viror omnium plantarum designatur." This sense agrees with the others, and a Maid "viret," and is in bloom like the May of which she is queen. "A maioribus" can have no acceptance by the side of this; those who would alledge the climate of Italy to be much in advance of our May, can take off two months and reduce the year to the old ten.

> To gather May buskets* and smelling brere.
> Spenser, Shep. Cal.

> Among the many buds proclaiming May
> Decking the fields in holidays array,
> Striving who shall surpass in bravery,
> Mark the fair blooming of the hawthorn tree;
> Who finely clothed in a robe of white
> Feeds full the wanton eye with May's delight;
> Yet for the bravery that she is in,
> Doth neither handle card nor wheel to spin,
> Nor changeth robes but twice; is never seen
> In other colours than in white or green.
> Brownes Britannias Pastorals, II. ii.

1041 *a*. QUAKE : see art. 607, 695. TWINCKLE is a diminutival frequentative, for in old dutch it was Quincken, micare, motitare, dubio et tremulo motu ferri (Kilian). Will o' th' Wisp with his twinckling light is called in Friesland Quinkjacht, Quegjacht, Tweigjacht, the earwig Quinkstjert 'wagtail.' WINK = germ. Winken; it "dicitur autem sensu latissimo, primo quidem de oculis, mox etiam de capite et manu" (Wachter, whose account of its origin is on wrong principles); agls. Wincettan 'to nod, beckon' (Leo. cit.); agls. Wancol, instabilis etc. (Lye); dan. Wink 'sign, motion, signal, beck with the hand.' WAG, Vacillare in art. 374. WAVE with its wagging motion. BECK, BECKON agls. Becnian, may be concluded from the similar forms. BOB = agls. Beofian = germ. Beben : an earthquake is germ. Erdbeben = agls. Eorþ-beofung.

> Twink with his eye.
> Percy S. vol. xx. 21. Wit and Folly.

1042. In the following we have apparently a confusion of meanings and of forms, Nose, Nasus, Næse, Nasc, Nâsâ, Nef, art. 166, Nares, NIB, NEB, SNUFF, SNIFF, SNIVEL, SNUFFLE, SNORT, SNORE, SNARL, SNIPE with long bill, SNOUT, SNOT, swed. Snibb 'a nib,' germ. Schnabel 'a beak,' Schnauben,

---
* Buskets = small bushes.

Schnaufeln, Schnaufen, Schnieben, Schnüffeln = swed. Snufva, Snufla, Snofla = danish Snive, Snue, Snofte, Snuse, meaning 'snort, snuff;' germ. Schnarchen = isl. Snörla = swed. Snarka = dan. Snorke, meaning 'snore;' germ. Schnarchen = dan. Snærre, meaning 'snarl;' dan. Snive 'the glanders;' isl. Sneffi, Snudr = dan. Snuden 'a dogs nose;' isl. Snîti 'emungere;' isl. Snîta = dan. Snot 'snot.'

> Now awaketh Wrathe
> With two white eighen
> And nevelynge with the nose
> And his nekke hanging.
> Piers Ploughman, 2730.

See art. 676. The explanation is, we may confidently say, that an older radix is found in Πνειν 'to breathe,' of which we have a trace in the saxon Fnæst 'breath,' Fnæstiað 'aspera arteria' the windpipe, Fneosung 'sternutatio' = Fnora, perhaps in isl. Fnasa 'fremere,' Fníkr 'gravis odor.' The welsh, where many old roots are preserved, has Ffynned 'respiration,' Ffwn 'a puff, a sigh.' Dutch Fniezen, in an old lexicon, 'gravedo,' friesic Fniese 'sneeze loud,' in an old danish song Fuyse 'sneeze' (Outzen).

1043. It may be suspected that Af in the mœsog. Afar and Afta, our After, is οπ in Οπισω and P in Post. The essential idea in the use of the mœsog. is the same, and one of those words is the proper translation of οπισω. So also in germ. Abend = agls. Æfan = Even, Evening is perhaps the οπ in Οψε, late. Οπωρα may be the after season, with loss of aspiration in the compound.

Besides the mœsogothic Afar, there existed also a collateral form with T, as our After, which is equally found in the mœsogothic, where Afta translates τα οπισω, Aftana οπισθεν, Aftaro οπισω, Aftra παλιν, Aftuma εσχατος, Iftuma means 'next, successive.' The analogy of the greek Οπωρα makes it quite clear that the two last adjectives are identical with Antumnus, 'the after season.' It will not be a violent conjecture to add Antumare, to draw after-conclusions. The agls. form Eft is translated by the trusty Lye, 1. Iterum, denuo, rursus; 2. Item; 3. Postea. I have therefore no doubt but that AFTER = Αυταρ = Autem = Αταρ = At: and Aut is inseparable from the group.

1044. CLAMMY, CLING, CLEAVE, CLAY are apparently related to Κολλα, perhaps to Clamber, art. 1035. In Γλημη = Gramiæ = Glama, and Λημᾶν, perhaps the same sense resides. So Γλισχρος. See the words cited under Lithe, art. 872; also Clod, 568. CLUMP, LUMP, see 1021.

1045. WORM, see art. 244; also CREEP, art. 274; Crimson, Vermillion, art. 971. Serpere, רָמָה having lost initial: cf. רמש reptavit. Worm, I think, appears again in Formica = Βυρμακας (Hesych.) = Μυρμηκας, and this cannot be distant from MIRE in Pismire. Mire 'formica' (Bensons Somner), as agls. = dan. swed. Myre = dutch Mier. The former element is determined by the following illustrations from modern european languages: pld. Miegeempte from Migen = Mingere and Emmet; dutch Pismiere and Mierseycke from Seycke 'urina;' finnish Kusi 'urina,' Kusta 'mingere,' Kusiainen, Kusibainen 'a pismire;' esthon. Kussi 'urina;' Kussi-kuklane 'an emmet' (Mr. E. Adams). In Bavaria they are Mieg-emerken, Mieg-cemken, where the latter element is another shape of Emmeten. "Their abdomen is furnished with a poison bag in which is secreted a powerful and venomous fluid, called formic acid, which when their enemy is beyond the reach of their mandibles (I speak here particularly of the hill ant or Formica rufa), standing erect on their fore legs, they ejaculate from their anus with considerable force, so that from the surface of the nest ascends a shower of poison, exhaling a strong sulphureous odour, sufficient to overpower or repel any insect or small animal" (Kirby and Spence). Every thing that creeps, emmet, snake, or dragon, is a Worm, and Μορμω may be only a Worm, a crawling thing, like μυρμηξ. The old romances constantly speak of monsters as worms. In the Hexameron in agls. after Adams expulsion from paradise, "him bit lice and lyfty (airy) gnats, and also likewise fleas and other like worms (Hex. xvii.). Wormwood is so called because placed in chests and drawers to keep away moths, worms; in german it is Ware-moth, Wermuth.

Syr, at grete Rome, as y the telle,
Ther lythe a dragon ferse and felle;

* * * *

Wyth the grace of God Almyght
Wyth the worme ȝyt schalle y fyght.
Sir Eglamour of Artois, 694, 706.

Where chamber is sweeped and wormwood is strown
No flea for his life dare abide to be known.
Tusser, July, p. 172.

1046. CHINK should have been compared with Yawn, and Χαινειν: it is agls. Cinu. Homil. vol. ii. p. 154.

1047. The uncontracted Sol is found in the mœsog. Sauil. It may or may not be from †καυ-ειν = Καιειν.

1048. GANDER, Goose for Ganse, HEN, germ. Hahn = mœsog. Hana, the masculine of Hen, Anas, with a T germ. Ente, SWAN, Κυνα = Canem = Hound, Ciconia, Cuniculus have a singular resemblance to one another. That Swan expresses 'white' it seems impossible to doubt: art. 694. Wachter thought that Gander takes its origin from its whiteness. "Plinius, N. H. x. 22, Candidi anseres in Germania verum minores Ganzæ vocantur. Auctor vitæ seti Waldeberti, § 5, Anseres agrestes, quos a candore et sonitu vocis Gantas vocamus." Homer says Αργην χηνα, Od. ω. 161. A wild goose is grey, generally. Ciconia is to be compared with Πελαργος, which exactly expresses the mixture of lead (535) and white. Here by the way Stork like Stride is for Scork, from †car 'a leg,' like Crane = Γερανος, Heron, Ardea for †gar-dea. Cuniculus and Goose are white in the tame varieties. Κυνα originally as Canem shews †kwan means white just as much as Swan, and the sanskrit form of it is Shwan, Çwan. Homer, Λ. 50. Σ. 283, speaks of κυνες αργοι and elsewhere describes them as ποδας αργοι. The old interpreters made out of these passages a sense for αργος which will explain Homer, 'swift,' but which, as far as I can recollect, is quite unsupported by the language in general. Αργος means white in αργεννος, αργινοεις, αργης, αργυφος, αργυρος, argentum, εναργης, στομαργος (την σην στομαργον, ω γυναι, γλωσσαλγιαν, in the Medea), in the erse Arg, the sanskrit Râj. Are we then to conclude that Homers dogs were white? How then could he say ποδας αργοι? I have shewn that the true form of αργος is †barg (1030), and I believe that a solution of this Homeric difficulty will be found by referring all these roots, greek, erse, english, latin, to the hebrew בָּרָק 'lightning,' which is Bright, 'white,' and 'swift.'

1049. Grow, Crescere are of course the intransitive forms of Gar, Car, 279, see Girl, 282. Churl was originally used in a good sense; Kaerle, keerle, vir fortis et strenuus, vir proceræ staturæ et grandis corporis, qualem fuisse Carolum primum scribunt (Kilian). Kaerle, keerle, vir, homo, maritus (id.). Karl, 1. vir, 2. senex. Karl maþr, 1. mas, 2. vir fortis (Haldorsen). It seems probable that to these harder forms are related Virere, Ver, Vir, Virginem (acc.), Virga, as growths.

1050. The welsh Gâr, latin Crus, hebrew dual כְּרָעַיִם, seem to contain the radix of the names of birds of the Crane kind, Grallatores, and of Gradus, Gradi, Stride, Stork, art. 690.

1051. גלל, Κυλιειν have been considered in arts. 220, 269, 915. Welter is a frequentative form; to Welter, to Wallow, or lie groveling (Kersey). A sibilation of this is Swelter.

> And all the knights there dubb'd the morning but before
> The evening's sun beheld there swelter'd in their gore.
> Drayton, Polyolbion, XXII.

Well and Boil from the rolling motion. Ἅλως 'a threshing floor,' from the old wise of treading out the corn by oxen driven round and round. I heard the word Wyll used (1861) at Carew Castle, in Pembrokeshire, in its proper sense, 'a spring:' digging a well is in fact digging to a well: even in book english Well head, Well spring, retain the ancient sense.

1052. Lee: for Αλεη, Αλεεινος, see Epistola Alexandri ad Aristotelem in Englisc, Notes, fol. 112, b. 13; Lee side is sheltered from the wind, and Lee shore is lee-side-shore; the saxon Hleo shews the root to exist in †kal 'cover,' art. 291.

1053. SCELVS. Wrong is from Wring, meaning screwed, perverted; in the same manner Scclus is related to Σκολιος, Σκαληνος. The sense exists in the agls. Sceoleged 'strabo;' so that the word is still teutonic and must be reconciled with Shall. Halliwell out of the glossaries is much more copious on this root than the agls. dictionaries: " SKELLED, anything twisted or warped out of a flat or straight form into that of a curve (North). SKELLERED, warped; made crooked (North). SKELLY, to squint or look awry (North). SKELVE, to incline; spoken of a pot or pan that has slipped from its upright position;" thus they say "It's all skelved to aside and run over" (Linc.). In the elder Edda, at Skelfa is used actively of the sideway motion of the shield and spear in battle: B. H. has at Skæla, detorquere, and Skældr, Valgus, a word which is to be compared here. The agls. contains the root further in Scilhrunge 'balance,' properly the skelving rod, the second member being the moesogothic Hrugga, Rod (607 a), which still exists with us in the Rungs, that is, the stails of a ladder. Of Scylfan 'vacillare,' I am able to give an example, as Lye and Manning give none, from an unpublished MS.: "Awacie se cristendom, sona scylfþ se cynedom," 'Be the christianity weakened, soon skelves the kingship.' Our word SCOWL evidently represents the saxon english Sceoleged. Perhaps an unsibilate form may be Κλινειν, with Heal in 1061.

1054. BREATH. The agls. Bræð is very often used of sweet smells. It seems to establish a connexion between Spirare and Fragrare, breath and fragrance. "The house was filled with a wonderlike breath, so that all the lichmen were filled with the winsom stench." Homil. vol. ii. p. 98. The saxon Sworetan, 'sigh, draw a long breath,' suggests that its parallel Spirare is akin to the root Swee, art. 1016, and SIGH, SOUGH are clearly changed from Sweg, 'a sound.'

1055. That Συκον = Ficus, seems due to an older form with σφ. The agls. Swæc=Smæc, a Smack, a taste, by the convertibility of W and M. Now the mœsog. for Fig is Smakka, whence after that example we may assume a root †swak; by vocalization συκ, and by rejection of the sibilant †fac, fic: the long vowel being in some way connected with the double K. If the fruit be so named from its savour, our SMACK is connected with Συκον, Ficus. Loss of W as in Canem, and change of guttural to labial would produce Sapor.

1056. 'Εσπερα would be as natural an expression for last evening, as Morrow for next morning. Α. Τὸν δ' υἱὸν, ἔφη, ἑώρακας αὐτοῦ, ὡς καλός ἐστι; Β. Τί οὐ μέλλω; καὶ γὰρ ἑσπέρας ξυνεδείπνουν αὐτῷ. ' I was dining with him yesterday.' Xen. Hellen. IV. i. 6.

> T. Ἡμᾶς δὲ δὴ τί δρᾶν παρασκευάζεται;
> E. οὐκ οἶδα πλὴν ἕν, ὅτι θυείαν ἑσπέρας
> ὑπερφυᾶ τὸ μέγεθος εἰσηνέγκατο.
> Aristoph. Pax, 227.

' He brought in a monstrous big mortar last night.'

> ἦν δὲ καὶ πυός τις ἔνδον καὶ λαγῷα τέτταρα,
> εἴ τι μὴ 'ξήνεγκεν αὐτῶν ἡ γαλῆ τῆς ἑσπέρας.
> Ibid. 1150.

' If the cat didn't make away with one of em last night.' These examples may content us. It follows that 'Εσπερα is the same word as YESTER, and that WEST (art. 575) has been rightly compared with Vesper. There is also a reasonable probability that, as an evening comer would want shelter, the radical element is the same in GUEST.

1057. LEATHER may be Διφθερα, see 755. Δεφειν = Λεπειν = Glubere : if the mœsog. Hleipra ' a tent, σκηνη,' be truly of the same pedigree. In Διφθερα the θ was intrusive as in Εσθιειν, Εσθλος, Μαλθακος, Λοισθος. It may, on the contrary, be connected with Cloathe, and †kal ' cover,' but these roots meet, art. 291.

1058. Καρφος, CRUMPLE. The shrivelling effect of dryness makes it proper to compare the words in art. 1006, with those in 893.

1059. SPEER, art. 681, has affinity also with germ. Fragen, lat. Rogare, eng. Crave, etc.

1060. LEAF = agls. Leaf = norse Lauf = germ. Laub, with LEVEL which in agls. Læfel signified "libella, scyphus," Gen. xliv. 2, remembering that ancient cups were saucer shaped, in Læfeldre fæt, "a level vat," was ' a dish,' with agls. Læfer one of the broad bladed rushes, 'sword grass, swords,' cutting the hand when drawn across it, also 'a plate of metal, a metal plate' in Homil. vol. ii. p. 498, contain evidently within them some such root as would produce †laf-men, Lamina; this root may be CLEAVE = agls. Cleofian = norse Kliúfa. As Scindere, Findere have a common origin, so CLEAVE, CLIP, Glubere are from one source and nearly identical.

1061. HEAL over, usually said of ships, tubs, and the like, is constantly employed by Laȝamon, in the sense of lean: thus "Inne Deorfeter' Locrin deað polede. On arwe him com to heorter' þat he adun hælde" (v. 2474). 'In Dorset Locrin suffered (tulit) death: an arrow came for him to (his) heart, (so) that he adown healed.' In the last saxon dictionary the verb is given as Healdan; it should be Healan: þat cild bið hoforode and healede (MS. Cott. Tiberius, A. III. fol. 41). 'That child is humpbacked and healed.' This exhibits the monosyllabic root of Κλινειν, Lean, Clivus, and Proclivis.

1062. YAMMER is a verb not quite extinct; see it in the glossaries with ȝomer = agls. Geomrian, and cf. lat. Gemere.

& sæt & biheold æuore; æmne burinæsse *.
And hire ȝeddes † sæide; ȝeomere stefne ‡.
Laȝamon, 25851.

Olibrius þe luðere reue buten reowðe
hwil me ȝerdede hire þus ȝeomerliche ȝeide §.
Seinte Marherete, fol. 41. 14.

1063. YEAR. In art. 256 on Ceres the passage was worth citing.

Gép býþ ȝumena hiht· ðon ȝob læteþ
haliȝ heofones cýninȝ hrurjan ryllan
beophte bleba beopnum anb ðeappum·

'Year (harvest) beeth (is) hope of grooms (men) when god

* A burying place. † Songs.
‡ With plaintive voice, σφωνη = φωνη: should we amend the rhythm by ȝeomerlichre?
§ The bad grieve without ruth, while man girded (see arts. 354, 541) her thus, groaningly cried.·

letteth, holy heavens king, the ground sell (give) bright blades (fruits) to barons and to poor.' Compare: K'. ıannaꝑnuꞃ ʒıꝼ he bıþ on ꞅunnan dæʒ þonne bıð ʒod pınꞇeꝛ ꞇ pındıʒ lencꞇen ꞇ dꞃyʒe ꞅumoꞃ· ꞇ ꞅpyþe ʒod ʒeaꞃ bıð þy ʒeaꞃe· MS. 'If the kalends of January fall on a Sunday, then there will be a good winter, a windy lent (spring), and a dry summer, and there will be a very good harvest that year.' In the saxon word G is pronounced as Y, and in the norse disappears:

> Á'r er gumna góði.
> Get ec at ör var Fróði.
> Norse Runesong, 10.

'Harvest is the good of grooms (men). I hear that Froði was liberal,' where the second line is a mere rime to the former. That Ceres = Geres is at least to be compared with this word cannot be denied; a larger space has been allotted to it because the sense is wholly absent from all saxon dictionaries. YEAR is also connected with YORE, YARE a shakspearian word, ERE and EARLY, and probably with Γεροντα (acc.) and its sanskrit relatives. HARVEST seems to be GARB-fest, the fisting of sheaves (art. 1026), and belongs to Καρπος 'fruit,' Καρπος 'wrist,' probably once 'hand,' Grab, Carpere, Δρεπειν, Reap, and the rest of that family.

SANSKRIT INDEX,

EMBRACING words above mentioned as illustrating the English, Greek, Latin, and sometimes the Teutonic and Hebrew, with some others. This Index is not professed complete, nor very sceptical, though much has been rejected. The able scholars who treat of the Sanskrit never intended to assert all that presents itself in their books : they desire us only to compare this with that, and, according to our knowledge and amount of instruction, form an opinion. Their general doctrine is, that the Sanskrit has a very far back relationship to very many other tongues, but they would not insist strongly upon some of the instances alleged. They stand, therefore, in a different position to others : they make it their business to adduce examples of possible similarity : it is the duty of ourselves to select, to refuse, to hesitate. For a few of the words I am myself responsible, because the phenomena of letter change have struck me in a different way to what is commonly taught.

अंश: 'shoulder.' cf. mœsog. Amsa.
अक 'pain, affliction.' cf. $A\chi o\varsigma$.
अक्ष: for अक्षि "in fine compositorum" (Bopp) = oc-ulus, EYE, etc. Also in the senses of rota, currus, cf. Axis, $A\xi\omega\nu$.
अगरु = अगुरु 'aloe' = אֲהָלִים = Agallochum.
अगि्न = Ignis.
अघ sin; 2. pain. cf. $A\gamma o\varsigma$.
अङ्क: 'the flank or part above the hip.' cf. Haunch, and Clunis, etc. See art. 873.
अङ्कुश m. or n. 'the hook used to drive an elephant.' cf. Vncus, Hook.
अङ्गार m. or n. 'charcoal.' cf. $A\nu\theta\rho\alpha\kappa\epsilon\varsigma$.
अङ्गुरि 'a finger,' अङ्गुल: 'the thumb.' cf. Fangen and art. 1026.
अन्ज् 'to anoint.' cf. Vngere.
अद् 'to eat.' cf. Edere, $E\delta\epsilon\iota\nu$, Eat.
अन् 'to blow.' cf. $A\nu\epsilon\mu o\varsigma$, Animus, Ond. अनिल: is 'wind.'
अन्त: or neut. = End. mœsog. Andeis.
अन्तर = Inter. cf. Endo, old latin.
अन्तरं = $E\nu\tau\epsilon\rho o\nu$. Secondly = germ. Ander.
अनि obsolete except in derivatives = $A\nu\tau\iota$, Ante.
अन्य: 'another.' cf. Alius, $A\lambda\lambda o\varsigma$. L for N.
अप् 'water.' cf. Aqua.
अप implies privation, separation, etc. cf. $A\pi o$, Ab.
अपर as fem. 'the west,' as neuter 'the hind quarter of an elephant.' cf. mœsog. Afar, engl. After.
अभि in the Vedas with I long; as implying 'presence.' cf. Ob. In form $E\pi\iota$ is close.
अभ्र 'a cloud.' cf. $O\mu\beta\rho o\varsigma$, Imber.

अमा *áma*. See art. 985.

अम्बा mother. אם.

अबु 'water.' cf. Amnis, irish Amhan, 'water,' and art. 891. The derivation of Amnis from Am 'around' is false; it relies on poetic dreams about the Meander.

अम्भस् water. cf. Amnis, as in the preceding: $Ομβρος$.

अयस् germ. Eisarn, Iron (Bopp).

अलं *ἅλις*.

अविः Ovis, Ewe.

अश्मन् 'a stone.' cf. $Aκμων$, Hammer.

अश्व: Equus.

अष्ठ lip. cf. Os, Ostium.

अष्टौ $Oκτω$, Octo, Eight.

अस् or अष् 'shine,' אש 'fire.'

अस्थिं $Οστεον$.

अस्मद् the theme of the plural forms of the first person. cf. $αμμες$, $αμμιν$.

अस्मि 'am.' cf. †$εσομι$, the earlier form of Sum, $Ειμι$. angls. Eom = Am.

अहि $Eχις$, $Οφις$, Anguis.

आप् 1. obtain; 2. arrive, reach. 1. Ap- in Adipisci; 2. Hap, Happen.

आयुः 'age, duration of life.' $Αιων$, Ævum. See the art. on Quick, 1024.

आर्यः venerandus. cf. angls. Ar (a long) = germ. Ehre. But it is to be considered whether the teutonic forms at least be not reductions of the mœsog. Sweran = lat. Vereri, the long vowel being compensative.

आलिप् anoint. See लिप्.

आशु quickly. $Ωκυς$.

आस्यं 'face, mouth.' cf. Os.

आस् 'to sit.' cf. $ἦμαι$, $ἦσται$ (Bopp).

इ 'to go,' Ιεναι (Bopp). The mœsogothic Iddyan, the welsh Aed 'a going,' Addu 'to go.' Some old greek forms, Ιθματα, perhaps Ισθμος, shew that the greek has probably lost a dental. This opinion Bopp rejects: it would make it reasonable to suppose that the Sanskrit had lost a letter.

इन्यं, Ita.

इतर 'alius.' cf. Iterum; irish, Itir (Bopp). Then must the sanskrit be a diminution of Δευτερον.

इन्घ् to shine. Αιθειν (Bopp).

इभः 'an elephant.' cf. Ebur.

उक्षन् Ox.

उदरं Venter. ऊधम् Udder. उधसं Udder. See art. 574, 516. Also ऊधसः.

† उद्र् an obsolete word, ύδωρ. Water, occurring in the compound समुद्रः 'ocean.' cf. art. 891.

उद्रः Otter.

उन्द् 'to wet.' Vdus=Vvidus for Vdvidus, like Suavis for Suadvis (Bopp). Rejecting N, उदं 'water.' cf. art. 891.

उप Sub.

उपरि Super.

उभौ Αμφω, Ambo. See art. 788, whence it seems that the second syllable is two=Both: the first may be Con, άμα, in which case the sanskrit has rejected M.

उरणः Αρνειος, Ram.

उरु Ευρυς.

उप् Vrere (Bopp). ष्ष.

उमासा Aurora.

एक 'one.' זהא. See art. 976, &c.

एकचरः 'rhinoceros;' one-horned. Κερας, Horn.

एकतर: ʽΕκατερος, Either. See art. 976, &c.
एकदा Quondam.

वृष: Vrsus, Αρκος, Αρκτος, keltic, Arth, Eirth.

क: Quis; interrogatively का, Quæ. On the neuter see art. 962, &c.
कक् Vac-illare.
कख् Cachinnari, Cackle; diminutive Giggle. These may be imitations of sound.
काट: gula, 'guttur,' seems to have relation to Χανειν, Yawn; this will bring it within the group discussed in art. 1026. Χασκειν, Χαος, the norse, Ginnungagap, Os for † kaos, Chasm, GAPE, GAP = gaelic, Cab, touch upon one another.
कतर: Ποτερος, Vter, Hwæper.
कथ् 'narrare.' mœsog. Kwiþan, our queath, in Bequeath, Quoth. See art. 1016.
कदा Quando. That N is rejected by the sanskrit seems clear any way; for the neuter of the pronoun is the base.
कन् Splendere. cf. Candere, etc.
कपाल m. or n. skull. cf. Κεφαλη.
कपि: Ape; Κηβος, Κηπος. hebrew, Kôf.
कम् erse, Caemh, 'love.' Amare.
कर: Χειρ: cf. art. 279.
करका 'hail.' בָּרָד, with? Κεραυνος, בָּרָק.
ककेट: Καρκινος.
कर्पास m. or n. 'cotton,' carbasus, כַּרְפַּס, Esther i. 6.
कस्य: 'integer, sanus.' cf. Well. See art. 1008.
काव: Corvus. cf. Croak, imitative words.
कार: 'pain, affliction.' Care = mœsog. Kara, lat. Cura.

काल: 'black.' cf. old engl. to Colly 'to blacken;' Coal.

कास् to Cough.

कुब्ज: Gibbus. See art. 1026.

कस्तीर 'tin,' cf. $Κασσιτεριδες$.

गिर् $Γηρυς$; also गिरा.

किरि $Χοιρος$.

कुप्यं 'base metal, any but gold or silver.' cf. Cuprum.

कुम्भ: 'a water jar,' See art. 1026.

कृ Creare, Gar. See art. 279. cf. चर् in the sense of 'agere.' Shall we derive $Χειρ$ in its shorter form † $χερ$ hence, or shall this root be a verbal from † $χερ$?

कृमि: Vermis. cf. also Creep. कृपया: a Worm. क्रिमि:.

केश: 'hair.' erse, Cas, 'hair of head.' Cæsar, Cæsaries: perhaps angls. Feax, 'hair,' whence the republican Fairfax; so केशर: 'a lion's mane,' $Χαιτη$. See art. 705. cf. कच: 'the hair.'

कोल: lame, $Χωλος$. See Halt.

क्रन्द् = क्रन्द् to Greet, Cry.

क्रव्य, $Κρεας$, Carnem (acc). A root कृप् 'to cut,' perhaps existed; whence कृपाण: 'a knife, sword.' cf. also कर्दमं 'flesh.'

क्रमेल: Camelus. According to art. 1026. 755. the R would not be an insertion, but a conversion of the V. Similarly Crum in an equivalent of Cam, 'bent.'

क्री 'buy,' erse, Creanaim, $Περνημι$, $Πριασθαι$, Pretium (Bopp).

क्रुश् 'to call, cry, weep.' $Κραζειν$ (Pott).

क्रूर: 'cruel.' Radix कृ obsoleta est, extat etiam in क्रव्य, Crudus in latino Crudelis, et in $Κρεας$ (Lassen).

क्लप् 'lædere, occidere.' cf. Clades (Bopp) and Lædere.

क्लम् 'fatigari.' cf. $Καμνειν$ (Bopp). If art. 1026 be well suggested, the L is a change of the V, not an insertion.

क्षिद् 'humectari.' cf. Κλυζειν (Pott). The agls. Læcan is 'humectare,' whence our Leak.

क्क 'where?' cf. Vbi for cubi, Qua.

क्षण 'sound:' an unsibilate form of स्वन.

क्षि 'dwell.' cf. Κτιζειν, ευκτιμενον, περικτιονες (Pott).

क्षिण् 'kill or hunt.' Κτεινειν (Pott).

क्षुर: 'a razor.' cf. ξυρος, κουρευς.

खलिन:=खलीन: Χαλινον.

खोल, खोड, खोर Χωλος? See कोल.

गण्ड: 'cheek, temples.' cf. Genæ; agls. Wang, Wong.

गम् 'go.' cf. mœsog. Gaggan (gangan) = agls. Gangan. Gan. The third person singular is गच्छति.

गर m. n. Virus.

गर्भ: 'womb:' agls. Hrif.

गल: Gula. गिलि: 'swallowing;' गल् 'to eat:' see art. 1017. Believed akin to the synonyms with R, गिरि: 'swallowing;' गृ 'to swallow;' γαργαλιζειν; Gurgulio (Pott). See Wilson's Gram. p. 248.

गुप् 'cover.' cf. Κευθειν, Cutem (acc.).

गुरु Gravis.

गुह् 'hide, cover.' cf. Κευθειν, Hide, welsh, Cuddio.

गृध् 'desire.' cf. mœsog. Gredon, used impersonally, Gredop mik, πεινω: with adj. Gredags, 'hungry,' whence engl. Greedy.

गृ 'swallow, eat.' cf. Vorare, Brook, art. 423. 3d pers. sing गिरति.

गो Cow, perhaps Bovs.

गौ: Γαια.

गौर: yellow. cf. Aurum, Crocus, Cera.

गौरी girl. Κορη. Girl, in old English, is used for either

sex, in that respect answering to Κουρος, Κουρη. Gör, in the friesic, is a very young woman-child, (ein junges, noch unverstandiges Mädchen.) It is hard to see any affinity with Churl, Carline, Karl, which, in the oldest known usage, are applied to old men or women of the peasant class. Yet we are surprised to find so little trace of Girl in the teutonic languages.

> Thorugh wyn and thorugh wommen
> Ther was Loth acombred,
> And there gat in glotonie
> Gerles that were cherles.
>
> "*Piers Ploughman*," 526.

(The gerles are Moab and Ammon). The Glossary illustrates by "knave gerles," of the male children in the slaughter of the innocents at Bethlehem.

ग्रस् 'devour,' 'swallow.' cf. Gramen, Grass, and the words above, Gula, Brook.

ग्रह् for ग्रभ् Grab.

ग्रीवा Cervix. See Swere, and art. 1017.

ग्लान: 'wearied.' cf. Lassus.

घर्म 'heat.' cf. Warm, Θερμος (Bopp).

चद् 'cleave.' Scindere.

चतुर् Quattuor.

चद् 'to shine.' cf. Candere. चन्द्र:, चन्द्र: 'the moon,' चण्ड: 'hot.'

चन an affix giving an indefinite sense: mœsog. Hun.

चम् 'go.' cf. Κιεν, Κιων (Bopp).

चर् 'go.' cf. mœsog. Faran, Fare.

चत् a root not in use. cf. agls. Geotan, lat. Gutta.

चौर: 'a thief.' cf. Fur, Φωρ. चुर् 'to thieve.'

छद् 'tegere.' cf. Shadow, Shade; agls. Sceadu.

छाया 'shade,' Σκια.

छिद् Scindere.

जङ्घा 'crus.' cf. Shank. See art. 1015.

जन् 'be born.' cf. †gnasci = Nasci, Γενος, Kin.

जलः 'frigidus.' cf. Gelu, Chill, Cold.

जानुः Knee, Γονυ.

जारः 'adulterer.' cf. mœsog. Hors. Art. 533.

जीव् 'Vivere.' cf. Quick, etc.

जॄ grow old, Γηρασκειν. जरा Γηρας.

जॄ 'celebrare.' Garrire, Γηρυειν.

ज्ञा 'know,' Ken, etc.

फिर्झिका Gryllus.

दिप्, डिप् 'throw,' Δικειν.

तष् 'to cover, skin, peel, plane.' cf. Tegere, तष्कः = तष्न्, Τεκτων.

तत्र and similar adverbs of place are parallel to the latin adverbs in —tra.

तद् That.

तन् 'expand, extend,' Τεινειν, Tendere, Dehnen.

तनुः Tenuis, Thin.

तप् 'to heat.' cf. Tepere.

तमस् darkness = तमं, cf. Dim, Tenebræ, etc.

तरः Tree = तरु Δορυ, Δρυς.

तारा Star.

तुल्, तुलय् 'weigh, lift.' Tollere, Ταλαντον.

तृप् 'saturare.' Third person तर्पति. Τερπειν in the same sense occasionally in Homer; so that 'delight' is a derivative sense.

तृप् 'thirst.'

नृ traiicere. cf. Trans, Intrare (Bopp).

नं as a termination, marking the instrument with which aught is done, answers to —τρον, —trum, as in αροτρον, feretrum.

त्रस् 'timere.' Τρεω. Perhaps Timere is for tremere,

त्रा 'servare,' Τηρειν (Pott).

त्रुप् ferire, occidere. cf. norse at Drepa; engl. Drub.

त्रि Three.

तं Thou, Tu.

दंश् mordere. cf. Δακνειν, which is from Οδαξ. The sanskrit is also plainly a derivative root, and has lost the initial vowel, a short Α.

दक्ष: dexterous. cf. Δεξιος, Dexter, etc., Take.

दन्त: Dens. In the second edition of his Glossary, Bopp has observed that this may be 'mutilatum' for the participial अदत्, that is, Etend, Eating. Sanskrit scholars would do well to consider whether other sanskrit words and reputed roots have not lost initials.

दम् Domare or Domitum esse. cf. Tame, etc.

दम्पती 'husband and wife.' cf. Δαμαρ (Lassen).

दर:, दरं 'fear, terror.' cf. Terrere, Dread.

दशन् Decem. agls. Tigun.

दह 'to burn.' Δαιειν. Lassen thinks olim दघ to be akin to Daw, Dawn, Day.

दा Dare. दानं Donum; the sanskrit is 'ut videtur, obsoletum, pass. part. ab radice दा" (Bopp). To confess passive participles of an obsolete form is to confess the sanskrit has undergone changes. Since the old latin Duim, and the adjective Duonus = Bonus, a derivative active participial, shew that the older present was DVOMI, it will be probable that the sanskrit has lost the V. So I have argued in † ekwant art. 976. seqq. And there is fair philological evidence that for six, the welsh Chwech is older than षष्. The latin Quis stands in the same position as regards its sanskrit equivalent. It seems to follow, that in the combinations DW, KW, the sanskrit has sometimes rejected the W.

दिव m. or n. 'day.' Dies. दिव् 'lucere,' shews the meaning, and दिव्, fem. 'air, sky,' the connexion with Divus, Divinus.

दिश् Δεῖξαι. cf. Dicis causa; Indicare, etc.

दुग्ध 'milk;' see the altered root below, and cf. Dugs. If in the auslaut, gutturals and labials will change place, then the mœsog. Daddyan 'give suck,' seems of the same origin, and it brings with it Teat, etc. The greek, Θηλυς, Θηλαζειν, require change of dental to L; or the dd may indicate a † dag-dyan, and the long vowel a † θαγ-λυς. By sibilation of the sanskrit Dug, we can obtain Suck, Sugere.

दुस् or in practice दुर्=Δυς.

दुह 'to milk.' cf. Dugs.

दुहित् DAUGHTER. It is thought that this is a derivative of the preceding. Filia, quæ mulgendi officium habuit in vetusta familiæ institutione (Lassen). In general, in ancient times, men milked: cattle that roam over unlimited pastures are very wild, and it was never convenient to send the maidens far from home. The word also is correlative, the maiden is not daughter either to the cow or to the family. The irish Dighim is 'suck the breast,' and in this sense the assigned root may be held correct.

दृभ् 'fear;' 3d pers. दृभति, Ταρβειν.

दृश् Δερκεσθαι = welsh, Edrych; irish, Dearcaim (1st pers.) = δερκομαι; Dearc, 'the eye.'

दृप् 'be proud, confident.' θαρσειν.

दृ Tear, mœsog. Tairan, Δρυπτειν.

देव: Deus.

देव:, दोवृ 'husband's brother,' Δαηρ, Levir.

द्यु 'a day.' cf. Dies.

द्रु 'run.' cf. Δραναι, Δραπετης.

द्रु: Δρυς, Tree.

द्रुम: tree. cf. Dumus for †drumus. (?)

द्रै 'to sleep.' cf. Δαρθανειν, Dormire.

द्वन्द्व 1. a pair; 2. together. cf. the agls. probably ancient form for 'two,' Twegen; engl. Twain, which here appears doubled. Vincire, Bind, with their sanskrit equivalent, seem derivable from this form of the numeral with loss of the initial, like Bini.

द्वार् Door. The vowels of the english and greek by vocalization of the vau. The verb द्वृ, with 3d pers., द्वरति is 'operire.'

द्वि Duo, in comp. sometimes द्वा. The vowel for the G in Twegen, as in the mœsog. Twai, and engl. Twain, Twin.

धरा Terra. Dorr, Dry, seems not to be sanskrit.

धा τιθεναι (Bopp). Another form of दा, answering to the latin sense of Dare in the compounds 'put,' as circumdare. (?)

धाव् 'run.' Θειν (Bopp).

धृप् 'be proud.' Θαρσος. Another form of दृप्.

धु 'shake, agitate.' cf. Θυειν, Θυελλα (Bopp).

धूम: Fumus. cf. Θυμος.

धे lactere, धेनु 'vacca lacteus.' cf. $T\iota\theta\eta\nu\eta$. $\Theta\eta\lambda\nu\varsigma$ may have an adjective L from this root.

ध्वन् 'sonare,' the equivalent of क्रण्, and of स्वन्, with perhaps स्तन् all which see.

ध्रुव: 'certus.' cf. True. Horne Tooke was nearly right in his treatment of True, the mœsog. Triggws is $\pi\iota\sigma\tau o\varsigma$, and the verb Trauan $\pi\epsilon\pi o\iota\theta\epsilon\nu\alpha\iota$, our Trust is a sibilate form.

न as negative, see on Ne. art. 164.

नक्त Noctu. The usual substantive निशा Nox, is further removed from the European languages. Properly $\Delta\nu o\kappa$—related to $\Delta\nu o\phi o\varsigma$

नक्ष् Nancisci. Related to the next word?

नख m. or n. Germ. Nagel = Engl. Nail = $O\nu\nu\chi a$ = Vnguem (acc.) The same word as Fangs, Fangen. (?)

नग्न: Naked, by contraction Nudus: the passive participle of some verb: the agls. sometimes Hnacod.

नद् 'shine.' Nitere.

नप्तृ filius, Nepos. cf. $A\nu\epsilon\psi\iota o\varsigma$ (Pott). (?)

नभस् aer, cælum. $N\epsilon\phi o\varsigma$, etc. Irish, Neamh; Welsh, Nef, 'heaven.' An. for $\Delta\nu\epsilon\phi a\varsigma$.

नर: $A\nu\eta\rho$: "proprie dux, quo seasu in Vedis interdum usurpatur: नृ ducere." Lassen.

नरक m. n. Tartarus. cf. $E\nu\epsilon\rho\theta\epsilon\nu$, $E\nu\epsilon\rho o\iota$.

नव: Novus.

नवन् Novem.

नश् destroy. cf. Necare.

नह् Nectere. G or K initial lost.

नाग: Snake.

नामन् Nomen. G or K initial lost.

नाभि: Navel, Nave of wheel: $O\mu\phi a\lambda o\varsigma$, etc. Root नह् 'bind.'?

नासा Nasus, Nose. One may suspect all these words to mean breathers, and to have lost the initial in Πνεῖν. agls, Fnæst, 'breath;' norse, Fnasa, 'to snort.' Then the initial S in so many words would be an alteration of the labial.

निघा Nit. That Nit has lost a K, see art. 332.

निन्द् 'reprehendere.' cf. Ὄνειδος.

निञ्ज् 'purificare, lavare.' Νίπτειν (Bopp).

नी Νέεσθαι (Bopp).

नीड m. or n. Nidus. The Greek Νεοττια, as connected with Νεοσσος, and that with Νεος, Novus, seems to point to the true origin.

नीरं 'aqua.' cf. Νηρευς.

नु Num.

नुद् 'send.' cf. Nuntius (Bopp).

नून Nunc, Νυν.

नौ: Navis, Ναυς.

पच् Coquere. Πέσσειν.

पच्चन् Πεμπε, for † pempem.

पट् 'spread,' पाट: 'breadth.' cf. Patere.

पदं 'Foot,' Pedem, etc. cf. पथ: Path.

पत् Πεσειν. for † πετειν; so Πιπτειν for † πιπετειν.

पति: 'a master, an owner, a husband.' Ποσις (Bopp.) mœsog. Faþs.

पत्र 1. 'wing,' Πτερον, Πτερυξ. 2. 'leaf.' Πεταλον.

पर: 'secundus, alius.' Par. 2. ulterior, Περαν.

परा Παρα.

परशु: Πελεκυς.

परि Περι, Περιξ.

पर्दे Παρδειν.

पलित: Πολιος (Bopp).

पश् 'ligare.' cf. Fascia, Fas (Pott). Fascis.
पशु Pecus.
पश्चात् Postea; the abl. of an obsolete पश्च (Lassen). Seems to have lost a vowel, οπισθεν. See art. 1043.
पा, पो Bibere, Πιvειν. cf. Poculum.
पिन्ज् 'to tinge or colour.' Pingere (Pott).
पितृ Pater.
पिष् Pinsere.
पुत्र: son. cf. Puer (Bopp).
पुष् nourish as a tame animal. See Pecus above.
पूय् Putere.
पूर्व: '1. prior; 2. matutinus.' cf, Πρωϊ.
पृथु 'latus, magnus, largus.' cf. Πλατυς with L for R.
प्यै 'pinguescere.' cf. Πιων, etc.
प्र Pro, Præ, Προ, etc.
प्रछ् germ. Fragen, Rogare, etc.
प्रति Προτι, whence Προς, also ejecting R, Ποτι.
प्रथम: Primus.
प्री 'to love.' mœsog. Friyon. ?
प्रु Fluere.
प्लु Salire. cf. Ludere for † pludere. Art. 840.

फुन्ज् Florescere.
फेन: Foam.

बन्ध Bind.

भक्ष् Φαγειν.
भन्ज् break, Fαγνυναι.
भर: Burden. Φορτιον.
भा 'shine, be luminous.' cf. Φαος (Bopp).
भु Be.
भुज् 'bow.' mœsog. Biugan; agls. Bugan=Bow.

भृ Bear.
भृष्ट Frictus, Fried. भर्गः 'cooking, frying.'
भ्रम् Roam, Ramble.
भ्राज् 'shine.' cf. Bright; with loss of initial राज्, so that Bright is of the same root as Argentum.
भातृ Brother. etc.
भ्र Brow, etc.

मख् 'sacrifice.' cf. Mactare.
मघ् Moveri.
मज्ज् or मन्ज् Mergere.
मज्जा Marrow. See art. 902.
मन्च् 'abstergere.' cf. Emungere, Ἀπομυττεσθαι, מחה.
मणि m. f. 'a pearl.' माणव: 'a necklace of sixteen strings.' cf. Monile; norse, Men, 'a necklace.' cf. मराड् 'ornare.'
मति 'animus, mens.' cf. Μητις.
मद् 'to be drunk, insane.' cf. Mad. मद: 'drunkenness.' मद्य 'wine, intoxicating liquor.' मधु 'honey, Mel'=The erse, Mil=Welsh, Mêl with derivative Melyn 'honey.' See art. 618.
मध्य: Medius; a very exact parallel.
मन् 'cogitare, opinare.' cf. Mentem, etc. मनसं 'mens.' मति: 'mind.'
मरकत:=मरक्तं Σμαραγδος.
मल m. n. 'sordes.' cf Μολυνειν. See also File, art. 439.
मशक: Musca=मशिका. See Midge, art. 718.
मस् 'to measure.' cf. मा measure. मानं Mensura. It is not to be hastily said whether in Metiri an N is suppressed, or in Mensura inserted.
मह् 'amplificare,' with 3rd pers. मंहते 'augeri, crescere.' cf. Magnus, Mag. art. 19, 834.
मा μή. Ne.

मातृ Mother.
माया 'magic.' cf. Magus.
मास् Moon. मास: Month.
मिथ्या frustra. cf. Ματην.
मिश्र् = मिस् Miscere; ग़टप, so that S is radical.
मिह् 'effundere;' also Mingere, Meiere, especially in derivatives. "Olim मिघ्" (Lassen).
मुखं 'mouth.' The mœsog. Munþ-s represents the teutonic forms. Whether some similar root existed in the greek and latin, see art. 747, 875, cf. the familiar MUG; these fay words deserve attention.
मुर 'surrounding, encircling.' cf. Murus. ?
मुष् = मूष् 'steal.' Hence after, the sanskrit grammarians all agree to derive मूषिक m. f. 'mouse, rat.' In the latin and greek a participial termination was to be expected, or some affix; and is there nothing in common between Mouse and Titmouse? See agls. Máse.
मूक: Mutus.
मूर्खः 'stupidus.' cf. Murk, 'dark.'
मृ Mori, with numerous derivatives.
मृज् 'wipe.' cf. Ομοργνυναι (Curtius).
मेघ: 'nubes.' cf. Ομιχλη, Muggy weather, Fog. Muggy = friesic, Muskig = danish, Muske, used in the same sense; isl. Mugga, B. H. explains 'caligo pluviosa vel nivosa, Snefog.' Smoke = agls. Smóka, Smée = welsh, Mwg = irish, Much, seems the same in form.
मेदस् Medulla (Bopp).
म्ना 'to fix in the memory by frequent repetition.' cf. Μνημων. The original radix must be min or men, cf. art 153.

य or यत् the reputed base of the relative = Qu—Quid.

यकृत् Iecur. That the sanskrit has lost D, see art. 787.

यवस: Cibus. ?

यामातृक:, यामातृ:, जामातृ:, Γαμβρος, Gener. Lassen says, "यामि vel, जामि f. is 'soror;' while यम mfn. is Geminus, cujus vocis vetusta scriptura, गम fuit." cf. cæterum γαμεω, γαμβρος." See art. 792, where it is made probable that the root has lost D.

यु Jungere; युग् Jugum, Yoke, etc. In art. 791 it is argued that these words are derivatives of Duo = Twegen, and have lost D.

युवन् Juvenis; युवीयस् Junior; यविष्ठ Youngest, where the sanskrit has eliminated N. Lassen observes that यवन 'the name of the people of the west,' is alien. But cf. the hebrew Jāvān, Ionia.

रज् 'shine;' राजत: Αργυρεος. cf. Argentum. This root seems to have lost an initial labial, Bh.

रञ्ज् Regere, in the Vedas (Lassen). I argue from the welsh Brenin, 'a king,' the historic Brennus; the agls. Brego, that the latin and sanskrit have lost B.

रथ: currus. cf. Rheda, Rota, Ride, Road.

रुह 1. ascendere; 2. crescere, Grow. ?

रूक्ष: Rough. But Rough seems to have lost some initial. See art. 799.

लक्ष् observare, notare, animadvertur. cf. Look.

लङ्घ् 'go by leaps.' cf. mœsog. Laikan, and art. 840.

लप् Loqui, Λεγειν; for †gloqui, glegein, art. 1017.

लभ् 'obtain, get, acquire.' cf. Λαβειν. If the irish Lamh, 'a hand,' be literally correct, Λαμβανειν is the older form, and †lab has lost an M; but the irish mh is pronounced V or W.

लस् 'fall.' cf. Labi.

लस् 'ludere,' with प्र and वि 'procacem esse.' cf. mœsog. Laikan and Lascivus. See art. 840.

लिप् 'illinere, ungere.' cf. Ἀλείφειν, which has lost a guttural initial: art. 1012. So that the sanskrit has lost an initial syllable.

लिह् Lick, for † glick. Art. 1017.

लिश् 'to be Ὀλίγος' (Bopp).

लुप् Rumpere (Bopp).

लुभ् 'cupere,' Lubet. It has been argued that Lubet = Placet.

लोक् videre. cf. Look.

वच् 'loqui.' cf. Vocem. But Vocem is from † kwak, † kwek, and the sanskrit has lost K, art. 1016.

वत्स: Vitulus.

वन् colere, venerari, amare. cf. Win—some.

वप् Weave.

वम् Vomere.

वर: 'husband, bridegroom.' Vir.

वराह: 'boar.' cf. Verres.

वर्म्मन् Arma.

वश् 'wish.' cf. Ϝέκων.

वस् 'habitare,' a sibilate form of Ϝικειν, Οικειν.

वस् 'tegere, induere.' cf. Weed, Vestis.

वह Vehere. वाह: Wagon.

वा 'or.' cf. Ve.

वा 'blow.' cf. Ἀηναι (Pott) cf. mœsog. Waian = germ. Wehen and Ventus, ' wind,' as participles = वात: ' wind.'

वाञ्छ ' wish '=germ. Wunschen.

वास: 'habitatio.' cf. Ϝαστυ. Sibilations of Wick.

वि an inseparable prefix 'dis, se.' cf. Ve, as in Vecors. (?)

The radix of Dis is Two, as in διακοσιοι we see di for dw; perhaps Vi is for dwi.

वि Avis. "A initio elisum videtur." (Lassen.) Nom. वि:, masc. or वी fem.

विद् to wit, Ειδεναι.

विधवा Vidua, Widow.

वीर: Vir, Ἥρως.

वृ 'tegere, operire.' cf. agls. Wreon.

वृत् 'versari, esse, fieri.' cf. agls. Weoðran. With आ 'reverti,' cf. Vertere.

वृष् 'to sprinkle.' cf. Εερση (Pott).

व्रज् 'go, travel.' cf. mœsog. Wraton.

श This letter is understood to be always a conversion of a guttural: it is often represented by ç.

शङ्ख: a sacred Conch shell. cf. Cochlea, etc. (Pott.)

शण Hemp, Cannabis.

शत Centum, Ἑκατον. It has been argued that the two first syllables were † ekwant; if so, the sanskrit has lost the initial vowel, the W and the N.

शर: Arrow. Bopp compares Κειρειν.

शकॆरा Saccharum, Sugar.

शर्द् a Fart: root शृप् Παρδεῖν. Then Παρδεῖν is a softening of † kard.

शाल् 'to flatter.' cf. Κολαξ.

शाल Hall.

शिरस् Καρα. ?

शी 'jacere, dormire.' cf. Quies.

शुष्म Siccari, शुष्क: Siccus.

शुभ: 'neat, clean.' cf. agls. Syfer, 'neat, clean, sober.' Sobrius.

शून्य: 'vacuus.' Κενος for † kwenos.

शूर् ' to be valiant, powerful.' cf. Κυριος.
श्रम् 1. laborare. 2. defatigari.' cf. Καμειν. If art. 1026 be well suggested, the R is for V.
श्रि 'ire.' cf. Gradi, Schreite, Stride (Bopp).
श्रवस् 'an ear;' the irish Cluas—L, R interchanged. 2 in the Vedas Gloria, ΚλεFος.
श्रु 'hear.' Κλυειν.
श्रोणी=श्रोणि 'femur.' cf. Clunis.
श्वन् Hound, Κυνα, Canem (acc.).
श्वसृ Sister.
श्वेत=सित m. f. n. agls. Hwít, White. cf. Wheat, Σιτος; Welsh, Gwyn; Lat. Candere; Creta, with R for V.

षष् Sex, Six.
षिवु Sew, Suere.
ष्ठा Stand, Stare.

सखिन् Socius. nom. —खा.
सच् Sequi.
सज्जा armour, mail. cf. Πανσαγια.
सत्य m. f. n. true. cf. mæsog. Sunþs=agls. Soþ=engl. Sooth.
सद् Sidere.
सद् ire. cf. Ὁδος (Bopp).
सना Semper.
सप्तन् Septem.
सम् Συν. समः 1. æqualis, 2. Ὁμοιος.
सपः Serpens.
सलं water. सलिलं ' water.' cf. Ἁλς, Θαλαττα, Saliva.
सवितृ 'sun.' See art. 1047.
सस्न् ' adhærere.' cf. Viscus.
सायः evening. cf. Serus (Bopp).

सायक: Sagitta.
सारस: a kind of Heron, Grus, Crane.
सिन्दुरं minium rubrum; Cinnabar.
सिव् Sew, Suere.'
सु Eu.
सूनु: 1. agls. Sunu, Son; 2. agls. Sunne : the Sun.
सेव् 'serve, gratify by service.' cf. $\Sigma \epsilon \beta \epsilon \iota \nu$ (Bopp).
सृप् with third person सर्पति Serpere. A sibilation of Creep.
स्रन्ध: shoulder. Art. 1015.
स्तन् Thunder,' Tonare, cf. Stun. $\Sigma \tau \epsilon \nu \tau \omega \rho$ (Pott)—

"By the whirlwind's hollow sound,
By the thunder's dreadful stound."—*Drayton.*

स्तन: 'mamma; woman's breast.' agls. Spana. cf. $\Sigma \tau \epsilon \rho \nu o \nu$. ?
स्त्रैण: 'produced from or by a woman.' cf. agls. Strynan, Streonan, 'procreate':

"Then the emperour and hys wyfe,
In yoye and blysse they lad ther lyfe,
That were comyn of gentyl strynde."
Le Bone Florence, 2172.

"As when a greyhound of the rightest straine
Let slip to some poore hare upon the plaine."
W. Browne's Br. Pastorals, II. iii.
Shakspeare, "*Much Ado about Nothing*," II. i. end. "*Henry VIII.*" iv.

स्थग् = ष्ठग् 'cover.' cf. $\Sigma \tau \epsilon \gamma \epsilon \iota \nu$.
स्थल् stare. cf. Germ. Stellen, $\Sigma \tau \epsilon \iota \lambda \epsilon \iota \nu$ (Bopp).
स्था Stare, Stand; $\Sigma \tau \eta \nu a \iota$.
स्नुषा 'daughter-in-law;' agls. Snoru; Latin, Nurus; $N \upsilon o \varsigma$.
स्पृह् 'wish, desire, long for.' cf. $\Sigma \pi \epsilon \rho \chi \epsilon \sigma \theta a \iota$, Sperare.
स्मि Smile, स्मेर: 'ridens,' Smirk = agls. Smeorcian.
स्मृ Memoria tenere.

स्यन्द् ooze, flow. cf. a Sound = agls. Sund; the river Indus.

सु 'flow, drop.' cf. 'Ρεω.

स्व: suus. cf. Σφε. The S is probably a sibilation of K.

स्वन् Sonare.

स्वप् 'dormire,' Sleep with L for V. cf. Sopire, Sompnus, 'Υπνος, etc.

स्वर: 1. air breathed through the nostrils. 2. sound in general.' cf. Susurrus (Bopp).

सशुर: Socer, 'Εκυρος. स्वश्रु Socrus, 'Εκυρη.

स्वसृ Sister = Germ. Schwester = agls. Sweostor; nom. -सा.

स्वादु Sweet, Suavis for † suatvis, 'Ηδυς.

स्विद् to Sweat, Sudare, Ιδιειν for † swid.

हंस: Anser for चंस. cf. Gander, etc. art. 1048.

हद् Χεσειν for † χεδειν. cf. Κεχοδα, and the sibilate forms; as Σκατος, also the forms with final guttural, as Caccare.

हन् kill. cf. Καινειν.

हनु: ' the jaw.' cf. Gena, etc. chin.

हरित: Viridis.

हि to go. 2. to send. cf. κιειν, Ciere (Bopp).

हिम: cold: as subs. Himan, 'cold, snow, frost.' Χειμων, Χιμετλον, mons Hæmus, Hiems, the Himâlayas.

हृ 'take.' cf. Αιρειν (Bopp). Αγρα (Pott), with उद् it is Αιρειν, 'lift,' with उद्, it is Φειρειν, 'say.'

हृद् Cor, Heart, Καρδια; gaelic, Cridhe.

हृष् Φρισσειν.

ह्लाद् to Gladden. cf. welsh, Llawd, ' pleasure, delight.'

ह्यस् Χθες, Yesterday.

X

ENGLISH INDEX.

Ache, 76.
Acquaint, 63.
Acre, 356.
After, 1043, 1064.
Again, 765.
Agee, 262.
Ail, 77, 829.
Ajar, 1026.
Aleppo, 1012.
All, 1008.
Ancle, 1026.
Aneal, 79.
Angle, 357.
Answer, 1016.
Ant, αντι, 78.
Ape, 263.
Apple, 543.
Arabia, 1006.
Arm, 80.
Arrow, 81.
Ass, 82.
Axe, 83.
Awn, 358.
Aye, 84.

Bag, 394.
Bairn, 400.
Ball, 395.
Bandy, 405.
Bane, 396.
Bar, 649.
Bargain, 397.
Barley, 406.
Barm, 943.
Barrow, 1026.
Barton, 417.
Basket, 398.
Bath, 616.
Bay, Bays, 49.
Bays (berries), 358 a.
Be, 299, 1024.
Beak, 1038.
Bear, 400.
Beard, 567.
Beathe, 616.
Beaver, 401.
Beck, 403, 1041.
Bee, 404.
Beech, 402.
Beer, 406.

Beigh, 64.
Belch, 802.
Belly, Bellow, 394.
Bend, 405, 518.
Bere, 406.
Berg, 1026.
Berry, 627, 756.
Berth, 417.
Bid, 407.
Bilge, 394.
Bill, 408.
Billiards, 395.
Billow, 394.
Bind, 409.
Birch, 409 a.
Birth, 400.
Bladder, 411.
Blaze, Blast, Blank,
 Blanch, Black, Blush,
 Blowzy, 410, 529.
Bleach, 410, 529.
Bleat, 597.
Blister, 411.
Blithe, 861.
Bloom, 412.
Blossom, 412.
Blow (flo), 413, 817.
Blow (flog), 414, 1036.
Blue, 535.
Boar, 415.
Bob, 1041.
Boll, 395.
Bolster, 394.
Bore, 416.
Borough, 417.
Borrow, 417.
Both, 418, 788.
Bottom, 419, 862.
Box, 420, 1026.
Bran, 421.
Branch, 859.
Brand, 456.
Bray, 359.
Break, 804, 598.
Breathe, 654 a, 1054.
Breeches, 422.
Breme, 730.
Brim, 456.
Broak, 805.
Broker, 393.

Brook, 423.
Brow, 425.
Brown, 426.
Browse, 423.
Buckle, 49.
Budget, 394.
Bullet, 395.
Bunny. 521.
Burden, 400.
Bury, 1026.
Buss, 547.
Butt, 428.
Button, 31.
Buxom, 12, 49.

Cack, 86.
Calf (of leg), 292.
Calf (of cow), 1012.
Call, 85.
Cam,Camber,Cambrel,87.
Camel, 1026.
Camp (kæmpfen), 744,
 1026.
Camp (castra), 1026.
Can=ken, 63.
Can (white), 1025.
Can (vessel), 1026.
Cardoel, 612.
Care, 88.
Carve, 89, 264, 663.
Chafer, 863, 1026.
Chaff, 900, 1038.
Chaffer, 90.
Champion, 1026.
Chap (change), 90, 864.
Chap (cheek), 522.
Chaste, 708.
Cheapen, 90.
Cheek, 522, 1033, 268,
 1016.
Cherub, 1010.
Chesil, 628.
Chew, 268, 522.
Child, 315.
Chill, 265.
Chin, 266.
Chink, 1016.
Chip, 91.
Chirp, chirk, chirm, 267.
Choke, 522, 1038.

2 A

Choose, 268, 522.
Chop (κοπ), 91.
Chop (barter), 864, 782.
Churl, 92, 1049.
Clamber, 1035.
Clammy, 1021, 1044.
Clap, 840.
Clay, 1021, 1044.
Claw, 93.
Clear, 322, 529.
Cleave (adhærere), 1021, 1044.
Cleave (scindere), 1060.
Climb, 94, 458.
Cling, 1021, 1044.
Clod, 568.
Clog, 459.
Clue, 269, 568.
Coal, 535.
Cob, 305.
Cod, 518.
Coddle, 70.
Cold, 265.
Colt, 523.
Comb, 95.
Come, 270.
Cool, 265.
Coomb, 589.
Cop, 297.
Core, 299, 1026.
Corn, 271.
Corner, 307.
Couchgrass, 1024.
Cough, 590.
Couth, 70.
Court, 272.
Cover, 1037.
Cow, 526.
Crab, 97.
Craft, 856.
Crane, 1050, 273.
Crank, 893.
Crave, 542, 1059.
Crawl, 274.
Creep, 274, 525, 650.
Cress, 275.
Crimp, 893.
Croak, 99.
Crop, 98, 651.
Cross, Crutch, 607 a.
Crumple, 893, 1058.
Cry, 267.
Cuckoo, 100.
Cuddle, 63.
Culver, 535.
Cumbh, 1026.
Cunning, 63.
Cup, 865, 1026.
Curl, 281.
Cushot, 599.

Daffodil, 19.
Dare (dream), 101.
Dare (audere), 470.
Daughter, 471.
Daw, Dawn, 360.
Day, 360, 830.
Deal, 472, 739.
Dear, 591.
Deek, 652, 1039.
to Deck, 486.
Deem, 102.
Deep, 557.
Deer, 558, 473.
Deftly, 460.
Dew, 109, 479, 613.
Dim, 796, 474.
Din, 493.
Dingle, 589.
Dip, 559.
Dive, 559.
Dole, 472.
Doom, 102.
Door, 475.
Dote, 554.
Dough, 653.
Doughty, 104.
Dove, 535.
Downs, 1026.
Drag, 827, 476.
Draw, 831, 476.
Dream, 101.
Dregs, 477.
Drill, 563, 1026.
Drink, Drench, Drown, 49.
Drite, 654.
Dry, 478, 592, 667, 1019, 1033.
Dumb, 479 a.
Dumpy, 1026.
Dunk, 474.
Dwarf, 1026.
Dye, 479.

Ear (arare), 105.
Ear (auris), 106, 276.
Early, 1063.
Earn (eagle), 107.
Ease, 709.
Egg, 361, 543.
Egg on, 362.
Eight, 1004.
Either, 976.
Eke, 364.
Elbow, 109.
Eleven, 617.
Elm, 114.
Elope, 840.
Else, 110.
Eme, 111.

Errand, 113, 383, 1016.
Ethel, 710.
Eve, 1005.
Evening, 1043.
Ever, 112, 1024.
Ewe, 115.
Ey (island), 363.
Eye, 363, 544.

Fagot, 365.
Fallow, 1023.
Fang, 1026.
Fare, 116, 429.
Fast (fasten), 116 a.
Fast (festinare), 531.
Fat, 600.
Father, 431, 502.
Fear, 117.
Feather, 503.
Fee, 432.
Feel, 433, 1035.
Fele, 434.
Fell, 435, 394.
Fennel, 439 b.
Fern, 504, 849.
Ferry, 116.
Fers (Chaucer), 534.
Fever, 436.
Few, 437, 545.
Fight, 438, 1026.
File (filth), 453, 439 a.
Fillip, 118.
Filly, 445.
Film, 435.
Fin, 439 b.
Finch, 655, 826.
Find, 440.
Fine, 560, 866.
Finger, 1026.
Fire, 441.
Firth, 441 a.
Fish, 806.
Fist, 438, 1026.
Fire, 1001.
Fizz, Fizzle, 446.
Flabby, 546, 1022.
to Flag, 1022.
a Flag, 442.
Flail, 118.
Flange, 442, 873.
Flank, 873.
Flap, 818, 1022.
Flash, 611, 711.
Flask, 819.
Flat, 442, 601.
Flax, 442 a.
Flay, 435.
Flea, 840.
Fleece, 443.
Flitch, 442, 873.

ENGLISH INDEX. 347

Float, Fleet, 850.
Flock, Floss, Floo, 443.
Flog, 118, 1036.
Flow, 119.
Flush, 410.
Flutter, Flicker, 444.
Fly, 444.
Foal, 445.
Foam, 656.
Foist, 446.
Fold, 447.
Folk, 448.
Fond (try), 440.
Foot, 449, 506.
For, 450.
Ford, 116.
Fore, 451.
Forlorn, 626.
Four, 851.
Frame, 731.
Frayne, 807.
Freeze, 712.
Freight, 116.
Fresh, 808.
Fright, 117.
Frog, 452.
Froth, 120.
Froward, 450.
Fry (φρύγειν), 452.
Fry of fish, 656 a.
Full, 453.
Fuller, 121.
Further, 451.

Gag, 1016.
Gall, 277, 527, 1012.
Gallop, 840.
Gambril, 87.
Game, 1026.
Gammon, 528.
Gander, 278, 1048.
Gap, 351.
Gape, 278 a, 351.
Gar, 279.
Garb (sheaf), 1026.
Garden, Garth, 272, 1011.
Gas, 446.
Gasp, 278 a.
Geotan, 280.
Ghost, 446.
Gird, 281, 1011.
Girl, 282, 1049.
Glad, 283, 507, 821.
Glade, 672.
Glance, 322, 529.
Glare, Glass, Gleam, Glisten, Glitter, Gloss, Gloze, Glede, Glim, Glimmer, Glimpse, 322, 529.

Glib, 672, 1020.
Glove, 326.
Glow, 322, 529, 657.
Gnat, 284.
Gnaw, 266.
Goat, 316.
Gold, 277, 527, 1012.
Good, 508, 867.
Gore, 285.
Gourd, 286, 1026.
Gout, 280.
Grab, 287, 1026.
Grass, 122, 275.
to Grate, 271, 1031.
Gratings, 877.
Grave, 658, 664, 1031.
Great, 868.
Greet, 267.
Grid, Griddle, 877.
Grin, 783.
Grip, 287, 1031.
Grit, 271.
Groom, 827 a, 943.
Grope, 287, 1026.
Grow, 1049.
Grub, 658, 664, 1031.
Grunt, 664 a.
Guest, 1056, 289.
Gulf, 256.
Gulp, 1017.
Gurkins, 1026.
Gush, 852.
Gust, 446.

Hack, 83, 306.
Hail, 1008, 1028.
Hair, 290, 530.
Hal, 291.
Hall, 659.
Halm, 292.
Hals, 293.
Halt, 291, 840.
Ham (cham), 1009.
Ham (home), 532, 1026.
Hamper, 1026.
Hanap, 1026.
Hand, 123, 295, 1026.
Harns, 296.
Harvest, 1063.
Hart, 16, 307.
Hasten, 531.
Have, 461, 1026.
Hawker, 364.
Head, 297, 857, 1026.
Heal, 125, 1008.
Heal (over), 1061.
Heap, 298, 1026.
Hear, 629.
Heaven, 1026.
Heel, 300, 1028.

Hemp, 301, 770.
Hen, 1048.
Heron, 124, 273.
Hew, 306, 83.
Hide (κεύθειν), 302, 510.
Hide (cutis), 303, 509.
Hill, 1028.
Hillier, 291.
Hirn, 307.
Hive, 304.
Hoard, 772, 630.
Hobby, 305.
Hockey, 1026.
Hoe, 306.
Hogg, 306.
Hold, 1026.
Hole, 125, 1008.
Holt, 660.
Home, 532.
Hook, 1026.
Hoop, 1036.
Hore (whore), 533.
Horn, 16, 307.
Hornet, 308.
Horse, 534.
Host, 524.
Hound, 310.
Huckster, 364.
Hummock, 1026.
Hump, 869, 1026.
Hunch, 1026.
Hundred, 981, 870.
Hunt, 311.
Hurdle, 877.
Hurry, 312.

I, 366.
In, 126.
Inter, 127.
Interloper, 840.
Ipswich, 258.
It, 510 a.

Java, 645, 790.
Javelin, 313.
Jaw, 522.
Jericho, 1014.

Keep, 128, 1026.
Ken (γεν), 315.
Ken (know), 314, 129, 63.
Kennel, 310.
Kent, 130.
Kernel, 1026.
Key, 822.
Kid, 316.
Kin, 315.
Kindle, 1009, 1025.
Kiss, 131, 317, 547, 713.
Knead, 331.

2 A 2

ENGLISH INDEX.

Knee, 318.
Knit, 320.
Knot, 319.
Know, 319 a, 63.
Knuckle, 132.
Kringle, 339.

Lack, 137.
Ladder, 320 a.
Lake, 135.
Lakken, 548.
Lane, 133.
Lap, λαπτειν, 134.
Lap, Lappet, Lappel, 461a, 548.
Lappe, λαβειν, 348.
Larky, 840.
Lash, 1036.
Latch, 348.
Lather, 135.
Laugh, 832.
Law, 549.
Lax (salmon), 840.
Lay, 140, 367, 549.
Lead, 777.
Lead, ducere, 320 a.
Leaf, 1060.
Leak, 135.
Lean, 323, 1061.
Leap, 840.
Leather, 195, 1057.
Leave, 462, 550, 957.
Lee, 1052.
Left, 136.
Leme, 322.
Less, 137.
Level, 1060.
Lewd, 853.
Ley, 138.
Lick, 139, 323 a, 871, 1017.
Lid, 291.
Lie, 140, 367, 603.
Lift, 321.
Light, 322, 551.
Like, 809, 814.
Limp, Limber, 872, 1021.
Limpet, 291.
Lip, 464, 872, 1017.
Liquorice, 258.
Lisp, 810.
List, 714.
Listen, 324.
Lithe, 872, 1021.
Little, 137, 604.
Lizard, 704.
Loaf, 325.
Lobster, 840.
Lock (allicere), 141.
Lock (claudere), 833.

Lock (of hair), 810 a.
Loin, 873, 784.
Long, 139.
Loof, 326.
Lot, 604 a.
Lowe, 322.
Lug, 324.
Lust, 715.
Lustre, 322.
Lute (lie hid), 142.
—ly, 957.

Mad, 511.
Madden, 854.
Maggot, 50.
Maid, 834.
Main, 368, 834.
Malachi, 1013.
Mallet, 454.
Malt, 147.
Marches, 143.
Mare, 1040.
Margaret, 144.
Marjorum, 72.
Mark, 143.
Marrow, 902, 786, 674.
Marsh, 148.
Mart, 636.
Mate, 903.
May, 1041, 19.
Mead, μεθυ, 511, 618.
Meadow, 145.
Meal, 146, 454.
Mean (min), 153.
Meat, 50.
Meed, 716, 904.
Melt, 147.
Mere, 148.
Mesh, 149.
Mette, 874.
Mettle, 874.
Mickle, 368.
Mid, 151, 512, 717.
Midge, 718, 835.
Might, 834.
Milk, 152.
Mill, 29, 146.
Min (memini), 153, 746.
Min (minor), 154.
Mind, 874. 153.
Mingle, 836.
Minnow, 155.
Mire, 148, 1045.
Mite, 50.
Mock, 155.
Moist, 145.
Mole, 837, 454.
Monger, 150.
Mood, Moody, 874.
Moon, 156.

Moor, 148.
Moss, 157.
Moth, 50.
Mother, 158, 513.
Mothery, 742.
Mouldy, 742.
Mound, 1026.
Mourn, 159.
Mouse, 160.
Mouth, 747, 875.
Mow, 161.
Much, 368.
Mud, 145.
Mug (face), 155.
Murder, 162.
Musty, 742.
Muzzle, 619.

Nail, 838.
Naked, 839.
Name, 163, 327.
Nap, 328.
Navel, 769.
Ne, 164.
Neb, Nib, 1042.
Need, 605.
Neigh, 329.
Nephew, 569.
Nest, 719.
Nettle, 330.
Neve, 331.
New, 165.
Nibble, 601.
Night, 369.
Nits, 332.
Nook, 1026.
Nose, 166, 631.
Not, 342.
Nought, 342.
Now, 167.
Nut, 333, 606.

Oak, 168.
Oar, 169, 732.
Of, 463 a.
Offer, 4.
Ogee, 262.
Oil, 170, 1012.
Old, 171.
One, 172, 985, 976.
Only, 957.
Open, 173, 552, 748.
Orchard, 272, 383.
Ord, 174.
Otter, 815.
Out, 720.
Oven, 404.
Ox, 363.

Paddock, 564.

ENGLISH INDEX. 349

Pude, 564.
Pain, 676.
Pansy, 828.
Paps, 561.
Path, 449.
Paunch, 394.
Peel, 1040.
Persia, 435.
Piggesnie, 828.
Pillow, 175.
Pinnoc, 655.
Place, 3.
Play, 840.
Plum, 740, 535.
Poacher, 394.
Pocket, 394.
Poke, 394.
Pool, 176.
Prate, 177.
Pumpkin, 1026.
Purse, 905, 632.

Quaint, 63.
Quake, 607.
Quappe, 518.
Quean, 334, 315.
Queen, 334.
Queme, 270.
Quench, 335 a.
Quern, 336.
Quick, 21, 304, 335, 1024.
Quill, 292.
Quince, 1026.
Quiver, 607.
Quoin, 130.
Quoth, 1016.

Raddling, 877.
Rag, 178.
Rain, 179, 841, 811.
Rajah, 1030.
Rake, 722.
Raven, 337.
Reach, 370.
Ready, 513 a.
Reap, 797.
Red, 778, 570.
Reech, 371.
Rich, 372.
Rid, 877.
Riddle, 338, 877.
Ridge, 798.
Rime, 779.
Rimple, 893.
Rind, 180, 1006.
Ring, 339.
Ripple, 893.
Rivel, 893.
Rob, 465, 733.
Rod, Rood, 607 a.

Roof, 780.
Root, 181.
Rough, 799.
Rover, 465.
Row, 732.
Rub, 800.
Ruddy, 570.
Ruffians, 465.

Sack, 182, 1029.
Sad, 183, 514.
Saloon, 659.
Sallow, 1023.
Salt, 184.
Salve, 1012.
Same, 185, 662.
Sanm, 662.
Sand, 648.
Sap, 553.
Saunter, Sawney, 185 a.
Say, 1016.
Scabbard, 1015.
Scale, 1015.
Scantling, 1015.
Scar, 1032.
Scathe, 186.
Scatter, 187.
Scoff, 188.
Scoop, 537, 1026.
Scorch, 640.
Score, 663, 1032.
Scour, 696.
Scowl, 1053.
Scratch, Scrape, Scrawl, 664, 1031.
Scream, 664 a.
Screen, 877.
Screw, 592 a, 13, 1026.
Scum, 536.
Scut, 665.
Scuttle, 1015.
Seal, 701.
Seam, 844 a.
Seek, 645.
Seely, 666.
Seneschal, 188 a.
Sere, 667.
Set, 183, 203.
Settle, 183, 514.
Seven, 466, 1003.
Shaft, 757, 1015.
Shake, 668, 842 a.
Shale, 1015.
Shall, 189.
Shank, 1015.
Shape, 189 a.
Shard, 190.
Share, 663.
Shave, 757.
Shaw, 1029.

Sheaf, 757.
Shear, 749, 663, 1032.
Sheath, 1015.
Sheep, 757.
Shell, 1015.
Shelter, 1029.
Shide, 1015.
Shield, 1015.
Shin, 1015.
Shine, 669.
Shingle, 1015.
Ship, 191.
Shirt, 663.
Shoot, 193.
Shoulder, 1015.
Shovel, 537.
Shred, 663.
Shrew, Shrewd, 13.
Shrink, 893.
Shrivel, 893.
Sickle, 53.
Sieve, 571.
Sigh, 1054.
Sill, 1015.
Sip, 906.
Sister, 633.
Sit, 183.
Six, 194, 1002.
Skates, 1015.
Skell, Skelve, 1053.
Skid, 1015.
Skiff, 1026.
Skill, 1015.
Skin, 195, 1029.
Skink, 1015.
Skirmish, 640.
Sky, 1029.
Slack, 670, 842, 1022.
Slade, 672.
Slash, 1036.
Slate, 1015.
Slattern, 1022.
Slay, 118, 518, 671, 1036.
Sledge, 1020.
Sleek, 1020.
Slide, 672, 1020.
Slime, 673, 1020.
Slink, 673 a, 1020.
Slip, 672, 1020.
Slobber, Slaver, 1017.
Slough, 1021.
Slow, 1022.
Sludge, 1021.
Slut, 1022.
Smack, 1055.
Smuggle, 175.
Sneeze, etc., 676, 1012.
Snow, 677.
Solomon, 1008.
Some, 199.

Sore, 678.
Sough, 1054.
Sound, 200.
Sow, 198, 758.
Spade, 537, 1015.
Span new, 1015.
Spand, Spandrel, 1015.
Spank, 1015.
Spar, 649.
Spare, 679.
Sparrow, 634, 680.
Speed, 201.
Speer, 681, 1059.
Spider, 859.
Spill, 1015.
Spillikins, Spills, 1015.
Spin, 682, 1015.
Spindle, 1015.
Spink, 655.
Spit, 1015.
Spit, Sputter, 202, 683.
Split, 1015.
Splinter, 1015.
Spool, 1015.
Spoon, 1015.
Spoor, 681.
Spunk, 1015.
Spur, 683 a.
Squeamish, 683 a.
Squint, 684, 130.
Stagger, 372 a.
Stails, 372 a.
Stand, 203.
Star, 685, 204.
Starling, 680.
Steaks, 686.
Steep, 372 a, 518.
Steer, 687.
Step, 372 a, 518.
Sting, Stick, Stitch, 205, 878.
Stink, 687 b.
Stir, 688.
Stockade, 689.
Stork, 1048.
Storm, 688.
Straw, 206.
Streak, 843.
Strew, 206.
Stride, 690, 1050.
Struggle, 844.
Stumble, 887.
Stun, 493.
Sty, 372 a, 518.
Such, 897.
Sulk, 207, 691.
Sultry, 621.
Sumpter, 844 a.
Sup, 906.
Swab, 907.

Swallow (down), 692, 1017.
Swallow (bird), 693.
Swan, 694, 1024.
Sway, 695, 879.
Sweal, 621.
Swear, 1016.
Sweat, 515.
Sweet, 208, 697.
Swelter, 621, 1051.
Swere, 698.
Sweren, 880.
Swill, 1017.
Swing, 879.

Take, 373, 480.
Tame, 481.
Teach, 482.
Tear, 483.
Teat, 209, 561, 608.
Ten, 484, 845.
—th, 958.
Thames, 51.
That, 485.
Thatch, 486.
The, 494.
Their, 487.
Thick, 562.
Thin, 488.
Think, 881.
Thirst, 478.
Thole, 489.
Thou, 490, 699.
Three, 491, 997.
Through, 563.
Thrash, 492.
Throng, 882.
Thrush, 680.
Thumb, 1026.
Thump, 572, 723, 885.
Thunder, 493.
Thursday, 885 a.
Thus, 494.
Thuster, 883.
Tickle, 609.
Tile, 26.
Till, 593.
Tilt, 737.
Timber, 495.
Tin, 700.
Tines, 925.
Tinder, 594, 884, 1025.
Tingle, 210.
Tipple, 554.
Tire, 211.
Toad, 564.
Token, 212, 496, 701.
Tolls, 213.
Toom, 1026.
Toot, 579.

Tooth, 886, 925.
Top, 595.
Top (spin), 1026.
Topple, 1026.
Tor, 214.
Touch, 497.
Tread, 573.
Tree, 498.
Trim, 734.
Trip, 573.
Trouble, 735.
True, 596.
Trundle, 1026.
Tug, 499, 846.
Tumble, 887, 1026.
Turn, 610.
Twain, 1027.
Twelve, 622.
Twenty, 888.
Twig, 1026.
Twigger, 1027.
Twin, 792.
Twinckle, 1041.
Two, 500, 991.

Udder, 574, 516, 892.
Un, 215.
Uncouth, 70.
Under, 216.
Urchin, 915.
Ure, 626.

Vails, 432.
Vat, 455.
Vie, 438.

Wade, 217.
Wag, 218, 374, 695, 847.
Wagon, 376, 847.
Wainscot, 27, 828, 1015.
Wake, 377, 1024.
Wall, 27, 219.
Wallop, 840.
Wallow, 340, 220.
Wamble, 221.
Wan (hwan), 962.
Wan, Wane, 1025.
Ward, 222.
-wards, 223.
Wart, 224, 377.
Wasp, 725.
Waste, 341.
Watch, 377.
Water, 891.
Wave, 225.
to Wax, 1024.
Way, 375.
a Wear, 272.
to Wear, 635.
Weasel, 636.

Weather, 891.
Weave, 226.
Wed, 227.
Weed, 724.
Weigh, 227 a, 759 a.
Well, Wyll, 457, 1051.
Well (hole), 1008.
Welter, 340, 1051.
Wend, 889.
Were (vir), 228.
Wet, 891.
Whale, 457.
What, 342.
Wheat, 702.
Wheel, 220.
When, 343, 890.
Whence, 345.
Whether, 344.
While, 346, 229.
Whirl, 336.
Whisky, 726.
Whit, 342.
White, 759.
Who, 347.
Whole (hole), 1008.
Whom, 348.

Whore, 533.
Whoop, 236.
Wick, 231, 727, 1024.
Widow, 232.
Will, 233.
Willow, 703.
Win, 234.
Wind, 235, 891.
Wine, 236.
Winnow, 237.
Wipe, 907.
Wisk, Wisp, 907.
Wit, 517.
Wite, 238.
With, 262, 990.
Withy, 728, 239.
Woe, 240.
Womb, 576, 1026, 892.
Wool, 241, 443.
Word, 577.
Work, 242.
Worm, 244, 1045.
Worry, 1017.
Worse, 350.
Wort, 812.
Worth, 243.

Wound, 623.
Wriggle, 1026.
Wring, 592 a, 1026.
Wrinkle, 893, 611.
Write, 540, 578, 664.
Writhe, 1026.
Wroth, 245.

Y, 261.
Y, as prefix, 520.
Yammer, 1062.
Yard (garden), 354, 272.
Yard (virga), 541.
Yawn, 351.
Year, 1063.
Yeast, 446.
Yellow, 527, 1012, 1023.
Yesterday, 352, 1056.
Yet, 353.
Yode, 852 a.
Yoke, 378, 791.
Yolk, 527.
Yon, 355.
Yore, 1063.
Young, 246.
Youth, 894.

LATIN INDEX.

Abominari, 922.
Acies, 362.
Acuere, 83.
Acus (aceris), 358.
Adeps, 612, 1012.
Adolescere, 79, 170, 621.
Adversus, 860.
Æternus, 112.
Ævum, 112.
Ager, 356.
Aio, 84, 1016.
Alapa, 258.
Albus, 1012.
Alere, 1008.
Alius, 110.
Amare, 1009.
Amb-, 214 a.
Ambo, 418.
Amita, 111.
Amnis, 891.
Anas, 278, 1048.
Animus, 171.
Ansa, 123.
Anser, 1048, 278.
Aper, 249, 415.
Aperire, 173, 552, 748.
Apex, 297.
Apis, 404.
Aqua, 726, 891.
Ar, 760 a.
Arare, 105, 1031.
Arcus, 81.
Ardea, 124.
Arca, 1006.
Arena, 628.
Arere, 1006.
Argentum, 1030.
Arista, 81.
Armus, Armilla, 80.
Ascia, 85.
Asinus, 82.
Audire, 760 a.
Augere, 364.
Aula, 659.
Auris, 106, 276.
Aurum, 308.
Auscultare, 324, 629.

Bacca, 358 a, 627, 756.
Balæna, 457 a.

Balare, 597.
Barba, 567.
Bascauda, 398.
Basium, 547.
Bellua, 457 a.
Bilis, 527.
Bonus, 915.
Bos, 526.
Bucca, 1038.
Bufo, 564.
Bulbus, 395.
Bulga, 394.
Bulla, 395.
Bullire, 395, 457.
-bundus, 923, 935.
Burere, 427.

Caballus, 305.
Caccare, 86.
Calamus, 292.
Calare, 85.
Calculus, 1034.
Calx, 300, 1028.
Cambire, 864.
Camera, 391.
Campsare, 87.
Campus, 95.
Camurus, 87.
Cancelli, 877.
Candere, 594, 660, 694, 749, 1025.
Canis, 310, 1025, 1048.
Cannabis, 301.
Cantium, 130.
Canus, 1025.
Capere, 128, 1026.
Capo, 91.
Caput, 96, 297, 595, 857.
Carcer, 1026.
Cardo, 1026.
Carduus, 566 a, 915.
Carmen, 279.
Carpere, 780, 1026.
Carihago, 1011.
Carus, 591.
Castus, 590, 915.
Cauda, 605.
Caulis, 292.
Celare, 291, 603.

Cella, 291.
Centum, 870.
Cera, 308.
Cerebrum, 296.
Ceres, 256, 1063.
Cernere, 338, 877.
Cernuus, 338, 915.
Certare, 744.
Cervix, 608.
Cervus, 307.
Ciconia, 1048.
Cincinni, 1026.
Circulus, 281, 330.
Circum, 281, 1011, 1026.
Civis, 304.
Clam, 291.
Clamare, 85.
Claudere, 833.
Claudus, 294.
Clava, 450.
Clinare, 323, 1061.
Clivus, 458, 1061.
Clunis, 873, 1026.
Clypeus, 915.
Cœlum, 1026.
Cohors, 272.
Colere, 593, 691.
Collis, 1028.
Collum, 293.
Coluber, 672.
Columba, 535.
Columen, Columna, 292.
Con, 261, 520, 662, 979 seqq.
Consul, 261.
Contemplari, 474.
Copia, 298, 1026.
Cor, 299, 1026.
Corona, 1026.
Cornix, 99, 337.
Cornu, 307, 1026.
Corvus, 99, 337.
Crabro, 308.
Cras, 352.
Crates, 877.
Creare, 279.
Creperus, 1007.
Crepusculum, 1007.
Crescere, 279.
Creta, 759.

LATIN INDEX.

Cribrum, 338, 877.
Crocire, 99,
Crocus, 308.
Cruor, 285.
Cubitus, 1026.
Cuculus, 100.
Cucumis, 286.
Cucurbita, 286, 1026.
Culmus, 292.
Cumulus, 1026.
Cuneus, 1015.
Cuniculus, 1025.
Cunnus, 315, 1026.
Cura, 88.
Currere, 312.
Curtus, 89, 663, 1032.
Curvus, 1026.
Cutis, 303, 509.
Cymba, 1026.

Damnare, 102.
Dapes, 554.
Decem, 484, 845.
Decet, 460, 486.
Deus, 886, 925.
Dextra, 480.
Dicere, Dicare, 496.
Dies, 830.
Dignus, 104, 486.
sub Dio, 360.
Distinguere, 205.
Docere, 482.
Domare, 481.
Dominus, 928.
Dormire, 101, 554.
Dorsum, 704.
Ducere, 499, 846, 881.
-ducre, 846.
Duodecim, 622.

Edere, 108.
Ego, 366.
Endo, 126.
-ere, 934.
Erinaceus, 258.
Eructare, 371.
Ex, 720.
Exercere, 920.

Faber, 401.
Fagus, 402.
Famulus, 532.
Fascis, 365.
Fatuus, 391.
Fauces, 522.
Febris, 436.
Fel, 527.
Felix, 666.
Femur, 528.
Fendere, 396.

Fenestra, 883.
Feniculum, 439 b.
Fera, 558.
Ferina, 558.
Ferire, 69, 397.
Ferre, 400, 429.
Ferrum, 69.
Fervere, 436.
Fiber, 401.
Fibula, 1026.
Ficus, 1055.
Filix, 504.
Findere, 1026.
Firmus, 654 a.
Fiscus, 149, 398.
Flaccus, 516.
Flagellum, 118, 414.
Flamma, 410, 529.
Flare, 413.
Flavus, 527, 1023.
Fligere, 414.
Flos, 412.
Fluere, 119.
-focare, 522.
Follis, 394.
Forare, 416, 563.
Forceps, 391.
Forma, 391, 731.
Formica, 391, 1045.
Formido, 117.
Formus, 391, 436, 456, 565.
Fornax, 436.
Fragrare, 1054.
Frangere, 598.
Frater, 424, 501.
Frequens, 882.
Fretum, 441 a.
Frigus, 712.
Fringilla, 655.
Frui, 423, 656 a.
Frumen, 423.
Frumentum, 656 a, 423.
Frustum, 423.
Fui, 399, 1005, 1024.
Fulgere, 410, 529.
Fuligo, 410, 529.
Fullo, 121.
Fulvus, 527, 1023.
Funda, 638, 1015.
Fundere, 1015.
Fungus, 638.
Furfur, 421.
Futuere, 602.

Garrire, 267, 664 a.
Gelu, 265.
Gena, 266.
Genu, 318.
Genus, 315.

Gerere, 518.
Gibbus, 869.
Gignere, 315.
Glama, 1044.
Gleba, 568.
Globus, 256, 568, 1026.
Glomus, 256, 568, 1026.
Glubere, 258, 291.
Gluma, 291.
Glutire, 1017.
Gnoscere, 314.
Gradus, 690.
Grallator, 124.
Gramen, 122.
Gramiæ, 1044.
Grandis, 868.
Granum, 271.
Gravis, 678.
Grunnire, 664 a.
Grus, 273.
Gubernare, 297.
Gula, 692, 1017.
Gutta, 280, 852.

Habere, 461, 1026.
Hamus, 1026.
Heri, 352.
Hiare, 351.
Hibernus, 257.
Hiems, 257.
Hir, 257. Hir is neut. and without inflexion.
Hinnire, 329.
Hircus, 290.
Hirsutus, 290.
Hirtus, 290.
Hiscere, 351.
Hoedus, 316.
Homo, 943.
Horrere, 519.
Hortus, 272.
Hospes, 289.
Hostis, 289.
Humilis, 1026.

Id, 510 a.
-idus, 917.
Iecur, 279.
Illustris, 322.
In, 126.
In (un), 215.
Inter, 127, 216.
Interpretari, 177.
Invitare, 407.
Invitus, 407.
Ire, 852 a.
Irritare, 245.
Iugum, Iungere, 378.
Iuvenis, 216.
Iuventus, 894.

354　LATIN INDEX.

Labium, Labrum, 463, 872, 1017.
Lacerare, 614.
Lacere, allicere, 141.
Lacerta, 704.
Lacrima, 613.
Lactare, 141.
Lacus, 135.
Lætus, 203, 507.
Lambere, 872.
Lamina, 1060.
Lancinare, 614.
Languere, 139 a, 1022.
Lapis, 554.
Lappa, 548.
Laqueus, 548.
Lascivus, 840.
Latere, 142, 321, 603.
Latro, 321, 554.
Latus, 873.
Lavare, 135, 121.
Laverna, 554.
Laxare, 670, 842, 1022.
Lectus, 140.
Legare, 1013.
Lenis, Lentus, 673 a, 872 a, 1021.
Levis, 551.
Lex, 549.
Liber (free), 320 a.
Liber (bark), 258, 291.
Lictor, 1013.
Limax, 673, 1021.
Limus, 673, 1021.
Lingere, 139, 323 a, 871, 1017.
Lingua, 139, 323 a, 615, 1017.
Linquere, 550.
Lippire, 391.
Liquet, 135.
-lis, 349, 957.
Loligo, 612.
Longus, 139 a.
Lubricus, 672, 1020.
Lucere, 322.
Lucerna, 322.
Lucina, 367.
Lucus, 138.
Ludere, 840.
Luere, 670, 1022.
Lumbi, 568 a, 873.
Lumen, 322.
Luna, 1012.
Lux, 322.
Luxus, Luxare, Luxuria, 670, 1022.

Macerare, 902.
Mactare, 74.

Macula, 149, 837.
Madere, 145.
Magnus, 19, 368, 834.
Maius, 1041.
Malleus, 29.
Mandare, 1026.
Mandere, 619.
Manducare, 875.
Mango, 150.
Manifestus, 116 a.
Manus, 763, 1026.
Mare, 148.
Margarita, 144.
Margo, 143.
Mater, 158.
Meditari, 612.
Medius, 151.
Mel, 511, 618.
Memini, 153.
Memor, 746.
Mensis, 156.
Mentem, 153.
-mentum, -men, 936.
Merces, 904.
Min, Memini, 153.
Mirari, 30.
Miscere, 836, 858.
Mœrere, 159.
-mo, -monia, 936.
Mola, 146.
Monere, 153.
Mordere, 747.
Mors, 162, 903.
Mucor, 742.
Mucus, 902.
Mulcere, 152.
Mulgere, 152.
Multus, 391.
Mus, 160.
Musca, 718, 835.
Muscus, 157.
Mutare, 151.
Mutuus, 151.

Nares, 631, 1042.
Nasus, 166, 676.
Ne (not) 164, add Nullus, Nunquam, Nemo, Nolle.
Necesse, 605.
Nectere, 320.
Nepos, 569.
Nidus, 719.
Nix, 677.
Nodus, 319.
Noscere, 314.
Nomen, 163, 327.
Novus, 165.
Nox, 369.
Nudus, 839.
Nunc, 167.

Nuper, 167.
Nux, 333, 606.

Obscœnus, Obscurus, 745, 1029.
Occare, 306.
Occulere, 291.
Oculus, 363, 544.
-olescere, 1008.
Oleum, 79, 170.
Olim, 229.
Omen, 922.
Operire, 1037.
Opitulari, 489.
Oportet, 261.
Opportunus, 261.
Orbis, 272, 1026.
Ordiri, 174.
Oriri, 174.
Os, 317.
Osculum, 317, 709.
Ostrea, 317.
Otium, 709.
Ovis, 115.
Ovum, 361, 543.

Pagina, 402.
Pallium, 435.
Palpare, Palma, 433, 1035, 1036.
Palumbes, 535.
Palus, 176.
Pampinus, 1026.
Pandus, 405.
Papillæ, 561.
Parcere, 679.
Parens, 42.
Parere, 400.
Parsimonia, 704.
Passer, 634, 680.
Pater, 431, 502.
Paucus, etc., 437, 545.
Pecus, Peculium, 432.
Pedere, 901.
Pellere, 840.
Pellis, 394, 435.
Per, 450, 563.
Pera, 905, 632.
Perna, 300, 683.
Persona, 729 a.
Pes, 449.
Pestis, 706.
Petere, 428.
Petorritum, 518.
Pila, Pilula, 395.
Pileus, 435.
Pinguis, 562.
Pinna, 439 b.
Placet, 714, 809.
Planus, 442.

LATIN INDEX. 355

Plebs, 434.
Plenus, 453.
Plere, 439 a.
Plicare, 442 a, 447.
Polluere, 391, 439.
Populus, 434.
Porcus, 415.
Post, 1043.
Precari, 542.
Prehendere, 123.
Pro, etc., 451.
Proclivis, 1061.
Promulgare, 391.
Prunum, 740.
Pugil, Pugnare, 438, 1026.
Puleer, 23.
Pulex, 840.
Pullus, 445, 523.
Pulvis, 454.
Pungere, 1026.

Quærere, 681, 683 a.
Qualis, 349, 485.
Quando, 343.
Quatere, 607, 668.
Quem, 348.
Queo, 1024.
Queri, 267, 664 a.
Quinque, 866.
Quis, 347.
Quod, Quid, 342.

Radix, 181.
Rapere, 287, 465, 733.
Rastrum, 722.
Regere, 370, 372, 1030.
Regere in Porrigere, 370.
Remus, 732.
Repere, 274, 650.
Rogare, 542, 1059.
Ruber, Rufus, 570.
Ruga, 611.
Rumen, Ruminare, 371.
Rumor, 359, 931.

Sacculus, 182.
Sacer, 639.
Sagaris, 1032.
Sagitta, 193.
Sal, 184.
Salvus, 1008.
Sanus, 200.
Sarpere, 1026.
Satis, Satur, 183, 514.
Satus (serere), 198.
Scamnum, Scandere, Scandula, 1015.
Scapula, Scalæ, 1015.
Scelus, 189, 1053.
Scindere, Scintilla, 1015.

Scobæ, 539.
Screare, 383.
Scribere, 540, 578, 664, 1031.
Scrobs, 658.
Sculpere, 1031.
Secare, 1032.
Secere, Sector, Sectio, 1016.
Segnis, 185 a.
Semel, 199, 229, 985.
Semper, 199, 985.
Senex, 188.
Sentina, 687 b.
Septem, 466.
Sequi, 1016.
Serere, 758.
-serere, 1016.
Serpere, 650.
Serum, 638.
Seta, 705.
Sevisse, 198.
Sex, 194, 1002.
Sic, 897.
Signum, 701.
Siliqua, 642.
Silva, 660.
Similis, 185, 349, 662.
Simul, 185, 229, 662.
Singuli, 199.
Socer, Socrus, 639.
Sol, 383, 1047.
Sollus, 639, 1008.
Solvere, 670, 842.
Sompnus, 880.
Sonus, 638, 687 a, 1016.
Sorbere, 906.
Soror, 633.
Spatula, 1015.
Spirare, 654 a, 1054.
Splendere, 648.
Spolium, 648.
Sponda, 1026.
Spuere, 202, 638.
Spuma, 202, 536, 638, 656.
Stannum, 700.
Stare, 203.
Statim, 203, 229.
Stella, 204.
Sterilis, 1006.
Sternere, 206.
Sternutare, 638.
Stimulare, 878.
Stirps, 203.
Strenuus, 844.
Stria, 843.
Strobilus, 1026.
Stupere, 203.
Sturnus, 680.
Suavis, 208, 697.
Succus, 553, 638.

Sudare, 621, 639, 515.
Sulcus, 207, 638, 691.
Sus, 197.

Tacere, 644.
Tæda, 884, 1025.
Talis, 349, 485.
Tardus, 554.
Taurus, 687.
Taxus, 57.
Tegere, 486, 637, 652, 1039.
Templum, Tempestas, 474.
Tendere, 737.
Tenuis, 488, 560.
Tergere, 478.
Terminus, 739.
Terra, 1019.
Tertius, 998.
Testa, Testis, 706.
Tingere, 479.
Tinnire, Tintinare, 210.
Titillare, 609.
Titubare, 887.
Tolerare, Tollere, 489.
Tonare, 493, 885 a.
Topper, 468.
-tor, 626.
Tornus, Torquere, 610, 1026.
Torpere, 101.
Torrere, 478, 1006.
Toxicum, 57.
Trabs, 498.
Trahere, 476, 831.
Tranquillus, 259, 346.
Tremere, Trepidus, 391.
Tres, 491, 998.
Tritavus, 998.
Triturare, 492.
Truncus, 498.
Tu, 699.
Tunc, 487.
Tundere, 572, 885.
Turbare, 688, 735.
Turbo, 610, 1026.
Turdus, 680, 723.
Turma, 734.
Turris, 214.
Tus, 582.
-tus, 907.
Tussis, 590.

V, 270.
Vacillare, 218, 374, 695, 879.
Vadere, 617, 449, 889.
Væ, 240.
Valere, 1008.
Vanus, 259, 335 a.

Vanescere, 335 a.
Vannus, 237.
Vapor, 259, 745.
Varius, 422.
Vas, Vadis, 227.
Vastare, 341.
Vates, 517.
Vber, 574.
Vbi, 258.
Vdus, 891.
Vehere, 759 a.
Vehiculum, 376.
Velle, 233, 566.
Vellere, 554.
Vellus, 443.
Venari, 311.
Venire, 270.
Venter, 259, 315, 576, 892.
Ventus, 235, 891.
Venus, 315.
Verberare, 354, 409 a.
Verbum, 577.
Vereri, 243.
Vermis, 244.
Verrere, 638, 907.
Verres, 415.
Verruca, 224.

Versus, 223.
Vertere, 222, 336, 1026.
Veru, 336.
Vesci, 704.
Vespa, 225, 725.
Vesper, 575, 1056.
Vestigium, 681.
Vestis, 635, 724.
Via, 375, 847.
Vibrare, 695.
Vicus, 1024, 231, 727.
Videre, 517.
Viduus, 232.
Vigere, 1024.
Vigilare, 377, 1024.
Viginti, 888.
Villus, 241.
Vincere, 234.
Vincire, 409.
Vinum, 236.
Virere, 1049.
Virga, 409 a, 541, 1049.
Virgilius, 242.
Virgo, 1049.
Vis, 1024.
Viscera, 704, 745.
Visire, 446.

Vitex, 239.
Vituperare, 238.
Viverra, 636.
Vivus, 335, 1005, 1024.
Vlmus, 114.
Vena, 109.
Vmbo, 1026.
Vncus, 357, 1026.
Vnda, 891.
Vnde, 258, 345.
Vndecim, 617.
Vnguis, 838.
Vnquam, 258.
Vnus, 172.
Volare, 444.
Voluere, 220, 340.
Vomere, 683 b.
Vox, 230.
Vrbs, 272, 1026.
Vrsus, 704.
Vt, 258.
Vter (whether), 258, 344, 976.
Vter (bag), 892.
Vulgus, 448.
Vultus, 245 a.
Vulva, 394.

GREEK INDEX.

A copulative, 261, 985.
— intensive, 520.
αγαθος, 503.
αγγελος, 1031.
αγγος, αγγουρον, αγγλιθες, 1026.
άγιος, 159.
αγκιστρον, 357, 1026.
αγκυλη, αγχου, 1026.
αγκυρα, 1026.
αγρος, 356.
αιει, 112, 383, 1024.
αιρα, 383.
αισθεσθαι, 383.
αιφνιδιος, αιψα, 383.
αιων, 112, 383, 1024.
ακουειν, 276.
ακυλος, 168.
αλγειν, 77.
αλεη, αλεεινος, 1052.
αλειφειν, 1012.
αλεκτρυων, 258.
αλινδεισθαι, 258.
αλλος, 110.
άλς, άλες, 184.
αλσος, 660.
άλως, 1051.
άμα, 261, 980, seqq.
αμβροτος, 215.
αμβων, 1025.
αμειβειν, 864.
αμφω, 418.
αναγκη, 605.
ανεμος, 171.
αντι, 78.
άπαξ, 979.
απο, 463 a.
απομυττεσθαι, 902.
απροτιμαστος, 1026.
αργος, αργυρος, 1030, 1048.
αρουν, 105, 1031.
άρπαζειν, 257, 732.
άρπη, 1031.
ασκηθης, 186.
αστηρ, 204.
αστραγαλος, 74.
αστραπη, 204.
αστυ, 1024.
ασφαραγος, 423.
αυλαξ, 691.
αυλος, pipe, 292.
αυξανειν, 364.
αυταρ, 1043.
αφρος, 120.
αχος, 76.
αχυρον, 358.

Βαδιζειν, 449, 889.
βαθος, 419, 557, 862.
βαλανειον, 616.
βανα, 518.
βαπτειν, 559.
βατραχος, 452.
βεη, 30, 1024.
βενθος, 862.
βηξ, 524, 554.
βιβρωσκειν, 423.
βιος, 21, 1024.
βληχαν, 597.
βλιττειν, 753.
βυθρος, 419.
βυρα, 406.
βουλεσθαι, 233.
βους, 526.
βραδυς, 554.
βριζειν, 554.
βρογχος, 423.
βροτος, 752.
βρυκειν, 423.
βρυχασθαι, 359.
βρωμασθαι, 359.
βυσσος, 557, 862.

Γαζα, 630.
γαλα, 1012, 1017.
γαληνη, 259.
γαστηρ, 705.
γελαν, 832.
γελειν, 1018.
γενειον, γενυς, 266.
γενναν, γενος, 30, 315.

γερανος, 124, 273, 1050.
γερων, 1063.
γενεσθαι, 268, 520.
γιγνωσκειν, 314.
γλυφειν, 1031.
γλωσσα, 323 a, 1017.
γναθος, 266.
γναφευς, 328.
γογγυλος, 1026.
γομφος, 1026.
γονυ, 318.
γραφειν, 540, 644, 1031.
γραστις, 275.
γυνη, 334.
γυρος, 281, 336.
γωνια, 130.

Δαηρ, 612.
δακρυ, 30, 483, 613.
δαμαζειν, 481.
δαρθανειν, 101.
δας, 884, 1025.
δεικνυναι, 496, 701.
δεκα, 484.
δελτος, 554.
δελφυς, 554.
δεμειν, 495.
δενδρον, 495.
δεξια, 496.
δερκεσθαι, 30.
δευειν, 103.
δεφειν, 755.
δεχεσθαι, 486, 899.
διδασκειν, 482.
digamma, 381 to 388.
διφθερα, 755, 1057.
δνεφας, 474.
δοκειν, 881.
δορυ, 498.
δραττεσθαι, 1026.
δρεπειν, 797, 1026.
δυο, 500.
δυσπεμφελος, 1026.
δωδεκα, 622.

Εγγυς, 1026.

358   GREEK INDEX.

εγω, 366.
εδειν, 108.
εδνα, 227.
ειδεναι, 383, 517.
εικειν, 383.
εικοσι, 383, 888.
ειπειν, 1015.
ειρειν, 1015.
εις, 126.
εις, 172.
εκαστος, 977.
εκατον, 870.
εκει, εκεινος, 355.
ελαιον, 70, 170, 1012.
ελασσων, 137.
ελαφος, 840.
ελαφρος, 551.
ελευθερος, 320 a.
ελθειν, 258, 320 a.
ελισσειν, 220.
εμβρυον, 30.
εμειν, 221, 683 b.
εν, 126.
ενα, 172.
ενδεκα, 617.
εννυναι, 724.
εντερον, 126.
εξ, 194, 720.
εξαιφνης, 383.
επιλησμων, 705.
επτα, 466.
εργον, 242.
Ερεβος, 1007.
ερεικειν, 383.
εριπτειν, 258, 780.
ερεσθαι, 383.
ερεσσειν, 169.
ερετμειν, 732.
ερευγεσθαι, 371, 383.
ερκος, 1026.
ερπειν, 650.
ερυθρος, 570, 383.
ερωδιος, 273, 1059.
εσθης, 724.
εσθιειν, 108, 705.
εσθλος, 710.
εσπερα, 1056.
ετι, 353.
ευαδε, 383.

Ζητειν, 645.
ζυγον, 378.

'Ηδυς, 697.
ηεριος, 1007.

ηλιος, 383.

Θαμβειν, 471 a.
θαρρειν, 470.
θελειν, 566.
θεραπων, 644.
θερμος, 565.
θηρ, 473, 558.
θιγγανειν, 497.
θολος, 612.
θορυβειν, 088, 735.
θρονος, θρηνος, 498.
θυγατηρ, 471.
θυειν, 582.
θυμος, 582, 554.
θυρα, 475, 544.
θωραξ, 612.

Ιασθαι, 30.
ιδειν, 517.
ιδιειν, 515.
ιδιος, 383.
ιδρως, 383, 515.
ιεναι, 852 a.
ιμασθλη, 705.
ιμερος, 1025.
ιπνος, 464.
Ιρις, 113, 383, 1016.
Ιρος, pr. n., 113, 383.
ισθι, 705.
ισμεν, 705.
ισταναι, 203.
ιτεα, 239, 728.

Καθαρος, 708, 1002.
καιειν, καυσαι, 383.
καλαμος, 292.
καλειν, 85.
καλος, 1008.
κιλυξ, 291.
καλυπτειν, καλυβη, 291.
καμπτειν, 87, 1026.
κανθαρος, 863, 1026.
κανθηλιος, 1026.
κινθος, 130, 684.
κανναβις, 301.
καπηλος, 90, 864.
καπνος, 259.
καπτειν, 278 a.
καρα, 296, 98, 755.
καραβος, 97.
καρδια, 290.
καρπος, 1026.
καρφος, καρφειν, 1006
  1058.

κεαζειν, 1015.
κεινος, 355.
κειρειν, 663, 1032, 89,
  263.
κεισθαι, 259.
κελαινος, 535.
κελευθος, 320 a.
κελλειν, 259.
κελυφος, 291.
κενος, κενεων, 259, 315,
  335 a, 1026.
κεντειν, 867.
κεραμος, 1026.
κερας, 307.
Κερβερος, 1010.
κευθειν, 30, 302,
  510.
κεφαλη, 296, 857.
κηπος, 263.
κηρ, 290.
κιγκλιδες, 877.
κικυς, 1024.
κιρκος, 339.
κλαιειν, κλαυσαι, 383.
κλειειν, 833.
κλεπτειν, 321.
κλιβανος, 325.
κλιμαξ, 94, 458.
κλινειν, 323, 1061.
κλυειν, 30, 324.
κλωθειν, 262.
κναπτειν, 328.
κνιδη, 330.
κοιλος, 1026.
κοινος, 261.
κοκκυξ, 100.
κολλα, 1021, 1044.
κολοιος, κολωο 8 5.
κολοκυνθις, 1026.
κολωνη, 1028.
κονδυλος, 132, 331, 295,
  1026.
κονιδες, 332.
κοννειν, 129, 314.
κοπτειν, 91.
κοραξ, 99.
κορειν, 696.
κορη, 282, 92.
κορυφη, 98.
κορυστης, 705.
κπυριξ, 290.
κοσκινον, 599, 915.
-κοσιοι, 912.
κραζειν, 99.
κραμβος, 1006.

GREEK INDEX. 359

κρανιον, 296.
κραστις, 275.
κρατα, 856.
κρεας, 89.
κρηγυος, 596.
κρινειν, 338, 877.
κριος, 307.
κτεις, 924.
κυβη, κυβερναν, 296.
κυβισταν, 296, 1026.
κυκλος, 281, 898.
κυκνος, 278, 694, 1048.
κυλιειν, 220, 340, 915, 1051.
κυμβαχος, 1026.
κυμβιον, 865, 1026.
κυπελλον, 865.
κυσαι, 131, 317.
κυσθος, κυστις, 705.
κυων, 310, 1048.
κωλυειν, 30.
κωμη, 532, 1026.
κωνος, 1025.
κωνωψ, 284.

Λαγαρος, 873.
λαγων, (flank), 873.
λαθειν, 321, 603.
λαικαζειν, 840.
λαιμασσειν, 1017.
λαιος, 136.
λαμβανειν, 1035, 326, 518, 548.
λαμπειν, 321.
λαμπη, 673.
λανθανειν, 142.
λαξ, 258, 300.
λαπαρη, 873.
λαπτειν, 1017, 134.
λαφυσσειν, 1017.
λαχειν, 604 a.
λαιος, 853.
λαυκανιη, 1017.
λεγειν, λεγεσθαι, 367, 549, 1017, 140.
λεγειν, gather, 1035, 518.
λειπειν, 462.
λειχειν, 30, 871, 1017, 139.
λεπας, 291.
λεπειν, 258. 291.
λεπτος, 291.
λευκος, 322.
λευσσειν, 258, 322.

λημη, 258.
λιγνυς, 322, 410.
λιθος, 544.
λιπα, 1012.
λοβος, 461 a.
λογγαζειν, 139 a.
λουειν, 121.
λυγδος, 322.
λυειν, 670, 842.
λυκιος, 322.
λυχνος, 322.

Μαινειν, 511.
μανθανειν, 874.
μαργαριτης, 144.
μαρπτειν, 1026.
ματηρ, 158.
μαχεσθαι, 74 *.
μεγαλα, μειζων, 251, 19, 368, 834.
μεθυ, 511, 854.
μειδιαν, 620.
μελδειν, 147.
μελι, 618.
μεσος, 151, 717.
μετα, μεταξυ, 151, 512.
μηδεσθαι, 874.
μηνη, μην, 156.
μητηρ, 158.
μιμνησκειν, 153.
μινυνθα, 154.
μισγειν, 836, 858.
μισθος, 716, 904.
μοιχος, 675.
μολυνειν, 439.
μορμω, 1045.
μορφη, 731.
μυελος, 902.
μυια, 718, 835.
μυλη, 29, 146.
μυρμηξ, 1045.
μυρον, μυρρα, μυρεσθαι, 674.
μωκος, 155.

Νεος, 165.
νεοττια, 710.
νεφος, 474.
νησσα, 258, 278.
νιφειν, 677.
νους, 319 a.
νυν, 167.
νυος, 858.
νυξ, 369.

Ξηρος, 592, 667, 1006, 1033.
ξυλον, 660.
ξυν, 662.
ξυνος, 261.
ξυραν, 663.

'O, ἡ, το, 494.
οβελος, 313.
ογκος, 1026.
οδους, 886, 925.
οδυνη, 925.
οιγειν, 173, 552.
οιδα, 383.
οικος, 231, 304, 383, 727.
οινος, 236, 383.
οις, 115.
οισυη, 383, 728.
οκελλειν, 259.
ολιγος, 137, 604.
ολος, 125, 1008.
ομβρος, 891.
ομου, 261.
ομφαλος, 1026.
ομφη, 859.
ονομα, 30, 163, 327.
ονυξ, 838.
οπισω, 1043.
οπος, 553.
οπωρα, 1043.
οξυς, 83.
ορεγειν, 370.
ορυσσειν, 258, 1031.
ορφνη, 1007.
ορχεισθαι, 1026.
ορχις, 1026.
ός, 347, 348.
οσσα, 706.
οσσε, 544, 706.
οσσεσθαι, 706.
ουθαρ, 516, 891.
ουλος, 443.
οφθαλμος, 363.
οφρυς, 425.
οψ (eye), 363.
οψ (vox), 1016.

Παρα, 450.
πας, 520.
πατειν, 449.
πατηρ, 431, 502.
παυειν, 259.
παυρος, 437, 545.
παχυς, 562, 600.
πελαγος, 121.

πελεκυς, 408.
πελλος, πελιδνος, Πελοψ, etc., 535.
πελτη, 435.
πεντε, 860.
πεποσθε, 705.
περαν, 429.
περδειν, 430.
πηγη, 403.
πηνιον, πηνιζειν, 682.
πηρα, 905.
πιπρασκειν, 30.
πλαξ, πλακους, 442, 601.
πλειν, 121, 850.
πλεκειν, 442 a, 447.
πλεος, 453.
πληθος, 434.
πληρης, 453.
πλησμονη, 705.
πλησσειν, 671, 1036.
πλισσεσθαι, 840.
πλοκαμος, 447.
πλους, 447.
πλυνειν, 121.
πνειν, 1042.
ποθεν, 345.
πολος, πολευειν, 395.
πολυς, 434, 448.
πορνη, 533.
πορος, 429.
πορρω, 451.
ποτε, 890.
πους, 449, 506.
Πριαμος, 426.
πριασθαι, 30.
πριν, 451.
προ, 451.
πτερις, 504, 849.
πτερνα, 300, 683 a.
πτερον, 503.
πτυειν, 683.
πυθμην, 419.
πυκνος, 562.
πυνθανεσθαι, 440.
πυξ, 1026.
πυξος, 420.
πυρ, 427, 441, 456.
πυργος, 417.
πυρετος, 436.
πυρος, 406.
πυρρος, 426.
πωλος, 445, 523.

'Ραδιος, 179 a, 513.
ραινειν, 179, 841.

ρακος, 178.
ρηγνυναι, 598.
ρινος, 180, 1000.
ρυσσος, ρυτις, 611, 893.

Σαιρειν, 638, 907.
σακκος, 182.
σαλευειν, 184.
σαττειν, 844 a.
σειειν, 842 a.
σελας, σεληνη, 657, 1018.
σελμα, 612.
σιαλος, 30.
σιτος, 702.
σκαληνος, σκολιος, 1053.
σκαμβος, 1026.
σκανδαληθρον, 1015.
σκαπτειν, 537.
σκατος (σκωρ), 192.
σκαφη, σκαφος, 191, 1026.
σκεδασαι, 187.
σκελος, 1015.
σκευος, 189 a.
σκηνη, 195, 1029.
σκια, 1029.
σκνιψ, 661.
σκολοψ, 1015.
σκυφος, 1026.
σκωπτειν, 188.
σκωρ, 190.
σμυχειν, 196.
σπαθη, 537.
σπαν, 848.
σπανιος, 1015.
σπενδειν, 1015.
σπερχειν, 758 a.
σπευδειν, 201.
σπινθηρ, 1015.
σπινος, 655.
σπογγος, 638.
σπονδυλος, 1015.
σταις, 653.
σταχυς, 648.
στεγειν, 486, 637, 652, 1039.
στειρα, 667, 1006.
στειχειν, 372 a.
στενειν, 493.
στεφειν, 518.
στηναι, 203.
στιβαρος, 203.
στιζειν, 205.
στρατος, 654.

στρεφειν, 74, 592, 13, 1026.
στρογγυλος, 74, 390, 592, 1026.
στρομβος, 390.
στρουθος, 680.
στρωννυναι, 206.
στυεσθαι, 203.
συ, 699.
συκον, 1055.
συν, 662.
συς, 197.
σφαιρα, 69.
σφην, 1015.
σφηξ, 725.
σφονδυλος, 1015.
σφυρον, 69, 30.
σχεδη, 1015.
σχιζειν, 1015.
σχινδαλαμος, 1015.

Ταλαντον, 489, 915.
ταλας, 489.
ταρασσειν, 735, 688.
ταφη, 1026.
ταυρος, 687.
τεγγειν, 103, 479.
τειρεα, 685.
τειρειν, 211.
τειχος, 680.
τεκειν, τικτειν, 1039, 579.
τεκμωρ, τεκμηριον, 212, 496.
τελαμων, 942.
τελειν, 472.
τελη, 213, 472.
Τεμπη, 589.
τερηδων, 938.
τερμων, 739.
τερσαινειν, 478.
τεταγειν, 373, 480.
τετασθην, 705.
τετταρες, 851.
τηγανον, 686.
τηκειν, 686.
τικτειν, 579.
τιλλειν, 554.
τινθαλεος, 884.
τιτθη, 209, 561, 608.
τληναι, 489.
το, 485.
τολμαν, 489.
τοξον, 57.
τορνος, 610.
τορυνη, 610.

GREEK INDEX. 361

-τος, 917, 920.
τρεις, 491.
τρεπειν, 610.
τριβειν, 211.
τριτος, τριτατος, 998.
τρυξ, 477.
τυ, 490.
τυμβος, 859, 1026.
τυμπανον, 885.
τυπτειν, 885.
τυρσις, 214.
τως, 494.

'Υβος, 257, 869.
ὑδωρ, ὑειν, 891.
ὑλη, 660.
ὑμην, 195.
ὑπνος, 880.
ὑφη, ὑφαινειν, 226.

Φλεγειν, 410, 711, 322.
φλενειν, 410.
φλυκταινα, 411.
φονος, 396.
φραζεσθαι, 177.
φρασσειν, 649.

φρατρια, 501.
φρισσειν, 519, 530.
φρονειν, 177.
φρυγειν, 452.
φρυνη, φρυνιχος, 452.
φυναι, φυειν, 399, 30.
φωνη, 638 a, 687 a, 1016.

Χαινειν, see χασκειν.
χαιρειν, 312, 641.
χαιτη, 705.
χαλαν, 670, 842, 1022.
χαλβανη, 256.
χαλεπος, 277.
χανδανειν, 1026.
χαος, 317, 351.
χαραξ, 1031.
χαρασσειν, 664, 1031.
χασκειν, 278a, 317, 351, 1046.
χειν, 852, 280.
χειρ, 279, 257, 1026.
χειρων, 350.
χελιδων, 693.
χερσος, 592, 667, 1006, 1033, 1019.

χηλη, 326.
χην, 278.
χηρα, 641, 667, 1006, 1019.
χθες, 352.
χιτων, 258.
χηλη, 93.
χλευη, 832.
χλωρος, 277.
χοιρος, 288.
χολη, χολος, 277, 527, 1022.
χορος, 641.
χορτος, 272.
χρυσος, 729a.
χυτλον, 852.
χωλος, 294.
χωρα, 592, 1006, 1033, 667.

Ψαρ, ψαρος, 680.
ψηλαφαν, 433.
ψυλλα, 840.

Ωλενη, 109.
ωον, 361, 543.

THE END.

Printed by Taylor and Francis, Red Lion Court, Fleet Street.

BY THE REV. O. COCKAYNE.
1861.
ANGLO-SAXON.
NARRATIUNCULÆ ANGLICE CONSCRIPTÆ.
1. Epistola Alexandri ad Aristotelem.
2. De Rebus in Oriente mirabilibus.
3. Passio Sanctæ Margaretæ Virginis, etc.

Only 250 printed: and a right to raise the price of the last-sold Copies will be reserved.

JOHN RUSSELL SMITH, SOHO SQUARE.

By the same.

In the Press,

SEINTE MARHERETE þE MEIDEN ANT MARTYR.

In Alliterative Rhythm and Old English of about 1200: from the skin books.

WITH

SEINTE MARGARETE.

A Poem in Riming English of the fourteenth century: from the Harleian Collection, hitherto unpublished.

WITH REMARKS AND ILLUSTRATIONS.

JOHN RUSSELL SMITH, SOHO SQUARE.

By the same.

A GREEK SYNTAX.

WITH EXAMPLES SUITED TO MEMORY.

Price 3s. 6d.

PARKER, SON, AND BOURN, 445 STRAND.

Note.—Some Philological Papers by the same author may be procured direct from himself for twelve postage stamps each.

www.ingramcontent.com/pod-product-compliance
Lightning Source LLC
Chambersburg PA
CBHW020224240426
43672CB00006B/408